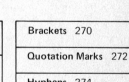

D0107754

The Able Writer

A Rhetoric and Handbook

John P. Broderick
Old Dominion University

HARPER & ROW, PUBLISHERS, New York
Cambridge, Philadelphia, San Francisco,
London, Mexico City, São Paulo, Sydney

1817

For Carol, Julie, and Amy

Sponsoring Editor: Phillip Leininger
Project Editors: Matthew Collins/Linda Buchanan
Designer: Frances Torbert Tilley
Production Manager: Marion Palen
Compositor: Progressive Typographers, Inc.
Printer and Binder: Halliday Lithograph Corporation
Art Studio: Vantage Art, Inc.

The Able Writer: A Rhetoric and Handbook

Copyright © 1982 by Harper & Row, Publishers, Inc.

Library of Congress Cataloging in Publication Data

Broderick, John P.
  The able writer.

  Includes index.
  1. English language—Rhetoric.   2. English language—
Grammar—1950–   I. Title.
PE1408.B69866   808'.042   81-2913
ISBN 0-690-00891-0   AACR2

Contents

v

Preface

To the Student

The premise of this book is that anyone can become an able writer. *You* can become an able writer. It takes work, of course, but you do not have to start from scratch. You bring to this composition course an amazing array of language skills—and not just those learned in school. Since the day you were born, you have listened to English: in conversations, on television, in classes, and elsewhere. You have spoken English: to friends and strangers, to individuals and groups, face-to-face and over the telephone. You have read English: in letters, newspapers, magazines, and textbooks. And you have written English: in notes, in school assignments, and maybe graffiti. Your job in the composition course is to learn which aspects of that experience can help you to develop skills in English composition and which aspects may work against the development of such skills. The aim of this book is to help you with that job.

This book was written to be used as either a classroom text or a reference book. As a text, it assumes that the composition course has content. That is, it seeks not only to guide you as you practice writing; it also tries to teach you something about the process of English composition: how to plan essays, how to analyze essays, and how to evaluate the effectiveness of essays. The chapters have been written to be read, and enjoyed, in sequence. As you work through the book, you should make it a point to read all the samples of writing, for these samples usually exemplify the explanations they accompany. The same holds true for exercises. Even if your teacher does not assign all of the exercises, you should read them and think them through. They often extend the explanations they accompany. Sometimes, they even introduce new concepts. They will always give you practical and concrete experience with the issues being taught. If you are not using this book as a course text but as a reference, the index, the table of contents, and the guide to *The Able Writer* along with the correction chart, both found inside the covers of the book, will help you find those sections treating your specific questions about English composition. It will be easiest to find useful answers if you read the entire chapter subsection to which you are referred.

To the Teacher

This book is rooted in the long tradition of composition instruction that, in many ways, has remained unchanged since the time of Ancient Greece. I do, however, take a reasonably specific stand on just which aspects of that tradition are most important for today's students. The emphasis in this book is on language. My aim is to have you teach your students how to communicate their ideas effectively in formal, standard written English (which I call *edited English*). Able writers often exercise considerable freedom in applying the norms of edited English, but they usually know what the norms are and how they have creatively tested them. To become able writers, students must master those norms, and the college composition course very likely presents the last opportunity to study them explicitly and carefully.

This book is for teachers who teach the English language when they teach composition. It is for teachers who, in addition to teaching broader rhetorical principles, also take time to teach the rhetoric and structure of the paragraph, the inner dynamics of the sentence, the subtleties of word choice, and the appropriate uses of spelling and punctuation. In developing ways to do all of these, I have drawn some insights from contemporary linguistics. From sociolinguistics, I have enlisted help in defining edited English. I use the descriptive linguist's distinction between paradigms (sets of language elements that share a function) and syntax (principles for arranging those elements in a linear order) as the basis for treating the sentence and problems writers have with the sentence. The distinction between paradigms and syntax also underlies my treatment of categories and predications as the two major types of ideas that writers need to create and control. Linguistic research has also influenced my treatment of the social impact of words, the relationship between spelling and pronunciation, and the functions of punctuation marks in paragraph structure, sentence structure, and word structure.

Throughout the book, the learning needs of student writers and the inner dynamism of the writing process are paramount. Matter from the rhetorical tradition and from linguistics always appears in service of these. My firm belief is that teachers who are committed to teaching students to write will be comfortable with this book. Those whose commitment is to a particular rhetorical, linguistic, or literary theory may not be so comfortable, for my presentation seeks to avoid dogma and jargon.

Chapter One, on language, delineates the subject matter of the book, edited English, as accurately as a preliminary chapter can. For a fully adequate definition, however, the entire book must be covered. Chapter Two, on ideas, describes some language-oriented prewriting techniques that can help students use their own experiences to generate ideas. But neither an awareness of what edited English is nor an ability to call forth creative ideas will guarantee mastery of edited English. Students need to learn about and to practice many specific skills to earn the title of able writer. Chapter Three, which treats organization, shows that explicit and careful attention to audience, purpose, and plan is a key defining characteristic of edited English.

Chapters Four through Eleven treat the language of edited English. Once ideas are organized, they must be expressed in paragraphs (Chapter Four), sentences (Chapters Five through Seven), words (Chapters Eight and Nine), spellings (Chapter Ten), and punctuation (Chapter Eleven) that conform to the very specific requirements of edited-English style. Each of these chapters emphasizes the special structural features of edited English, while at the same time aiming to show how knowledge of other styles of English can help master the special requirements of edited English.

Chapter Twelve, which treats the writing of research papers, is in some ways a review of the entire book. It extends the treatment of ideas from Chapter Two by discussing the library as a research tool. It extends the treatment of organization from Chapter Three by showing how to take, arrange, and write from research note cards. And it extends the treatment of the language of edited English from Chapters Four through Eleven by describing very specific formats for the research paper's text, notes, and bibliography.

The Appendix, which is a glossary of edited-English usage, lists a number of very specific requirements concerning word choice and sentence structure in edited English.

The following diagram may serve as a visual representation of the structure of this book. The core is edited English (the inner circle). The contents of the circle show that edited English is the style most closely associated with the art of written composition, that it has its own organizing principles, that it has its own modes of expression, and that it has its own special set of usage requirements. But the edited-English circle is enclosed in an outer circle (the English language). This shows that it shares with other varieties of English most of its principles of organization and expression. The diagram also attempts to show that edited English requires access to bright and original ideas if its principles of organization and expression are to produce truly interesting writing.

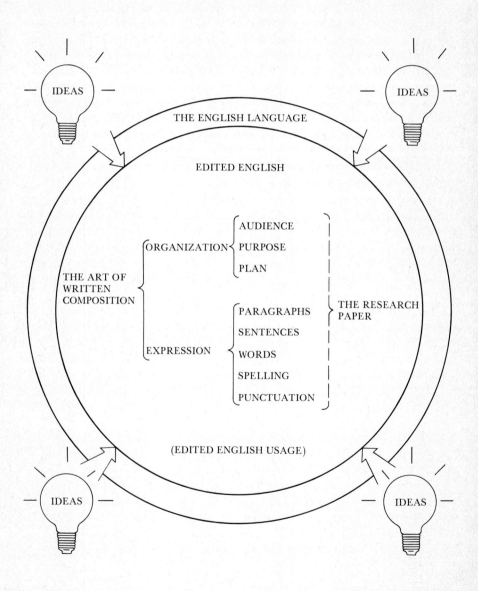

To Those Who Helped

This book was long in the making. Erika Lindemann, Christopher Reaske, and Richard Beal each reviewed more than one draft of the entire manuscript and provided exceptionally sensible and usable advice. Others who read part of the manuscript and provided valuable written comments were Michael Squires, James Raymond, Ross Winterowd, and Carolyn Rhodes. Tony Ardizzone provided me with samples of his students' writing. Terence Walton provided the photograph of the COM-CAT entry on page 291. I thank them all. The book is better because they helped. Any remaining deficiencies are my responsibility alone.

I wish also to thank Walter Paulits, who taught me to write. The memory of his achievements as a teacher sustained my belief in this book's thesis: that the resources to be an able writer are latent in any student.

My daughters, Julie and Amy, were patient and understanding throughout the years of work on this book. My wife, Carol, not only bore with me and encouraged me, she also proofread the typescript and did extensive research for the usage glossary. Even the dedication cannot adequately thank Carol, Julie, and Amy. But they already know exactly how much their help has meant to me.

John P. Broderick

One | *Language*

Writing is an art like painting, ballet, or basketball. Newcomers to any art are often surprised to discover that they may need months or even years of very hard and sometimes monotonous exercise before they can approach the mastery of experienced practitioners. Picasso did not start out painting the abstractions for which he became famous; like any art student, he did his share of realistic landscapes and portraits. The great Russian ballerinas spent years practicing very basic foot positions and body movements before they could take flight before an audience. And no fast-break artist in professional basketball began with behind-the-back passes. Most coaches, in fact, would ignore a prospect who did not show a thorough mastery of the basics of the game. The same is true of the writer. You cannot hope to develop an effective and personal writing style unless you master the basics of the craft. This book seeks to teach you those basic principles and to guide you in adapting them to your own personality and your own goals as an able writer.

Explicit discussion of the composition process begins in Chapter Three. It will show you how to adapt your ideas to the needs of a specific reading audience, how to focus on a specific purpose, and how to choose an organizational plan suited to your audience and purpose. Chapters Four through Eleven discuss in detail all aspects of the language of written composition: paragraphs, sentences, words, spelling, and punctuation. Chapter Twelve focuses on a very specific task: the writing of research papers.

These matters form the heart of a course in written composition, but before any of them can be taken up effectively, two preliminary matters must be treated. Chapter One will discuss language structure and language variation as part of a definition of the special style of written composition: edited English. Chapter Two will give you several suggestions about how to find ideas to write about, how to shape them to suit your own needs as a writer, and how to record them in a writer's notebook so that they will be handy when you need them.

Language Structure

Exactly what is language? How does it work? What do we do with it? How do we adapt it to the many needs of human life? These are some of the questions addressed in this chapter. None of them can be treated comprehensively here, but you will have an opportunity to examine many important issues raised by such questions. The aim is to define the special style of language that is the subject of this book: the language of formal written communication, here called *edited English*. Edited English shares with all styles of English four kinds of structural principles: discourse structure, sentence structure, word structure, and sound structure. Each of these is discussed briefly in this section. However, edited English also has its own special requirements concerning all four types of structure. These requirements are introduced in the second section of this chapter and examined in great detail in later chapters of this book.

Discourse structure

Knowing how to use the English language is a lot like knowing how to play a card game. Just as in a game like poker you know whose turn it is and whether to fold or play a given hand, so too in a conversation you know whether it is your turn to speak, whether or not to take your turn, and, if you take it, what kind of sentence to "play." If someone says to you, *What did you get for Christmas?*, you recognize the sentence as a question, you know it is your turn to speak, and you know that you should "play" a statement to answer the question. Those principles of the game of English grammar that control the taking of turns in spoken English and the correct ordering of sentences in both spoken and written English are its principles of discourse structure.

Whenever you carry on a conversation or write a letter, you constantly select sentences that appropriately follow those that went before. Consider the following few sentences from the beginning of an informal letter:

It's raining today, so I thought I'd write you about school. My subjects are not interesting this year. Maybe they will be next year. At least, I hope so. . . .

Now suppose we tried to rearrange the same perfectly good English sentences as follows:

At least, I hope so. Maybe they will be next year. My subjects are not interesting this year. It's raining today, so I thought I'd write you about school. . . .

The same sentences turn into nonsense as discourse. You have no difficulty recognizing the disorder in the second letter, but you might find it hard to explain the exact sources of the difficulty. Even young children know such principles of discourse structure and use them to tell stories before they learn to write. Later in this book, in the chapter on organization and in the chapter on the paragraph, you will have an opportunity to examine closely the principles of English discourse structure and to work at identifying the ones you already know and those you must learn in order to write more effectively.

Exercise

Here is an example of a letter where the writer paid little heed to the principles of discourse structure:

Dear Mr. Jones:

She told me she knew about my record. I try to explain a problem I have, but I am not listened to. Peggy, you have no idea how hard I had it growing up. But she wouldn't listen. That's when I quit my job. The unemployment checks stopped coming two months ago. If I'm given another month, I'll find some money. I have nowhere else to go. The rent will get paid.

Sincerely,
John Smith

Evidently, the writer of this letter wanted to ask his landlord for more time to pay his overdue rent. But even this basic point is not clear. And the arguments to support the writer's plea are strewn randomly about the page.

The principles of written discourse structure require that people mentioned be clearly identified (thus, a pronoun should normally follow the mentioning of a person's name). Events should be narrated in an orderly way (thus, the tense of the verbs should clearly show the sequence of events). Connections between people, places, and things should be clear (thus, expressions such as *because, as a result,* and *therefore* should be used when one thing is presented as the cause of another). The writer of the above letter violated each of these principles and other discourse principles as well.

Study the letter and prepare to discuss why you think its discourse structure is weak. Rewrite the letter, making all the required points clear and organizing the argument more effectively.

Sentence structure

There is more to the structure of English than discourse structure, just as there is more to playing a card game than knowing when and how to take your turn. To play the game of English, you also need to use the principles of sentence structure. As a card player, you know how to arrange the *cards* into *hands,* such as straights, flushes, and full houses. As a speaker of English, you know how to arrange the *words* into *sentences,* which might be statements, questions, or commands. Because you have such knowledge, you readily recognize the following as English sentences:

> Skiers speed on mountains.
> Diplomats lie during negotiations.
> Politicians bargain at meetings.

These sentences can be likened to the following playable hands:

(a)   (b)   (c)

The three sentences in the first set have different words, but they are all *statements;* by the specified order of the words that compose them they are qualified to be sentences (noun, verb, preposition, noun). Similarly, the three hands in the second set have different cards, but they are all *straights;* by the specified order of the cards that compose them (2, 3, 4, 5, 6) they are qualified to be playable hands. However, if we take the same twelve words and try to arrange them as indicated below, they are no longer usable sentences because the words are no longer in a "playable" order; they can be likened to the card hands printed on the following page, which no longer qualify as straights:

> mountains on during speed
> negotiations lie bargain diplomats
> meeting at skiers politicians

(a)   (b)   (c)

Notice that in the earlier set of playable sentences, the words *skiers, diplomats,* and *politicians* were interchangeable (just as the twos of spades, hearts, and diamonds were interchangeable in the earlier set of playable straights). As a result of this interchangeability, all of the following are perfectly fine English sentences: *Diplomats speed on mountains; Politicians lie during negotiations; Skiers bargain at meetings. Speed, lie,* and *bargain* are similarly interchangeable. So are *on, during,* and *at.* But no member of these sets of three can be interchanged with a member of another set.

Because *skiers, diplomats,* and *politicians* are interchangeable, we can label them "nouns." Because *speed, lie,* and *bargain* cannot substitute for any noun but do substitute for one another, they get a different label: "verbs." And because *on, during* and *at* substitute for one another but not for nouns or verbs, they get yet another label: "prepositions." The words *mountains, negotiations,* and *meetings* are also nouns. Part of knowing the principles of sentence structure in English is knowing the parts of speech into which all of the words are grouped (just as part of knowing how to play cards is knowing the classes according to number and suit into which all of the cards fall).

To know the principles of sentence structure fully, you must also know how to group parts of speech together into meaningful sequences. In a card game it is not enough to know that the two red sixes and the two black sixes are the same in having a value higher than a five but lower than a seven; you must also know that all straights are defined according to the following pattern: $2 + 3 + 4 + 5 + 6 + 7 + 8 + 9 + 10 + J + Q + K + A$. Similarly, you are able to recognize *Skiers speed on mountains* as a sentence not only because you recognize *skiers* as a noun, *speed* as a verb, *on* as a preposition, and *mountain* as a noun, but also because you know that the following part-of-speech pattern defines a sequence of words as a sentence: NOUN + VERB + PREPOSITION + NOUN (this is of course only one of the many sentence patterns English allows). Later in this book, in the chapters on the sentence, you will have an opportunity to examine closely the principles of sentence structure in English and to work with as many of the types of cards (parts of speech) and as many of the hands (sentence patterns) as you need to know in order to play that special brand of language game called edited English.

Exercise

Here are the first few lines of the King James version of the Bible:

In the beginning God created the heaven and the earth. And the earth was without form, and void; and darkness was upon the face of the deep. And the Spirit of God moved upon the face of the waters.

Here are lists of all the words in the above passage grouped according to part of speech:

Nouns (N): beginning, God, heaven, earth, form, darkness, face, deep, Spirit, waters

Verbs (V): created, moved

Linking Verb (LV): was

Adjective (Adj): void

Article (Ar): the

Prepositions (P): in, without, upon, of

Conjunction (C): and

Using the part-of-speech labels given in parentheses above, write the sentence patterns for each of the three sentences in the passage. The pattern for the first sentence is:

```
P  +  Ar  +    N    +  N  +   V   + Ar  +   N    +  C  + Ar  +   N
In    the   beginning  God  created  the   heaven   and   the   earth.
```

After you have done this, try to create other English sentences using only the vocabulary from the above passage and only the sentence patterns (or parts of them that are also sentences) that occur in the passage. Here is such a sentence based on the pattern of the first sentence:

```
P  +  Ar  +  N  +    N    +   V   + Ar  +   N   +  C  + Ar  +    N
In    the   deep  darkness  moved   the   earth   and   the   waters.
```

After you have worked on this for a while, go on to invent other English sentences that follow the patterns in the passage but use other vocabulary. Here is such a sentence based on the pattern of the first sentence in the passage:

```
P   + Ar + N  +   N   +  V   +  Ar   +  N   +  C  +  Ar  +  N
From   a   spy   Henry   heard   some    truth   and   some    lies.
```

This exercise aims both to give you a feeling for how systematic the principles of sentence structure are and to show you how complex they are. Even though the above passage is one of the simplest you will ever encounter in written English, the sentence patterns in it are relatively complex. (There are infinitely more sentence patterns in English than there are playable hands in even the most complex of card games.)

Word structure

In addition to discourse structure and sentence structure, English has a third kind of structure: word structure. We are so familiar with the vocabulary of English that we often fail to notice that the words we are using have meaningful parts that are put together in principled ways. Consider the word *nondrinker*. When you hear it in a sentence, a single idea comes to mind: that of a person who does not drink alcoholic beverages. But parts of the idea are in fact communicated by parts of the word: *non-*, *drink*, and *-er*. Furthermore, your knowledge of word structure in English would cause you to take notice if someone started talking about a "*drinknoner*": You know that *non-* must appear before *drink*, not after it.

The analogy with card games can help with understanding word structure just as it did with discourse structure and sentence structure. Here are two drawings of the seven of hearts. One of them is analogous to *nondrinker* and the other to *drinknoner*. Can you guess which is which?

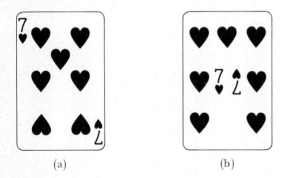

(a)   (b)

The one on the left is obviously a real card (just as *nondrinker* is a real word). The one on the right is not a real card, even though it is composed of exactly the same parts as the one on the left; like *drinknoner*, it fails to arrange the parts according to the rules of the game. But notice that both in cards and in language the phrase "rules of the game" has an entirely different sense here: it refers neither to rules that control taking turns and playing the correct hand (discourse structure) nor to rules for arranging the cards into playable hands (sentence structure) but to rules that specify the content and arrangements of the symbols *on* the cards (word structure).

Perhaps you have never noticed before now that five of the seven hearts on the seven of hearts face one way, and only two hearts face the other way. Still, you had no difficulty recognizing which card had the correct arrangement of hearts and numbers. You also know that the heart and the number seven can appear on other cards, having the same values they have on the seven of hearts. Similarly, you know that the meaningful parts of the word *nondrinker* can recur in other words. Here are some lists where the words on each list contain one of the meaningful parts of *nondrinker:*

*non*conformist	*drink*	employ*er*
*non*smoker	*drink*able	travel*er*
*non*political	*drink*ing	writ*er*
*non*drip	*drink*s	build*er*

And just as you know that the value of a playing card appears in two corners, (with the small suit symbol under the number or letters), and that the large suit symbols appear specifically arrayed in the central area of the card, so too you know that word parts are of specified types and must appear in specified arrangements. For instance, *non-* is a PREFIX; *drink* is a ROOT; and *-er* is a SUFFIX. Using these terms, we can make this general statement about one type of word structure in English: There are many words in English (such as *nondrinker*) that are structured according to the following pattern:

PREFIX + ROOT + SUFFIX

Here are some other words like *nondrinker* that follow this pattern:

Prefix	+ Root	+ Suffix
mis	+ treat	+ ment
re	+ tract	+ ion
re	+ deep	+ en
dis	+ bar	+ ment
ex	+ press	+ ion
en	+ light	+ en
dis	+ color	+ ation

These words, and the patterns they represent, illustrate only one of very many such patterns of word formation in English.

Knowledge of English includes knowledge of the lists of English word parts (prefixes, roots, suffixes), knowledge of what each individual word part on each list means, and knowledge of a wide array of patterns for arranging these word parts into real English words. But much of your knowledge of English word formation is now probably implicit (like your knowledge of how to tie a shoe—you know how to do it, but would have a hard time explaining exactly what you do). Later in this book, in the chapter on words, you will have an opportunity to examine in detail the issues of word structure and word meaning and to sort out what you already know about English vocabulary from what you need to learn in order to use words most effectively in edited English.

Exercise

Here are two well-known poems. You may have studied them closely in the past, focusing on the ideas they express. But the poems also reveal interesting patterns of word use—patterns that contribute to the artistic impact of the poems. This exercise aims simply to have you look closely at the patterns of word formation favored by each poet. The words in the Williams poem employ much simpler patterns of word formation than those in the Roethke poem; Williams' words have fewer prefixes and suffixes than Roethke's.

Take a look at the vocabulary of each poem, especially at the words I have underscored. Find out what you can about the patterns of prefixes, roots, and suffixes in these words. I will make some additional suggestions about how to do this below, but first read the poems.

The Red Wheel Barrow

So much depends
upon

a red wheel
barrow

glazed with rain
water

beside the white
chickens

—WILLIAM CARLOS WILLIAMS

Dolor

I have known the inexorable sadness of pencils.
Neat in their boxes, dolor of pad and paper-weight,
All the misery of manilla folders and mucilage,
Desolation in immaculate public places,
Lonely reception room, lavatory, switchboard,
The unalterable pathos of basin and pitcher,
Ritual of multigraph, paper-clip, comma,
Endless duplication of lives and objects.
And I have seen dust from the walls of institutions,
Finer than flour, alive, more dangerous than silica,
Sift, almost invisible, through long afternoons of tedium,
Dropping a fine film on nails and delicate eyebrows,
Glazing the pale hair, the duplicate gray standard faces.

—THEODORE ROETHKE

These poets use the principles of English word formation in very different ways. Most of Williams' words have one meaningful part; most of Roethke's words have more than one. Start with the underscored words and make lists of other English words that use each of the meaningful parts you can identify in the word you are working with. Here are some examples:

beside:	*be*hind	*a*side
	*be*tween	*sid*ing
	*be*fore	*side*d

unalterable:	*un*thinkable	*alter*	break*able*
	*un*proven	*alter*ing	conceiv*able*
	*un*substantiated	*alter*ed	suit*able*

Do not expect to find easy answers. One of the purposes of this exercise is to demonstrate how intricate the principles of English word formation can become.

As you work on the exercise you may wish to think about the relationship between each poet's patterns of word formation and the artistic meaning of the poems. How especially do Roethke's word choices contribute to the ideas he is trying to communicate in the poem?

Sound structure

The fourth and final type of English structure is sound structure, which in written English roughly relates to spelling. The principles of English sound structure function simultaneously with the principles of discourse, sentence, and word structure. As with these other types of structure, the card game analogy can be helpful. There are some things you know about the cards in a deck that have little to do with their symbolic values in a given game. You know for instance that none of the suits of cards is colored green: Two are red and two are black. You know that no card in the deck has the number one on it. In a similar way, you know certain things about English words that have little to do with their meanings or uses in sentences. You know for instance that no English word makes use of the guttural sound that German uses in the pronunciation of the last two letters of *Bach*. And you know that the Russian letter И never appears in a written English word.

Similarly, as you know that a club and a spade never appear on the same playing card, and neither do the letters Q and K, so you know that the sounds (and letters) *m* and *b* never appear in that order at the beginning of an English word. It is important to note that you can *play* cards perfectly well even if someone paints all the hearts green, and you can understand English even if it is spoken with a German accent, and even if many of the words are misspelled. But in each instance you *know* that some kind of rule of the game is being broken.

Since this book is about written English, there will be discussion of the sound structure of English only when sound structure relates to spelling. In a later chapter on spelling, you will have an opportunity to study the English spelling system in detail and to study those patterns of spelling that reflect principles of English sound structure.

Exercise

I have just compared knowledge of English sound structure and of the English spelling system with knowledge of the colors and arrangements of the numbers and suit symbols on playing cards. However, whereas you never have to draw a playing card from memory, you do in effect have to draw words from memory when you spell them. Therefore, the more you can learn about the highly systematic nature of English sound structure and its relation to the spelling system, the better off you will be. You will work on this extensively in Chapter Ten. For now, let us just try to get a more concrete impression of the fact that there are indeed systematic principles governing both English pronunciation and English spelling. For instance, when an English word begins with the sound usually spelled with the letter *s*, then only certain consonants may immediately follow that *s*. And when a word ends with the sound spelled *th*, only certain consonants may immediately precede *th*. Try to learn something about the principle governing just which consonants can immediately follow an *s* at the beginning of a word and the other principle governing just which consonants can precede *th* at the end of a word. Here are two groups of words to help you in your search. The lists are not necessarily complete:

(1) sky, scream, stale, slate, snake, spare, smear, swear
(2) sixth, tenth, twelfth, fifth

Language Variation

In the first section of this chapter, we looked at four kinds of structure in English: discourse structure, sentence structure, word structure, and sound structure. We compared the kinds of language structure to kinds of rules in a card game: rules for taking turns (discourse structure), rules for arranging cards into hands (sentence structure), rules for arranging symbols on cards (word structure), and rules determining the shapes and colors of the symbols on the cards (sound and spelling structure). We can make one more use of the card game analogy before we leave it. Many card games have slightly different sets of rules depending on where the game is played, how many players there are, and why they are playing. Sometimes in poker, only three cards are dealt before betting begins; at other times, five cards are dealt. Sometimes twos are wild; at other times, they are not. The same is true of English. Sometimes the game of English is played according to slightly different rules from those appropriate at other times. There are different varieties of English, determined by where and why it is being spoken and by the speaker. Some of these varieties are called *dialects* of English; others are called *styles* of English. Dialects tend to be systematically associated with particular groups of speakers of English. Styles tend to be systematically associated with particular situations in which English is used. A given person, who *speaks* a certain dialect virtually all of the time, may *use* a certain style on some but not on all occasions. Edited English is a style of English. Before we try to define it and distinguish it from dialects of English and from other styles, let us look at some dialects and styles of English, beginning with dialects that are determined by where English is spoken: regional dialects.

Regional dialects

The distinction between British English and American English may serve as a very obvious example of a regional dialect distinction. The groups of people who speak the one or the other dialect can be identified according to where they come from. Differences among dialects in discourse structure are few. In sentence structure, British and American English differ in a number of ways. Americans tend to say, *The class is studying Shakespeare; The committee is discussing policy. Class* and *committee,* because they are grammatically singular—i.e., have no plural *s* ending—take the singular form of the verb, *is.* The British, on the other hand, consider group nouns like *class* and *committee* to be plural and tend to use the plural form of the verb with them: *The class are studying Shakespeare; The committee are discussing policy.*

In word structure, dialect differences usually show up as differences in the lists of words rather than as differences in word parts or the principles for combining them; i.e., British English does not have any prefixes or suffixes that American English lacks. Here are just a few of the many differences in vocabulary between British and American English:

British	American
lorry	truck
lift	elevator
disc	record
petrol	gas

to motor	to drive
garage	service station
cinema	movie
coach	bus
cheerio	good-bye

Can you think of other instances where the British tend to use a different vocabulary item from the one Americans use?

There are also systematic differences between British and American English pronunciation. The most noted difference is the absence of the consonant sound *r* at the end of many syllables where most Americans pronounce it, as, for example, when the British pronounce *far* as "fah." There are of course other differences in the sound systems of the two dialects, but the differences in the spelling systems will have a more direct bearing on the subject matter of this book. Here are just a few examples:

British	**American**
colour	color
centre	center
defence	defense
paediatrician	pediatrician

Differences such as these, and problems they can cause you when you are writing edited English, are discussed in greater detail in the chapter on spelling.

All varieties of English (dialects and styles) share the great majority of all four types of structural principles. A given variety is usually defined by listing just those structural features that are peculiar to it. What sets off a given dialect or style of English from all other varieties of English is that all the features on such a list tend to *go together*. For instance, a speaker of English who says *The committee are* will also favor the words *lorry* and *lift,* will also pronounce *far* as "fah," and will also favor the spellings, *colour* and *centre*. Even though there is widespread variation in English, the patterns in the variation are thus very systematic.

It goes without saying that formal written British dialect is in every way the equal of its American counterpart. But writers in America are expected to follow the grammatical conventions and spelling conventions of American English and to prefer American vocabulary where it differs from British vocabulary. For this reason, in this book edited English is considered a part of the American dialect of the English language.

Exercise

There are regional dialects within the American dialect of English. In a sense, there are as many regional dialects of English as there are places where it is spoken. Wherever a list of sound, word, and sentence structure features consistently correlates with the place of origin of groups of speakers of English, there is reason to speak of a regional dialect, or at least a subtype of a regional dialect. Here for instance are some features of language structure that in a very general way tend to distinguish the speech of Southerners and Northerners:

Sentence structure

Southerners	Northerners
Did you not eat?	Didn't you eat?
I might could do it.	I could do it.
You oughtn't to lie.	You hadn't ought to lie.

Vocabulary

Southerners	Northerners
y'all	you (youse)
grinder	sub, hoagie
low (What cows do.)	moo
bucket	pail

Pronunciation

Southerners	Northerners
here = "hee-*uh*"	here = "hee*r*"
tennis = "t*i*n-nis"	tennis = "t*e*n-nis"
creek = "kr*ee*k"	creek = "kr*i*k"
borrow = "bar-*uh*"	borrow = "bar-*oh*"

Not all Southerners or Northerners, of course, prefer all of the features listed above, and several are features of casual conversational style, not of careful spoken language or of written language. But they illustrate an important fact known to all Americans: that American English is composed of different regional dialects.

Think of your own experience with English, in the place you now live or in places you may have lived previously. Then try to make your own list of features of sentence structure, vocabulary, and pronunciation that characterize regions of the United States you have lived in.

Why do you think most of the regional dialect features in America are in the spoken language? Notice that there are no regional variations in the spelling of English words; why is this so?

Social dialects

In addition to regional dialects like the British and American ones, the English language also has *social* dialects. There are groups of people born and raised in a region whose speech differs from the speech of other people from the same region. The more a society succeeds in guaranteeing its citizens equal educational and occupational opportunities (thus leveling differences of social class), the less noticeable social dialect differences become. But they do exist in the English-speaking world, and you need to be aware of them.

Imagine two people watching a television news account of oil companies artificially inflating prices during a shortage. Both are natives of a large northeastern city. But one is a college-educated corporate executive and the other is a blue-collar worker who dropped out of high school. Both are upset by the news account. In their separate living rooms, the corporate executive exclaims, *I'm not going to tolerate any more corruption!,* and the blue-collar worker exclaims, *I ain't gonna put up wit' no more ripoffs!* Each of these sentences represents a different social dialect: each is the product of systematic choices in sentence structure, word structure, and sound structure made from distinct lists of features of social dialect.

The first sentence represents *standard* dialect; the second, *vernacular* dialect. In sentence structure, the use of *not . . . any* (avoiding a double negative) marks the first sentence as standard, whereas the use of *ain't . . . no* (using a double negative) marks the second sentence as vernacular. In word choice, both *tolerate* and *corruption* represent standard vocabulary, and *ain't* represents vernacular vocabulary; *gonna* and *ripoffs,* while not limited to use in vernacular dialects, are much more likely to occur in vernacular. Differences in sound structure do not usually show up in spelling, but I have tried to represent one sound feature of the vernacular sentence by departing from the standard spelling of the word *with:* Notice the final *t'* instead of *th* in the vernacular sentence.

Edited English, the special style of written English treated in this book, is part of the standard social dialect of English, and it carefully avoids any structural features that are explicitly limited to use in vernacular social dialects of English.

Exercise

Regional and social dialects tend to overlap. That is, in any given region, the structural features most common to the region tend also to show up mostly in the speech of those with less education and less income. But a given list of structural features usually does correlate more directly with either region or social class, regardless of region. For instance, the passage printed below contains many structural features associated with vernacular dialects from various parts of the United States. Other features clearly represent the vernacular dialect of the middle Appalachian region. Read it and then list features of discourse structure, sentence structure, word structure, and sound structure that seem to relate this selection to vernacular dialects generally. Then try to isolate structural features that seem to identify it as the regional vernacular of the middle Appalachian region.

> Some boys was a-walkin' down a road deep in a holler. One of 'em said, "Hit's a heap o' wild animals in them there woods, an' bein' we's 'thout of a gun, I b'lieve I'll not go in 'ere. You'uns can do what you wants, but I ain't a-goin' noways." His heart was a-beatin' up in his neck. Th' other two, they laughed; said, "Ain't nothin' to worry 'bout yonder. We heared the wild animals done made off from hereabouts."

Spoken style versus written style

Whereas English dialects, both regional and social, represent relatively invariant behavior of speakers of English, styles change to suit the occasion. If we compared dialects and styles with habits of dress, we might relate British English to the bowler hat and clothes that go with it and American English to the cowboy hat and clothes that go with it. British businessmen never dress like cowboys, and American westerners never wear derbies. But styles of speech might be better compared to the difference between, say, a dress and a swimsuit. The same person might wear both outfits, but on different occasions, and for drastically different purposes. Just as a person puts on a swimsuit to spend time in water and a dress to spend time out of water, so too does one "put on" written style to spend time on a sheet of paper, and spoken style to spend time off it.

In order to learn something about just how noticeable the differences between spoken style and written style can be, read the following short conversation, adapted from a TV soap opera, and compare it with the letter below it, giving a written version of the same ideas that Sam might have written, had he not been able to talk to Janet.

A conversation
SAM: (There are) some things about me that you don't know—that I'm not very proud of.
JANET: What?
SAM: (I've) been in a lot of trouble. (I) tried to clear it up. Peggy found out a lot of things about me.
JANET: What?
SAM: Things. Peggy found out . . . We almost split up.
JANET: Why?

A letter
Dear Janet,
I am writing, reluctantly, to explain why we must not see each other again. I am a married man, and I love my wife. We have a vow never to keep anything from each other. We made the vow a few years ago after I had gotten into a

lot of trouble. I tried to conceal it from her, but she found out. My deceit almost broke up our marriage. The only way I could save it was by promising never to hide anything from her again.

In many conversations, neither party has any special message to get across to the other; the two are simply spending time together, communicating. However, in the above conversation, Sam does have a message he wants to get across to Janet. Thus, their roles as sender and receiver of the message are similar in both the spoken and written discourses. For this reason, we may assume that the medium of communication (sounds in air vs. marks on paper) mainly accounts for differences in language structure between the conversation and the letter.

The basic unit of discourse structure in spoken style is the interchange: a pair of utterances, one by each of the participants in a conversation. Notice how the whole flow of discourse in the above conversation depends on Janet's completing each interchange in just the way Sam expects, so that he can then proceed to initiate a new interchange. The basic unit of discourse structure in written style is the paragraph: a series of smoothly flowing sentences treating one idea—an idea that is usually summarized in the first sentence of the paragraph. Notice that, in the letter above, Sam begins by telling Janet exactly why he is writing. This idea is not reached until very late in the conversation, in a portion of it that I have not even transcribed above.

In sentence structure, spoken style usually favors shorter sentences; written style, longer sentences. This is because a reader can see more words at one time than a listener can hear. A reader can also reread if a long sentence is not understood the first time. Notice that the sentences in the conversation above are generally shorter than those in the letter. There is another tendency that differentiates spoken and written sentences: speakers often leave out pronouns and contracted auxiliary verbs at the beginning of sentences; parentheses indicate this possibility in the conversation above. Written style never allows such omissions. Thus, Janet would hardly notice if Sam said, *Been in a lot of trouble,* instead of *I've been in a lot of trouble.* The context makes it quite clear *who* has been in trouble: the speaker; in this case, Sam. And the *-en* on the word *been* makes the tense of the verb clear enough: the contracted *have* in *I've* is clearly implied. Written English, on the other hand tolerates no such omissions, partly because the reader and writer are not face to face in the same room, where misunderstandings could be clarified by questions, and partly because the conventions of written English allow little deviation from established standards.

In word structure, the differences between spoken style and written style are tendencies rather than absolute distinctions. Certain words, like *don't, a lot,* and *split up* in the conversation above, tend to be used more in speech than in writing, and certain other words, like *reluctantly, deceit,* and *conceal* in the letter above, tend to be used more in writing than in speech.

The most radical difference between spoken and written style is in sound structure: written style does not have sound structure. Instead, it has what might be called *letter structure:* a set of principles for representing the language in symbols for the eye rather than in symbols for the ear. The sound system of English is called its phonology; the letter system, its orthography (or spelling system). There are certain relationships between the two systems, but there are just as many independent tendencies. The study of English spelling rules is clearly a central part of the study of written style in English. To remind yourself of just how dramatic this difference is, you must realize that the conversation *printed* above is not, strictly speaking, spoken style (because it has been written down and printed in this book); you must picture two speakers actually saying the words printed there. The letter, on the other hand, represents written style only when read silently; the words are not even sounded out, but perceived directly through the eyes.

Edited English is a written style of English. It conforms to all the structural tendencies that distinguish the letter printed above from the conversation transcribed above. We will see in the next subsection, however, that not all written English is edited English. But before you go on to that section, do the following exercise; it will give you additional insight into the distinction between spoken and written styles, and it will illustrate the fact that there are different types of spoken styles.

Exercise

The conversation between Sam and Janet printed earlier represents what is often called casual (or colloquial) spoken style, and sometimes simply conversational style. There is another type of spoken style, which we may call careful spoken style. It differs from casual spoken style chiefly in that one of the speakers tends to do all the talking. The other is limited to the role of listener—but a listener to whom the speaker pays close attention. The listener is expected to show attention and comprehension by nodding the head, or saying *yes, I see,* or *uh-huh* at appropriate intervals. Below I have printed two narratives by one person. The first represents careful spoken style; the second represents written style. Study them and attempt to determine just how they differ in discourse structure, sentence structure, and word structure. Technically, they cannot be compared in sound structure, since written style has no sound, but you might learn some additional things about the difference between pronounced and spelled English if you read the spoken version aloud several times and compare it with the impression many of the same words make on you when you read them silently in the written version.

A narrative in careful spoken style
(elements in brackets are interruptions by the listener)
> The girls are just sitting there eating lunch, and it looks like—like Charlie Brown and Woodstock and Snoopy were going to play—well, they were going to play baseball, but—but Snoopy ran off with the bat and ball and the skateboard. [Uh-huh.] So Charlie Brown sort of looks dejected—[Uh-huh.]—unhappy 'cause he can't play now. Snoopy took off with his stuff, [Uh-huh.] and he's—Snoopy's very happy, singing.

A narrative in written style
> Lucy and Sally were quietly sitting on the bench by Snoopy's doghouse, Sally eating lunch and Lucy drinking a soda, when Snoopy appeared on the scene riding his skateboard. Charlie Brown and Woodstock came up to Woodstock's tree looking sad; it seems Snoopy had broken up their baseball game by stealing the bat and ball and skateboarding away with it, feeling pleased with himself for his mischievousness.

After you have carefully compared the spoken narrative and written narrative, testing whether and how the claims I made about the difference between spoken and written styles are illustrated in them, go back and compare the careful spoken narrative with the casual spoken conversation between Sam and Janet given earlier. Can you discover any tendencies that support the distinction between two types of spoken style: casual and careful?

Edited English: formal written style

So far in this part of the chapter we have seen that edited English is part of the American dialect of English, that it is part of the standard dialect of English, and that it is a written style and not a spoken style of English. To complete our definition of edited English we need one more distinction: that between informal and formal written styles. Edited English is the formal written style. Informal written style, generally speaking, is the style used when people write quickly, with little forethought, and give little attention to applying the principles of writing taught in the schools. Formal written style (edited English) is the product of careful planning and the conscious application of special principles of discourse structure, sentence structure, word choice, spelling, and punctuation that have been developed, used, and passed on by good writers of the past. The distinction between informal written style and edited English has nothing to do with correctness; both are correct. Edited English is simply more effective and objective; its messages come through clearly to a very wide audience of readers. Here are two paragraphs written by a college freshman. She had listened to a recorded lecture, and she was asked to write down quickly as much as she could remember of what she had heard. In doing so, she used the informal written style. Later she was asked to think about the ideas in her notes and to plan a well-argued and well-written essay based on that information. She outlined, drafted, and revised. The paragraph in formal written style (edited English) resulted from those efforts. Read the two paragraphs. How do they differ?

Informal written style
The fact that a girl can earn her own living and may leave her husband to do so, brings out respect. Half the working women are married, which makes them an economic asset, something they haven't been since the days of the farm. Since they're out, the husband helps with the housework, which leads toward equality. In a marriage, there's either equality or the stronger personality takes over.

Formal written style: edited English
Today's women are in a position unique in their history. For the first time, they are not shackled by marriage; they can go out and earn their own livelihood. This fact has enhanced progress toward sexual equality. With wives spending more time outside the home, husbands assume more of the household responsibilities, and the two roles in marriage tend to equalize. Personality, rather than sex, now determines who will be the dominant partner in a marriage.

In discourse structure, the two paragraphs are very similar: they both express one idea, and the idea is summarized in the first sentence. Neither paragraph relies on interaction or requires the reader to be able to ask questions of the writer in order to understand the message; they are both clearly examples of written style. But they are different, and systematically so. The differences tend to be a matter of degree rather than of kind.

The writer of edited English works harder to make the sentences in a paragraph flow smoothly together. The informal paragraph above starts out talking about *a girl* (singular) but then switches to *women, they, them* (all plural); the formal paragraph starts with *women* and sticks with plural nouns and pronouns: *their, they, wives.* The informal paragraph uses contractions; the formal paragraph avoids them. The informal paragraph favors locutions that are also common in spoken styles: *brings out, there's, takes over.* The formal paragraph favors words that are not common in conversation and whose meanings are not worn out through overuse: *shackled, enhanced, responsibilities, determines, dominant.* The informal paragraph does not use punctuation to enhance meaning: The comma after *asset* should probably be replaced by a dash, which would relate what follows more closely to what just preceded. The formal paragraph does use punctuation to enhance meaning: The semicolon after *marriage* in the second sentence directs the reader to consider the close connection in meaning between the two clauses it joins. Features like these distinguish edited English from informal written style.

Edited English can express the whole range of human thoughts and emotions. It can be fitted to your own personality. It can be humorous or serious. But in every case it conforms to a number of very specific norms. To be truly literate, you must know what these norms are. You must work to learn them. After you have mastered the norms of edited English, you may on occasion choose to violate one or another of them. But you will be able to do so creatively and effectively only if you know them well.

Chapters Three through Eleven of this book are a detailed description of just those features of language structure that characterize edited English and thus distinguish it from informal written style and from spoken styles and that make it part of standard social dialect and American regional dialect. The diagram below summarizes the distinctions we have made to isolate and define edited English; keep in mind that edited English shares most of its structural features with other dialects and styles of English. You should especially remember this as you work through the rest of this book. In fact, you should seek to relate your study of edited English to the large store of knowledge you already have of the many other varieties that together with edited English make up the English language.

The English Language
- American Regional Dialect
  - Standard Social Dialect
    - Written Style
      - Formal: EDITED ENGLISH
      - Informal
    - Spoken Style
      - Careful
      - Casual
  - Vernacular Social Dialect
- British Regional Dialect

Exercise

The vocalist practices singing by intensive work with musical scales; the pianist starts with "Chopsticks" and works up to more complex but no less structured exercises; the football player works out with weights. The comparable exercise for the would-be writer is the 500-word theme. It is doubtful that anyone has ever written such a theme outside the composition classroom. But inside the composition classroom, the 500-word theme is the staple form of exercise for the student of edited English. The 500-word theme is long enough to give exercise in all four levels of edited-English structure, and it is short enough for the writing of several in a semester so that the student can learn by trial and error. Printed below is such a theme written early in the college semester by a student who had obviously learned much about edited English from his earlier schooling. As you read it, ask yourself how it is different (because it is written in edited English) from an informal letter describing the same experiences or from a conversational account. For that matter, consider how some of the theme's ideas might appear in vernacular dialect or even British dialect. That is, what is it about the language of this theme that makes it edited English?

ADAPTABILITY

Like many people my age, I had quite a few jobs before entering college. In all of my jobs, from paper carrier to industrial worker, I learned something besides simply how to do that job, but at one job in particular I underwent a definite character change. While employed at West End Car-care Center, I developed what I feel to be a broader sense of adaptability.

When I took the job at West End, it was like any other job; it was a way to make money. My primary responsibility was running the gasoline pumps, but there is much more to that task than just pumping gas. I had to service each customer's vehicle; check the oil, battery, and radiator levels; and visually inspect fan belts and water hoses for wear and possible replacement. I had to communicate with the customer about the condition of the vehicle—about things like badly worn tires or corroded battery terminals—and if necessary, I had to schedule a date for the car to be repaired or more thoroughly serviced. At the same time, I was supposed to do everything as quickly as I could so that business would flow smoothly. West End also advertised free pick-up and delivery of any vehicle scheduled for service; therefore, I frequently had to pick up or deliver a customer's car.

I learned to adapt to many different automobiles in a wide range of mechanical conditions. I have driven cars ranging from Cadillac Eldorados and Porsches to small imports and American compacts. Most of them had mechanical faults. Problems like worn shock absorbers or a misfiring engine were annoying at worst, but major problems such as extremely bad steering or faulty brakes were sometimes plainly dangerous. I learned to adopt an extremely defensive style of driving while behind the wheel of an unfamiliar vehicle. I assumed that nothing on the car would work, and I handled it accordingly. This course of action may seem overly pessimistic, but that is how I adapted to preserve both the vehicle and myself.

Because of the nature of my work, I would be constantly interrupted while doing one thing, only to have to perform some totally unrelated task; therefore, I had to adapt to a new method of working. I learned to concentrate on one job, for instance rebuilding a carburetor; switch to something else, perhaps refreezing an air conditioner; go on to yet another task; and then return to the carburetor without having lost my train of thought. This ability to adapt quickly to a change in my thought process and then return to my original point of concentration has definitely remained with me.

Direct contact with a large number of people in a relatively short period of time allowed me to learn to adapt in yet another way: I have learned to adapt quickly to different personalities. I tried to relate to customers as unique individuals, each with their own special problems and needs. I found that if I tried to serve all customers according to their individual personalities, then I would also find it easier to perform my job more efficiently. Business people, senior citizens, housewives, tourists, teenagers, blue collar workers—I treated no one as "just another customer."

West End Car-care Center taught me several kinds of adaptability: adaptability to changing physical situations, adaptability to sudden changes in lines of thought, and adaptability to people and their individual needs. The job itself was ordinary, but what it taught me was quite extraordinary.

> —Keith Williams, a student

Two | *Ideas*

Edited English has the same basic function as other varieties of English: the transfer of ideas from one mind to another. Thus, the study of ideas—what they are and how to create them—is not limited to the study of edited English. Although you should have clear ideas and important ideas in mind no matter what style of English you are using, edited English has a way of forcing you to confront ideas and to struggle with the really difficult task of finding good ideas. Students of English composition know better than anyone how the blank page can seem to mirror the content of the brain. The aim of this chapter is to help you confront the blank page not only with a ready-made store of ideas, but also with some confidence that you will be able to use them.

Language and Ideas

The discussion of ideas in this section is not intended as a philosophical one; instead, it is based on what language scholars have discovered about ideas through careful analysis of English and other languages. Since you already know a great deal about English, you should be able to evaluate many of the suggestions made here by careful attention to the words and sentences given as examples. Your aim should be to learn how to use language skills you already possess as a means to discover new ideas and ultimately to adapt them to your needs as a writer.

Categories and predications

Ideas are basically of two types: categories and predications. Categories are labels that classify things into groups because of some similarity of structure or function. Predications express connections among categories or their members. A category usually appears in language as a single word; a predication usually appears as a complete sentence. *Child, falcon, azalea, pebble,* and *malice* label categories. *Michelangelo created the Pietà, War disrupts life, Women suffer, Moby Dick is an archetype,* and *Jefferson was shy* are predications. Let us look closer at both types of ideas.

The word *pebble* is a category label that groups together certain things and sets them off from other things. Pebbles are concrete, not abstract (like *malice,* say). And they differ from other concrete things: Children, falcons, and azaleas are alive; pebbles are not. Statues, like pebbles, are both concrete and nonliving, but statues are products of human labor; pebbles are not. Even more specific features differentiate pebbles from bricks, from rocks, from stones, from shells. Examine your idea of a pebble. What exact size range does the idea require? Are your pebbles round? Are they of certain specific colors? Are certain uses implicit in your idea of a pebble? You probably have relatively definite answers to these questions, because you have a clear *idea* of what a pebble is.

I have given the statement, *War disrupts life,* as an example of a predication. This sentence connects war and life and also specifies the disruptive nature of the connection. The sentence calls on you to consider your idea of *war* (a category) and your idea of *life* (a category) and then to examine what the one has to do with the other. You are led to focus on just those aspects of the idea of war that can influence life (the portions of the idea that focus on valor and justice are not evoked). And you are led to think about just those aspects of life that war can disrupt: life as a way of life or daily routine. The sentence does not evoke the idea of life as the opposite of death (the statement, *War destroys life,* would make you think about death). The point is this: the very particular connection between war and life expressed in the statement, *War disrupts life,* is itself an idea, here called a predication.

Because categories are expressed most often in single words, you may tend to feel that they are somehow sacred and unchangeable. Like the sun, the moon, mountains, and oceans, they seem part of the world you were born into, things you must adapt to and learn to live with if you are going to survive. But this is not the case. It is true that you are limited in your power to create new *words* or do away with old ones. But you have more power than you may realize over the *ideas* that words label. A concrete word like *crab* or an abstract word like *feminism* can label an amazing array of ideas. Think what *crab* must mean to a Chesapeake Bay fisherman as opposed to a Denver insurance executive. How different an idea must the word *feminism* convey when expressed by the editor of *Ms.* magazine, a Kentucky coal miner, or an Irish peasant woman.

As for predications, most people do not feel the same limitations on their freedom of thought and expression as they might feel about categories. Whereas you have to pick from a fixed list of words to express categories, you are perfectly free to make up your own sentences to express predications. But predications are not all that different from categories. Some sentences express rich and original ideas; others are old and worn out, even meaningless. Compare the meaning of *An apple a day keeps the doctor away* with *Defrauding widows keeps money in the treasury.* The first is so familiar that, even after reading it several times, you may wonder just what kind of truly meaningful connection between apples and doctors it is trying to express. The second sentence, on the other hand, is thought provoking. You do not normally think of defrauding widows as a means of balancing a governmental budget, but the sentence forced you to relate the two and consider the irony of the relationship.

Exercises

a. Consider the words listed below. Probe the content of the ideas they label for you. Some of the words may evoke rich and detailed personal experiences of yours; others may be almost empty of meaning. Ask yourself why. (Have you had more experience with some of them than with others?) Then add your own words to the list. Look especially for words rich in content to you, and for other words empty of content—both abstract words and concrete words.

(1) aluminum	(8) crab	(15) peach
(2) azalea	(9) falcon	(16) piety
(3) arrow	(10) feminism	(17) shrub
(4) brutality	(11) fidelity	(18) surgeon
(5) child	(12) God	(19) tenderness
(6) conundrum	(13) hibiscus	(20) toad
(7) cook	(14) malice	(21) unicorn

b. Consider the sentences listed below. Determine the exact nature of the predication that each expresses. Is it original, or is it worn out? Might others disagree with your assessment? Who might? Why? Try to arrange the sentences in order of originality.

(1) Beggars can't be choosers.
(2) Pollution threatens our national survival.
(3) Life is just a bowl of cherries.
(4) A stitch in time saves nine.
(5) Crude oil will lubricate the electorate.
(6) A bird in the hand is worth two in the bush.
(7) Human rights are women's rights.

  (8) Stupidity decreed the world food crisis.
  (9) April showers bring May flowers.
(10) Fire frightens tulips.

Received ideas

From the day you were born, you began to develop an inventory of ideas. Categories probably came first: the idea of a face, a smile, mother, father. But predications were not long delayed. As a baby, you soon learned the connection between crying and food, between cooing and the smile it evoked. The vast majority of these earliest ideas were received from parents, family, peers, teachers, and television. This is really an advantage. What individual, after all, is capable of discovering afresh all of the categories and predications the human race has amassed over the centuries? What if you had to find out for yourself about the danger of fire, of wild animals, of poisons, of thunderstorms? What if your generation had to reinvent the family, rediscover agriculture, reestablish the sciences? It is clearly a boon that your cultural tradition provides a vast store of ready categories and predications.

But it is also true that full participation in your individuality requires you to personalize received categories, to give them your unique stamp, and even perhaps to make a special contribution to expanding the inventory and deepening the content of human ideas. Received ideas can, in fact, tyrannize your intelligence if you do not struggle with them and reshape and expand them in the light of your own experience. You have to infuse words like *radical, conservative, reactionary, racist, militant, bigot,* and *snob* with the content of your own experience, or such labels will become the masters of your thoughts instead of their servants. Often enough, this struggle will show you that words such as these, from thoughtless overuse, have lost contact with reality and should be dropped altogether —perhaps making way for terms that label ideas you yourself may have a role in creating.

Predications may also come precoded. Maxims are ready examples: *A penny saved is a penny earned.* But there are innumerable other received predications that play important roles in thinking. Here are some:

Those who live by the sword shall die by the sword.
All men are created equal.
Judge not and you shall not be judged.
Do unto others as you would have them do unto you.
The last shall be first.

These are among the greatest ideas of history. But unless you infuse them with your own experience, unless you learn their meanings anew and reassert them as though no one ever had before, then they too can come to control instead of serve your ability to think. Think, for instance, about the meaning of the sentence, *All men are created equal.* Jefferson had very specific notions when he included this assertion in the Declaration of Independence: He was concerned about the unjust tax laws that England was imposing on the Colonies. But many generations of Americans have given this sentence new meaning: To Lincoln it applied to the evils of slavery; to Susan B. Anthony it meant that women should have the vote; to Martin Luther King, Jr., it was a call to fight racism. What does it mean to you?

Exercises

a. Make a list of at least ten categories whose meanings for you have come mostly from others rather than from your own experiences. Words like *bigot, slob,* and *racist* are ready examples, though words like *truth, democracy,* and *socialism* can also label mostly received meaning. After you make the list, ask youself what kinds of concrete experience you would need to have in order to give the words your own meanings. (Unless you have truly suffered from bigotry, you may not know what *bigot* really means; unless you have exercised your right to vote, or been denied it, you may never fully know what *democracy* means.)

b. Make a list of at least five maxims or famous quotations you know well (e.g., *Early to bed, early to rise makes one healthy, wealthy, and wise* or *An eye for an eye; a tooth for a tooth*). After you list them, ask yourself what they really mean to you. Then ask yourself what kinds of experiences you would need to have to infuse such received predications with new life. (If you have never worked hard for long hours, the first maxim above can mean little to you; the second will have meaning to the extent that you have experienced "justice" without mercy in your own life.)

Created ideas

Of course, not all ideas are received. Many categories and predications come fresh and crisp from probing minds in every generation. Some new categories are true discoveries of phenomena simply unknown to exist before, for example, the discovery of oxygen in the seventeenth century and the discovery of x-rays in the nineteenth. But other new categories result from creative regroupings of facts known before-hand but not fully understood. Freud's positing of the unconscious mind as an explanation for dreams and other psychic phenomena is an example. And there are more ordinary, but still inventive, creations of new categories. Think of the many new categories that appeared in our culture as a result of the invention of the automobile or television.

As for predications, there is a sense in which every sentence represents the creation of a new idea. Even a sentence as often repeated as *I don't know how I'm going to make ends meet* represents an essentially different idea every time it is spoken. This is because the "I" is different every time, the "ends" are different every time, and the situation to which the sentence refers is a unique event. But there is no denying that some sentences express more creative and original predications than others. Poets are masters of such originality.

Word

The word bites like a fish.
Shall I throw it back free
Arrowing to the sea
Where thoughts lash tail and fin?
Or shall I put it in
To rhyme upon a dish?

> —STEPHEN SPENDER

How is a word like a fish? The question either seems silly or reads like the first line of a dumb joke. But Spender's answer to this question is a splendid example of a fresh and stimulating idea—a predication perhaps never asserted before by anyone.

Many of the great discoveries of science are of the same stamp. It was not until the turn of this century, for instance, that the connection between dirt on a surgeon's hands and the infection that invariably followed operations was first noted—by the American surgeon, William Stewart Halsted. And other, though less dramatic, inventions of new predications bombard us every day, from television ads that relate house odors to bad breath ("house-a-tosis") to popular lyrics that sing of "the back roads by the rivers of my memory."

Exercises

a. Make a list of at least five categories (words) whose meanings for you have come mostly from your own experience. If you have a serious hobby, or if you ever worked really hard on a school science project, or if you ever struggled to learn anything well, then such experiences will provide the words for your list. You will probably not find many words whose meanings are entirely based on your own experience. When you finish your list, try to decide which words come closest to the most original category you have ever discovered.

b. Make a list of at least five predications (sentences) that you feel you have learned on your own from your own experience and have not received from others. These sentences may express a simple concrete predication, such as *Peanut butter tastes good on pickles,* or a more abstract predication, such as *Failing a test can improve your social life.* Just be sure to look for predications you have discovered for yourself.

Creating Ideas for Writing

In later chapters you will learn how to organize your ideas when you write edited English and how to structure your ideas into effective paragraphs and clear sentences. But none of that information will be of any real use unless you have something interesting to write about. Interesting ideas are original ideas. Whenever you write, you should have something new to say. Your reader should gain special insight into the categories and predications that form the substance of what you write. This section describes several specific and practical activities you can use to harness your mind's basic powers to think creatively. As you examine them and practice them, do not worry too much about just how you will use them to help you with specific writing tasks. Think of them as warm-up exercises. The section on the writer's notebook, later in this chapter, will give you some suggestions on how to adapt them to specific written assignments. And other suggestions on how to use them will be given throughout the book.

Free association

Psychologists use free association to help patients discover ideas and emotions which lie just below the surface of consciousness and play a powerful role in triggering responses to people and situations, but which may have been repressed or simply forgotten. Free association can also lend practical assistance to writers. It can help you discover the store of experiences that form the content of any category. It is perhaps most useful for probing the content of your concrete categories. To use free association you must suspend the basic tendency of your mind to formulate predications. Pick an idea, hold it firmly in mind, and do not let yourself follow the implications of any word or assertion that would lead you too far from the idea itself. Here is a free association I wrote about fire; I wrote it in a classroom while my students were also practicing free association:

fire
the smell of ashes lingers on, days after
looking at it hypnotizes
for some it is a necessity, not a luxury
yet it's not really warm in a room heated by fire
smoke
smoke doesn't always come from fire
it can come from an overheated engine
what if I can't make it to an exit?
matches
we take them for granted
stone-age people really had to labor for fire

it's constantly changing
maybe it evokes the flux of human existence
fire
fire
summers in the '50s
and singing and eating by fires on summer nights
and fireworks
Thanksgiving weekend in a mountain cabin
the smell of a fire from outside
the mixture of dark winter cold and bright warmth
if fire is an archetype, might it lose its status to electricity?
smoking cigarettes
pain and coughing
my uncles were firemen
what would they think of it?
I've never needed it or suffered from it
to a picnicker, it's a scorched hotdog
what was it to my parents?
what's it like to bank a coal furnace?
what's it like to put out a fire in the cellar?
to think what might have happened?
what's it like to chop wood from need and not for exercise?

Several things happened to me as I wrote the above lines. One of the most important was that I *remembered* some experiences that I had not even thought about for a long time: a fire in the basement of my home when I was about seven, a campfire at a fourth of July picnic when I was in high school, a Thanksgiving weekend in a mountain cabin the year after I graduated from college. I also rediscovered that my idea of fire is singed with fear: the basement fire, fearful stories told by my firemen uncles, the fear I felt when my car once began smoking on an interstate highway. Certain philosophical overtones in my concept of fire also surfaced: the idea of fire as a symbol for the flux in the human condition and as a reminder of the daily struggle for survival.

Exercise

Try writing free associations about a few of the words listed below. Let your pen run free, and do not stop writing until you are sure that you have toured every hollow and hill of your idea.

(1) air	(7) leaves	(13) summer
(2) clouds	(8) pain	(14) tears
(3) flowers	(9) rain	(15) trees
(4) grass	(10) sleep	(16) water
(5) kisses	(11) snow	(17) wind
(6) laughter	(12) spring	(18) winter

Existential sentences

A second activity you may find useful as a tool for creating or refining categories is the forming of existential sentences. An existential sentence simply relates an abstraction to a slice of life. It is especially useful for probing the concrete content of abstract categories. Just what, for instance, do you mean when you use the words *love, justice,* or *democracy*? How much of the content of such categories have you received from others and how much have you added from your own experience? Here are some existential sentences treating democracy:

Democracy is the feeling of privacy in the voting booths.
Democracy is the recurrent suspicion that more than half of the people are
  right more than half of the time.
Democracy is the *don't* in *don't shove.*
Democracy is an idea which hasn't been disproved yet.

All of the above sentences were written by E. B. White almost forty years ago in an editorial in the *New Yorker*. They express a part of *his* idea of democracy. What about your idea? Try writing some existential sentences about democracy. If you find yourself writing sentences like the following, then you may not yet have infused this word with content drawn from your own daily experience:

Democracy is the flag waving.
Democracy is fireworks on the fourth of July.
Democracy is the President giving the State of the Union Message.

And if you have trouble writing *any* existential sentences, then you have not yet begun to create a personal idea of democracy. But the building blocks of such an idea are probably there in your experience. Try now to use the existential sentence as mortar and if necessary start building a personal concept of democracy from the ground up. If you already have the structure of an original concept under way, then use the existential sentence to build it higher. Here are some more existential sentences on democracy to help you get started:

Democracy is being bothered by campaign workers on the way to the polling
  place.
Democracy is a four-hour town council meeting about how to enforce the
  leash law.
Democracy is finding a job even if you don't belong to a movement.
Democracy is staying home on election day.
Democracy is a news correspondent being flippant with the President.

In this subsection and the last we have looked at free association and existential sentences as means to help you discover your own ideas. But what if you need to create an entirely new category or have to deepen the content of a shallow category? What you need to do, of course, is *research*. The last chapter of this book treats research in great detail. Put simply, research comes down to going out and finding out what you need to know. Suppose you are assigned to write a paper about slums or one about mysticism. You try free association, but few words appear on the page; you try existential sentences but the page remains white. If you do not know about slums, go to one. Look; listen; feel; smell; experience the place. If you cannot do that, then talk to someone who has, or read books about slums. As for mysticism, do the same. Ask about it, and especially—since it is a human experience—observe those who practice it. Watch what they do; listen to what they say; read what they write.

Notice that research is rooted in perception, in the exercise of the senses: seeing, hearing, touching, smelling, and tasting. Perception is the absolutely essential ingredient in the formation of new ideas. But neither raw perception nor reading and experimentation—the kind of perception called research—can automatically guarantee that new or creatively revised categories will result, just as the mere act of purchasing pasta, spices, and tomatoes does not automatically result in a spaghetti dinner, and most especially not in a memorable one. The creative thinker, like the creative chef, has to learn to mix the ingredients in a way that no one else does, if truly memorable ideas are to result. Chapter Twelve, on research, is a cookbook for ideas. In many ways, its content belongs here, but a full treatment of research also requires reference to many ideas yet to be treated in other chapters. When you do study the last chapter, remember that even the writing of a research paper must be an exercise in creating ideas.

Exercise

Here is a list of some abstract terms. Use existential sentences, as you did with *democracy* above, to break into the supply of experiences that are stored with these words in your mind. With words like *selfishness* and *tenderness*, you will probably find a rich supply of concrete personal experiences; with a word like *freedom*, you may discover a high proportion of received content, and with words like *sanctity* and *humility* you may find very little meaning at all.

(1) authority	(6) freedom	(11) sanctity
(2) chauvinism	(7) honesty	(12) selfishness
(3) confusion	(8) humility	(13) suffering
(4) faith	(9) impulsiveness	(14) tenderness
(5) fear	(10) mysticism	(15) virtue

Question words

Free association and existential sentences help you to probe the content of categories. The third idea-generating technique, the use of question words, can also help in probing the content of categories, but it does so in a more structured way, and it can also help you to generate predications about a topic based on your experience with the topic.

The question-word technique is a simple one. It has long been used by journalists, who know that any reporter must find out and then inform the reader about the *who, what, where, when, why,* and *how* of any news story. And that is exactly what I now suggest that you do when you are faced with a writing task. Before you begin to plan, and certainly before you begin the writing task itself, always ask *who, what, where, when, why* and *how.* Let me exemplify the technique using a familiar and concrete topic: my bicycle.

My bicycle. *Who or what is it? What are its qualities? What is it like?* [Notice that I have subdivided and slightly expanded the questions about *who* and *what.* I will do the same with the other questions in the following paragraphs.] My bicycle is a vehicle; it's metal; it's red; it has handle bars, pedals, two wheels, spokes, no gears, no fancy decorations. It seats one. It's my main source of exercise in the warm months; it's my ticket to freedom from life's worries. It's my tour guide to the seasons: as I ride by the same yards and woods, I breathe in the smells of burning leaves, then of falling snow, then of blooming flowers. My bike is a source of adventure and even of danger. Sometimes, it's like an airplane. At other times, it's like a roller coaster. Peddling against the wind, it's like running up stairs; peddling with the wind, it's like sledding down an icy slope.

Where is it located? Where did it come from? Where is it going? It's in my garage, but it's also on my mind a lot. It's on my mind when I'm studying, when I'm driving to school, when I'm stuck at a desk. I bought it at a Schwinn store, but I also got it from the hands of factory workers. Did they enjoy making it? Were they paid enough? Is my use of it worthy of their care and skill? It's also the product of some very clever industrial production processes. Somebody designed it. Somebody refined the metals in it. Somebody produced the rubber in its tires. Somebody etched the serial number on it. Somebody painted it. Where is it going? It's going wherever my legs will take it. There are lots of places I have yet to take it to. Where will it go when I'm done with it? Will someone else fix it up and use it? Will it become scrap? Will its steel be made into something else? I wonder what? Maybe it will become another bike that my great grandchildren will ride. Is there any religion that believes in the reincarnation of vehicles?

When did it come into existence? When does it do what it does? When will it cease to exist? I bought it three years ago. It was fully assembled and waiting for me in the show room. It couldn't have been more than a few months old at the time. I brought it home in the summer, and I rode it every day until the winter cold got too much for my face to stand. While riding it, I watched a whole new neighborhood appear; I watched new families move in; I watched their grass grow in; I watched them make friends over rakes and lawn mowers; I waved and said, "Hi," as I rolled by. In the two years since, I have watched many of

them move away, selling their custom homes for twice what they paid for
them. I've also watched my tires get bald. But it's a good bike; with a new set
of tires, it will last several more years. It was stolen from my garage once, on a
rainy night, but I found it less than a block away the next morning. It probably wasn't fancy enough for the thieves—no gears, no racing stripes, no fancy
handle bars.

Why does it exist? Why is it the way it is? Why should I write about it? It exists because the Schwinn people thought there was a market for it. It exists in my
garage because I wanted a bike and had the money to pay for it (and because
those thieves didn't like it). It also exists because I like to go places that my
legs don't have time to take me to. And it exists because of the gas shortage:
There was a time when I drove to a lot of places that I now ride my bike to. It
also exists because some very clever person (I wish I knew who and when) invented the bicycle. Why is it the way it is? I guess that means, among other
things, why does it have two wheels and not three? For one thing, I don't
know how to ride a unicycle, and I'd feel foolish on a tricycle. Why doesn't it
have gears? Because I'm conservative. I learned to ride a bike with foot brakes
and no gears, and I just didn't want to have to adapt to hand brakes and
gears. I also bought it just for exercise, not to ride cross country. Besides, it's
very flat around here, so I don't need low gear to peddle up hills. Why should
I write about my bicycle? Before I started writing answers to these questions, I
think I would have had a hard time saying why, but I have found myself
blurting out some interesting things. I could write about what my bike has
taught me. I said above that it showed me how fast the world changes—new
houses, new people, new social networks. But even in the morning, when no
one is stirring as I ride, my bicycle is like a movie theater on wheels: it plays
the world for me. It takes me by homes of the rich, every house with two cars
and a boat, and it takes me by homes of the poor, some with two cars—but
only three wheels between them. It takes me by people's trash. It takes me by
churches, which will spend the day empty, and by schools, which will spend
the day overcrowded. It lets me think. It lets me ride into my future. It lets
me escape my past. It lets me breathe deep. It lets me live.

How does it work? How does one use it? How does one understand it? My feet turn
the pedals, which are attached to a chain, which in turn makes the back wheel
go around. It's that simple. Of course, it takes a little practice to learn how to
balance, but once you've mastered that, there's not much more to it. I guess if
I were more mechanically inclined, I could write another page or two about
how a bicycle operates, but I'm not.

And so, there you have an example of how to use question words to
generate ideas. Did you notice that this technique has a lot in common
with free association? The main difference is that you are guiding your
thoughts and thus assuring that you probe the content of your experience more fully than free association might lead you to do. Another important difference is that the question words force you to generate predications, which are ideas expressing connections between your topic and

other aspects of your experience. Some of these predications may surprise you. Often they will become key ideas to be used when you eventually sit down to organize and to write in earnest. Here are just some of the interesting predications that surfaced as I answered the above questions about my bicycle:

My bicycle is the product of the labor of real people.
It is the product of the imagination of its inventor and designer.
It may be reincarnated as another bicycle.
It is a movie theater on wheels.
My bicycle helps me to escape from the past.
It gives me time to think.
It guides me to my future.
Riding my bicycle against the wind is like climbing stairs.
Riding it with the wind is like sledding down hill.

In the above exercise, I used question words to help discover what I thought about an object (my bicycle). The technique can also be used with persons, events, or abstractions. Let us try it together this time, using question words to examine the abstract idea expressed by the word *enthusiasm.* Read the questions at the beginning of each paragraph, and then write your own answers before you read mine.

Enthusiasm. *Who or what is it? What are its qualities? What is it like?* It's a feeling or state in humans that makes them excited about and committed to an idea or a cause. It's the feeling fans have about their favorite team. It's the feeling joggers have about jogging. It makes people want to go out and win converts. But they always have smiles on their faces. We do not say that sour-faced apostles are enthusiastic. What are its qualities? One quality is innocence. Enthusiastic people haven't experienced a let-down yet; they only know the bright side of their cause. Enthusiasm is youthful, even in older people. It makes you feel young. It's a happy feeling. It's also energetic. What's it like? It's like love, but it's not so possessive. It's like loyalty, but it's not so serious. It's like a dog wagging its tail. It's like children waiting for Santa to come.

Where is it? Where does it come from? Where does it lead? It's in people, but we experience it by watching how they act. You can see happiness in people's faces, but you see enthusiasm in how they talk and act. The students who come to a school's basketball games and cheer are the enthusiastic ones. Those who only buy tickets or who just argue about how great the team's outside shooters are don't show enthusiasm. Enthusiasm comes from the need humans have to belong, to be part of something bigger than themselves. It gives them a way of proving to the group that they should be accepted as full members. Where does it lead? It can lead to excesses, but it usually doesn't. When attachment to a cause leads to excesses, we don't call it enthusiasm; we call it fanaticism. That's why we don't generally call people enthusiastic when we think their cause is unjust or evil. Enthusiasm fills them with the good in their cause. Enthusiasm generally leads to good things. At worst, it sometimes tests the patience of the nonenthusiastic.

When did it come into existence? When does it show itself? When will it cease to exist? Enthusiasm has probably been around as long as humans have. As for me, I guess I first experienced it playing sports. I really felt it when I started rooting so passionately for the Philadelphia Phillies that I listened to or attended and scored every game they played and talked about them constantly to just about anyone who would listen. I later felt it about the study of languages, and even tried to convince many of my college friends to switch their majors. I would like to think that I will never grow too old for it, but I must confess that I would have to look hard to find a lot of it in my life nowadays. Is that a sign that I'm getting old?

How does it work? How does one use it? How does one understand it? Enthusiasm works by getting people to talk and do a lot about the source of their enthusiasm. It gets them to want to win converts. I suppose that people have to continue to feel fulfillment from their cause, or their enthusiasm would burn out. Thus, it is a more superficial feeling than love, or honesty, or truthfulness, all of which can remain strong even when they are not fulfilled. That may be why it doesn't seem quite correct to call enthusiasm a virtue; virtues are more permanent, more substantive. How to understand enthusiasm? I guess by examining my own experience, by closely observing others, by talking to others about it, or even by studying about it. In fact, I remember reading once in the *Oxford English Dictionary* that *enthusiasm* originally meant "possessed by a god." I think the word still connotes the kind of irrational commitment that its original meaning suggested.

In both of the above examples of the use of question words to generate ideas, I purposely did not choose the topics until I was about to write, and I have resisted the temptation to do much revision of what I wrote so that you can see the kinds of comments you might expect yourself to write when you use the question word technique. Notice that in both the *bicycle* example and the *enthusiasm* example I expanded and reworded the basic questions. Feel free to do the same. If you let the question words *who, what, where, when, why,* and *how* work freely on your mind—asking them in several ways, as I did above—you may be amazed to discover just how much information you have available on a given topic, and just how original your perspective on the topic is.

Remember, when you use the question words, you are not yet explicitly planning or writing for another reader; you are simply thinking on paper. To some extent, you are probing the content of categories, as you also do with free association and existential sentences, but you are also pushing your mind through the use of the question words to discover connections and to express them as predications. Here are some of the predications about enthusiasm that I discovered while doing the above exercise:

Enthusiasm is a feeling that must usually be expressed in action.
Enthusiasm cannot really be called a virtue.
Enthusiasm makes one feel young.
We don't usually apply the term *enthusiasm* to people we think are com-
    mitted to evil causes.
There's an aspect of irrationality about enthusiasm.

Exercise

When you know a lot about a topic, the use of question words can help you get
your knowledge down on paper and will even begin to organize that knowledge,
under the question-word headings. When you know little or nothing about a
topic, and have not yet decided just what perspective you want to take in writing
about it for others, the question words can guide your preliminary reading and
research. Suppose, instead of bicycles, the first topic above had been autogyros?
And suppose, instead of enthusiasm, the second had been anorexia? The page
would not have filled up so fast in either case. But I would have discovered the
kinds of answers to look for when I headed to the library. Below are listed some
topics for you to investigate by the use of question words. Try as many as you can.
Some of them will require you to do some reading; others need only your own
experience. Try to work on at least a few of each type.

(1) trees	(5) diligence	(9) ingenuousness
(2) Queen Victoria	(6) vacations	(10) the Reformation
(3) generosity	(7) cooking	(11) anorexia
(4) autogyros	(8) your favorite high school teacher	(12) your bed

Scrambled perception

This fourth activity to help you create ideas differs from the other
three because it forces you to gather new raw material for ideas and to
combine the material in original ways. It aims to help you sharpen your
senses: to see, hear, touch, smell, and taste more actively, that is, to *notice*
more about what is going on around you. And it combines practice in
sharpening sense awareness with a conscious withholding of your mind's
inclination to categorize.

Here are some examples of how it works: Turn the sound off when
you are viewing a television show; tell yourself that it is not a television
show at all, and then *watch*. Watch every movement, every gesture, every
aspect of every scene. Make notes about what you are seeing if there is
time, but above all start noticing. Force yourself to do this for five full
minutes. Then, and only then, try to create a written interpretation of
the sights you have observed. Or try closing your eyes at a sporting event
and telling yourself that it is not an athletic event. Force yourself for five

full minutes to listen to everything, to notice every sound. Then, and only then, try to write an interpretation of the sounds you have just heard. You can do the same with the other senses. Close your eyes and feel, smell, or taste an object, but do so attentively, and do not draw conclusions about what your senses are experiencing until you have given them several minutes to send raw data to your brain.

Whenever you can, practice viewing familiar people, objects, and situations as though they were wholly different from what they are. Look at a service station attendant and say to yourself, "This is not a service station attendant; who is it, then?" Look at a tree and say to yourself, "This is not a tree; what then might it be?" Observe the dinner hour in a college cafeteria and tell yourself, "This is not a meal; what then might it be?" In each case the question will force you to see, to hear, to feel, to smell, and even to taste things you might otherwise not even notice. You might see indications of *gracefulness* in the way the service station attendant washes your windshield. You might see indications of *intelligence* in the way the tree turns its leaves away from the wind or gently lowers its outer branches as a squirrel scampers along them. You may see *ritual* in the college cafeteria. Write descriptions of such perceptions—on the spot. Describe the college dinner hour as if it were indeed a religious ceremony, seeing the servers as priests or priestesses, the trash as offerings to a god, the food as the god's response to the offerings. The possibilities are endless. When such perception games are done, you can then recall that the person is, after all, a service station attendant; the object is, after all, a tree; the situation is, after all, a college cafeteria at meal time. But you will, in each case, have enriched the content of a category and possibly discovered some wholly new predications.

Exercise

The key to the scrambled perception technique is to withhold judgment while at the same time forcing your senses consciously to handle as much raw perceptual data as possible. This technique can be practiced at any time and in any place. And it can serve your needs when you are preparing to write about a variety of subjects. Here are just a few suggestions for becoming more familiar with the technique:

(1) Pour ink on a folded page and press the fold together to make an ink blot. Study the ink blot. Write several separate descriptions of the shapes in the ink blot.

(2) Hold any picture upside down—a photograph, a magazine, a newspaper. Describe in great detail the shapes and arrangements in the picture. Turn it right side up. Have you discovered anything about what's in the picture that you did not notice before?

(3) Stand on your head and describe what you see. Listen as you look. Do the sounds in the situation seem any different when the world is upside-down?

(4) Close your eyes and feel the furniture in your room, the faces of your friends, the plants around you. Have a friend give you an unknown object to feel. When you open your eyes to see what it is, ask yourself whether you learned anything new about it by playing the game.

The Writer's Notebook

The techniques discussed in the last section did not present a coherent process that automatically results in a written product to be read by others. Instead, each one in its own way probed the resources of your mind with a view to mining creative insights that might ultimately be refined into a piece of organized discourse. If the suggestions made there for discovering and deepening categories and predications are to be of lasting usefulness to you, they must become *habitual concerns*. Even when no particular writing assignment is on the horizon, you should be building and revising your inventory of categories and processing your perceptions and asking questions in the hope of creating new predications. The writer's notebook will help this to happen. Keeping such a notebook should be an integral part of the writing course. And if you use the notebook successfully in the course, you may come to decide that keeping one will become an integral part of your life after the course has ended.

Think of your writer's notebook primarily as a place to practice the four techniques described in the last section. You should write something in it every day. Carry it with you when you go to all your classes and to meals. Write free associations outdoors as you experience the feel and the smell of the seasons. Let the particulars of a place and time suggest a theme for a group of existential sentences: If it is snowing, write a group of existential sentences about solitude, all in terms of snow. When you are studying for a test in any course, use question words both to test your knowledge and to aid your memory. Write descriptions of people and events as if they were really something else, focusing on the perceptual detail and reserving judgment about generalities as much as you can.

If you write every day, if you begin to look at life, hoping to discover something to write about in your notebook, you will not only develop certain mental skills that are absolutely essential to good writing; you will also build an inventory of ideas in rough-draft form that will solve in advance the problem of finding a topic when you are faced with a particular writing assignment.

Here is a sampling of entries from writers' notebooks. All the writers cited kept notebooks for the very same reasons I am urging you to keep one: as an incentive to perception and as a way to adapt the creative resources of language to the creation of new ideas. Only one of the writers is explicitly doing one of the four techniques described in this chapter (the third entry is a free-association exercise). Nevertheless, as you read their notebook entries, it will be clear to you that they are indeed engaged in the same kind of language-oriented mental exertion that the four techniques call for. Some writers keep notebooks all of their lives, making one or more entries such as these each day. Read the selections, enjoy them, and resolve to begin your own notebook today.

I hear the sound of Heywood's Brook falling into Fair Haven Pond, inexpressibly refreshing to my senses. It seems to flow through my very bones. I hear it with insatiable thirst. It allays some sandy heat in me. It affects my circulations; methinks my arteries have sympathy with it. What is it I hear but the pure waterfalls within me, in the circulation of my blood, the streams that fall into my heart? What mists do I ever see but such as hang over and rise from my blood? The sound of this gurgling water, running thus by night as by day, falls on all my dashes, fills all my buckets, overflows my float-boards, turns all the machinery of my nature, makes me a flume, a sluice-way, to the springs of nature.

—HENRY DAVID THOREAU

April 8—The ashtree growing in the corner of the garden was felled. It was lopped first: I heard the sound and looking out and seeing it maimed there came at that moment a great pang and I wished to die and not to see the inscapes of the world destroyed any more.

. . .

July 22—Very hot, though the wind, which was south, dappled very sweetly on one's face and when I came out I seemed to put it on like a gown as a man puts on the shadow he walks into and hoods or hats himself with the shelter of a roof, a penthouse, or a copse of trees, I mean it rippled and fluttered like light linen, one could feel the folds and braids of it—and indeed a floating flag is like wind visible and what weeds are in a current.

—GERARD MANLEY HOPKINS

Student nurses
    Tiredly ironing my permanent press uniform at 2:00 A.M. and burning my finger . . . Polishing my shoe heels to pass inspection . . . Soaking my shoelaces in Clorox only to have them turn yellow . . . My first male patient stripping in front of me and I close my eyes . . . My first injection with an IM syringe where I missed my target—the orange navel . . . My first experience with death—I had to close her eyes, but they wouldn't . . . The rewarding feeling of having helped a sick person, or having eased their pain and suffering just a little . . . The warm smile of gratitude and appreciation from a patient . . . The vastness of science and the wonder of the human body . . . The trip to Maryland where we made a sign on a Burger King

crown, "Student Nurses do it Better," and showing it to every car we passed—and the truck that followed us . . . Those long nights of cramming and the early morning alarm clock . . . Seeing my first and last cadaver . . . Dissecting a grossed-out cat . . . Rejection and fear and giving up the idea of becoming a nurse . . . Changing my mind and wanting more than anything to earn that cap and pin.

—TERESITA MEJIA, A STUDENT

Sundays are good days to write, they seem so appropriate, and with pencils—always with pencils; they talk back to you making that grinding abrasive noise and vibration. Oh yes, and you can always scrub words away with the eraser when you don't like them or when they're illegible, but who cares? You know you never read most of the things you write, especially the things you write with a pencil. Maybe it's because you always render the mood that comes over you when you have a pencil in your hand—and that stupid impression, no, dent—that's exactly what it is—in your finger. Why doesn't someone figure out a way to make pencils or hands so that you don't get that ridiculous, unreasonable, yes, even painful dent in your second finger?

. . .

I bought a book today. My favorite kind. A paperback. Paperbacks are so much better than hardbacks; they're not so heavy; they bend. But what is most peculiar about paperbacks is the way they never lie flat after they've been opened and read from a few times. It's almost as if they were inviting you to jump back in, make a return visit, maybe get really acquainted this time. Hardback books are so big—cumbersome too, and they're always just too big to go into your biggest pocket. They seem to try to be impressive with their squared off corners and their unnecessary thickness. I sometimes feel as if a hardback book is trying to scare me away and then laugh! And there's another thing hardbacks can't do—they never quite take on the appearance of their owners. You know the way a paperback gets because you carry it around all the time—full of papers, notes about assignments, scribbles and comments and underlinings. And the corners always get bent up and begin to separate into layers, and they always get dirty around the edges, and better than that, they're full of funny little memories like coffee stains and little pieces of cocoanut and sometimes even bubble gum. Paperbacks can be almost like friends because you get to know them so well, I guess; that's probably the reason I have a house full of them. But hardbacks, they're hopeless. You never get to know them; they're just too damned impersonal. Maybe they just don't approve of me; they're probably even snobbish in a bookish kind of way towards my paperbacks that always surround and outnumber them. I bet they don't like having to be so close to the swinish multitudes. But I bet my paperbacks have more fun.

—DOUG WEBB, A STUDENT

Exercise

Here is another selection from Doug Webb's notebook; he wrote it during the break between classes and simply described his trip from one classroom building to another. But notice how rich it is in perceptual detail. Read it and then plan to pay similar attention to sights, sounds, and smells the next time you walk about campus; plan also to write about your experiences, even if you literally have to scribble your impressions.

Hot and cold, never comfortable, those are the corridors of the English Building. Through the door the wind whips papers at its will. There is a dull whistle in the Administration Building tunnel and another unbalancing gust at its end. Over the chain and through the grass I walk in hopes of warmth only to grasp an icy door knob. While I'm buying a coke, my nose informs me that the machine has been recently oiled, but it never gives the right change. The stairs and a cigarette steal my breath. I rest at my uneven chair and notice the hole in the instructor's shiny black tie-up shoes, and a wrinkle that goes all the way across.

Three *Organization*

The last chapter gave you some tools to help you discover interesting ideas and begin to develop them. However, edited English style requires that even the most creative ideas must be rigorously evaluated and carefully organized before and during the process of committing them to paper. If you want to write effectively, you must make several conscious and thoughtful decisions before you write, and you must reevaluate these decisions as you write.

Whether you are planning a term paper, an essay, a paragraph, or simply a sentence, you should learn to ask and answer these questions: Who is my reader? What is my role in relation to my reader? Why am I writing? How should I present my ideas? In this chapter I discuss the organization process, suggesting that you use these questions in a step-by-step approach to specific writing tasks. However, the set of questions treated here should not become a straitjacket. Their answers are interrelated. You should get used to asking each question over and over until all your answers work together to produce the best possible organization.

You must also remember that the possibilities for organizing a piece of edited English are as varied as experience and as complex as the human mind. The suggestions made here are only tools. Nevertheless, they represent a reasonably complete set of tools. When you learn to use them, you can create structures of language capable of expressing even your most creative ideas.

Audience

In the discussion of written vs. spoken styles in Chapter One, I said that the great challenge of written style is the impossibility of interaction between the writer and the reader. Unlike a listener, a reader cannot interrupt to ask for clarification. Furthermore, conversations usually take place between people whose roles are well defined from the social context in which the conversation takes place. Your special challenge as a writer is (1) to fix your reader so firmly in mind that you see in advance any need for clarification the reader may have and (2) to make your role so clear in the way you write that the lack of conversational context does not weaken communication.

Your reader

The first question to ask yourself is, Who is my reader? Sometimes you write for yourself, in a diary or in your writer's notebook, but when you write edited English you are usually writing for someone else. Ask yourself, Is it someone I know or someone I do not know? Then ask, How well do I know my reader? Answers to such questions determine how much information you should include and how you should express it. Other related questions are, Is my reader friendly to me? Is my reader friendly to my views?

Suppose you need to write a letter about the physical conditions of the house you live in. (Your ultimate purpose is to obtain help.) If you are writing to a close friend who has visited it several times you might begin like this:

The seals on the living room window are leaking air. I have badgered the builder about fixing them. I don't know if he'll ever get around to it. I'm really bugged!

But if you are writing to the local Better Business Bureau, your letter might begin something like this:

I live in a two-year-old house that is equipped with double-paned weather-proof windows. The seals on the living room window are leaking air. I have asked the builder four times to repair it, but he has not yet done so.

Notice that the second version, written to people whom you do not know, contains more information and does not reveal that the situation has you emotionally upset. You want to build your case on facts so that they will support your cause.

When you sit down to write, the lens of your imagination must bring the image of your reader into sharp focus, and you must keep the resulting picture firmly in mind throughout the whole process of planning and writing.

Exercise

You are a twenty-two-year-old college graduate (choose your own field). You are also the single parent of a two-year-old child. You have sought employment for one whole year since graduating from college but have failed to find any. You want help in finding a job. Pick any audience from the list below; then write a letter in which your audience is clearly focused throughout.

(1) Your federal congressman
(2) The president of your local Chamber of Commerce
(3) A local newspaper
(4) An uncle who owns a business but with whom you have not gotten along in the past
(5) Your best friend from college, who is doing well and who has many contacts

Be prepared to discuss how your audience determined both *what* you wrote in the letter and *how* you wrote it.

Your role as writer

The second general question to ask yourself is, What is my role in relation to my reader? Unless you are writing your autobiography, you are not writing simply as *you:* you are writing in some particular *role* or as a representative of some *group*. I am not writing this book as a husband, a father, a homeowner, or even as a concerned citizen; I am writing it as an educator. If I were writing as a concerned citizen to a local newspaper, I would emphasize the benefits of good writing to society. In this book, I try to emphasize the benefits to you, the student.

Questions of audience can cause problems in the writing course. In fact, your audience is a teacher who is interested in how well you write as well as in what you have to say, and your role is that of a student who aims primarily to demonstrate mastery of edited English. Such a situation can make your writing artificial. If you write only to please your composition teacher, you may not learn enough about effective writing in the real world. However, it is possible to turn this problem into a powerful learning tool. Whenever you write a composition, include with it a brief statement in which you describe an imaginary audience and in which you state explicitly your role as writer. Then your teacher can evaluate not only your ideas, your plan, and your language, but also your ability to bring your reader clearly into focus and to define your role as writer.

Here is a 500-word theme where the student writer did just that. Read the statements about audience and role. Then, as you read the paper, notice how her decisions about audience and role affected both the ideas and the language of the paper. How would the paper have been different if she were writing for her fellow college students? How would it differ if it were written for an alumni magazine? How would it differ if it were written for her parents and other parents of college freshmen?

HIGH SCHOOL AND COLLEGE

Audience: The students, especially juniors and seniors, at my former high school.

Role: Myself as an individual, but mainly as a student.

There are many truisms about the differences between high school and college. Everyone knows that college is more difficult than high school: Courses cover more difficult material and do it faster. Everyone knows that college schedules differ: There is more free time and thus the need to use it effectively. And everyone knows that college students need more discipline: No one makes you attend class or do your work. But there are a few important aspects of attending college in the eighties that seem to be well-kept secrets. One of them is that the world is not the ordered place high school texts and teachers make it out to be. The other is that many university professors are just as disordered as the world they try to teach you about.

Half way through my first semester in college it became clear to me that I was overwhelmed by a feeling of confusion. At first, I blamed it on being away from home, and on having to make new friends while at the same time doing the work for six courses. But even as I got these problems under control, the feeling of confusion seemed to increase. I began to notice that the feeling was strongest in class and while studying. It wasn't my life that was confusing me; it was ideas.

In high school I thought I had learned that a good English composition was one that avoided errors in grammar, spelling, and punctuation. Why then did my errorless first theme earn a D? Was I supposed to accomplish something as well as avoid errors when writing? In high school I thought I learned that matter was composed of neatly packaged little atoms: perfectly round clumps of protons and neutrons circled in neat orbits by shiny round electrons. Why then did my Chem prof say it was not that way at all? In high school I thought that good and evil forces in history and in the history of ideas were pretty well defined. Why then did both my history and philosophy professors say such nasty things about many of my heroes?

The confusion about ideas I think I could have tolerated—after all, college was supposed to be more difficult, and there were new insights to be learned. But what added to my confusion was the seeming unwillingness or inability of my teachers to help. My English teacher told me that my error-less paper earned a D because it lacked "focus" and reeked of "vapid diction." She just raised her eyebrows when I asked what to do about it—I should have learned that in high school. My Chemistry professor told me he had been doing advanced research that confirmed the weaknesses in classical atomic theory, but I didn't have enough experience to understand his arguments. And my History and Philosophy professors just smirked when I asked them how people and events could be good and bad at the same time.

I am tempted to find somebody to blame for not warning me about the complexity of ideas and the incompetence of those who push ideas in colleges. But, in spite of it all, I am beginning to turn my confusion into excitement. Maybe it's up to me and not my teachers to make order out of the confusion. Maybe I'm supposed to become my own best teacher from now on. Maybe that's the difference between high school and college that is the best kept secret of them all.

—Tricia Bernard, a student

Exercise

Imagine again that you are a twenty-two-year-old college graduate, facing the same problems as those defined in the exercise on p. 46. But this time you aim not only to focus your audience clearly as in that exercise; you aim also to write with a well-defined and consistent role throughout. The same five types of audiences as were listed in the last exercise are repeated here. But below them are listed five different roles you might play as writer. There are twenty-five different combinations of audience and role. Thus you can write twenty-five different letters about this one problem. Try at least four of the twenty-five possible combinations of audience and role. Be sure that your decisions about what to say and how to say it are, in each case, closely keyed to the audience you have chosen and the role you are playing.

Your Audience:
  (1) Your federal congressman
  (2) The president of your local Chamber of Commerce
  (3) A local newspaper
  (4) An uncle who owns a business but with whom you have not gotten along in the past
  (5) Your best friend from college, who is doing well and who has many contacts

Your Role:
  (1) President of a group of unemployed college graduates
  (2) President of a group of unemployed single parents
  (3) A highly trained individual whose talents are being wasted
  (4) A parent whose child needs food, shelter, and clothing
  (5) An individual human being with hopes and needs

Purpose

The third question to ask yourself as part of the organization process is, Why am I writing? Whenever you write you are primarily either *informing* or *persuading* your reader. It is impossible to do one of these without doing a little of the other, but one of these purposes must dominate if your reader is to get your message. Compare the following two passages:

The house is the second on the left after you enter the court. It is a one-story brick ranch with green shutters and has an ivy-covered lamppost near the driveway. You can't miss it.

The house is a spacious and beautiful brick ranch on a quiet court. It is plushly landscaped and has an elegant ivy-covered gas lamp adorning the entrance walkway. Don't miss this once-in-a-lifetime opportunity!

The purpose of the first passage is simply to give some visitors the information they need to find the house. The second passage, while it has some descriptive information in it, is obviously intended to persuade the reader to consider buying the house.

When you write, you must decide in advance which of these two general purposes should control other aspects of the organization process and also the actual writing and revising of the paper. Then you should stick with the choice until the final draft is completed. Writing that primarily gives information is called *exposition* or *expository writing;* writing that primarily aims to persuade is called *argumentation* or *argumentative writing.* Let us now look more closely at each of these two types of edited English.

Informing the reader: exposition

Expository writing usually focuses on a specific purpose. It seeks to give information mainly about persons, places, or events. Let us look closer at each of these specific purposes.

If a stranger wishes to meet you at an airport and needs to make it easy for you to identify him, he might write you this note describing himself:

I am six feet tall, weigh 195 lbs., have brown hair, and will be wearing blue and white plaid pants and a red sweater.

In the note, he provides you with useful information. He does not try to persuade you to meet him or to like him or to agree with him. Here is a passage describing a person taken from a short story by Eudora Welty. It is not as bland as the above description. Through its choice of words, it subtly leads us to form a positive impression of the person described. But its main purpose is clearly to give us a sharp picture of that person:

She wore a dark striped dress reaching down to her shoetops, and an equally long apron of bleached sugar sacks, with a full pocket; all neat and tidy, but every time she took a step she might have fallen over her shoe-laces, which dragged from her unlaced shoes. She looked straight ahead. Her eyes were blue with age. Her skin had a pattern all its own of numberless branching wrinkles and as though a whole little tree stood in the middle of her forehead, but a golden color ran underneath, and the two knobs of her cheeks were illuminated by a yellow burning under the dark. Under the red rag her hair came down on her neck in the frailest of ringlets, still black, and with an odor like copper.

—EUDORA WELTY, "A Worn Path"

Expository prose may also focus on a thing. Suppose you have lost a mechanical pencil in a hotel room. The management will need a description of it to find it; this is what you send them:

It is made of translucent turquoise plastic, uses thick lead, and has a worn blue eraser.

The sentence does not attempt to persuade the hotel management to find it and send it to you; it simply gives them the information they need to recognize it. Here is a passage from a historical novel describing the eleventh-century crown of England. Notice that while its purpose is clearly to give the reader information about a thing, it also inspires awe and alludes to the symbolic values of the jewels in the crown:

> The golden crown was fashioned like a victor's diadem of old, but with an arch above betokening the overlordship of all Britain. Every stone spoke of a royal virtue. Foremost shone a great ruby for valor; round about were set emeralds for justice, sapphires for chastity, amethysts for a king's love of his people and his duty towards them; chrysolite was there for wisdom, chalcedony for fortitude, sardonyx for lowliness, mercy and truth. All these and more adorned the crown of England, and set above was a great matchless pearl, the likeness of a tear.
>
> —HOPE MUNTZ, *The Golden Warrior*

A place is an arrangement of persons and things. Here is an expository passage about a place:

> My mother sat at the head of the long table, my two sisters and I looking at her expectantly. Photographs of my grandparents were arranged behind her on the buffet. The candles in the chandelier flickered overhead.

Notice that the emphasis in a place passage is not so much on describing the people and things mentioned as on making clear where they are in relation to one another. Here is a passage from a student theme which describes a place. Notice how effectively the writer shows us the relationships between things and people:

> The fraternity house had a front walkway of worn bricks. Unkempt bushes and tall bare trees were scattered about the yard. It looked like an ordinary house in an ordinary neighborhood. It was a dark red brick house, its windows trimmed with black shutters and its porch lined with a black railing. As I approached the porch, I noticed a yellow tabby cat crouched by the door. It was a plaster doorstop. In the doorway stood what seemed to be half of the fraternity waiting to greet me.
>
> —KAREN O'NEIL, A STUDENT

An event may be defined as persons or things acting or undergoing change. If you tell a story or describe a process simply to give your reader information, you are writing expository prose about events. Suppose you have a friend who plans a visit to Ecuador, a country you have visited. You might include the following story in a letter to her:

> When I was in Ecuador, I traveled from Quito, the capitol, to the head waters of the Amazon. A group of us left Quito early one morning and drove three hours south to Ambato, where we had lunch. From there we drove all afternoon southeast to Baños, where we spent the night. The next day we rode six

hours along a narrow road through a canyon until we reached Puyo, whose streams ultimately drain into the Amazon.

Your purpose in this passage is simply to give your reader enough information to decide for herself whether she might be interested in such a trip during her visit to Ecuador. Here is a passage from a student theme that describes an event. Like many stories, it has an implied argumentative purpose as well: we are warned about the dangers of drag racing. But the basic purpose is clearly expository: The author is telling us a story, and an interesting one.

It was midnight on a deserted strip of four-lane highway, and my weekly drag race was about to start. The starter flashed his light and pandemonium broke loose. Tires squealed and smoked; engines wailed so loud that I thought people a mile away could have heard them. I was behind through first gear, but as I hit second, I pulled side-by-side with the other car. Then it happened. As I caught a leaping third gear and started to pull away, I saw a man walking along the road ahead of me. I thought of braking, but knew it would be no use; I couldn't stop in time. I was barely ahead of the other car, but the only thing to do was swerve in front of it and pray that the guy I was racing would have enough time to stop. It happened so fast; everything I did was by reflex. I looked in my rear view mirror and saw the shocked face of the other driver only feet behind me and closing fast. Luckily, he slid to a screeching stop just as I barely got out of his way. When I finally stopped, I thought of what might have happened. That turned out to be my last drag race.

—DON SEXTON, A STUDENT

Whereas stories like the two above recount particular events, process narratives recount generalized events, usually relatively familiar and repeated activities. Here is a passage that gives information about the process of preparing soil for planting a garden:

First you plow the land to a depth of twelve inches. Then you add peat, mulch, and fresh topsoil, and plow them in thoroughly. Then you sprinkle lime and fertilizer over the surface. When you rake the surface smooth, the ground is ready for planting.

Notice that both types of events, stories and processes, include information about persons and things and their arrangements. But in both stories and processes the emphasis is on action and change ordered by a time sequence. Stories focus on action and change at a specific time and place; processes focus on generalized action and change. Here is another process passage. Notice that the generalized subject word *you,* which was used in the above process passage is not used here. But by using the simple present tense (*pulls, brushes, begins*) and a few appropriate adverbs (*first, then*) the author makes it clear that she is talking about any act of swimming, not just the act of one person on a given day.

Let's begin with the right hand. First it pulls down to the side. When it brushes by the right leg, the left hand begins to move down toward the left leg, and as the right hand goes around to make the full circle and come back to the original position, the left hand is moving down the left leg. Then the right hand proceeds down and brushes by the right leg again while the left hand pulls around and comes back in a full circle to the original position. In other words, each arm moves around in a circle but the arms are a *half circle* apart.

— VIRGINIA HUNT NEWMAN, *Teaching Young Children to Swim and Dive*

Once you decide to write an expository rather than an argumentative paper, you must further specify your decision. You must decide whether your purpose will focus on (1) persons, (2) things, (3) places, (4) stories, or (5) processes. All of these types of information can be part of a passage, but a truly informative passage will clearly emphasize only one of them.

Exercise

Write five short expository passages, each one of which focuses on one of the purposes listed below. Some suggested topics are given in parentheses beside each purpose.

(1) Purpose: to give the reader information about a person (a member of your family, a teacher, a friend, a famous person, yourself)
(2) Purpose: to give the reader information about a thing (your car, a household appliance, a tool, a piece of sporting equipment)
(3) Purpose: to give the reader information about a place (your room, a place on campus, a vacation spot, a night spot)
(4) Purpose: to give the reader information about a specific event by telling a story (how you met someone who means a lot to you, how your life was once in danger, how you once got the best of someone, how someone helped you when you really needed help)
(5) Purpose: to give the reader information about a generalized event by narrating a process (how to put something together, how to take something apart, how to operate something, how to act in a certain situation)

Persuading the reader: argumentation

We saw in the last section that even expository prose, which aims primarily to pass on information, often has a secondary persuasive purpose. We call a piece of writing argumentative when the persuasive purpose clearly dominates: when the writer is very obviously trying to recruit the reader, to win over the reader, or to move the reader to act. Argumentative writing can in fact be divided into three subtypes: *reasoning, evaluation,* and *exhortation.* If you present statistics and case studies in such a way as to persuade your reader to agree that most people who sample cocaine become addicts, then yours is the first kind of argumentation: *reasoning.* If you emphasize the terrible consequences of drug addiction—loss of health, of dignity, even of life—in order to have your reader condemn drug abuse as evil, then yours is the second kind of argumentation: *evaluation.* If you present both the facts and the consequences but make it clear that you are doing so in order to get your reader to *do* something about drug abuse (contribute money, write to Congress, give up the habit), then yours is the third kind of argumentation: *exhortation.*

Reasoning calls on the reader to agree or disagree, in a sense to say yes or no to what the writer asserts. Here is an example passage whose purpose is clearly argumentative reasoning:

> Human virtue is a habit perfecting man in view of his doing good deeds. Now, in man there are but two principles of human actions, namely the intellect or reason and the appetite. . . . Consequently every human virtue must be a perfection of one of these principles. Accordingly if it perfects man's practical intellect in order that his deed may be good, it will be an intellectual virtue, but if it perfects his appetite, it will be a moral virtue. It follows therefore that every human virtue is either intellectual or moral.
>
> —ST. THOMAS AQUINAS, *Summa Theologica,* I–II, 58, 3

Your response to this passage is clearly expected to be agreement or disagreement. If, for instance, you do not agree that "in man there are but two principles of human actions, namely the intellect or reason and the appetite," then you will not agree that "it follows therefore that every human virtue is either intellectual or moral." If, on the other hand, you accept the premises, then your response will be to agree with the conclusions of the argument in the passage.

Evaluation calls on the reader to like or dislike something, to evaluate it as good or bad. The writer does not necessarily come right out and say, "This is good," or "That is bad," but the evaluative function of the passage is usually clear nonetheless. Notice, in the following passage from a student paper, that the writer obviously wants you to like the idea of a year of national service by every young American, even though the passage never actually asserts that it is a good idea:

> Several members of Congress have sponsored legislation to require a year of national service from every young American, male and female. The service year would take place immediately after high school. Such a year of service would benefit both the nation and the young people themselves. Their youth and creativity would not only upgrade the armed forces, where many would serve, but could also brighten the lives of many hospital patients, or even move important ecological projects forward. The young people themselves

would learn that the freedoms they take for granted require some sacrifice to preserve, and they might also learn some valuable skills which they could use to their own advantage later in life.

—JEFF ANDREWS, A STUDENT

Exhortation calls on the reader to act or avoid acting, to get up and do something, or to avoid doing something. Not every argumentative exhortation is so obvious as the one that follows, but most exhortations do tend to be pretty explicit:

Come to Canada. Enjoy your favourite activities in the midst of beautiful, unspoiled scenery. Then join in the life of our exciting cities. Experience dining at its international best. Or, relax in a quiet setting where a friendly greeting is still a way of life. You'll find it easy to be as active and busy or just as peaceful as you want. Come for a weekend or come for a month. There's so much to come for. Canada.

—Advertisement in *Time* (May 23, 1977)

Once you decide to write an argumentative rather than an expository paper, you must further specify your decision. You must decide whether your focus will be on reasoning, evaluation, or exhortation. All three types of arguments may be part of a passage, and various types of information about persons, things, places, and events may also be present, but a truly successful argument will not only clearly be an argument; it will also focus on just one of the three types of argumentation.

Exercise

Write three short argumentative passages, each one of which focuses·on one of the purposes listed below. Some suggested topics are given in parentheses beside each purpose.

(1) Purpose: to persuade the reader by the use of reasoning (give reasons why students should have a voice in forming college curriculum, why politicians should be paid less, why the terms of Senators or Congressmen should be changed, why marijuana should or should not be legalized).

(2) Purpose: to persuade the reader by the use of evaluation (show that the following are good or bad: smoking, drinking, the medical profession, the legal profession, motorcycle helmets, politicians).

(3) Purpose: to persuade the reader by the use of exhortation (get the reader to do something about hunger in the world, birth defects, poverty, low pay for workers, or child abuse).

Plan

The fourth question to ask yourself as part of the organization process is, How should I present my ideas? This is perhaps the most complex question of all. To answer it, you need to determine as specifically as you can what your *topic* is (the topic is usually a word or phrase expressing the main *category* your paper treats). To answer it, you also need to determine what your *thesis* is (the thesis is a sentence expressing the main *predication* your paper treats). And to answer it, you need to determine the *organizational plan* that best fits not only your topic and your thesis, but also your audience and purpose.

Take another look at the theme entitled "Adaptability," on p. 22. Its audience was the writer's fellow college students. Its purpose was expository: to give the reader information about events (the writer's experiences working at West End Car-care Center). Its topic was adaptability. Its thesis was expressed in the last sentence of the first paragraph: "While employed at West End Car-care Center, I developed what I feel to be a broader sense of adaptability." Its organizational plan was narration. You should also take another look at the theme entitled "High School and College," on p. 47. Its audience was the juniors and seniors at the writer's former high school. Its purpose was expository: to give the reader information about a place (college) and events that take place there. Its topic was high school and college, but mostly college. Its thesis was expressed in the fifth sentence of the first paragraph: "But there are a few important aspects of attending college in the eighties that seem to be well-kept secrets." Its organizational plan was comparison and contrast, supported by narration.

Your topic is what you are writing about. Your thesis is what you want to say about it. Your plan determines how you develop your thesis. The section on outlining, which follows this section, will give you some practical suggestions about specifying your topic and formulating a thesis and then coordinating your choice of organizational plan with your topic and thesis, but for those suggestions to make sense, you need to have a thorough understanding of the various types of organizational plans that are available. The remainder of this section will look at the most common ones and attempt to exemplify them. You will examine more than a dozen planning principles, but all of them can be grouped under these five headings: (1) description, (2) narration, (3) definition, (4) induction, and (5) deduction.

Let us take a brief preliminary look at each of the five. Description simply draws a picture in words:

It has an eighteen-inch-square horizontal wooden surface supported by two twenty-inch wooden legs on the front and two similar legs on the back that extend twenty-four inches above the horizontal surface and are joined by two boards each a half-inch thick and four inches wide.

These words attempt to do what might be done graphically something like this:

Narration presents a motion picture in words:

The child picked up the chair and threw it to the ground, breaking it into several pieces.

Notice that at least these three frames are included in the above verbal movie:

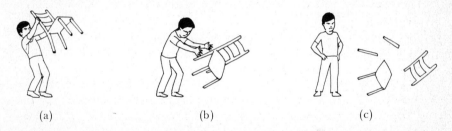

| (a) | (b) | (c) |

Definition puts the picture into a verbal frame:

A chair is a piece of furniture having a horizontal surface for one person to sit on and some kind of back support.

The above sentence did not *describe* any particular chair; instead, it talked about the idea of a chair in the abstract. The dotted lines in the following drawings represent the "frame" that constitutes the definition of a chair:

  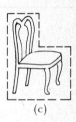

| (a) | (b) | (c) |

Induction is the verbal process of constructing a frame:

This thing (a) has a horizontal surface for a person to sit on and a back support; that thing (b) does too; so does that other thing (c). There must therefore be a class of such things. I'll call them chairs.

Graphically, the process of induction might be represented like this:

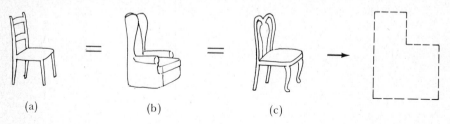

(a)   (b)   (c)

Deduction takes a preexisting verbal frame and finds something to put into it:

(a) A piece of furniture with a horizontal surface to seat one person and with back support is a chair.
(b) This has a horizontal surface to seat one person and back support.
(c) Therefore, this is a chair.

Graphically, the above deductive process might be represented like this:

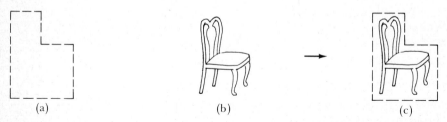

(a)   (b)   (c)

Your choice of a plan of organization is often very closely related to your purpose. Description and narration are most naturally employed when your purpose is to inform. Induction and deduction lend themselves more readily to persuading the reader. Definition serves either purpose more or less equally. In expository prose the subject to be discussed (the topic itself) is the first thing the reader generally wants to know, so definition is a suitable plan. On the other hand, it is a necessary part of any argumentative paper to define the things the writer wants the reader to believe, or like, or do.

Questions of purpose and questions of plan are nonetheless distinct. Your purpose is determined by the effect you want your paper to have on your reader. Plan is determined by the subject matter and the need to provide the best means for packaging your ideas. The follow-

ing diagram may serve as a preliminary representation of the relationship between purpose and plan. (The thirteen numbered subtypes of
organizational plans are discussed and exemplified on the following
pages.)

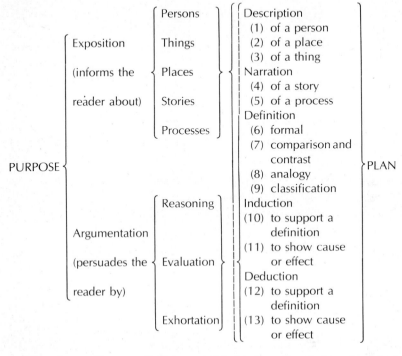

The above diagram indicates (with broken lines) that description and
narration may also serve the purpose of persuading the reader—for
instance, in an exhortation paper appealing for aid to the needy that
includes a description of the effects of hunger on children. Broken
lines also indicate that induction and deduction may serve the purpose of informing the reader—for instance, in an expository paper
about a court proceeding that includes accounts of the lawyer's arguments.

When you have finished studying description, narration, definition,
induction, and deduction in the next several pages, come back and reexamine the diagram above. It should then tell you even more about
the relationship between purpose and plan.

Description

Here is a student theme that is a good example of description. As
you read it, notice that it contains some narration as well. Notice also

that its purpose, while essentially expository (to give information about a person), includes an undertone of argumentation (the author is also using evaluation to get the reader to dislike the person being described). The topic of the theme is "Mrs. Gross." The thesis is expressed in the last sentence of the first paragraph: "Indeed, Mrs. Gross's name appropriately described her repulsive character."

THE NAME OF GROSS

Mention of the name Maude Gross revives vivid images of the woman who lived in the apartment next door to my family in the summer of my thirteenth year. Knowing how children tend to tease about names, my mother harshly warned my younger brother and me to refrain from any taunts or insulting comments concerning the Gross's family name. After meeting Maude Gross, however, we ignored the warning and secretly referred to her as "Gross Mud." This nickname stemmed not so much from cruelty as from honesty. Indeed, Mrs. Gross's name appropriately described her repulsive character.

True to her name, Mrs. Gross was massive in size with unsightly folds of bulging fat. Her body seemed to consist of loosely connected mounds of drooping flesh. Pudgy cheeks hung down so low that they were almost indistinguishable from her fleshy double chin, and her shoulders slumped forward causing her huge bosom to sag as well. The best indication of her gross obesity, however, was her belly; to keep her enormous stomach from interfering with her heavy legs, Mrs. Gross had to spread her legs apart when she sat.

My mother explained Mrs. Gross's flabby physique by suggesting that perhaps she had a hormonal problem, but this did not excuse the unhygienic aspects of her appearance. I never saw Mrs. Gross in anything but a dingy cotton, knee-length housecoat of gawdy orange and pink flowers. The hem was tattered and the underarm seams were splitting from the strain of her overweight condition. Sweat marks stained the underarm area. The only thing dirtier than her housecoat was her hair. I seriously doubted that either was washed more than once a month. Mrs. Gross's dyed red hair was unbelievably greasy; as a result, it lay plastered to her head. Beads of perspiration from her brow gave her face a wet, shiny look that added to the impression of disgusting uncleanliness.

The unclean appearance of Mrs. Gross seemed to extend to her household as well. The bare floor was littered with food crumbs and stained with faded red Kool-aid spots. The sparsely furnished room was cluttered with dirty, crumpled clothes and spilled trash. In the midst of the filth, Mrs. Gross sprawled ungracefully in a grimy yellow armchair in front of her small black-and-white television set. Her enormous body was squeezed into the confines of the chair, and her flab seemed to flow over the torn edges. Her life seemed to revolve around this one chair. I always saw her seated there, reading a magazine or watching television, oblivious to the noise of screaming kids and buzzing flies.

Occasionally, however, Mrs. Gross would heave her great weight out of her undersized chair to lumber after her three bickering kids. Puffing and wheezing, she would yank up her unsuspecting child and shake him till he quieted. She would press her red, angry face close to her child's so that her bad breath puffed explosively as she yelled. Her bellowing roar was certainly enough to strike terror in the hearts of the neighborhood children as well. Her language was often crude, even with adults. Indeed, every aspect of her appearance and her behavior lived up to her name: the name of Gross.

—Shirlyn Kowalczyk, a student

The most important thing to notice about the above description is that it is ordered. The writer first described Mrs. Gross's physical appearance, then her dress and personal habits, then her furniture, then her actions to people around her. Whether you decribe a person, a thing, or a place, you should do as Ms. Kowalczyk did in the above paper: adopt a point of view and then follow a pattern of description based on it. You may move outward, from the person or thing described to the surroundings, as in the above paper, or you may move from near to far, from top to bottom, from largest to smallest, from background to foreground;

these are only a few of the descriptive plans you may adopt, but *do* think about your plan before you start to describe and *do* adopt a point of view and stick to it.

The passage from Eudora Welty on p. 50 described a person; the passage about the eleventh-century crown of England on p. 51 described a thing; the passage about the fraternity house on p. 51 described a place. Reread each of these passages carefully. Try to discover the descriptive plan of each passage. As the descriptive information is presented, does the author move in a certain spatial direction? Does a descriptive principle other than spatial order, such as size or color, determine the plan by which the descriptive details are arranged? As you read and analyze each passage, notice how rich it is in concrete detail and notice how the details are presented in some carefully planned sequence.

Exercise

Write three descriptive passages, one for each subtype of description listed below. Be sure to think about audience and purpose before you write, but concentrate on writing a detailed concrete description in which you carefully and consistently maintain a given point of view by following a well-chosen descriptive plan:

(1) Description of a person
(2) Description of a thing
(3) Description of a place

Narration

Here is a passage that is essentially a narration. Since it speaks of people and animals and places, it has a certain amount of description as well. But narration is clearly the controlling organizational plan.

I could not see where don Juan was. The squealing of the rodents became extremely loud and finally it was so dark that I could hardly distinguish the general features of the terrain. I heard a sudden and close sound of soft steps and a muffled catlike exhalation, then a very soft growl and the squirrel-like rodents ceased to squeak. It was right then that I saw the dark mass of an animal right under the tree where I was. Before I could even be sure that it was a mountain lion it charged against the trap, but before it reached it something hit it and made it recoil. I hurled my bundle as don Juan had told me to do. I missed, yet it made a very loud noise. At that instant don Juan let out a series of penetrating yells that sent chills through my spine, and the cat, with extraordinary agility, leaped to the mesa and disappeared.

—CARLOS CASTANEDA, *Journey to Ixtlan*

This passage illustrates quite well the central principle of good narration: Let the reader know the sequence of events. The verb *became* in the first sentence shows this passage of time. So do expressions such as *then, it was right then, before,* and *at that instant.* Once you decide to write narration, keep the action moving. The plan of your paper must be determined by the sequence of events, rather than by any one of the people, things, or places you talk about. The same holds true when you are narrating a process; for example, if you are giving directions about how to bake a cake, do not be afraid to use expressions such as *first, second, third,* and *finally,* or *the most important, the next most important,* and *the least important.*

The passage about the drag race on p. 52 narrated a story, and the passage about how to teach children to swim on p. 53 narrated a process. Study each passage and notice that while both of them also describe persons, things, and places, it is the time order of events that controls the plan of organization. In each passage, identify all of the words or expressions that play a role in making the time order clear and thus give each passage its narrative character.

Longer narrative passages sometimes use time order in a more complex way. In a flash-back the narrative may begin at one point and then jump back in time and move up to the starting point again. Or two events or processes may be narrated together, with alternate passages treating each one. But the essential skill you need to write any narrative passage is the ability to make time order clear to your reader.

Exercise

Write narrative passages of each of the following types in which you make the time order of the events in the story and the steps in the process as clear as you can. (The several subtypes of planning principles will be numbered consecutively throughout the set of exercises following the five subsections in this section.)

(4) Narration of a story
(5) Narration of a process

Definition

There are several ways of defining something, and you will have an opportunity to examine some of them in this subsection. The first is called *formal definition,* and the brief definition of a chair given earlier is an example of it. Formal definition puts the item or abstraction being defined into a class and then distinguishes it from all other members of the same class. Thus a chair *is* a piece of furniture (class) that seats one person and has back support (a table is also a piece of furniture, but it seats no one; a bench seats two or more; a stool has no back support). Here is a 500-word theme I wrote myself some time ago to use as an example with my own students. Its basic organizational plan is formal definition. In its very first sentence it puts the topic (a student of English) into a class: "The student of English is a reader and a writer." The remaining paragraphs of the theme seek to specify the particular kind of reading and writing that English majors do, which sets them apart from just anyone who might happen to pick up a book to read or a pen to write with. The theme's basic purpose is expository, but it also seeks subtly to suggest that one should consider majoring in English, and is to that extent argumentative exhortation as well as exposition.

WHAT IS A STUDENT OF ENGLISH?

The student of English is a reader and a writer. A reader probes the mind of another human being in a way that no amount of talk can allow. The reader has time to test and measure ideas from many perspectives, to weigh and analyze words with critical care. In the process, the reader will often discover insights that the writer was not even aware of during the composing process. This happens because a writer creates structures of ideas that take on an existence of their own. A written text thus becomes a living extension of the mind that created it.

As readers, students of English specialize in the interpretation of literary texts. Poems, stories, and plays epitomize the independent nature of written texts: They challenge readers to live the life portrayed in the text, to think its thoughts, to feel its emotions—in short, to become more human by encountering the soul of the writer in and through the work of literature. Anyone who has traveled with Chaucer to Canterbury, or suffered with Shakespeare the plight of Romeo and Juliet, or stopped by those wintry woods with Robert Frost knows how much imagination and insight literature demands of a reader.

The close reading of literature also provides exercise in a more practical skill: the reading of life. It trains the mind for perceptive and critical reading of political speeches, newspaper editorials, business memoranda, letters

---

of all types, and even the trivial advertisements that daily flood the brain. No one is better prepared to distinguish fact from fiction, truth from trash, or worth from worthlessness than a student of literature.

The writing program of an English major centers on rhetoric: the art of persuasion. Through practice and analysis, the student learns to write with purpose for any audience, to plan detailed logical arguments, and to marshall concrete evidence in support of those arguments. The study of poetic language refines the precision of the writer's word choices; the study of grammar and linguistics sharpens the clarity of the writer's sentences.

English majors also have opportunities to write poetry, fiction, and drama. Although only a specially talented few will pursue creative writing as a career, all students of English learn that no profession is nearer to the frontiers of the human spirit than that of the creative writer. They learn what Shelley meant when he called poets mirrors of the gigantic shadows that futurity casts upon the present.

Skills in critical reading and imaginative writing are essential not only for those who would write or teach professionally, but also for those who would hold positions of responsibility in government, business, or industry. As readers, English majors prepare to interpret the world they will live and work in; as writers, they prepare to reshape and perhaps even to recreate it.

An extended formal definition usually relies heavily on description and narration because concrete details and examples are needed to see how the thing being defined works, or how it differs from those other entities in the same class with it. The above theme relied heavily on process narration. Much of it narrated the general process (set of activities) that a student who majors in English engages in.

The second subtype of definition is *definition by comparison and contrast.* Instead of explicitly putting something in a class and then distinguishing it from everything in the same class, the thing to be defined is implicitly placed in a class and simply compared to one or a few other things that are like it. It may also be contrasted with something else. Or some combination of comparison and contrast is used. The basic principle is to compare or contrast your topic with something you think your reader knows better than your topic, thus to help your reader understand something unfamiliar by reference to the familiar. Here is a passage that uses comparison and contrast effectively. Its assumption is that most readers have more experience with electric fans than with airplane propellers, and so it defines the latter by reference to the former.

> Because the propeller is driven by a motor, it is almost the same thing as an electric fan; the two look slightly different only because they are used differently. In the propeller you don't use the backward blast of air, but you use the kick and you allow it to make plenty of noise. The electric fan is designed not to make too much noise; you use the blast of air and you don't use the "kick-back." In fact, most people don't know that an electric fan has a kick just like a propeller. But just set your electric fan on a toy wagon and watch it propel.
>
> —WOLFGANG LANGEWIESCHE, "Why an Airplane Flies"

The third subtype of definition, *definition by analogy,* is similar to definition by comparison. However, in an analogy, the two entities being compared do not belong to the same class; they are in fact usually completely unrelated, or at least seemingly so. In this book, you have already seen an extended use of definition by analogy: In the first section of the first chapter, I used analogy with a game of cards to help define language and its structure. There, the analogy was *explicit.* I came right out and said that language was *like* a card game. And I often made statements to the effect, "Just as in cards, so too in language." Analogy is often used most effectively when it is *implicit.* That is, the writer does not come right out and say that something is like something else. Instead, the writer uses words and expressions that relate to one thing (usually more familiar) in describing and thus defining another thing (usually less familiar).

In the following example, notice that the authors never say, "Writing is like fighting a war," but they effectively use that analogy by talking about the "strategy" and "tactics" of good writing.

> We contend that good writing is good strategy first and foremost. The wholeness of the whole composition we must first secure or all is lost; poor strategy loses wars, poor tactics only battles. Too often we are concerned only with the tactics of "correct" grammar, too seldom for the strategy of good design in writing. While we fuss with formalities, we lose the war. Sentences in Class A uniforms, Fowlered, Perrined, and Webstered, gallop off to annihilation like Tennyson's Six Hundred. The art of war is strategy first, tactics second. The art of writing cannot improve this wisdom.
>
> —GORDON ROHMAN AND ALBERT WLECKE, *Pre-writing: The Construction and Application of Models for Concept Formation in Writing*

The fourth subtype of definition is *definition by classification.* If several things are defined at the same time as subdivisions of some larger thing, definition by classification is being used. The essential principle governing definition by classification is that the groupings should be exhaustive. If you are classifying types of living things and you list only humans and animals, you have violated this principle because you missed plants. One of the most well-known classifications is the animal-vegetable-mineral groupings used in parlor games where one has to guess through a process of elimination what another player is thinking. If this classification were not exhaustive in regard to concrete things, the game would get nowhere. Here is the opening paragraph from a student theme that used classification as its organizational plan. The remaining paragraphs simply described in detail each of the three types of housekeepers listed in this paragraph. It is the author's contention that every houskeeper falls into one of these three classes.

There are three types of housekeepers. The first has dirt-o-phobia and must keep the home forever spotless and immaculate. (This individual keeps a germ-free hospital, not a home.) The second has dust-a-phobia and is compelled to wipe and brush and sweep the dust out of sight, but without deep cleaning. (This individual keeps a lot of throw rugs around for handy dust disposal.) The third has clean-a-phobia and is likely to leave things unkempt but cozy and comfortable. (This individual keeps a home, not a house.)

—DEBRA DAUTRICH, A STUDENT

All four subtypes of definition overlap to some extent. Formal definition begins with classification (putting the thing defined in its class) and ends in contrast (distinguishing the thing defined from other members of the class), but it focuses squarely on the thing defined. Classification necessarily entails comparison and contrast—the former, if similarities are emphasized among classified items; the latter, if differences are emphasized. Analogy does a little of everything, but it seeks to define indirectly. When you are writing definitions, your organization will be more effective if one of the four subtypes clearly dominates: formal definition, definition by comparison and contrast, definition by analogy, or definition by classification.

Exercise

Write several definition passages, one for each of the subtypes of definition listed below. You may use the passages given in the body of this subsection as models, but select topics that interest you. Remember to think about audience and purpose before you write.

(6) Formal definition
(7) Definition by comparison and contrast

(8) Definition by analogy
(9) Definition by classification

Induction

Here is a passage that is essentially an example of induction. Notice that it begins by discussing a long series of concrete facts. Only at the end is a generalization stated, based on the evidence.

The chimpanzee employs one unit of sound in social play, another when a juvenile is lost, a third when attacked, and so on—but two or more calls cannot be combined to generate additional messages. In contrast the 13 sounds of Hawaiian can be combined to form 2,197 potential three-sound words, nearly five million six-sound words—and an astronomical number if the full repertory of 13 sounds is used to form longer words. In the same way, a speaker of English can select three units of sound out of his store of 45—such as the sounds represented in writing by *e*, *n*, and *d*—and then combine them into such meaningful words as *end, den,* and *Ned.* But the chimpanzee cannot combine the three units of sound that mean play, lost juvenile, and threat of attack to form some other message. Nor can the chimpanzee's call that means "Here is food" ever be changed to talk about the delicacies it consumed yesterday or its expectations about finding certain fruits tomorrow. Generation after generation, as far into the future as the chimpanzee survives as a species, it will use that call solely to indicate the immediate presence of food. Thus, chimpanzees with their 25 units of sound are incapable of speech, while Hawaiians, with only 13 units, possess a very expressive language.

—Adapted from PETER FARB, *Word Play*

Induction is the basic plan of organization used in the sciences. Inductive discourse begins with a series of specific observations: statements about the behavior of specific things at specific times and in specific places. These statements are followed by a general statement that expresses similarities among all of the specific things just discussed.

The use of induction requires considerable discipline on the part of the writer, for it is the tendency of all humans to generalize too soon —to "jump to conclusions." When you are using induction to organize a paper, be sure you know the difference between your facts and your generalizations. Present your facts clearly and systematically. Then draw your conclusion. In the passage above, notice that Farb first presented a number of irrefutable observations: Both chimpanzees and humans make meaningful sounds; humans combine them and give the combination new meanings, but chimpanzees do not. Only after detailing his facts did he draw his conclusion: Chimpanzees are incapable of speech. An important thing to remember about inductive reasoning is that it simply recaps past experience; it does not emphasize predications about the future. All it would take is one English-speaking chimpanzee to turn Farb's whole argument on its head!

There are two uses you can make of induction as an organizational plan. You can use it to support a definition or to show cause or effect. In Farb's paragraph, he was implicitly developing the definition of the human species by showing that language is a characteristic that distinguishes humans from other mammals (he was defining by contrast). If, instead of the last sentence he actualiy wrote, Farb had written, "This is why Hawaiians have achieved a highly developed culture but no group of chimpanzees ever has," then he would have been using the facts in his paragraph to show the causes of cultural development in humans rather than to add substance to the definition of the human species.

Here is a student theme that very effectively uses induction to show cause and effect. Specifically, it argues that *because* the risk is minimal, nuclear power should be continued. Even though the conclusion is stated explicitly at the end of the first paragraph, the paper is clearly inductive, for the remaining paragraphs painstakingly develop the facts on which the conclusion is based. The author then very cleverly alludes to his conclusion in the final sentence.

RISK

Recent events at the Three Mile Island nuclear plant have raised serious questions about the risk caused by reactor plants. The primary risk to be considered is the release of radiation and the exposure of the public to this radiation. When the amount of radiation released at Three Mile Island is examined in a rational manner, the risk of nuclear power still appears to be reasonable.

In order to understand radiation, the terms in which it is measured must be understood. The term REM stands for Roentgen Equivalent in Man and is a unit which is used to measure biological damage due to radiation exposure. The term milirem (MR) means 1/1000 of a REM. The National Academy of Science has stated that 25,000 to 50,000 MR will cause growth disturbances in unborn children, and that 600,000 MR would cause death if the entire dose were received in a short period of time.

Each of us is exposed to approximately 15,000 MR during our lifetime. This 15,000 MR is received from sources such as

sunlight, color television, and medical x–rays. If we live in
a location that has a high elevation, such as Denver, we can
expect to receive an additional 100 MR per year. Another 100
MR per year could be expected if we operated a nuclear plant
on a submarine. One of the most significant increases in radiation exposure is caused by smoking. In March, 1979, Admi-
ral H. G. Rickover asserted to the House Armed Services Committee that people who smoke one pack of cigarettes a day can
expect to receive 5,000 MR of radiation for each year they
smoke.

Rickover also asserted that, in a typical group of
10,000 people, 1600 will die of cancer. If the typical group
of 10,000 people were exposed to 1500 MR of radiation, the
cancer death rate would possibly increase by one or two.
<u>Newsweek</u> magazine (April 9, 1979) reported that the radiation
levels at the Three Mile Island reactor were 30 MR. When this
30 MR is compared to the 1500 MR, which <u>may</u> cause two additional deaths per 10,000 people, the risk of radiation from
reactor plants appears reasonable. This comparison is not intended to justify the design, or the mechanical and human
failures that caused the Three Mile Island accident, but only
to put the radiation levels released there into proper perspective.

We are confronted with risk every day. An annual increase of approximately 65 in the automobile death rate would
be proportional to the two additional deaths caused by a radiation release of 1500 MR; however, a release of 1500 MR has
never occurred. Surely more than 65 people died last year due
to the faulty design, construction, and operation of automobiles. Should all manufacture and use of automobiles be discontinued? You decide.

—J. H. Shoemaker, a student

Exercise

Write an inductive passage of each of the two types listed below. You may use
the samples of induction given in the body of the section as models, but choose

your own topics. Make certain that you keep your facts separate from your conclusions, and that you provide enough specific facts to support your conclusion.

   (10) Induction to support a definition
   (11) Induction to show cause or effect

Deduction

    Here is a passage that is essentially an example of deduction. Remember that deduction takes a general principle, assumes that it is true, and then applies it to some specific situation. As you read the following passage, try to determine the general principle on which St. Paul bases his argument. What is his argument? That is, what specific conclusions does he draw from the general principle he begins with?

Now, since our message is that Christ has been raised from the dead, how can some of you say that the dead will not be raised to life? If that is true, it means that Christ was not raised; and if Christ has not been raised from death, then we have nothing to preach and you have nothing to believe. More than that, we are shown to be lying against God, because we said of him that he raised Christ from death—but he did not raise him if it is true that the dead are not raised to life. For if the dead are not raised, neither has Christ been raised. And if Christ has not been raised, then your faith is a delusion and you are still lost in your sins. It would also mean that the believers in Christ who have died are lost. If our hope in Christ is good for this life only, and no more, then we deserve more pity than anyone else in all the world.

         —From the *Good News For Modern Man,* 1 Cor 15: 12–19

Deductive arguments can usually be reduced to the form of a logical syllogism. St. Paul's argument reduces to what is called a hypothetical syllogism. Here is an outline of such a syllogism:

If *A*, then *B*.
A
Therefore, *B*.

Here is a hypothetical syllogism which expresses a key argument in the passage above:

If <u>Christ has risen</u>, then <u>all the dead will rise</u>.
       A   *B*

<u>Christ has risen</u>.
     A

Therefore, <u>all the dead will rise</u>.
          B

Notice that St. Paul never actually asserts in the above passage that Christ has risen. It is common in deductive argumentation to leave one of the premises understood. But when you write a deductive paper, you should know all your premises, and you should be sure that they work together validly to support your conclusions.

A deductive argument, like an inductive one, can serve two different planning functions: it may primarily apply a definition or primarily show causes or effects. The above passage by St. Paul was of the latter type: he argued that the dead will rise *because* Christ has risen. Below is a passage that uses deduction to apply a definition. Its argument reduces to another type of logical syllogism called a categorical syllogism. Here is an outline of such a syllogism accompanied by a very common example:

A is B.   All men are mortal.
                          A B

C is A.   Socrates is a man.
                          C A

Therefore, C is B.   Therefore, Socrates is mortal.
                                    C B

As you read the following passage, try to discover the logical syllogism that lies at the heart of its argument.

A teacher who creates an atmosphere where students are stimulated to ask their own questions and seek their own answers is a successful teacher. My tenth-grade English teacher was such a person. She didn't lecture us endlessly; she didn't make us take reams of notes; she didn't make us memorize irrelevant dates. Instead, she led us in the experience of good literature. When she read plays and poems to us, they came to life, and we wanted to read more. When she explained movies of great novels, she led us to seek out the books and read them on our own. She led me to see that literature could take me anywhere I wanted to go and let me be anyone I wanted to be. I even began to ask her for titles that treated ideas I had become interested in. Before she taught me, I had never read literature for pleasure; since then, I have not stopped doing so. "Successful" is really an inadequate word to describe the lasting effect she had on me.

—MICHAEL SIMMONS, A STUDENT

Here, in the form of a categorical syllogism, is a summary of the argument in the above passage:

A stimulator of questions is a successful teacher.
$\underbrace{\text{A stimulator of questions}}_{A}$ is $\underbrace{\text{a successful teacher.}}_{B}$

$\underbrace{\text{My tenth-grade teacher}}_{C}$ was $\underbrace{\text{a stimulator of questions.}}_{A}$

Therefore, $\underbrace{\text{My tenth-grade teacher}}_{C}$ was $\underbrace{\text{a successful teacher.}}_{B}$

Notice that the first sentence in the passage could be part of the definition of a successful teacher. But the passage does not go on to develop such a definition as its principal purpose. Like any deductive argument it assumes that the reader already agrees with the general assertion in the first sentence. The purpose of the passage is to use deductive argumentation to apply the assertion from the first sentence, to prove that a particular person, the author's tenth-grade English teacher, fits into the class defined in the opening sentence (the class of successful teachers).

Your deductive papers will be stronger if you decide in advance whether you are applying a definition or showing cause or effect. Try hard to argue clearly and to adopt a form of syllogistic reasoning that is appropriate to your argument.

Exercise

Write a deductive passage of each of the two types listed below. You may use the passages given in the body of this subsection as models, but choose your own topics. If you can, outline your arguments in the form of logical syllogisms before you begin to write.

(12) Deduction to apply a definition
(13) Deduction to show cause or effect

Outlining

You must ask the questions in the previous sections and answer them carefully, whenever you are planning strategy for a selection in edited English. But what about tactics? How do you put the plan into effect? The remainder of this book will deal with this question in detail. You will learn how to organize effective paragraphs and clear sentences, how to choose the right words, and how to punctuate for understanding. These are questions of style, and they will be taken up beginning in the next chapter. But before we leave the pre-style phases of the composition process (finding ideas and organizing them), let us take some time to look at outlining, a practical tactic that many writers find helpful throughout the process of both finding ideas and planning how best to present them.

It is important to consider questions of audience and purpose before and during the outlining process, the aim of which is to help you focus on a topic, formulate a thesis, and produce a carefully structured written version of your organizational plan. The following three subsections will treat the three phases of the outlining process in some detail. These are: (1) the preliminary phase, (2) the development phase, and (3) the revision phase.

The preliminary phase

The first step in the preliminary phase is to jot ideas about your tentative topic randomly on a sheet of paper in the manner of a free-association exercise. During this phase you must keep your audience, purpose, and—to the extent you will have specified it—your topic firmly in mind, for each of these may contain the seeds of just the right plan that are ready to burst forth if you just give them room to grow.

Suppose you are faced with the task of writing a paper for a composition course and you are free to determine topic, audience, and purpose. You have no burning desire to write about anything in particular but you do have an interest in and a fairly good knowledge of cars. You start by jotting random ideas on a piece of paper. On the following page is a representation of how such a sheet might look after a few minutes of random jotting about cars.

The next step is to look for a pattern or patterns in your jottings. Often enough as you jot, one word will suggest another or a series of others. You may wish to use different colored pencils on your jotting sheet, or you may wish to copy lists onto another sheet, but in examining the sheet represented on the next page you will notice groupings such as the following:

engines	accidents	back seats	Indy 500	Pinto
wheels	pollution	first love	A. J. Foyt	
ignition	clunker	convertible	sports	
color	repairs	vans	race cars	
	drunk drivers			
	cost			

The first column suggests descriptive features of cars; the second, problems with cars; the third, a particular cultural role of cars; the

pinto
Indy 500
A. J. Foyt
transportation
sports
race cars
accidents
back seats
first love
convertible
vans
repairs
dents
engines
color
ignition
insurance
electronics
wheels
pollution
gas
(lack of)
stupid
drivers
drunk
drivers
luxury
necessity
tickets
police
cost
clunker

fourth, the sport of car racing; the fifth, a particular type of car (the beginning of a classification).

Exercise

As you study the sample outline that is being developed in the three subsections of this section, you should also work on some outlines of your own. If you cannot think of a topic, here are some to start you thinking: air, clouds, fall, flowers, grass, kisses, laughter, leaves, pain, rain, sleep, spring, summer, tears, water, wind, winter. (If you have begun one, a writer's notebook will provide you with other topics.) Pick a general topic and then begin jotting ideas randomly on a piece of paper. Work on it for several minutes, at least until you have written a few dozen things on the sheet. Then use colored pencils to mark related items on the sheet, or make lists of related items on a second sheet. When you finish, set your work aside and continue reading; the exercise at the end of the next section will call on you to continue work on the outline or outlines you have just begun.

The development phase

The purpose of the preliminary phase was very much like that of a free-association exercise: to probe your mind to find out what information there is to work with. It also sought, by making the lists, to begin the process of organization. The main purposes of the development phase are to discover what aspect of the topic you know most about, and then to narrow the topic accordingly and formulate a thesis statement.

Notice that the longest of the five lists developed in the previous section from the jotting sheet was the one treating problems with cars. Let us use that list to illustrate how the development phase of outlining works. The first step in the development phase is to use more free association to expand the list. But now the focus of attention is on a more specific topic: the idea of problems associated with cars.

accidents . . . injury, death, medical costs, law suits
pollution . . . air pollution, noise pollution
clunker . . . that Corvair I owned
repairs . . . scheduled maintenance, body work, defective workmanship
drunk drivers . . . reckless drivers, aged drivers
cost . . . initial purchase, gas, licenses, insurance

When you finish this expanded list, study it carefully. Try to discover in it a planning principle that dominates. Do the ideas listed lend themselves best to description, narration, definition, induction, or deduction? Notice that it is impossible to answer this question without considering the questions about audience and purpose. To whom am I writing about cars? Why am I writing? Suppose you work for General Motors and you are writing an owner's manual. Suppose, on the other hand, you work for a consumer group and are writing to Congress. In the first instance you might simply wish to inform the prospective buyer about how to avoid problems, how to deal with them, or even simply how to recognize them. In the second instance, you might want to persuade Congress to pass legislation that would eliminate at least some problems.

Let us assume that you are writing this paper simply to inform the prospective car owner of the types of problems associated with car ownership. You are thus faced with the task of defining the problems —specifically, of classifying them by type. Examine the whole list of problems listed in the last paragraph. Try to group them into two or three mutually exclusive categories. Think about this for a few minutes before you read on. Here are a few possibilities; did any of these occur to you?

I. Problems in buying a car
II. Problems in operating a car

I. Problems caused by machinery
II. Problems caused by people
  A. The driver
  B. Others

I. Legal Problems
II. Personal Problems
III. Mechanical Problems

I. Serious Problems
II. Minor Problems

Check for yourself to see how many of the terms listed in the previous paragraph fit under the headings of these four suggested outlines. My choice is the second outline, and I will use it in the next subsection to illustrate the final phase in the outlining process. When the choices of audience, purpose, and plan have reached the stage represented by a general outline like the one just chosen, it is time to formulate the paper's thesis. The audience for the paper we are planning consists of prospective new-car owners. The purpose is to inform them about the problems of new-car ownership. According to the draft outline, these problems will be grouped under two major headings: Problems caused by machinery, and Problems caused by people. In view of these decisions, what do you think of the following as a thesis statement?

> The prospective new-car buyer should be fully informed about the problems that may come with the car, both those caused by machinery and those caused by people.

It actually names the audience, even states explicitly that the paper aims to inform them, and then lists the two major headings under which all the paper's ideas will be grouped.

In any paper you write, you should experiment with a number of general outlines, constantly reevaluating your answers to questions about audience and purpose. When you choose the general outline best suited to your specified topic, your audience, and your purpose, formulate your thesis and move on to the revision phase of the outlining process.

Exercise

Continue working on the outline or outlines you began in the exercise at the end of the previous subsection.

(1) Choose the longest list from those you developed during the preliminary phase (in doing so you will automatically be specifying your topic).

(2) Copy the list onto another sheet of paper, and expand it by writing related words and expressions beside each item on the list.

(3) Study your expanded lists to discover ways of grouping the ideas.

(4) Make several general outlines that fit the ideas you have developed.

(5) Choose the one you want to work with, and then formulate a thesis statement that fits not only the outline you have chosen, but also your audience and purpose.

The revision phase

There is no sharp division between the development phase and the revision phase. You will probably need to revise your outline several times, especially after you begin the actual writing of your paper. Throughout the revision process, learn to use the most generally acceptable enumeration format for outlining. The major headings in your outline should be indicated by upper-case Roman numerals:

I.
II.
. . .

Divisions under each Roman numeral are indicated by upper-case letters:

I.
  A.
  B.
  . . .

Divisions under the upper-case letters are indicated by Arabic numbers:

I.
  A.
    1.
    2.
    . . .

Divisions under the Arabic numbers are indicated by lower-case letters:

I.
  A.
    1.
      a.
      b.
      . . .

Only when you are writing a very long paper or a book will you need subdivisions in an outline more refined than these. [The next level is indicated by Arabic numbers in parentheses: (1), (2), ... Under that level, lower-case letters in parentheses are used: (a), (b), . . .]

Here is a revised and expanded outline based on the notes about car problems that were developed in the previous subsection. Notice that the topic specified there is expressed as the paper's title and the outline itself is preceded by an explicit statement of the paper's thesis. When you begin to draft the paper, you will need to decide whether the thesis will appear in this exact wording, and where it will appear.

    Title: Problems of Car Ownership
  Thesis: The prospective new-car buyer should be fully informed about the problems that may come with the car, both those caused by machinery and those caused by people.

    I. Problems caused by machinery
      A. Affecting the owner
        1. Maintenance
          a. Scheduled
          b. Unscheduled
        2. Breakdown
      B. Affecting society as a whole: pollution
    II. Problems caused by people
      A. Drivers
        1. Needless waste of fuel
        2. Needless wear and tear
        3. Needless damage to machines and people
      B. Others
        1. High purchase price
        2. High insurance costs
        3. High license fees

One way to assure that your outline is rooted in logic is to express all the subheadings under a given heading in parallel grammatical structure. Notice that the two major headings in the above outline follow the pattern, "Problems caused by _____" and the headings under the first section follow the pattern, "Affecting _____." The same principle holds true throughout the outline.

Another principle to follow in revising an outline is avoid single headings. The enumeration format exists for the purpose of subdividing. Thus, unless there are two or more subparts, you should not use a letter or number to label a single part. Notice, in the outline above, that only one problem under I. B. was listed (pollution). It was thus the whole content of I. B. (the colon indicated this) and was not given the number 1 under I. B.

The above outline, and the shorter ones in the previous subsection, are called *topic outlines.* You may occasionally find it useful, especially when planning an argumentative paper, to use what are called *sentence outlines* (where the parts are not words or phrases but whole sentences). Here is a short sentence outline of a paper arguing that big cars should be banned:

I. Large cars place needless economic burdens on the consumer.
   A. They cause needless expenses in both purchase and repair.
   B. They cause additional taxes.
   C. They feed the fires of inflation.
II. Large cars cause inefficiency in the automobile industry.
   A. For the same production costs, more small cars could be built.
   B. For the same labor costs, more workers could be hired.

Notice that a sentence outline relies on parallel structure too, and also avoids single headings.

Exercises

a. Work with the outline or outlines you have been developing in exercises at the end of the last two subsections. As you revise and expand them, take care to use parallel structure effectively and to avoid single subheadings. Include a title and a sentence expressing the thesis with each outline.

b. Below are some outlines. Read them carefully and evaluate them. Each one has one or more structural flaws—usually, lack of parallelism or unnecessary subdividing. Revise each one.

(1) Title: Effects of Poor Teaching

   I. Students do not learn
      A. Lack of attention in class
      B. Tests
   II. Alienation of students
      A. Loss of respect for adults
   III. Taxes are wasted

(2) Title: Colonial Williamsburg

    I. Plan
       A. Laid out in rectangular tracts
       B. Streets
   II. Architecture
       A. Of shops
       B. Houses
  III. Gardens
       A. Kinds of shrubs

(3) Title: Team Sports vs. Individual Sports

    I. Team sports teach cooperation
       A. Players must cooperate with other team members
   II. Individual sports teach discipline
       A. Must practice daily
       B. The coach's role

Four *Paragraphs*

The first three chapters of this book prepared you to write. This chapter and those that follow treat drafting and revising. As you read and write your way through the following chapters, you will probably find it easier to apply principles of paragraph structure, sentence structure, word choice, spelling, and punctuation as you *revise* your earlier drafts. But the more opportunities you give yourself to practice, the more you will incorporate many of these principles even in your early drafts. For now, plan to revise. Much of the discouragement felt by inexperienced writers comes from failure to realize that good writing takes work. If you know this and learn to use the writer's tools, you will even come to find pleasure in the work.

We saw earlier that edited English is addressed to an audience that is not intimately familiar with you or your topic, and that, like all written English, it is addressed to an audience that is absent. For these reasons, it must supply sufficient detail to familiarize the reader with the information it is trying to convey, and it must carefully and coherently make up for the lack of conversational interaction by anticipating and addressing any questions the reader might be expected to have. The structural device that has developed in our culture to fulfill these special requirements of edited English is the paragraph.

A paragraph can consist of one sentence or a hundred sentences, though most are between five and ten sentences long. The first line of a paragraph is usually indented, although some writers and book designers ignore this convention. No matter, because neither length nor visual appearance defines the paragraph. The paragraph is defined by its content: all of its sentences must treat one idea and do so coherently. In this chapter we will look closely at these two defining features of the paragraph: *unity* and *coherence.*

Only rarely will you ever need to write one paragraph in isolation. Usually, you write several as part of a larger plan. So before we go into the internal structure of the paragraph, let us see how you can take an outline and make a preliminary assignment of paragraphs to various parts of it. Below are the main headings of the outline that was developed at the end of the last chapter. Let us assume that it was developed as the plan for a 500-word theme. How many paragraphs would you expect such a paper to have? In considering this question, and in working with paragraphs throughout this chapter, you should generally plan to write paragraphs of at least five but no more than ten sentences. When the needs of a particular plan seem to call for shorter or longer paragraphs, you should of course feel free to write such paragraphs. With this in mind, to which headings in the outline would you assign separate paragraphs?

> Title: Problems of Car Ownership
> Thesis: The prospective new-car owner should be fully informed about the problems that may come with the car, both those caused by machinery and those caused by people.
> > I. Problems caused by machinery
> > > A. Affecting the owner
> > > B. Affecting society as a whole: pollution
> > II. Problems caused by people
> > > A. Drivers
> > > B. Others

This could be the outline of a book, or of just a page. How you assign paragraphs to an outline depends, of course, on how much information you wish to include for each heading and on the overall intended length of your paper. Given a length of about 500 words, here is a preliminary plan for converting the above outline into paragraphs:

> (1) An introductory paragraph that states the thesis of the paper and gives the reader a preview of its contents
> (2) I.A. Problems caused by machinery affecting the owner
> (3) I.B. Problems caused by machinery affecting society as a whole
> (4) II.A. Problems caused by drivers
> (5) II.B. Problems caused by others

Application of the principles of unity and coherence will, in the end, determine whether the above preliminary plan will hold up or whether some other division into paragraphs should be adopted. But making such an assignment even before beginning the first draft will probably save some revision time.

You will have to decide for yourself whether this type of preliminary assignment of paragraphs to your outlines is a useful tool for you.

Unity: One Idea

Every paragraph should express one and only one idea. This idea should be summarized in a topic sentence that is usually, though not always, the first sentence in the paragraph. All other sentences in the paragraph must relate to the main idea and therefore develop some aspect of the topic sentence. The paragraph should be long enough to fulfill all the expectations established in the topic sentence, but not so long that it begins to discuss issues not raised in the topic sentence. Unity also requires that only one organizing principle should control the development of the paragraph's main idea. The next three subsections treat each of these aspects of paragraph unity in detail.

The topic sentence states the idea

Here is a draft of the first paragraph of the paper outlined just above. Read it and notice that the first sentence summarizes the whole paragraph, and all of the other sentences simply give additional information about the ideas introduced in the first sentence:

The prospective new-car owner should be fully informed about the problems that may come with the car, both those caused by machinery and those caused by people. Mechanical failure will most certainly affect the owner: In addition to scheduled maintenance, unexpected inconvenience and expense can be caused by unplanned repairs and even breakdowns. Society as a whole can also be affected since failure to service the pollution control system contributes to pollution. The owner should also be forewarned that his own driving habits and even those of others on the road can cause him problems. Other problems, mostly in the form of increased costs, will come to the purchaser courtesy of assorted groups and individuals in society.

This paragraph is a preview of the whole paper. Notice that it contains five sentences. The first is both a summary of the paragraph (its topic sentence) *and* a summary of the whole paper (its thesis). Each of the other four sentences develops some aspect of the topic sentence. The second and third sentences give more information on the types of problems caused by machinery, and the fourth and fifth sentences give more information on the types of problems caused by people. If there were another sentence, for instance about the failure of Henry Ford to foresee all of these problems, the unity of the paragraph would have been weakened, because there is no hint of this idea in the topic sentence. We shall return to the above paragraph later, for it is indeed a first draft and needs revision for several reasons. But it does make a good unified beginning.

Here is a first draft of the second paragraph of the paper outlined above. This is the paragraph treating mechanical problems affecting the owner:

Unless the owner of a new car follows the manufacturer's scheduled maintenance suggestions, he will surely have a greater incidence of unscheduled maintenance, and will probably even experience a breakdown. The owner's manual specifies oil changes, and a variety of other checks at six-month or 6000-mile intervals. These are not cheap, but they are much cheaper than engine overhaul or major parts replacements, which would probably result if they were skipped. If years go by without attention to scheduled maintenance, the owner can count on a breakdown. Whether this happens in city traffic or on the open road, it will cause great inconvenience, and could even be dangerous. Imagine waiting even several minutes in rush-hour traffic on a hot summer day for a wrecker. The sweat would be the least of the problems. Tired and impatient drivers may not be ready to stop for either the driver or his stalled car. The danger of inattentive drivers failing to stop for a stalled vehicle is even greater on the open road.

This paragraph, like the previous one, will require further revision, but it is essentially unified. The topic sentence specifies that the mechanical nature of the automobile requires scheduled maintenance, and the sentence lists two major consequences of failure to provide that maintenance: (1) more unscheduled maintenance and (2) breakdown. All of the remaining sentences simply develop these ideas from the topic sentence. More information is given on just what the schedule of maintenance is; specific types of unscheduled maintenance are listed (engine overhaul and parts replacement); and specific types of breakdowns and their consequences are described.

Although the topic sentence is usually the first sentence in a paragraph, it does not have to be. It may be last, especially in inductive paragraphs where evidence is presented first and then a generalization (the topic sentence) is presented as a conclusion based on the evidence. Here is such a paragraph:

When a woman is viciously attacked, fifty neighbors watch without helping, without even calling the police. A farmer destroys his barn to keep a fire from spreading to his neighbor's property, but the neighbor won't help to compensate the farmer. An indifferent passer-by watches a baby drown. A motorist sees a wheel wobbling loose on the car in front of him but merely slows down to keep out of the way of a pileup. American and English law on principle do not have a "good Samaritan" provision (Germany, Italy, the Soviet Union, France do). The Anglo-American principle is "Mind your own business"; the law limits your obligation, you are responsible only for what you do—not for what you should or could have done. This is the prudence of self-centeredness and indifference, contrasted to the aggressive, questioning prudence of *agapē*.

—JOSEPH FLETCHER, *Situation Ethics*

The topic sentence may also occur somewhere in the middle of a paragraph, especially in a brief narrative where the climax is reached in the middle and then the consequences are presented. Here is such a paragraph (the topic sentence is italicized):

At the twenty-mile marker my legs, chest, and arms began to tighten up. I slowed down the pace and shook my arms loose, which is a tactic used to battle fatigue. I also stepped off the road to run on the grass when my feet started aching from the pounding they had received from nineteen miles of pavement. All of the attempts to stymie the fatigue were in vain. *I had hit, as some people refer to it, the "wall."* Distance runners humorously refer to it as "rigormortis," or "the wrath of God." It is the point when your body has used up its energy supplies and converts to burning body fat and tissue. It is also a point where many marathon runners ask themselves why they decided to run a marathon in the first place.

—KEN SLAYTON, A STUDENT

The topic sentence may even be implied, especially in descriptive paragraphs, where the main idea is simply, "I am describing this person or thing or place," and you would waste words and even insult the reader by coming right out and saying so. Here is an example of such a paragraph; it begins with a description of Thomas Jefferson's suite at Monticello and ends in a brief narrative of how he used the suite. It is a unified description of the suite and its use, but there is no topic sentence that summarizes the remaining sentences in the paragraph:

The library suite contains his architect's table, made in the Monticello cabinet-shop, and the polygraph with which he was able to make copies of his correspondence. Books that he owned have been given or purchased, and identical editions to those he was known to have on his shelves have been collected over the years to fill the bookcases. Jefferson's bed is set into an opening between his bedroom and his "cabinet" (one of the three rooms in the library suite), thus giving him access to it from both rooms, and improving the circulation of air in hot weather. His clothes were kept in the closet above his bed. He was an early riser, and for one who was up with the dawn it is perhaps curious that he designed for himself such a lofty and elaborate bedroom. It was his inner sanctum; here he could escape from his visitors and still be able to get at his books and also walk straight out into the garden beyond.

—DESMOND GUINNESS AND JULIUS TROUSDALE SADLER, JR.,
Mr. Jefferson, Architect

Exercise

Read several of the paragraphs numbered (1) through (14) on pp. 91–95 below. As you read each one try to determine its unifying idea. Then find the topic sentence of the paragraph and underline it. Does the sentence express what you thought was the unifying idea of the paragraph? If not, revise the topic sentence. Be prepared to discuss why you think the topic sentence of each paragraph is or is not effective.

Other sentences develop the idea

The unity of a paragraph derives in large part from a balance between the topic sentence and the content sentences. As you write a paragraph, you may find that you want to mention certain points that you did not hint at in the topic sentence. If you do, then go back and revise the topic sentence so that it does hint at these ideas. Or you may find that the topic sentence hints at so much that one paragraph is not enough to say all that you want to say. In that case, go back and shorten the topic sentence. As I wrote the draft of the second sample paragraph in the previous section, I found myself wanting to go into great detail about the consequences of a car breakdown. I was tempted to tell one or two stories about broken water hoses that caused me hours of delay on trips I have taken. But I decided that the purpose of the paper would not be served by going into such detail and that such information would weaken the unity of the paragraph by delivering more information than the topic sentence promised. If I thought the paper would be strengthened by such detail, then I would give the idea of breakdowns a paragraph of its own and go ahead and tell the stories.

Here is the third paragraph of the paper outlined above. As you read it, critically evaluate the *balance* between the expectations established in the topic sentence, and the details delivered in the content sentences:

The mechanical nature of an automobile unavoidably affects society as a whole, since no means has yet been found to eliminate the polluting effects of the internal combustion engine. Thus, the buyer of a new car is also purchasing an extra degree of social responsibility. The car will come equipped with a pollution control system that can greatly reduce pollution in the car's exhaust. It must be serviced periodically to remain effective. And most cars require the use of unleaded gasoline for efficient operation of the pollution control system. Both of these requirements add to operating expenses. But these amount to a small price to pay when weighed against the dangers to society of uncontrolled automobile pollution, and when one considers that, even with the control system, the car continues to pollute the environment.

As you were reading the paragraph, were you surprised by any of the sentences—i.e., did they treat ideas that the topic sentence had not led you to expect? On the other hand, were there any topics you did expect but that the paragraph did not get around to treating? The answer to both of these questions is yes. There is great emphasis in the body of the paragraph on the social responsibility of the owner, but no hint of this in the topic sentence. On the other hand, the topic sentence talks about the polluting effects of the internal combustion engine, which leads the reader to expect some discussion of just how such an engine goes about polluting. But no discussion of this appears in the paragraph. How might this weakness in unity be corrected? The answer depends on the purpose of the paper. According to the outline of the paper, the purpose is to persuade the reader of the need to know about the problems of buying a new car. To achieve this purpose, it is probably not necessary to treat in detail the mechanics of the internal combustion engine. But it is useful to stress the idea that car ownership entails social responsibility. Thus, the topic sentence, rather than the content sentences, should be reworded to correct the weakness in unity. Before you read the suggested revision of the topic sentence printed below, read the paragraph again and try to think of a topic sentence of your own that more accurately summarizes the content of the paragraph and thus sets up more valid expectations in the reader's mind. (Do this now, before you read on.) How does your revised topic sentence compare with this one?

> An automobile is a machine that pollutes the air that all members of society have to breathe.

There are still a number of other revisions needed in the paragraph, but a revision such as the one just suggested clearly strengthens its unity.

Exercise

Study each paragraph in the 500-word theme printed on pp. 64–65 above, entitled "What Is a Student of English?" Circle each sentence in each paragraph, and then, in the margin beside it, write the word or phrase in the topic sentence it develops. Then evaluate each paragraph. Was enough information given about the ideas presented in the topic sentence? Was information given in the body of the paragraph that was not adequately foreshadowed in the topic sentence? Here is the first paragraph of that theme, circled and labeled:

The student of English is a reader and a

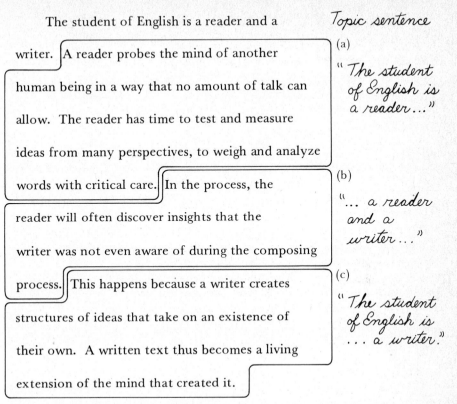

Topic sentence

writer. A reader probes the mind of another human being in a way that no amount of talk can allow. The reader has time to test and measure ideas from many perspectives, to weigh and analyze words with critical care. In the process, the reader will often discover insights that the writer was not even aware of during the composing process. This happens because a writer creates structures of ideas that take on an existence of their own. A written text thus becomes a living extension of the mind that created it.

(a)

" *The student of English is a reader...* "

(b)

" *... a reader and a writer...* "

(c)

" *The student of English is ... a writer.* "

One organizational plan controls development

So far, we have seen that a unified paragraph has one idea expressed in a topic sentence. It also has a balance between expectations set up in the topic sentence and the details delivered in the content sentences. But paragraph unity requires one more thing: The entire paragraph should develop according to one organizational plan. Here are drafts of the final two paragraphs of the paper outlined at the end of the last chapter and assigned paragraphs at the beginning of this chapter. Read each paragraph and see whether you can discover the organizational plan that controls the development of each one. It will, in each case, be one of the thirteen subtypes of planning principles discussed in the last chapter:

(1) Description of a person
(2) Description of a thing
(3) Description of a place
(4) Narration of a story

(5) Narration of a process
(6) Formal definition
(7) Definition by comparison and contrast
(8) Definition by analogy
(9) Definition by classification
(10) Induction to support a definition
(11) Induction to show cause or effect
(12) Deduction to apply a definition
(13) Deduction to show cause or effect

Now, here are the two paragraphs for your analysis:

> An uninformed new-car owner could be his own worst enemy. Accelerating unevenly and driving at high speeds will waste fuel unnecessarily. Driving on dirt roads and leaving a car out at night will cause undue wear both to the engine and to the paint. Careless driving habits not only shorten the useful life of the car; they also pose serious dangers to the driver himself, to other drivers, and to pedestrians.
>
> Prices of new cars are higher than ever before. The new car buyer can expect to pay twice what he would have paid five years ago. Automobile insurance costs are higher than ever before. Even the cost of obtaining a license has increased significantly. Thus, the new-car buyer should be prepared to handle financial problems from a variety of sources.

Both of these paragraphs have problems with coherence (a subject we will deal with later), but they are essentially unified. Did you spot the topic sentence in each one? It is the first sentence in the first paragraph and the last sentence in the second paragraph. Did you detect a proper balance between the topic sentence and the other sentences? And were you able to determine which organizational plan controlled the development of each paragraph? The first paragraph used deduction to show cause or effect; the second paragraph used induction to support a definition, and it was a definition by classification.

So far in this section, we have looked at drafts of five essentially unified paragraphs for a paper on the topic, Problems of Car Ownership. In the next section we will reexamine and revise all of the paragraphs in light of the requirements of coherence. But before turning to coherence, you should take some time to read the following paragraphs; they have been selected from a variety of works by good writers and translators. Some of them have appeared earlier in this book; others have not. Some are by student writers; some are by published writers. As you read them, notice that one organizational principle tends clearly to control the development of each paragraph, even though other principles may play minor roles.

(1) Description of a person

My mother explained Mrs. Gross's flabby physique by suggesting that perhaps she had a hormonal problem, but this did not excuse the unhygienic aspects of her appearance. I never saw Mrs. Gross in anything but a dingy cotton, knee-length housecoat of gawdy orange and pink flowers. The hem was tattered and the underarm seams were splitting from the strain of her overweight condition. Sweat marks stained the underarm area. The only thing dirtier than her housecoat was her hair. I seriously doubted that either was washed more than once a month. Mrs. Gross's dyed red hair was unbelievably greasy; as a result, it lay plastered to her head. Beads of perspiration from her brow gave her face a wet, shiny look that added to the impression of disgusting uncleanliness.

—SHIRLYN KOWALCZYK, A STUDENT

(2) Description of a thing

It stands just sufficiently short of vertical that every leaf of shingle, at its edges, and every edge of horizontal plank (blocked, at each center, with squared verticals) is a most black and cutting ink: and every surface struck by light is thus: such an intensity and splendor of silver in the silver light, it seems to burn, and burns and blinds into the eyes almost as snow; yet in none of that burnishment or blazing whereby detail is lost: each texture in the wood, like those of bone, is distinct in the eye as a razor: each nail-head is distinct: each seam and split; and each slight warping; each random knot and knothole: and in each board, as lovely a music as a contour map and unique as a thumbprint, its grain, which was its living strength, and these wild creeks cut stiff across by saws; and moving nearer the close-laid arcs and shadows even of those tearing wheels: and this, more poor and plain than bone, more naked and noble than sternest Doric, more rich and more valiant than watered silk, is the fabric and the stature of a house.

—JAMES AGEE AND WALKER EVANS, *Let Us Now Praise Famous Men*

(3) Description of a place

The lake had never been what you would call a wild lake. There were cottages sprinkled around the shores, and it was in farming country although the shores of the lake were quite heavily wooded. Some of the cottages were owned by nearby farmers, and you would live at the shore and eat your meals at the farmhouse. That's what our family did. But although it wasn't wild, it was a fairly large and undisturbed lake and there were places in it which, to a child at least, seemed infinitely remote and primeval.

—E. B. WHITE, "Once More to the Lake"

(4) Narration of a story

At the twenty-mile marker my legs, chest, and arms began to tighten up, I slowed down the pace and shook my arms loose, which is a tactic used to battle fatigue. I also stepped off the road to run on the grass when my feet started aching from the pounding they had received from nineteen miles of pavement. All of the attempts to stymie the fatigue were in vain. I had hit, as some people refer to it, the "wall." Distance runners humorously refer to it as "rigormortis," or "the wrath of God." It is the point when your body has used up its energy supplies and converts to burning body fat and tissue. It is also a point where many marathon runners ask themselves why they decided to run a marathon in the first place.

—KEN SLAYTON, A STUDENT

(5) Narration of a process

Cut the lead capsule and take it off completely. Take the cork out gently. Wipe the lip of the bottle. Hold the bottle (with or without the basket) in one hand and the decanter in the other, and pour steadily until you see the sediment (if any) moving into the shoulder of the bottle. Then stop. Having a light—a candle flame is ideal—behind or below the neck of the bottle makes it easier to see when the dregs start to move—besides adding to what should be a pleasantly sensuous ritual.

—HUGH JOHNSON, *The World Atlas of Wine*

(6) Formal definition

Joy is a delight of the mind, from the consideration of the present or assured approaching possession of a good; and we are then possesssed of any good, when we have it so in our power that we can use it when we please. Thus a man almost starved has joy at the arrival of relief, even before he has the pleasure of using it: and a father, in whom the very well-being of his children causes delight, is always, as long as the children are in such a state, in the possession of that good; for he needs but to reflect on it, to have that pleasure.

—JOHN LOCKE, *Concerning Human Understanding*

(7) Definition by comparison and contrast

There are many truisms about the differences between high school and college. Everyone knows that college is more difficult than high school: Courses cover more difficult material and do it faster. Everyone knows that college schedules differ: there is more free time and thus the need to use it effectively. And everyone knows that college students need more discipline: No one makes you attend class or do your work. But there are a few important aspects of attending college in the eighties that seem to be well-kept secrets. One of them is that the world is not the ordered place high school texts and teachers make it out to be. The other is that many university professors are just as disordered as the world they try to teach you about.

—TRICIA BERNARD, A STUDENT

(8) Definition by analogy

We contend that good writing is good strategy first and foremost. The wholeness of the whole composition we must first secure or all is lost; poor strategy loses wars, poor tactics only battles. Too often we are concerned only with the tactics of "correct" grammar, too seldom for the strategy of good design in writing. While we fuss with formalities, we lose the war. Sentences in Class A uniforms, Fowlered, Perrined, and Webstered, gallop off to annihilation like Tennyson's Six Hundred. The art of war is strategy first, tactics second. The art of writing cannot improve this wisdom.

—GORDON ROHMAN AND ALBERT WLECKE, *Pre-writing: the Construction and Application of Models for Concept Formation in Writing*

(9) Definition by classification

There are three kinds of sundae eaters: skimmers, miners, and slobs. Skimmers start with the cherry, then delicately eat all the whipped cream. Next they eat the topping with minimal disturbance to the ice cream, which they save for last to savor on its own. Miners also start with the cherry, then carefully tunnel into the whipped cream, through the topping, and down to the ice cream. Next they gradually widen the tunnel, working always from the top down, until all the precious delights are exhausted. Slobs ignore the cherry; they vigorously plunge their spoons into the nearest heap of whipped cream. Soon they create a swamp whose delights they love to wallow in.

—BARBARA MCNAIR, A STUDENT

(10) Induction to support a definition

When a woman is viciously attacked, fifty neighbors watch without helping, without even calling the police. A farmer destroys his barn to keep a fire from spreading to his neighbor's property, but the neighbor won't help to compensate the farmer. An indifferent passer-by watches a baby drown. A motorist sees a wheel wobbling loose on the car in front of him but merely slows down to keep out of the way of a pileup. American and English law on principle do not have a "good Samaritan" provision (Germany, Italy, the Soviet Union, France do). The Anglo-American principle is "Mind your own business"; the law limits your obligation, you are responsible only for what you do—not for what you should or could have done. This is the prudence of self-centeredness and indifference, contrasted to the aggressive, questioning prudence of *agapē*.

—JOSEPH FLETCHER, *Situation Ethics*

(11) Induction to show cause or effect

Anna Lyons, Mary Louise Lyons, Mary von Phul, Emile von Phul, Eugenia McLellan, Marjorie McPhail, Marie-Louise L'Abbé, Mary Danz, Julia Dodge, Mary Fordyce Blake, Janet Preston—these were the names (I can still tell them over like a rosary) of some of the older girls in the convent: the Virtues and the Graces. The virtuous ones wore wide blue or green moire good-conduct ribbons bandoleer-style, across their blue serge uniforms; the beautiful ones wore rouge and powder or at least were reputed to do so. Our class, the eighth grade, wore pink ribbons (I never got one myself) and had names like Patricia ("Pat") Sullivan, Eileen Donohoe, and Joan Kane. We were inelegant even in this respect; the best name we could show, among us, was Phyllis ("Phil") Chatham, who boasted that her father's name, Ralph, was pronounced "Rafe" as in England.

—MARY MCCARTHY, *Memoirs of a Catholic Girlhood*

(12) Deduction to apply a definition

A teacher who creates an atmosphere where students are stimulated to ask their own questions and seek their own answers is a successful teacher. My tenth-grade English teacher was such a person. She didn't lecture us endlessly; she didn't make us take reams of notes; she didn't make us memorize irrelevant dates. Instead, she led us in the experience of good literature. When she read plays and poems to us, they came to life, and we wanted to read more. When she explained movies of great novels, she led us to seek out the books and read them on our own. She led me to see that literature could take me anywhere I wanted to go and let me be anyone I wanted to be. I even began to ask her for titles that treated ideas I had become interested in. Before she taught me, I had never read literature for pleasure; since then, I have not stopped doing so. "Successful" is really an inadequate word to describe the lasting effect she had on me.

—MICHAEL SIMMONS, A STUDENT

(13) Deduction to show cause or effect

I am left with a very old-fashioned measure of a poem's worth—the depth of its sincerity. And it seems to me that the poets of our generation—those of us who have gone so far in criticism and analysis that we cannot ever turn back and be innocent again, who have such extensive resources for disguising ourselves from ourselves—that our only hope as artists is to continually ask ourselves, "Am I writing what I *really* think? Not what is acceptable; not what my favorite intellectual would think in this situation; not what I wish I felt. Only what I cannot help thinking." For I believe that the only reality which a man can ever surely know is that self he cannot help being, though he will only know that self through its interconnections with the world around it. If he pretties it up, if he changes its meaning, if he gives it the voice of any borrowed authority, if in short he rejects this reality, his mind will be less than alive. So will his words.

—W. D. SNODGRASS, *In Radical Pursuit*

(14) Restatement

In all thirteen of the paragraphs you just read, you should have noticed that other organizational plans besides the dominant one played
some role in development of the paragraph's ideas. And virtually any
combination of the above thirteen planning principles is possible. There
is even a common and important method of developing a unified paragraph that cannot be classified under any of the thirteen types you have
just examined, perhaps because it can combine with all of them. This
additional method may be called development by restatement. It is especially useful in opening paragraphs where you want forcefully to impress your reader with the main idea of a paper. It may be used anywhere in a paper where your intention is clearly to emphasize an idea.
Here is an example to add to the above list. Notice that in every sentence,
Langer simply reasserts how special a quality of the human species language is.

Language is the highest and most amazing achievement of the symbolical
human mind. The power it bestows is almost inestimable, for without it anything properly called "thought" is impossible. The birth of language is the
dawn of humanity. The line between man and beast—between the highest ape
and the lowest savage—is the language line. Whether the primitive Neanderthal man was anthropoid or human depends less on his cranial capacity, his
upright posture, or even his use of tools and fire, than on one issue we shall
probably never be able to settle—whether or not he spoke.

—SUZANNE K. LANGER, "The Lord of Creation"

A combination of developmental principles. It is extremely useful for you,
as a student of writing, to learn that there are distinct ways to develop a
unified paragraph and to practice using each one of them. At the same
time, you should be well aware that experienced writers generally combine methods of development. The more you practice, the more you will
learn to do just as they do. The trick is to combine the methods effectively so that the combination produces a unified paragraph. Here is a
paragraph that effectively uses such a combination of developmental
principles. Read it, and try to determine what they are.

Running is probably the world's most democratic sport. Runners are almost
totally lacking in discrimination based on race, sex, age, class or anything else.
At a recent race in New York City I saw a cardiologist, an orthopedic surgeon,
and a preventive medicine specialist for a major corporation, a foundry
worker and a printer, a retired postman and a shoe salesman, a judge, an author, and a film-maker, a Rockefeller Foundation executive and a man who
has long been on unemployment, along with an assortment of office workers,
housewives, students and senior citizens. If they met at a cocktail party instead
of a race I suspect they would not have much in common, but here there was
little if any sense of social hierarchy. Running is an egalitarian and distinctly

unsnobbish sport, one that meshes with much that is excellent in the American spirit.

—JAMES FIXX, *The Complete Book of Running*

The above paragraph starts out by stating a definition. It then goes on to develop according to the principle of formal definition, but in doing so, launches into a brief narrative: about the race in New York City. At the heart of the narrative, however, is a developmental tactic that works with just about any planning principle, and that is the use of examples; Fixx gives an extensive list of just the kinds of people who participated in the race. The variety of their occupations proves his point about running as a democratic sport. After his list of occupations comes a sentence that explicitly uses a hypothetical syllogism ("If they met at a cocktail party . . .") and is thus a brief excursion into development by deduction. At the end of the paragraph, Fixx ties all of this together by restating his main point that running is an egalatarian sport (and thus democratic). Thus, we have a paragraph that uses mainly formal definition, but in it, too, narrative, examples, and deduction all play a unified role.

Here is another paragraph that effectively uses a combination of developmental principles. Read it, and try to determine what they are.

Erasmus withdrew from a world estranged, a world which refused to keep the peace, a world which had slain reason by means of passion, and justice by means of violence. His heart was drowsy, but his hand was as vigorous as ever, his mind keen and bright as a lamp shedding immaculate rays in a wide circle about it, and penetrating to the remotest corners of the field of vision his incorruptible intellect surveyed.

—STEFAN ZWEIG, *Erasmus of Rotterdam*

The first sentence of the paragraph indicates that it is going to be a narrative paragraph, but even in doing so the sentence describes the world Erasmus withdrew from. Then it begins to describe Erasmus: "His heart was drowsy . . . his hand was . . . vigorous. . . ." The reader soon discovers that a description of Erasmus's state of mind is in fact the main idea of this paragraph (even though it is part of a longer narrative: his biography). But there is more: The second half of the paragraph, while describing Erasmus's state of mind, does so by a very effective use of analogy; it compares his mind to a bright light that penetrates even "the remotest corners of the field of vision his incorruptible intellect surveyed." Zweig has very effectively used several planning principles to develop a unified and interesting paragraph.

Exercises

a. Try writing paragraphs modeled after the various paragraphs listed in this subsection. You probably will not have time to write fourteen, but write as many as you can, or as many as your teacher assigns. In each paragraph, state the topic sentence clearly and be sure that the other sentences develop it adequately. Try to follow one planning principle throughout. Do not be afraid to follow closely the structure of one of the sample paragraphs in this subsection in writing any given paragraph. You might, for instance, want to reread paragraph (3), E. B. White's description of a lake, and then write your own description of a favorite vacation spot, trying to position your topic sentence and develop your ideas according to the same pattern as White's paragraph. Or you could do the same with any one of the fourteen sample paragraphs.

b. Try to find at least one paragraph that is developed according to each of the organizational plans labeled (1) through (14), above. Look in your textbooks, in magazines, in newspaper editorials, in your own writings. Most of the paragraphs you examine will not fit easily into one developmental category. This may be an indication that the paragraph is poorly written, but it may also indicate strength. If you find a paragraph that seems well written and interesting but is not easy to classify, try to discover the source of its strength. The author probably combined two or more organizational plans in a creative way to produce it.

Coherence

Language exists to convey ideas from one mind to another mind. In spoken conversation we use each sentence as a tool to convey a relatively specific piece of information to our listener. Suppose you say to me,

What do you want?

Your sentence gets me to think about wanting. And then suppose I answer,

I want a book.

The words *I want* in my sentence do not tell you anything new: you know I am there, because you just asked me a question, and you have wanting on your mind because you just asked me a question about wanting. The new idea in my sentence is conveyed by the word *book*. Notice that the central idea in both your question and my answer is expressed in the last word (*want* in your question, *book* in my answer). And if you read the question and the answer aloud, you will also notice that the last word in each is pronounced relatively louder than all of the other words in the sentence. *Want* in your question and *book* in my answer are clearly spoken more loudly than the other words in their sentences, even though they may not be "loud" in any absolute sense. And it was no accident that my answer actually overlapped with your question. Most conversations, in fact, tend to form a chain: You forge a link; I hook into your link and then add a link of my own; you hook into that and add another; and so on. A graphic representation of this process is given below. The capitalized word represents the new idea the speaker wishes to impress on the listener's mind; notice that it is pronounced louder and comes toward the end of the sentence.

You: What do you WANT?
     ↓
Me: I want a BOOK.
       ↓
You: A book on what SUBJECT?
         ↓
Me: The subject doesn't MATTER.
           ↓
You: If it doesn't matter, try THIS.

In a conversation we often rely more heavily on loudness than on word order to forge the links in our chain of coherence. For instance, I could easily have answered your opening question above by saying,

 A BOOK is what I want.

Here, the words *I want,* which link my answer to your question, actually occur at the end of the sentence, and the word *book,* which represents the new link I am forging in the information chain, actually occurs at the beginning of the sentence, but BOOK is still pronounced louder, in fact especially louder, to show that it is the new information.

For communication to *flow* from your mind to my mind, you have to link some part of your sentence to something already on my mind and then you have to get me to connect it with the new idea your sentence expresses. In conversational interaction you get your clues about what is on my mind from what you just heard me say. You then refer to that with words you generally pronounce softly and place toward the beginning of your sentence. The new idea you want to impress upon my mind you then express in words you pronounce loudly and generally place toward the end of your sentence.

Written sentences must also come linked in a coherent chain if communication is to flow between your mind and your reader's. But as a writer, you cannot easily signal the linking process with soft and loud pronunciation the way you can as a speaker. Thus, word order in written sentences plays an even more important role in forging the chain of coherence: The link with ideas already on the reader's mind comes early in the sentence; your new idea comes later. This is why it is often said that the end of the sentence is the position of emphasis, the place to put matter you want the reader to remember. Furthermore, as a writer, you must forge all the links in the chain without the reader's help. There are no clues, as in conversational interaction, about what is going on in your reader's mind. This is why the paragraph is so important in edited English: You need several sentences to treat one idea adequately enough to be sure the reader gets the message, you need unified paragraphs to help the reader see exactly what that idea is, and you need a very tight chain of coherence among the sentences of a paragraph to assure that the reader understands how the various aspects of the idea interrelate. Let us now look at some specific steps you should take to give your paragraphs this kind of coherence.

Repetition of key words and ideas

The chain of coherence in a conversation may be represented like this:

In a written paragraph, however, the chain of coherence is probably best represented like this:

Lines in the above diagrams represent sentences. In a conversation, the sentences alternate between one speaker and another. In a written paragraph, all the sentences are by the writer. Here is an example. Suppose you want to impress on me the idea that politicians are crooks. You might do so in a conversation as follows:

You: Politicians are CROOKS.

Me: They are NOT.

You: They EARN TOO MUCH.

Me: High pay doesn't PROVE ANYTHING.

You: It is proof because they DON'T WORK.

To make the same point effectively in a written paragraph, you would probably do better as follows (words in italics at the end of each sentence represent that sentence's new contribution to the developing idea):

Politicians are *crooks*.

A criminal *takes money without working for it*.

Politicians take money without working for it *too*.

Their crimes aren't *obvious*, but

Politicians and crooks certainly *behave alike*.

Notice that the sentences in the written paragraph tend to link up over and over again with the first sentence (the topic sentence), thus reminding the reader constantly just what the paragraph is about: *Politicians* is repeated twice and referred to once by a pronoun; *crooks* is repeated once and its idea is evoked two other times, once by *criminal* and once by *crimes*. You might even find it helpful to think of a paragraph as a web of coherence rather than as merely a chain. When you write paragraphs, do not bore your reader with needless repetition, but *do* work to use repetition to show your reader exactly how each sentence in the paragraph interrelates with the topic sentence.

The web diagram in the last paragraph represents a very simple example of how repetition of key words and ideas helps to create coherence in a paragraph. Here is a web diagram of passage (3) by E. B. White, given in the previous section of this chapter (p. 91) as an example of development by describing a place. The diagram shows that the structure of most paragraphs is more complex than the example in the last paragraph might indicate. But it also shows, quite clearly, that good writers—and White is a very good writer—do indeed repeat key words and ideas from earlier sentences and especially from the topic sentence in order to strengthen the coherence of their paragraphs. (See page 101.)

Exercises

a. Study the repetition of key words and ideas in each paragraph of the 500-word theme printed above on pp. 64–65 entitled "What Is a Student of English?" If you have access to some large paper (computer print-out paper will do fine), try to make web diagrams of one or two of the theme's paragraphs: (1) Show by underlining them the words in each sentence that seem to you to introduce new information into the paragraph, and (2) show by the use of vertical arrows the words that repeat ideas from earlier sentences and especially from the topic sentence. If you do not have time to work out such web diagrams, you could learn a

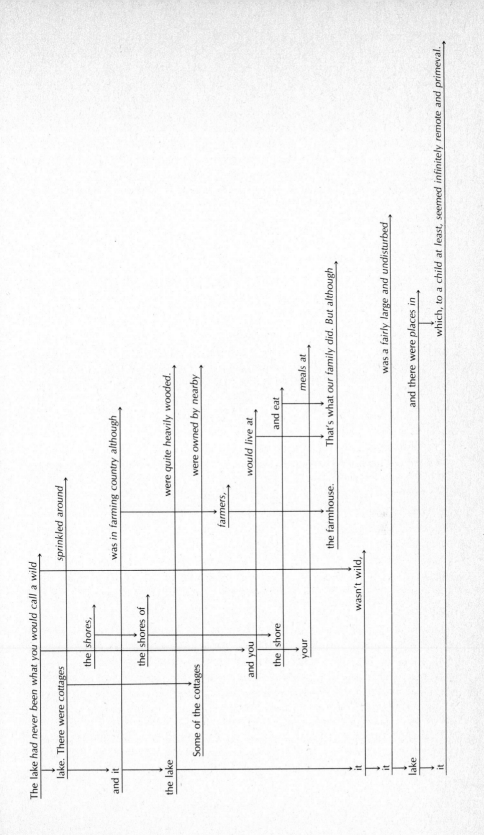

lot about each paragraph's repetition of key words and ideas simply by circling words and expressions that repeat earlier ideas and by taking note of the earlier idea each circled item repeats.

b. Revise the five paragraphs in the theme on problems of car ownership, printed below on pp. 106–108, by repeating key words and ideas where you think this would strengthen coherence in the paragraph.

c. Write a paragraph of your own; specify audience, purpose, and plan. In addition to attending to its unity, make a point of repeating key words and ideas as a way of strengthening its coherence.

Use of transitional expressions

The repetition of key words and ideas is not the only means available to you to strengthen the links in a paragraph's chain of coherence. English has words and expressions that exist to do just that. They are called transitional expressions.

Compare the two versions of a short paragraph given below. Notice how the second version flows more smoothly and seems to communicate its idea more effectively. This is because the connections between the sentences and the relationship of each to the topic sentence are expressed explicitly by transitional expressions. The transitional expressions are italicized.

Some say America does not have an energy problem; the facts prove otherwise. We do have undiscovered reserves of oil and natural gas. Even these will last only about fifty years. We have enough coal to supply our power needs for more than a century. Most of the coal does not burn clean. The price of coal's power is pollution. It will not last forever.

Some say America does not have an energy problem, *but* the facts prove otherwise. We do have undiscovered reserves of oil and natural gas. *However,* even these will last only about fifty years. *In addition to this,* we have enough coal to generate power for more than a century, *but* most of the coal does not burn clean. *Therefore,* the price of coal's power is pollution. *Besides that,* it will not last forever.

Notice that the paragraph has an argumentative purpose and uses induction to show cause and effect as its organizational plan (it lists the specific facts that are the causes of America's energy problems). But the paragraph develops the inductive argument by a special use of comparison and contrast called concession (*some say this, but I say that* is the basic formula). Concession contrasts the writer's view with the views of others who disagree. In the second version of the paragraph above, notice how the main idea is clarified and the evidence for it brought into clearer focus by using transitional expressions that indicate the contrastive nature of the argument (*but* is used twice; *however* once). The fact that the paragraph is indeed an argument is made clearer by the use of *therefore* to introduce the sentence that draws the conclusion. The fact that the opposition is having its second argument presented is indicated by the use of *in addition to this,* and the fact that the writer is adding a specific rebuttal to this second argument is indicated by the use of *besides that.* Without doubt the second paragraph is more coherent because of effective use of transitional expressions.

Did you notice that, except for the substitution of a few commas for periods or semicolons, all the wording of the second sample paragraph above remained the same as in the first? This shows that most transitional expressions are just that: they really do their work *between* sentences. If sentences are bricks, they are the mortar of paragraphs—a wholly different kind of language resource from the material sentences are made of. Following the next paragraph is a representative list of transitional expressions. It is not complete, but it is comprehensive enough to show you both the variety of types of transitional expressions in English and the large number of choices available to you when you need an expression of a given type. Like repetition of key words and ideas, these too can be overused. But do not be afraid to use them when you need them.

As you read the lists below, notice that the categories under which the transitional expressions are listed overlap to some extent with the organizational plans for paragraph development listed earlier in this chapter. But every organizational plan does not, in fact, have its own list of transitional expressions. The expressions that treat place are of course especially useful in descriptive paragraphs, and those that treat time are especially useful in narrative paragraphs. Transitional expressions of comparison and contrast will serve well in paragraphs that define by comparison and contrast. But notice that expressions showing cause may serve either inductive or deductive argumentation. And expressions of addition and exemplification may be used in paragraphs of description, formal definition, classification, and even induction and deduction. Summarizing expressions can play a useful role in just about any kind of paragraph. Here are the lists:

(1) Place

nearby, here, there, next to that, opposite to that, under that, beyond that, farther along

(2) Time

then, next, after that, just then, at the same time, previously, before that, finally, at last, first, second, soon, after a time, on another occasion, next day, an hour later, meanwhile, until then, at that moment, up to then, from now on

(3) Comparison

likewise, similarly, in the same way, in like manner, as, just as

(4) Contrast

aside from this, or, or else, otherwise, yet, though, only, but, however, nevertheless, despite this, on the other hand, by contrast, in fact, actually, as a matter of fact, at the same time, instead, rather, on the contrary, in any case, at any rate

(5) Cause

then, that being so, in that case, because of this, for, it follows that, on this basis, on account of this, as a result, in consequence, for this purpose, with this in mind

(6) Addition

and, and so, furthermore, further along, in addition, besides, incidentally, by the way, first, second, third, finally, neither . . . nor, not only . . . but also

(7) Exemplification

for example, for instance, in particular, specifically, that is, to illustrate

(8) Summary

to sum up, in short, briefly, in brief, on the whole, as I have said, in sum, indeed

Exercises

a. Study the use of transitional expressions in each paragraph of the 500-word theme printed above on pp. 64–65 entitled "What Is a Student of English?" Do the same with several of the fourteen paragraphs numbered (1) through (14) in the section on unity (pp. 91–95). Underline the transitional expressions in each paragraph you study and decide which type of transitional expression each represents. Analyze how the use of transitional expression contributes to the developmental plan of the paragraph as well as to its coherence.

b. Revise the five paragraphs in the theme (on problems of car ownership) printed below on pp. 106–108 by adding transitional expressions you think will improve the coherence of each paragraph.

c. Write a paragraph of your own; specify audience, purpose, and plan. In addition to attending to its unity and repeating key words and ideas, make it a point to use transitional expressions to strengthen its coherence.

Use of parallel grammatical structure

Whenever you are describing two steps in a process, or listing three causes of a problem, or noting three pieces of evidence to support a conclusion, do not be afraid to express such sets of items with similar language. Do not be afraid of sounding mechanical; usually the reader will appreciate the extra help you thus provide. The use of similar patterns of language to express similar or related ideas is called grammatical parallelism. It may be as simple as saying, *The first cause is . . . the second cause is . . . the third cause is . . .* , or it could be more complex, repeating a grammatical formula instead of exact words (*Students in a university should . . . the faculty of an educational institutional must . . .*).

Parallel grammatical structure strengthens the coherence of a paragraph the way using links of the same size and strength would improve a chain, or using bricks of the same size and shape would strengthen and improve the appearance of a wall. The reader can almost feel the smooth flow of ideas in the actual shape of the sentences when you use parallelism effectively.

Here is the paragraph that was given earlier in this chapter as an example of definition by classification. In it, grammatical parallelism helps the reader to keep track of which of three classified items is being discussed and also to compare the various parts of the descriptions of each of the classified items. Elements with the same number of underlines are expressed in parallel grammatical structure.

There are three kinds of sundae eaters: skimmers, miners, and slobs. Skimmers start with the cherry, then delicately eat all the whipped cream. Next they eat the topping with minimal disturbance to the ice cream, which they save for last to savor on its own. Miners also start with the cherry, then carefully tunnel into the whipped cream, through the topping, and down to the ice cream. Next they gradually widen the tunnel, working always from the top down, until all the precious delights are exhausted. Slobs ignore the cherry; they vigorously plunge their spoons into the nearest heap of whipped cream. Soon they create a swamp whose delights they love to wallow in.

—BARBARA MCNAIR, A STUDENT

Exercises

a. Study the use of parallel grammatical structure in each paragraph of the 500-word theme printed above on pp. 64–65 entitled "What Is a Student of English?" Do the same with several of the fourteen paragraphs numbered (1) through (14) in the section on unity in this chapter (pp. 91–95). Give the same number of underlines to sequences of words with parallel grammatical structure. Take note of how the use of parallelism contributes to the coherence of the paragraph you are analyzing.

b. Revise the five paragraphs in the theme (on problems of car ownership) printed in the next exercise by rewriting the sentences where appropriate to give related ideas parallel grammatical patterns.

c. Each of the three procedures discussed so far in this subsection strengthens the connections among the sentences in a paragraph. But they can also help you to hold an entire paper together. Where possible, key words and ideas from a paper's thesis (the topic sentence of its opening paragraph) should be repeated in the topic sentences of the other paragraphs of the paper. A paragraph can also begin with a transitional expression that relates it to the preceding paragraph. And parallel grammatical structure, especially in the formulation of the topic sentences of related paragraphs, can also create smooth transitions from one paragraph to another. Below are the draft paragraphs of the paper on problems of car ownership that were used earlier to illustrate various aspects of paragraph unity, and that you have been asked to revise in other exercises of this section to strengthen their internal coherence. But in addition to those problems with internal coherence, the five together do not read as a coherent essay. Read them and ask yourself how you can improve the coherence of the essay as a whole by repeating the key words and ideas from the paper's thesis sentence in the topic sentences of the other four paragraphs, by introducing a given paragraph with an appropriate transitional expression, or by expressing logically related topic sentences in parallel grammatical structure.

PROBLEMS OF CAR OWNERSHIP

The prospective new-car owner should be fully informed of the problems that may come with the car, both those caused by machinery and those caused by people. Mechanical failure will most certainly affect the owner: In addition to scheduled maintenance, unexpected inconvenience and expense can be caused by unplanned repairs and even breakdowns. Society as a whole can also be affected since failure to service the pollution control system contributes to pollution. The owner should also be forewarned that his own driving habits and even those of others on the road can cause him problems. Other problems, mostly in the form of increased costs, will come to the purchaser courtesy of assorted groups and individuals in society.

Unless the owner of a new car follows the manufacturer's

scheduled maintenance suggestions, he will surely have a
greater incidence of unscheduled maintenance, and will probably even experience a breakdown. The owner's manual specifies
oil changes, and a variety of other checks at six—month or
6000—mile intervals. These are not cheap, but they are much
cheaper than engine overhaul or major parts replacements,
which would probably result if they were skipped. If years go
by without attention to scheduled maintenance, the owner can
count on a breakdown. Whether this happens in city traffic or
on the open road it will cause great inconvenience, and could
even be dangerous. Imagine waiting even several minutes in
rush—hour traffic on a hot summer day for a wrecker. The
sweat is the least of the problems. Tired and impatient drivers may not be ready to stop for either the driver or his
stalled car. The danger of inattentive drivers failing to
stop for a stalled vehicle is even greater on the open road.

An automobile is a machine that pollutes the air that
all members of our society have to breathe. Thus, the buyer
of a new car is also purchasing an extra degree of social responsibility. The car will come equipped with a pollution
control system that can greatly reduce pollution in the car's
exhaust. It must be serviced periodically to remain effective. And most cars require the use of unleaded gasoline for
efficient operation of the pollution control system. Both of
these requirements add to operating expenses. But these are
small prices to pay when weighed against the dangers to society of uncontrolled automobile pollution, and when one considers that, even with the control system, the car continues
to pollute the environment.

An uninformed new—car buyer could be his own worst
enemy. Accelerating unevenly and driving at high speeds will
waste fuel unnecessarily. Driving on dirt roads and leaving a
car out at night will cause undue wear both to the engine and
to the paint. Careless driving habits not only shorten the
useful life of a car; they also pose serious dangers to the
driver himself, to other drivers, and to pedestrians.

Prices of new cars are higher than ever before. The new—

```
car buyer can expect to pay twice what he would have paid
five years ago. Automobile insurance costs are higher than
ever before. Even the cost of obtaining a license has in-
creased significantly. Thus, the new-car buyer should be pre-
pared to handle financial problems from a variety of sources.
```

Consistency

In order to maintain the unity and especially the coherence of any paragraph in edited English, you must be consistent in making certain types of grammatical choices throughout a paragraph. Writers tend to have trouble with consistency because spoken styles of English and even informal written styles do not ordinarily require the same level of consistency that edited English requires. This section will explain the three areas that are the most troublesome and then present some exercises: (1) consistency of pronoun reference, (2) consistency of tense and mood, and (3) consistency of voice.

Consistency of pronoun reference. Unless the idea changes, make it a point not to shift the person and number reference of a pronoun in any one paragraph. This point may seem obvious, but it is not. The problem is that the English language has several different kinds of *generic reference* in its pronoun system. When you want to talk about some activity or situation, and you are not interested in relating any specific persons to the activity or situation, you have several ways of referring to people in general (hence the term *generic*). Suppose you want to talk about the necessity to work in order to survive. You might say any one of the following:

People have to work if they are to survive.
One has to work if one is to survive.
We have to work if we are to survive.
You have to work if you are to survive.
A person has to work if he is to survive.

We and *you* can, of course, also have a specific reference, but I list them above as referring to nobody in particular. The use of *you* in this generic sense is probably not appropriate in edited English. The four other types of generic reference are appropriate, although the pronoun *one* seems a little stuffy. Consistency of point of view requires that, when you pick one of the above types of generic reference, you should stick with it throughout an entire paragraph.

The last example of generic pronoun reference on the list in the previous paragraph poses special problems. Until recently, the masculine forms of English pronouns (*he, him, his, himself*) were in very common use as generic pronouns and were considered by most people to have a neutral meaning in regard to the literal sexual sense when used generically. Thus, a sentence such as *A person should take care of his health* was said to apply equally to males and females. In recent years, many speakers of English have become sensitive to this feature of grammar to such an extent that it is now true that the masculine forms of the pronouns have largely lost their generic meanings and are limited in reference to male humans. This trend has not affected all Americans, but it has affected a sufficiently large number that you should learn how to avoid the use of generic *he, him, his,* and *himself* when you are writing edited English (remember, by definition, edited English is addressed to strangers, and you must therefore assume that at least some of your readers might take offense at the generic use of the masculine pronouns).

For many writers, this problem can be a formidable one. It is a problem, for instance, that recurs throughout the draft theme printed earlier in this chapter on pp. 106–108. Here are some of the sentences from that essay where the problem is evident:

. . . The prospective new-car *owner* should be forewarned that *his* own driving habits and even those of others on the road can cause *him* problems. . . . Unless *the owner* follows scheduled maintenance suggestions *he* will surely have a greater incidence of unscheduled maintenance. . . .

There are several other sentences in the theme where the problem recurs. And the problem is that many contemporary readers of such a paper will feel that it is directed to men who are buying cars—that it either assumes there are no women buyers or does not care to inform them. The simplest solution is to choose one of the other types of generic reference: (1) a plural indefinite noun and the pronoun *they* (or *we*) or (2) the pronoun *you* (or *one*). Here is an example of the first suggestion applied to the above sentences:

. . . Prospective new-car *owners* should be forewarned that *their* own driving habits and even those of others on the road can cause *them* problems. . . . Unless *owners* follow scheduled maintenance suggestions *they* will surely. . . .

And here are some of the other possibilities (their usefulness depends on the topic, the purpose, and the audience). The first version works when it is appropriate for the writer to play the role of a new-car owner:

. . . *As* prospective new-car *owners, we* should be forewarned that *our* own driving habits. . . .

The next version seems stuffy:

. . . The prospective new-car *owner* should be forewarned that *one's* own driving habits. . . .

The third version will work if it is appropriate to write the paper as though you are giving the reader directions. This is not the generic form, *you,* because the pronoun actually refers specifically to the reader (this is the device that I have used throughout this book):

. . . *As* a prospective new-car *owner, you* should be forewarned that *your* own driving habits. . . .

A fourth possibility is to avoid the use of pronouns altogether; however, this tends to make your writing too unspecific and your meaning too fuzzy.

. . . The prospective new-car owner should be forewarned that *personal* driving habits and even those of others on the road can cause problems. . . . Unless the owner follows scheduled maintenance suggestions, *there* will surely be greater incidence of unscheduled maintenance.

Some people have suggested various revisions of English grammar, ranging from the invention of new, truly neuter, pronouns to the relaxation of certain rules of English grammar. One is the rule that requires pronouns to agree with their antecedents. Pronouns referring to singular nouns must be singular and pronouns referring to plural nouns must be plural. If this rule were relaxed, then instead of *his,* which is grammatically correct, *their* would be acceptable in the following sentence: *The new-car owner should be forewarned that their driving habits.* . . . None of the suggestions for revising the language or its rules of grammar has yet achieved enough acceptance for me to advise you to follow them when you are writing edited English. There are already a sufficient number of options available to you within the tradition of edited English (as I hope I have just demonstrated) for you to handle the problem of avoiding generic *he, him, his,* and *himself,* while maintaining both clarity and consistency.

Consistency of tense and mood. Additional problems with consistency can arise from the fact that English allows different verb tenses to express the same time reference. In spoken English, it is common to tell stories that occurred in past time by using the grammatical present tense of a verb:

Yesterday, *I'm* walking down the street and this guy *comes* up to me and *says,* "Where's the post office?" So I *tell* him *it's* right across the street and he *looks* at me and *says,* "How could I be so dumb as not to see it?"

This use of the present tense to narrate past events is not appropriate in edited English, but it occasionally creeps in and weakens consistency in a paragraph:

Yesterday, I was walking through town, when a man approached me and asked where the post office was. I told him it was right across the street. Then he *turns* to me and *wonders* how he ever missed seeing it.

Just remember, do not change the verb tense in any given paragraph unless you want the time reference to change as well.

Similar problems can arise with mood in verbs. Mood has to do with your attitude as a writer: Are you stating, asking, commanding, requesting, guessing, or wishing? The typical inconsistency of mood occurs in paragraphs that treat process narrations, where you are giving the reader instructions. If you want to tell a reader how to put a piece of paper into a typewriter, you could do it in either of the two following ways, both of which mean pretty much the same thing:

You should first insert the paper in the slot in the carriage; then you should turn the wheel until the paper appears in front of the carriage. Next you should loosen the pressure lever and align the ends of the paper. Finally, you should tighten the pressure lever.

First insert the paper in the slot in the carriage; then turn the wheel until the paper appears in front of the carriage. Next loosen the pressure lever and align the ends of the paper. Finally, tighten the pressure lever.

The first passage gives the reader directions by saying *you should.* The second passage does so by using imperative sentences, where both *you* and the idea expressed by *should* are understood (imperative sentences begin directly with the verb). There would be no real problem *logically* if the two ways of giving instructions were mixed in one paragraph, but because of the grammatical inconsistency, such a mixture does weaken both unity and coherence when it occurs in edited English. So if you start a paragraph with the imperative, stick with it throughout the paragraph; if instead you start with *you* and a helping verb such as *should, must,* or *ought to,* then stick with that choice throughout the entire paragraph.

Consistency of voice. *Voice* is a grammatical term that, like tense and mood, relates to the verb. But unlike tense and mood, a full understanding of voice requires a look at the sentence as a whole. English has two voices: *active voice* and *passive voice.* In an active sentence the subject of the sentence (the noun in front of the verb) is the *doer* of the action of the verb, and the verb is not in its past participle form and preceded by the helping verb *to be* in any of its forms (*am, is are, was, were, be, being,* and *been*). *John stole the car* is an active sentence. In a passive sentence, the subject is not the doer of the action of the verb, and the verb *is* in its past participle form and preceded by some form of the helping verb *to be. The car was stolen by John* and *The car was stolen* are both passive sentences. Toward the end of Chapter Seven (pp. 176–177) there is a subsection advising you against the overuse of passives and explaining the problems such overuse can cause. The general point of this section is to warn you that switches from active to passive or vice versa in a paragraph create inconsistency and can weaken unity and coherence. Here is a paragraph illustrating the problem in its typical form. The paragraph begins in the active voice and then for no apparent reason switches to the passive. (Passives are italicized.)

My high school basketball team won the state championship when I was a senior. They were a team who had played together for three years and who had suffered through two losing seasons together. But then things finally began to click. Inventive game plans *were devised* and they *were executed* with spirit and skill. Every opponent *was destroyed*. When the season was over, the team had earned the glory that came with the championship.

The switch to passive in the three instances indicated not only weakens consistency; it also makes the paragraph less interesting. If the sentences were kept in the active voice they might have looked like this:

The coaches devised inventive game plans that the players executed with spirit and skill. Working together, the team destroyed every opponent.

You should guard against a tendency to shift to the passive voice, especially in paragraphs where the ideas call for active sentences.

Exercises

a. The following paragraph has a number of problems with consistency: pronoun reference, tense, mood, and voice. See if you can spot them and correct them:

Students at this university have to work together to solve their problems. We should tell the administration that a student cannot be expected to study on an empty stomach. Go to the dean of your college today and explain that one was not even able to read by the dim lights we have in our dormitory rooms. A student will improve his situation only if he joins with others. The problems will be solved only if something is done about them by the students.

b. Revise the theme about problems of car ownership that was given above on pp. 106–108 so that it no longer has inconsistencies in pronoun reference. It has several problems with the use of *he, him, his,* and *himself* as generic pronouns. Adopt a policy for solving this problem and stick with it throughout the entire theme.

c. Here are several topic sentences. For each one, write a unified and coherent paragraph. Develop it according to the organizational plan given in parentheses. Be sure to pay attention to all the specifics of unity and coherence: Maintain balance between what the topic sentence promises and what the content sentences deliver. Follow the same organizational plan throughout. Repeat key words and ideas. Use transitional expressions to strengthen coherence. Use parallel grammatical structure where appropriate. Maintain consistency in pronoun reference, in tense and mood, and in voice. To give yourself sufficient space to practice, plan to write several good-sized sentences in each paragraph.

(1) The building I live in is distinctive enough that you should have little difficulty recognizing it. (Description)
(2) My first day at college was hectic but interesting. (Narration)
(3) There are several easy ways to start a car. (Process)
(4) A doughnut is easy enough to define. (Formal definition)
(5) Spring and fall have as much in common as they have differences. (Comparison and contrast)
(6) There are three kinds of English teachers. (Classification)
(7) All young Americans should give one year to the service of their country immediately after finishing high school. (Induction or deduction)
(8) Uncontrolled population growth will cause an end to individual freedom. (Cause or effect)

Five | *Sentence Grammar*

A sentence can be a complete discourse all by itself. Here are a couple of famous examples:

It is much better to know something about everything than to know everything about one thing.

—BLAISE PASCAL, *Pensées*

The ear attentive to wholesome correction finds itself at home in the company of the wise.

—PROVERBS, 15:31

Writing such single sentence discourses requires the same kind of effort as does the writing of longer discourses. The author must carefully consider audience, purpose, and plan. But very few sentences are in fact independent discourses; most are parts of paragraphs that in turn are parts of larger written works. An able writer must know how to shape sentences to fit the contexts in which they appear. And the ability to do so is a skill you will often use most consciously when you revise early drafts of essays and papers. Let me show you what I mean. On page 115 is a revised first draft of one of the paragraphs from the theme entitled "What Is a Student of English?" that was given in Chapter Three (pp. 64–65) as an example of formal definition. First read the printed version; then read in the revisions. Try to pay close attention to the changes in sentence structure. I will comment on them below.

~~The student of English is also a writer.~~ ~~All~~ English majors have an oppor-
tunity to test their creative powers by writing poetry, fiction, and drama. ~~The~~ *Although only a specially talented* ~~truly talented~~ few earn the privilege to pursue creative writing as a career/, ~~All~~ *a*
English majors learn that no profession is so near the frontiers of ~~human intel-~~ *the* ~~lectual growth~~ *human spirit* as that of the creative writer. ~~The poet, Shelley, has even said~~ *They learn what Shelley meant when he called poets* ~~that poets are~~ mirrors of the gigantic shadows that futurity casts upon the
present.

The above paragraph underwent additional revision before the theme in which it appeared was complete, but I chose to show you this draft and this revision because it indicates well how sentences must be shaped and reshaped to fit coherently into paragraphs. In the first draft of the paragraph, the sentences were clear enough, but they did not fit together as well as they do in the revised version. By changing the third sentence into a dependent clause (starting with *Although only a specially talented few* . . .), I was able to make its connection to the following sentence much clearer. And by beginning the last sentence with *They learn,* I improved coherence, because *they* repeats the idea expressed in the phrase *all English majors* in the previous sentence, and *learn* actually repeats the verb of the previous sentence. But to make this change, I had to make major grammatical changes elsewhere in the sentence. The original draft had Shelley's idea expressed in a noun clause (*that poets are mirrors*) that was the direct object of the verb *to say.* In my revision Shelley's idea is part of an adverb clause (*when he called poets mirrors*) that is now part of an entirely new and different noun clause (*what Shelley meant*).

When I made the changes described in the previous paragraph, I neither thought of nor used the grammatical terminology contained in my description of the changes (*direct object, dependent clause, noun clause, adverb clause*). And when you first examined my changes, I am sure that you could feel the improvement even before I went on to discuss them using the grammatical terminology. But it is also true, I think, that you can understand such changes and use your understanding to make similar changes in your own writing when they are explicitly explained, and explained in terms you can understand.

You may not have a clear understanding of all of the grammatical terms I used in the last paragraph or of the terms your teacher may want to use to discuss problems you may have in writing and revising your own sentences. Thus, the purpose of this chapter is to explain and exemplify as many grammatical terms as space allows, so that you will have just such a vocabulary to talk about your sentences and about how to improve them. But this is only the first of three chapters on the sentence. The next chapter, entitled "Sentence Strategy," aims to give you practice in revising and reshaping sentences so that, when you are faced with the kind of need I faced in the sample paragraph above, you will be better prepared to generate a variety of revisions from which to choose the one best suited to the context. The chapter after next, entitled "Sentence Repair," describes problems that writers often have because edited English requires sentence structures that are different from those in conversational styles and informal written styles. But let us first turn to the matter of this chapter: sentence grammar.

Chapter One compared sentences to hands in a card game: Only certain arrangements of words are sentences, just as only certain arrangements of cards are playable hands. Actually, it is useful to think of sentences as arrangements of *groups* of words. In poker, we say that a full house consists of a pair and three-of-a-kind; so too we can say that a sentence like *The President has been negotiating* consists of two groups of words, *the President* and *has been negotiating*. But we cannot call the groups simply "a pair" and "three of a kind." Every group of words in a sentence needs two separate labels. One label states what the group does; this is its functional label. The other label states how the group is built; this is its structural label. Functionally, *the president,* is labeled the *subject* of the above sentence; structurally, it is called a *noun phrase*. Functionally, *has been negotiating* is called a *predicate;* structurally, it is called a *verb phrase*. The first section in this chapter defines the concept of function in more detail and reviews the principal types of functional groups that occur in English sentences. The second section defines the concept of structure in more detail and reviews the principal types of structural phrases that occur in English sentences. The third section discusses aspects of both function and structure in compound and complex sentences.

Functional Groups in Simple Sentences

Unlike most card games, where the number of cards in a hand is fixed, there is no limit on the number of words in a sentence. But there are relatively specific limits on both the number and the order of groups of words that compose English sentences. Below are the names for the main types of functional groups and typical functional patterns they appear in. Carefully examine the example sentences and the group labels that accompany them. Each type of group will be defined and exemplified further below. (The abbreviation in parentheses will be used in later diagrams.)

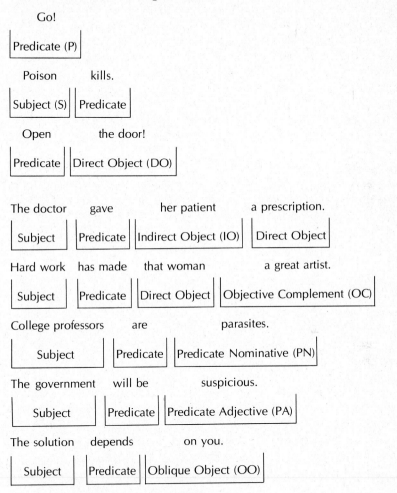

Go!

Predicate (P)

Poison kills.

Subject (S) | Predicate

Open the door!

Predicate | Direct Object (DO)

The doctor gave her patient a prescription.

Subject | Predicate | Indirect Object (IO) | Direct Object

Hard work has made that woman a great artist.

Subject | Predicate | Direct Object | Objective Complement (OC)

College professors are parasites.

Subject | Predicate | Predicate Nominative (PN)

The government will be suspicious.

Subject | Predicate | Predicate Adjective (PA)

The solution depends on you.

Subject | Predicate | Oblique Object (OO)

A predicate group ordinarily describes actions or states of being:

The ambassador *departed*. (Action)
Books *are* tools. (State of Being)
Truth *can appear* fuzzy. (State of Being)

A subject group ordinarily names persons, things, or ideas that perform the action or exist in the state described by the predicate:

The ambassador departed. (Person)
Books are tools. (Things)
Truth can appear fuzzy. (Idea)

A direct-object group ordinarily names persons, things, or ideas that are directly affected by the action described in the predicate:

The losers congratulated *the winners.*
Union members build *better homes.*
Many philosophers have described *love.*

An indirect-object group ordinarily names persons, things, or ideas that are indirectly affected by the action described by the predicate:

The judge granted *Elizabeth* a divorce. (*A divorce* is the direct object, the thing granted; Elizabeth is indirectly affected: She benefits from the grant.)
You should send *the bank* an explanation. (*An explanation* is the direct object, the thing sent; the bank is indirectly affected: It receives the explanation.)
The negotiators gave *peace* priority. (*Priority* is the direct object, the thing given; *peace* names the idea that is indirectly affected: It gets the priority.)

An objective-complement group ordinarily names persons, things, or ideas that are closely related to the direct object, and like it are directly affected by the action described in the predicate:

The voters elected him *president.* (*Him* is direct object; *president* is objective complement.)
The preacher called money *an evil thing.* (*Money* is direct object; *an evil thing* is objective complement.)
Some doctors make health care *a luxury.* (*Health care* is direct object; *a luxury* is objective complement.)

A predicate-nominative group ordinarily names persons, things, or ideas that are closely linked to the subject by predicates like *be* or *become* and that are often just another name for the same persons, things, or ideas named in the subject group:

Electric cars may be *a solution.*
Little leaguers become *solid citizens.*

A predicate-adjective group ordinarily names a quality or characteristic that is closely linked to the subject by predicates like *be, become, seem, look, appear,* and *feel* and thus describes the persons, things, or ideas named in the subject group:

Many college students are *lazy*.
Very bright people may become *pompous*.
Those children seem *quite happy*.
Some dishonest senators are feeling *very bad*.

An oblique-object group names persons, things, or ideas that, like indirect objects, are indirectly affected by the action described by the predicate; however, these persons, things, or ideas are introduced by a preposition like *to, at, on,* or *for:*

The judge granted a divorce *to Elizabeth*.
The guests were looking *at the exhibit*.
The solution depends *on you*.
I was hoping *for a bigger raise*.

At various places in all of the patterns listed earlier groups of another type may be added: these are called adverbial-modifier groups. Here are some examples:

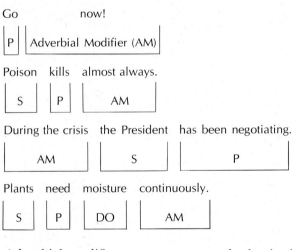

Go   now!

| P | Adverbial Modifier (AM) |

Poison   kills   almost always.

| S | P | AM |

During the crisis   the President   has been negotiating.

| AM | S | P |

Plants   need   moisture   continuously.

| S | P | DO | AM |

Adverbial modifiers may appear at the beginning or at the end of almost any of the patterns listed earlier. They may also appear between certain groups in those patterns:

The solution   depends   entirely   on you.

| S | P | AM | OO |

They may even appear inside of another group, usually the predicate group:

The senator has secretly sold his stocks.

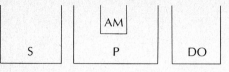

An adverbial modifier group ordinarily describes how, where, when, why, or how often the action or state described in the predicate group occurs:

The thieves removed the window *carefully*. (How)
In Canada, the supply of clean water is plentiful. (Where)
I didn't understand calculus *then*. (When)
For some reason, I have trouble with foreign languages. (Why)
Tourists have *often* complained about American unfriendliness. (How often)

The functional patterns presented so far in this section have all been exemplified with simple sentences. Simple sentences have one and only one functional pattern. (We will see in a later section that compound and complex sentences can have more than one functional pattern.) There are three types of simple sentences: declarative, interrogative, and imperative.

Declarative sentences make statements. In a declarative sentence, the subject group precedes the predicate group:

You can prevent heart disease.

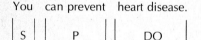

Interrogative sentences ask questions. In an interrogative sentence, the subject group is usually inside of the predicate group:

Can you prevent heart disease?

Imperative sentences give commands. In an imperative sentence there is no subject group:

Prevent heart disease.

All three types of simple sentences can be either *affirmative* (as illustrated in the above three sentences) or *negative:*

Negative Declarative
  You cannot prevent heart disease.
  You can't prevent heart disease.

Negative Interrogative
  Can you not prevent heart disease?
  Can't you prevent heart disease?

Negative Imperative
  Do not prevent heart disease.
  Don't prevent heart disease.

Notice that all negative sentences, whether declarative, interrogative, or imperative, contain either *not* or its contracted form *-n't* inside the predicate group.

Exercises

  a. Label each of the following sentences as *declarative, interrogative,* or *imperative* on the one hand, and as *affirmative* or *negative* on the other. Then identify and label the functional groups in each sentence. Here is the answer for the first sentence in the exercise:

The first astronauts   were   pilots.   (Declarative affirmative)

  (1) The first astronauts were pilots.
  (2) Have those packages been delivered yet?
  (3) Do not tell your parents about the accident.
  (4) Many drivers have been exceeding the speed limit.
  (5) Shouldn't you have eaten something?
  (6) The guards must have been sleeping during the burglary.
  (7) I will not give help to lazy students.
  (8) Margie seemed sad yesterday.
  (9) Explain the opera to those children.
  (10) Why are the American people skeptical?

  b. Write four sentences of each of the following types: declarative, interrogative, and imperative. Make two of each set of four affirmative and two negative. Identify the functional groups in each sentence you write.

Structural Phrases in Simple Sentences

As the brief definitions given in the last section indicate, terms like *subject, predicate, object,* and *adverbial modifier* label word groups according to what they *do* in a sentence. These are *functional,* or *role, labels:* The subject names persons, things, or ideas that perform an action or exist in a state; the predicate describes that action or state; objects name persons, things, or ideas affected by the predicate; adverbial modifiers describe how, where, when, why, or how often that action or state occurs.

There are other kinds of functional groups and other functional patterns besides those treated in the previous section, but surprisingly many English sentences represent some variation of one of the patterns exemplified there. When a sentence has a large number of words, this usually indicates that the groups composing it are complex in their structure, not that there are many more groups than usual. Therefore, to understand fully what a sentence is and how words work together in sentence structure, it is necessary to use another, and more complex, set of grammatical terms: These are *structural labels.*

Compare the following two sentences, which represent the same functional pattern, but in which the *structures* of the adverbial modifier groups are very different:

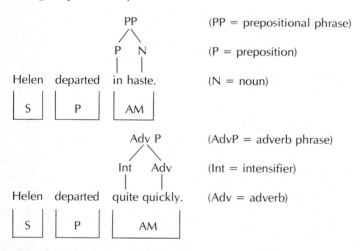

	(PP = prepositional phrase)
	(P = preposition)
	(N = noun)
	(AdvP = adverb phrase)
	(Int = intensifier)
	(Adv = adverb)

Both adverbial modifiers above describe *how* Helen departed. But notice that the adverbial modifier in the first sentence is structurally a *prepositional phrase,* i.e., a preposition (*in*) structured together with a noun (*haste*), but in the second sentence, the adverbial modifier is

structurally an *adverb phrase,* i.e., an intensifier (*quite*) structured together with an adverb (*quickly*). Prepositions, nouns, intensifiers, and
adverbs are different *parts of speech* in English, and all of them and
other parts of speech will be defined more specifically throughout this
section. When you compose a sentence, you combine parts of speech
in specific ways to form various kinds of *structural phrases.* For instance, you can combine prepositions with nouns, as in the sentence
above, to form a structural phrase, but you cannot combine them with
adverbs: there is no English sentence where *in quickly* could work together as either one functional group or one structural phrase. Nor
can intensifiers and nouns ever form a phrase: *Quite haste* cannot
occur as a structured part of an English sentence.

In the remainder of this section, you will have an opportunity to
study the parts of speech of English and to observe how you and
other speakers of English build them into the various types of structural phrases that play roles like subject, predicate, object, and adverbial modifier in English sentences. Remember, you already know how
to create English sentences. The study of grammatical terminology
does not of itself improve either speaking or writing ability. But by
learning such terminology you will be better able to use the information about sentence strategy and sentence repair presented in the next
two chapters, and you will be better able to discuss with your teacher
problems you may have in writing your own sentences.

Verb phrases

When you write a verb phrase, you use a *verb,* and sometimes you
use *auxiliaries* (also called "helping verbs" by some grammarians). Both
of these parts of speech have in common certain features that can
help you recognize them even outside the structural context of a sentence: they can change their spelling to show present tense, past tense,
present participle, and past participle:

Present Tense	Past Tense	Present Participle	Past Participle
break breaks	broke	breaking	broken
have has	had	having	had
am are is	was were	being	been

However, verbs and auxiliaries are most easily recognized and distinguished from one another according to how they fit into the structure
of the verb phrase.

Structurally, we can define the verb as that part of speech that may
constitute a verb phrase and thus function as a predicate all by itself.

Here are some sentences where the verb phrase is composed of a verb alone, unaccompanied by auxiliaries:

Henry Kissinger *negotiated* many treaties.
Primitive peoples *were* unaware of the need for progress.

A verb may also be accompanied by auxiliaries, which may be defined as parts of speech that cannot constitute a verb phrase on their own and must precede a verb when they occur in a verb phrase. Here are some sentences where up to four auxiliaries accompany the verb in the verb phrase:

British school children can conjugate Latin verbs.

We have been struggling with written English.

The Cuban people had been being prepared for an invasion.

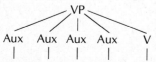

Those secrets should have been being guarded more carefully.

All the verb phrases in the above sentences, and most verb phrases in fact, function as predicates.

In negative sentences, the word *not* or its contracted form *-n't* appears immediately after the first auxiliary in a verb phrase:

Veterans are not protesting the lack of jobs.

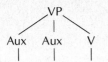

College students haven't been studying lately.

In question sentences, the first auxiliary appears at the beginning of the sentence and in front of the subject group, thus dividing the verb phrase:

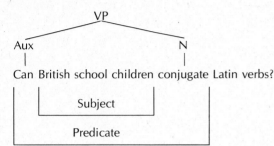

Exercises

a. Copy each of the following sentences onto a separate sheet of paper. Then identify and label the predicate below the sentence (also label the subject if it is inside the predicate), and analyze the structure of the verb phrase above the sentence. Here is the analysis of the first sentence:

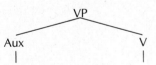

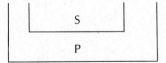

(1) Did the first Americans come to Alaska across a land bridge?
(2) Have those packages been delivered yet?
(3) Do not tell your parents about the parties in the dormitories.
(4) Many drivers have been exceeding the speed limit.
(5) Shouldn't you have eaten something?
(6) The guards must have been sleeping during the burglary.

b. Write six sentences of your own modeled after the six sentences in exercise *a.* Try to write some with two, three, or even four auxiliaries. Then analyze the verb phrases just as you did in exercise *a.*

Noun phrases

Noun phrases play the roles of subject, direct object, indirect object, objective complement, and predicate nominative.

Several parts of speech operate in noun phrases. The most important is the *noun*. Like verbs, nouns have certain characteristics that can help you recognize them even outside of the context of a sentence. They can change their spelling to show plural or possessive:

Singular	Plural	Possessive
teacher	teachers	teacher's
bush	bushes	bush's
love	loves	love's

But nouns are best defined and you can more surely identify them by noting how they fit into the structure of the noun phrase.

Structurally, we can define a noun as that part of speech that may constitute a noun phrase and thus fill one of the functions of a noun phrase all by itself. Here are some sentences with noun phrases composed of nouns alone, unaccompanied by other parts of speech:

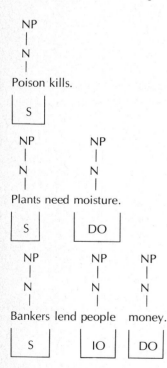

```
NP
|
N
|
Poison kills.
|__S__|

NP         NP
|          |
N          N
|          |
Plants   need moisture.
|__S__|      |__DO__|

NP         NP        NP
|          |         |
N          N         N
|          |         |
Bankers  lend people  money.
|__S__|      |__IO__|  |__DO__|
```

NP   NP
| |
N   N
| |
Professors are parasites.

[S]   [PN]

In most noun phrases, the head noun is accompanied by other words which may belong to a variety of parts of speech. Here are some sentences where nouns are preceded by determiners:

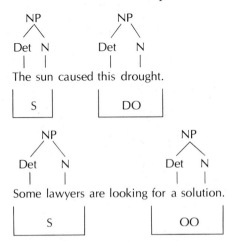

The sun caused this drought.

Some lawyers are looking for a solution.

Here are sentences where nouns are immediately preceded by adjectives (in the second sentence, the adjective *oldest* is in turn preceded by a determiner):

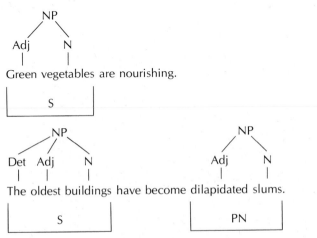

Green vegetables are nourishing.

The oldest buildings have become dilapidated slums.

Here is a sentence where both the subject and direct object noun phrases contain two adjectives:

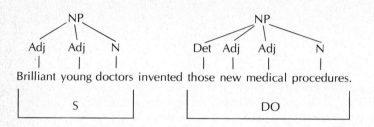

A noun phrase may also contain a possessive noun (N's), which will precede the head noun and any adjectives that may occur:

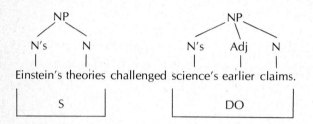

A possessive noun in a noun phrase may have its own determiner and adjectives, in which case we may analyze it as a possessive noun phrase (NP's) that is a part of another noun phrase and thus plays the role of *modifier* (M):

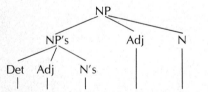

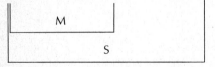

A noun phrase may also contain one or more other nouns preceding the head noun. When this happens, we may call the head noun and the nouns that accompany it a *compound noun:*

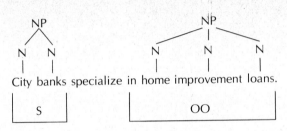

A noun phrase may also have another noun phrase following the head noun and related to the head noun by a preposition. (Prepositions are words such as *at, in, on, to, of, from,* and *through* that relate noun phrases to other elements of sentence structure. Relating a noun phrase to the head noun in another noun phrase is only one of the relational functions of prepositions; others will be discussed shortly.) Here are a few examples of noun phrases with prepositional phrases following the head noun. Notice that the noun phrase and the preposition that relates it to the head noun are labeled below the sentence as playing the role of modifier (M). *In Alaska* is part of the subject, but it cannot itself be called the subject; *of ice* is part of the direct object, but it cannot itself be called the direct object. Instead, both of these noun phrases participate in the modifying function of the prepositional phrase.

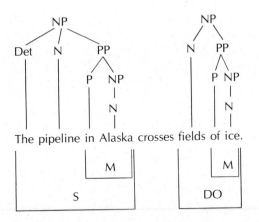

What about the function of a noun phrase *within* a prepositional phrase? In the sentence just above, it is the prepositional phrases that function as noun modifiers. The noun phrases participate in that function, but on their own they cannot be called noun modifiers. In fact, it is customary to describe the function of any noun phrase in any prepositional phrase as *object of a preposition* (OP). In the next several pages we

will examine several functions for prepositional phrases, but no matter
what the function of a prepositional phrase is, the function of a noun
phrase within it is object of a preposition.

   Noun phrases in modifying prepositional phrases are capable of all of
the structural complexity exemplified so far in this section. Here is a relatively complete functional and structural analysis of a sentence where
the noun phrases in modifying prepositional phrases show such structural complexity (the function of object of a preposition is labeled here,
but will not be in future sentence analyses unless there is a reason to do
so):

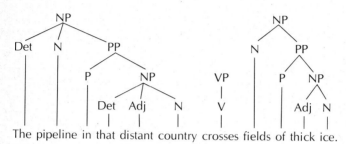

As was stated in the paragraph before last, prepositional phrases can
perform other functions than that of modifying nouns. A preposition
can serve to relate a noun phrase to the idea expressed in a verb. Such
prepositional phrases were said earlier (p. 119) to function as *oblique objects.* Here are two sentences that were used there to illustrate this function:

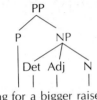

I was hoping for a bigger raise.

Noun phrases can also play roles in prepositional phrases that are parts of adjective phrases or adverb phrases; these two functions will be discussed later.

In all the noun phrases so far discussed, the head word has been a noun. But a noun phrase may also be headed by a pronoun. The following sentences contain noun phrases headed by *personal pronouns* (only the noun phrases with pronouns are italicized):

> *I* need love.
> Give *them* some information about *it*.
> *They* can help *us*.
> *We* have been communicating with *her*.

In analyzing sentences, pronouns can be given the same label as nouns (N), but it is useful to note that they are very limited in the kinds of noun-phrase structures they appear in; determiners, adjectives, and modifying prepositional phrases are in fact virtually prohibited from co-occurring with personal pronouns.

The following sentences contain noun phrases headed by *indefinite pronouns*. Notice that they do allow prepositional phrase modifiers to follow them in a noun phrase, but they generally do not occur with preceding determiners or adjectives.

> *Everybody* loves *somebody* sometime.
> *Someone from San Francisco* called.
> Have you ever met *anyone with perfect pitch?*

It is of course useful to a writer to be able to recognize noun phrases. But it is even more important to learn to control their structure when you write. The problem is that English allows an indefinite number of modifiers in front of a noun:

Those three lazy old English teachers should be fired.

And it also allows an indefinite number of modifying prepositional phrases to pile up after a noun:

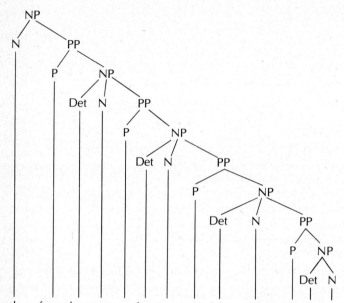

Teachers from the town on the river near the mountains in the West should be fired.

If you allow these two tendencies to run wild, as in the sentence below, you can force your readers to work so hard to identify the head noun in the subject group that they can lose interest in the sentence by the time the predicate comes along:

Those three lazy old English teachers from the town on the river near the mountains in the West should be fired.

Exercises

a. Copy each of the following sentences onto a separate sheet of paper. Then identify and label the function of each noun phrase below the sentence and analyze the structure of each noun phrase above the sentence. Here is the answer for the first sentence (label modifying prepositional phrases with an M, and label the noun phrases in them with OP):

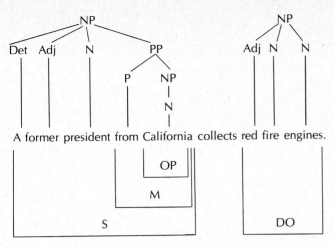

(1) A former president from California collects red fire engines.
(2) The world's great swimmers have practiced diligently from early childhood.
(3) The final evaluation depends on the quality of Mary's research.
(4) Throughout the centuries, the creative talents of large numbers of
women must surely have been wasted.
(5) Silence is the virtue of a fool. [—Francis Bacon]
(6) Distribute these pamphlets to anyone with a concern for conservation.
(7) True diplomats can negotiate treaties with their enemies in an atmosphere of skeptical frankness.
(8) The Smithsonian is filled with the precious junk of our history.
(9) Democracy substitutes election by the incompetent many for appointment
by the corrupt few. [—George Bernard Shaw]
(10) The capacity for self-deception derives from a basic flaw in human nature.

b. Write several sentences of your own like the sentences in exercise *a*. Try to
vary the structure of the noun phrases. Then analyze the noun phrases just as
you did in exercise *a*.

Adjective phrases

In the treatment of noun phrases above there were listed several sentences that contained adjectives playing a modifying role in noun
phrases. Adjectives may also head a structural phrase of their own, the
adjective phrase, which plays the functional role of predicate adjective.
Like verbs and nouns, adjectives may have certain characteristics that
can help you recognize them even outside of the context of a sentence.
Many of them change their spelling to show degrees of comparison:

Positive	Comparative	Superlative
big	bigger	biggest
happy	happier	happiest
red	redder	reddest

But adjectives are best defined by, and you can more surely identify them according to, the way they fit into the structure of noun phrases (as we have already seen) and adjective phrases.

Here are some examples of sentences with adjective phrases:

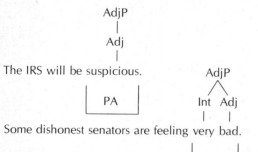

Notice that predicate adjectives follow verbs like *be, become, seem, look, appear,* and *feel.* These are called *linking verbs* because they connect the quality expressed in a predicate-adjective group to the subject. In the sentences above, the quality expressed by the adjective *suspicious* is thus connected to the noun *IRS* in the subject, and the quality expressed by *bad* is connected to the noun *senators.* In the first sentence, the adjective phrase that functions as predicate adjective consists of the single adjective, *suspicious.* In the second sentence, the head adjective is modified by an intensifier: *very.* (An intensifier is thus defined structurally as that part of speech that can precede adjectives in adjective phrases.)

An adjective in an adjective phrase can also be modified by a prepositional phrase that follows it:

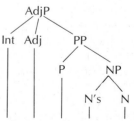

It is important for you to know not only the ways in which an adjective phrase can be expanded, but also the kinds of verbs that call for predicate adjectives. In edited English, sentences like the following (which uses *badly* instead of the adjective *bad*) are inappropriate:

The senators feel *badly* about their crimes.

People who write such sentences do so because they forget that *feel* is a linking verb that permits predicate adjectives to follow it and indeed requires an adjective rather than an adverb to express the idea that the above sentence seeks to convey.

Exercises

a. Copy each of the following sentences onto a separate sheet of paper. Then identify and label the predicate-adjective groups below the line, and analyze the structure of the adjective phrase above the line. Here is the answer for the first sentence:

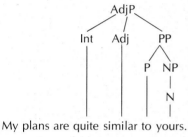

(1) My plans are quite similar to yours.
(2) I am not completely sure of that candidate's commitment to energy conservation.
(3) The laborer is worthy of his hire. [—Luke 10:7]
(4) My neighbors seemed happy about the price of their new car.

b. Write several sentences of your own like the sentences in exercise *a*. Try to vary the structure of your adjective phrases. Then analyze the adjective phrases just as you did in exercise *a*.

Adverb phrases

Adverb phrases function as adverbial modifiers. We saw earlier that adverbial modifiers may appear in a variety of places in English sentences. Adverb phrases are headed by adverbs. The adverb is a part of speech that can be defined structurally as that class of words that can occur as the only member of an adverb phrase, and that can thus function alone as an adverbial modifier. Here are some examples:

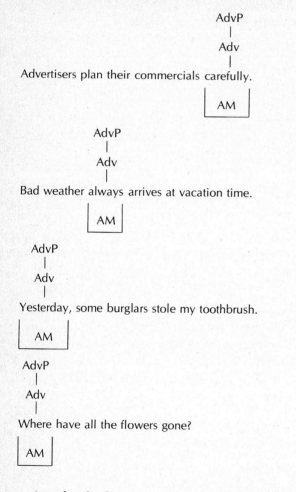

An adverb phrase may also consist of an adverb preceded by an intensifier:

Advertisers plan their commercials quite carefully.

Bad weather nearly always arrives at vacation time.

| AM |

Just yesterday, some burglars stole my toothbrush.

| AM |

AdvP
Int   Adv
| |
Exactly where have all the flowers gone?

| AM |

Notice that the adverbial-modifier function of adverb phrases such as *quite carefully* and *just yesterday* in the above sentences can also be performed by prepositional phrases:

Advertisers plan their commercials *with great care.*
In the morning some burglars stole my toothbrush.

Exercises

a. Copy each of the following sentences onto a separate sheet of paper. Then identify and label the adverbial modifiers below the line and analyze the structure of the adverb phrases or prepositional phrases that play the role of adverbial modifier above the line. Here is the answer for the first sentence:

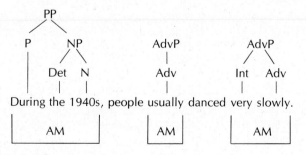

PP
P   NP
| Det   N   AdvP   AdvP
| | | Adv   Int   Adv
| | | | | |
During the 1940s, people usually danced very slowly.

| AM | | AM | | AM |

(1) During the 1940s, people usually danced very slowly.
(2) The world's great swimmers have practiced diligently from early childhood.
(3) The cost of living has quite literally doubled in the past ten years.
(4) Throughout the centuries, the creative talents of large numbers of women
must surely have been wasted.
(5) Diseases almost always attack during changes in the weather. [—Herod-
otus]

b. Write several sentences of your own like the sentences in exercise *a*. Include
various types of adverb phrases and also some prepositional phrases functioning
as adverbial modifiers. Then analyze both the adverb phrases and the prepositional phrases that function as adverbial modifiers, just as you did in exercise *a*.

Conjoined phrases

Two or more structural phrases in English sentences may join together to form one functional group. Here is a sentence where the predicate consists of two verb phrases joined by the word *and* (*come and go* is a
compound verb phrase; *and* is a conjunction, a part of speech used to
join two or more structural elements so that they behave as one):

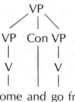

Citizens in a democracy come and go freely.

Verb phrases of more than one word may also be conjoined:

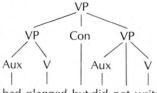

Pascal had planned but did not write a book in defense of religion.

A verb phrase may also have just the head verbs conjoined, in which
case the auxiliaries apply to both of them:

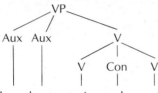

American farmers have been growing and exporting wheat for generations.

Or a verb phrase may have conjoined auxiliaries, both of which will apply to the verb:

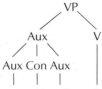

Automobile producers can and will produce cleaner engines.

Noun phrases may also be conjoined, and in any of the functional roles that noun phrases play. Here is a sampling:

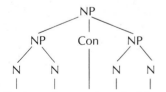

Dock workers and truck drivers are the arteries of commerce.

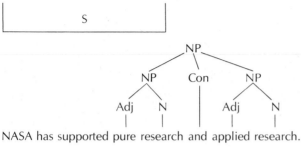

NASA has supported pure research and applied research.

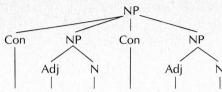

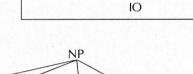

The legislature has given both clerical workers and professional staff a raise.

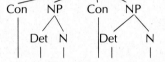

Our President is neither a liberal nor a conservative.

Conjunctions that operate in pairs (such as *both . . . and* and *neither . . . nor* in the two sentences above) are called *correlative conjunctions.*

English also allows conjoining in adjective phrases (only one of the example sentences will be diagrammed):

Balzac was *neither temperate nor prudent.*

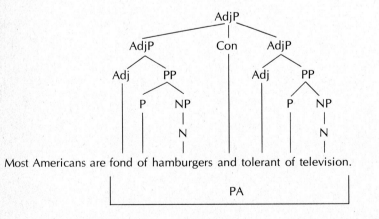

Most Americans are fond of hamburgers and tolerant of television.

Adverb phrases may also be conjoined (only the last of the three example sentences will be diagrammed):

The police department is sponsoring a crime-prevention workshop at the local high school *today and tomorrow.*
Very consistently and quite professionally, minority groups are increasing their political power.

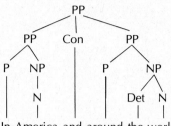

In America and around the world, the cost of fuel is high.

In edited English you must take care not to conjoin two different types of structural phrases. The following sentence, which attempts to conjoin a verb phrase and a noun phrase, shows the kind of confusion that can result:

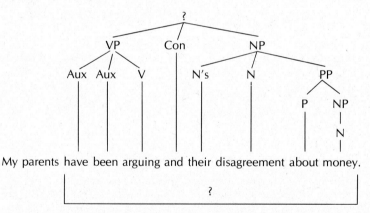

My parents have been arguing and their disagreement about money.

Most writers do not make such serious mistakes as that, but many do have trouble using conjunctions effectively in sentences. (See pp. 177–179 for a more detailed discussion of this problem.)

Exercises

a. Copy each of the following sentences onto a separate sheet of paper. Then identify and label the function of any conjoined group below the line and analyze its structure above the line. Here is the answer for the first sentence:

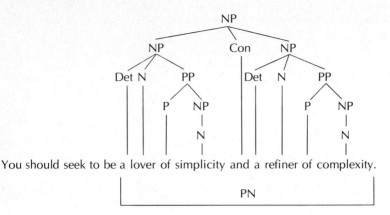

You should seek to be a lover of simplicity and a refiner of complexity.

PN

(1) You should seek to be a lover of simplicity and a refiner of complexity.
(2) Always and everywhere tyranny ultimately consumes itself.
(3) Inside the Magic Kingdom, a visitor to Disney World finds both imaginative adventures and misrepresentation of reality.
(4) The volcanoes of Ecuador are both simple and majestic.
(5) In Africa, neither the Arab governments nor the black governments have been the aggressors.

b. There is an additional function for noun phrases, which has not been discussed so far in this chapter. It is loosely related to the process of conjoining. Here are some examples. Ask yourself what the function of each italicized noun phrase is.

John, *my best friend,* arrives tomorrow.
Give it to your boss, *the woman in that office.*
One person, *the parent,* determines a child's self-confidence.

Did you notice that each italicized noun phrase seemed joined to the noun phrase preceding it, but without the help of a conjunction? In fact, such noun phrases are more than joined; each has the exact same referent as the noun phrase it follows: John *is* my best friend; your boss *is* the woman in that office; and the one person who determines a child's self-confidence *is* the parent. The italicized noun phrases thus share the functional role of the noun phrases that precede them. However, their primary functional role is a relational role *to* those noun phrases. Such noun phrases are usually called *appositives,* and they are said to be in *apposition* to the noun phrase preceding them. Here is an analysis of the first of the three sentences above, showing how appositives can be labeled (*AP* is an abbreviation for *appositive;* the *S* after the colon indicates that the appositive, *my best friend,* is in apposition to the subject):

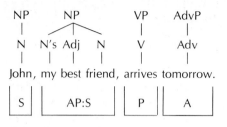

John, my best friend, arrives tomorrow.

Copy the second and third example sentences above onto separate sheets of paper, and then label the functional groups below the line (remembering to indicate the function of the noun phrase each appositive is in apposition to) and analyze the structure of all phrases above the line.

Compound and Complex Sentences

We saw in the previous section that a given functional group may contain two or more structural phrases joined by a conjunction. Conjunctions may also join whole sentences into larger sentences:

My father has retired, *and* my mother has bought him some knitting needles.

A sentence that functions as part of a larger sentence is called a *clause.* If a clause is able to function as a sentence on its own, it is called an *independent clause.* The two clauses joined by *and* in the above sentence are both independent clauses. Notice that each has its own subject and predicate group. The second clause also contains an indirect object and a direct object. Both clauses are declarative. Interrogative and imperative clauses may also be conjoined:

Can those doctors solve your problem, and will you listen to their recommendations?
Quiet that dog, or take it inside!

Conjoined sentences can consist of either affirmative or negative clauses. Here is a sentence where the first clause is affirmative and the second negative:

My neighbor planned a practical joke, but I didn't fall for it.

Whereas affirmative and negative clauses may be conjoined, declarative, interrogative, and imperative clauses ordinarily conjoin only with a clause of the same type.

A special type of conjoined sentence is the *comparative sentence.* It has its own special conjunctions (*-er than, more* . . . *than*) and usually short-ens the second clause. Here are some examples (the words in parentheses are often understood but not expressed):

Daisies are prett*ier than* marigolds (are pretty).
Working class students are often *more* serious about their studies *than* upper class students (are serious).
American astronauts trained *more* rigorously *than* the Russians (trained rigorously).

Notice that *-er* or *more* accompany a head adjective or adverb and the word *than* follows the entire adjective or adverb phrase.

In compound sentences two clauses stand side by side as coequal parts of a larger sentence. But one clause can also play a functional role *inside* another clause. When this happens, the combination of clauses is called a *complex sentence.* Here is a sentence where one clause (in italics) is playing the role of subject inside another clause:

That Paraguay is an officially bilingual country surprises some Americans.

In the following sentence, the clause in italics plays the role of direct object:

Many young people do not believe *that they are responsible for their actions.*

Notice that the last two example sentences were not composed of two independent clauses joined by a conjunction; rather, each italicized clause was part of another clause. Nor could the italicized clauses function alone as a sentence (a speaker of English would not say out of the blue, *That Paraguay is an officially bilingual country,* and expect that to make sense on its own to a listener). For this reason, such clauses are called *dependent clauses.* Dependent clauses like the two above, performing a functional role usually performed by a noun phrase (such as subject or direct object), are called *noun clauses.* At the top of page 145 is an analysis of a sentence that has a noun clause functioning as subject. Notice that no part-of-speech label is given in the diagram for the word *that;* when this word introduces a noun clause, some grammarians call it a *nominalizer* (*Nom*) and others call it a *complementizer* (*Comp*).

Dependent clauses may also modify nouns, thus occupying the same position in a noun phrase as a modifying prepositional phrase—the position immediately following the head noun:

I once climbed a tree *that was planted by my grandfather.*
Students *who plan a literary career* should read broadly.

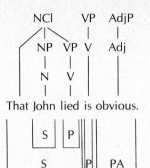

That John lied is obvious.

Such clauses are called *relative clauses.* Notice that a relative clause is *part of* a noun phrase and so differs from a noun clause, which alone constitutes a functional group in another clause. Thus, the entire direct object group in the first example sentence above consists of the words, *a tree that was planted by my grandfather,* and the entire subject group in the second sentence above consists of the words, *students who plan a literary career.* Here is an analysis of a sentence that has a relative clause modifying the head noun in its direct object group (the pronoun *that* in the following sentence, which is labeled N in the diagram, is more precisely called a *relative pronoun* and could thus be labeled *RPro*):

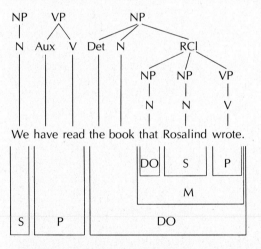

We have read the book that Rosalind wrote.

There are two kinds of relative clauses. *Restrictive relative clauses* specify a subgroup within the class named by the modified noun, or they help to identify or define the modified noun. In the following sentence the italicized restrictive relative clause limits the reference of the word, *adults,* to those attending school.

Adults *who attend school* need time to study.

Nonrestrictive relative clauses refer to the entire class named by the modified noun, or they provide incidental or nondefining information about the noun. In the following sentence the italicized nonrestrictive relative clause incidentally asserts that all adolescents attend school; it in no way restricts or defines the reference of the word, *adolescents*.

Adolescents, *who attend school,* need time to study.

Notice that nonrestrictive relative clauses are set off by commas. Restrictive relative clauses are not.

Dependent clauses may also function as adverbial modifiers. Here are some examples:

Pittsburgh was established *where the Monongahela meets the Allegheny.*
Vampires are most restless *when the moon is full.*
Crime is increasing *because parents don't teach values to their children.*

Notice that, just like other adverbial modifiers, all the above *adverb clauses* could appear just as easily at the beginning of the sentence. Here is an analysis of a sentence with an adverb clause at the beginning of it. The word *when,* which functions as an adverb within the dependent clause and is so labeled in the diagram, also helps to mark the clause as a dependent clause; for this reason it could also be called a *subordinating conjunction (SCon)*:

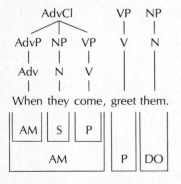

So far in this chapter, there have been many diagrams of sentences that labeled functional groups below the line and analyzed structural phrases above the line. The diagrams have not been presented as ends in themselves but as means of making concrete the very highly systematic nature of English sentence structure. Fortunately, you do not need to master a system of diagramming in order to master the art of writing clear and effective English sentences. For this reason, and also because this is not a book primarily about sentence structure, fewer diagrams will appear from this point on. When they do appear, study them to understand both the structure and the function of the sentence parts under discussion.

Exercise

Read each of the following sentences and decide whether the sentence as a whole is simple, compound, or complex. Then identify each clause in the compound and complex sentences and decide whether it is an independent or a dependent clause. Finally, determine which type of dependent clause each one is: a noun clause, a relative clause, or an adverb clause. (If you are especially brave, you might want to try diagramming some or all of the sentences.)

(1) A candidate who promises the impossible should be defeated.
(2) Why has American society rejected the elderly?
(3) Keep your eye on the tennis ball, and hold the racket very firmly
(4) It is now clear that water is humanity's most precious natural resource.
(5) While Rome burned, Nero supposedly played the fiddle.
(6) Approach your enemies with caution but also with the hope of possible friendship.
(7) The city government has not solved the waste-disposal problems, but a committee of citizens is working on a solution.
(8) I was teaching a Spanish class when I heard that President Kennedy had been shot.
(9) Samuel Beckett has written fiction and drama in both English and French.
(10) Sailors who enlist because they want to travel may be disappointed.
(11) Did Christopher Columbus discover America, or did Leif Ericson do it?
(12) Demand that people who offer you credit disclose the real interest rate.

Six | *Sentence Strategy*

The first few pages of the previous chapter examined a revised paragraph and described how changes in its sentences improved its coherence. The point of that discussion was that an able writer must know how to express the same idea in a variety of sentence structures in order to shape sentences to meet the needs of paragraph coherence and overall organization. During the long discussion of grammatical terminology in that chapter, you may have gotten the impression that sentence structure is so rigid that your flexibility as a writer of sentences will be severely limited. The purpose of that chapter was to introduce and explain as many grammatical concepts as possible in a short space, so little attention could be paid to flexibility in sentence structure. In fact, you have considerable flexibility when you write sentences. This chapter explains many of the strategies you can use to express your ideas in a variety of sentence structures. There are also many exercises that give you a chance to practice rearranging and combining sentences, so that when you need to reshape a sentence to fit the context, you will be better prepared to do so.

Rearranging Simple Sentences

In the previous chapter I attempted to demonstrate the essential orderliness of English sentence structure. Despite the fact that structural phrases, especially noun phrases, can expand to dozens of words, all the words in a sentence tend to belong to a reasonably small number of functional groups, and these groups tend to occur in predictable arrangements: the patterns laid out in the first few pages of the previous chapter. But the English sentence is not a straitjacket for your thoughts. While sentence parts do tend to pattern themselves in certain ways, there is a considerable amount of flexibility. We have already seen this in the patterning of adverbial modifiers; most may occur either at the beginning or at the end of a sentence:

Arms production is increasing *rapidly*.
Rapidly, arms production is increasing.

It is reasonable to wonder why English allows such flexibility in the ordering of sentence parts. Basically, it does so to serve the needs of discourse structure. Recall the discussion of coherence in the chapter on the paragraph (pp. 97–102). There we saw that both spoken conversations and written paragraphs had to be coherent to be intelligible, and that coherence required each sentence to be joined to preceding sentences just as links are joined in a chain. Each sentence must ordinarily make some explicit reference to what has gone before, and then clearly state the new information it is adding. I suggested that coherent writing generally requires the old information in a sentence to appear early in the sentence and the new information to appear toward the end of the sentence, in the position of natural emphasis. Thus, the first sentence above would fit best in a discourse context where arms production has already been mentioned or implied and where the idea of its increasing *rapidly* is the heart of the sentence's message. The second sentence would fit best in a context where the very fact of its increasing is being asserted for the first time.

Adverbial modifiers are the most mobile of the functional groups in English sentences, but they are not the only movable group. Sometimes the order of two oblique objects may be interchanged:

The Secretary of Labor will talk *to the unions about wage and price controls*.
The Secretary of Labor will talk *about wage and price controls to the unions*.

The first sentence above fits a discourse context where the following question is implied:

How is the Department of Labor going to deal with the unions?

The second sentence fits a discourse context where this question is implied:

Who is interested in the Department of Labor's position on wage and price controls?

Principles of English word order even allow a direct object group to appear before the subject if the needs of coherence are served by such an ordering:

Some industrialists believe in unlimited use of gas and oil. *That view,* I wish to refute.

The new idea in the second sentence is that expressed in the word *refute.* Thus, the passage achieves a tighter coherence by expressing the direct object (*that view*) first: It is the link to the ideas in the preceding sentence.

Often enough, English sentence structure serves the needs of coherence not by a mechanical reshuffling of groups but by allowing the same ideas to be expressed with different group structures. Compare the following two sentences:

All new administrations give *their political supporters special treatment.*
All new administrations give *special treatment to their political supporters.*

The first sentence follows the pattern, S/P/IO/DO; the second follows the pattern, S/P/DO/OO. But the ideas are the same. The ordering in the first sentence allows the direct object to hold the final position as the most significant new idea in the sentence. The second pattern allows a noun phrase that might otherwise have been an indirect object to hold this position. The first sentence above would fit coherently after a sentence like this:

Elected officials remember their friends.

The second sentence would fit coherently after a sentence like this:

Politicians have priorities about patronage.

In the first sentence *their friends* links up with *their political supporters,* thus leaving *special treatment* as the newest information in the last position. In the second set, *patronage* links up with *special treatment,* thus leaving *their political supporters* as the newest information in the last position.

Here is another pair of sentences illustrating how English allows the same idea to be expressed with a different group structure to serve the needs of coherence:

Jonas Salk perfected the cure for polio.
The cure for polio was perfected by Jonas Salk.

The first sentence follows the pattern, S/P/DO; the second follows the pattern S/P/OO. On the surface the two sentences are dramatically different in their structures. But on a deeper level any reader knows that they express the same idea: The thing that happened was somebody *perfecting* something; the one who did the perfecting was *Jonas Salk;* the thing that got perfected was *the cure for polio.* We know this despite the fact that *Jonas Salk* is the subject of the first sentence and an oblique object in the second, and despite the fact that *the cure for polio* is the direct object in the first sentence and the subject in the second sentence, and despite the fact that the predicate is a one-verb verb phrase in the first sentence but adds an auxiliary (*was*) in the second sentence. The second sentence is a *passive sentence.* Why should English allow two such different sentence structures to express the same idea? It does so primarily to serve the kinds of coherence demands that were discussed in the last chapter and in the preceding several paragraphs of this chapter. Passive sentences allow you to place the logical doer of a verb's action last when you want to indicate that its information is the new contribution to the on-going discourse. If someone asked you, *What did Jonas Salk do?*, you would probably answer with the active sentence, *Jonas Salk perfected the cure for polio* (the first sentence above), but if you were asked, *How did we eradicate polio?*, the more coherent answer would be the passive sentence, *The cure for polio was perfected by Jonas Salk* (the second sentence above). You can also use passive sentences when you wish to state what happened to something already mentioned (thereby putting it first) and thus to let the idea of the predicate occupy the position of new information at the end of the sentence:

Where's your car? *My car was stolen.*

The above sequence is more coherent than this possible alternative:

Where's your car? *Someone stole my car.*

The car was already mentioned in the question, so it is not the idea the questioner wants to hear (and is therefore not best positioned at the end of the answer). The passive provides a way of putting the car first and placing the information about stealing at the end of the answer.

These are some of the important ways in which English provides flexibility in the arrangement of sentence parts in discourse. It is useful to know something about them, but even more important to practice with them as a way of gaining greater control over your sentences as you forge the chains of coherence that well-written edited English demands. The following exercises will give you some opportunity for practice with them.

Exercises

a. Each of the following sentences contains an adverb phrase or a prepositional phrase functioning as an adverbial modifier. Identify it, and then rewrite the sentence, placing the adverbial modifier in another position. If it can appear in more than one other position, write a sentence for each of those positions. Here is the answer to number (1):

During our graduation ceremony, we had to listen to more than a thousand names.

(1) We had to listen to more than a thousand names during our graduation ceremony.
(2) Yesterday the mail carrier delivered my income-tax forms.
(3) Snow storms almost always happen at inconvenient times.
(4) The government has recently been trying to control inflation.
(5) Quite commonly, vacationers experience gas shortages.
(6) Most students study better in the morning.

b. Some of the following sentences have two prepositional phrases after the verb, each one functioning as an oblique object. Other sentences have no oblique objects, but do have direct objects. If you find two oblique objects, rewrite the sentence, interchanging the order of the oblique-object prepositional phrases. If you find a direct object, rewrite the sentence with the direct object at the beginning, set off by a comma. Here is the answer to number (1):

The parents' association should talk with the school finance committee about funding.

(1) The parents' association should talk about funding problems with the school finance committee.
(2) The treaty must safeguard democratic principles.
(3) Political candidates will argue with anyone about anything.
(4) The kindergarten teacher was reading to the children about nutrition.
(5) This crisis requires clear thinking.
(6) The governor is writing about the deficit to the legislature.

c. Some of the following sentences have indirect objects. If a sentence does have an indirect object, rewrite the sentence and place the indirect-object noun phrase into an oblique-object prepositional phrase. (Indirect objects convert to prepositional phrases with *to* or *for*). If, on the other hand, you find a noun phrase in a prepositional phrase (with *to* or *for*), which *could* be expressed as an indirect object, rewrite the sentence and express it as an indirect object. Here is the answer to number (1):

Joan and Danny's grandfather built them a beautiful new play house.

(1) Joan and Danny's grandfather built a beautiful new play house for them.
(2) The Supreme Court may grant that convicted murderer a stay of execution.
(3) Don't give them any hints.
(4) Can you give my neighbors the address of your mother's business?
(5) My grandmother used to bake me cookies on my birthday.
(6) One time I mailed my state income taxes to the federal government by mistake.

d. If a sentence is active, change it to passive; if it is passive, change it to active. Here is the answer to number (1):

The stranded child was rescued by a traveler from another state.

(1) A traveler from another state rescued the stranded child.
(2) A new plan of action was agreed to by the committee.
(3) The dance contest was won by a girl from another school.
(4) The long distance runners will determine the outcome of the track meet.
(5) Wars are won or lost by foot soldiers.
(6) The children of immigrants built the classic skyscrapers of Manhattan.

Combining Sentences

In order to make sentences fit coherently into the context of a paragraph, you will often find it necessary to revise their structure. Sometimes you will change two independent clauses into one complex sentence; at other times you may do the opposite. The revisions in the sample paragraph presented at the beginning of the previous chapter (p. 115) showed how combining sentences can improve coherence. The aims of this section are (1) to explain some of the many ways you can combine simple English sentences into a variety of more complex sentence structures and (2) to give you opportunities to practice using these sentence-combining techniques.

Sentences as nouns

These two sentences were given earlier as examples of complex sentences with noun clauses:

That Paraguay is an officially bilingual country surprises some Americans. Many young people do not believe *that they are responsible for their actions.*

These two sentences can be viewed as combinations of the following pairs of sentences:

Paraguay is an officially bilingual country. This surprises some Americans. People are responsible for their actions. Many young people do not believe that.

Only the context can determine whether to express such ideas as two simple sentences or as one complex sentence with a noun clause. Questions can also appear as noun clauses. Examine these two sentences:

The student government president is wondering about something. Can she win another term?

The question expressed in the second sentence can become a noun clause and replace the phrase *about something* in the first sentence. Here is how:

> The student government president is wondering whether she can win another term.

Notice that it was necessary to use the word *whether* and to take the subject (*she*) out of the predicate (*can she win* changed to *she can win*) in order to reshape the question into a noun-clause question. Notice also that a question mark does not appear after a sentence that has a question functioning as a dependent noun clause.

There are two other ways, not yet discussed, in which English grammar allows a sentence to be reshaped so that it can function as a noun does in another sentence. The structures that allow this to happen are not fully developed clauses, but in some ways they resemble clauses. In other ways, they resemble phrases and are in fact generally called phrases. The first is the *gerundive phrase (GerP)* and the second is the *infinitive phrase (InfP)*.

Gerundive phrases express ideas similar to those in noun clauses and they can perform the same functions in sentences as noun clauses and noun phrases. They are headed by an *-ing* form of a verb, which is given the name *gerund (Ger)*. Notice the structures and functions of the gerundive phrases in the sentences diagrammed on page 155.

Notice that the gerundive phrase *discussing problems* resembles a clause when analyzed internally (*discussing* is a predicate and *problems* is its direct object), but the phrase as a whole is more like a noun phrase because it functions as subject of the predicate *is*. Notice, too, that the gerundive phrases in the second and third sentences, while resembling clauses internally, function like noun phrases in the sentence as a whole (*building sand castles* is a direct object, and *listening to good music* is object of a preposition in a prepositional phrase functioning as an adverbial modifier).

There is another variety of gerundive phrase that even more closely resembles a noun clause. Compare the first sentence below, which illustrates this type of gerundive phrase, with the second sentence, where the same idea is expressed as a noun clause:

> *Ted's entering the race* was a sure thing.
> *That Ted entered the race* was a sure thing.

In the first sentence above, *Ted's entering the race* is a gerundive phrase where, structurally, the possessive noun *Ted's* precedes the gerund *entering*. Functionally, however, we can consider *Ted* to be the subject of the predicate *entering*, and we can consider *the race* the direct object of *entering*.

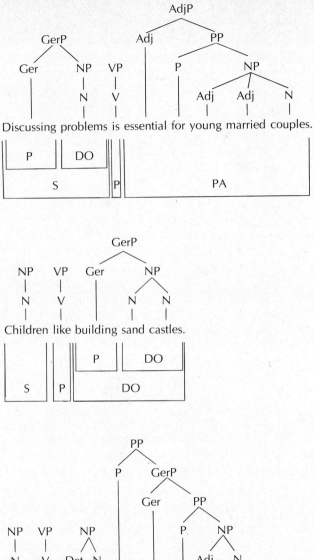

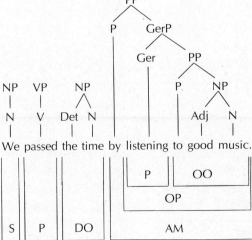

Infinitive phrases are like gerundive phrases because they express ideas similar to those in noun clauses and can thus perform the same functions in sentences as noun clauses or noun phrases. An infinitive phrase (InfP) consists of the preposition *to* structured together with a verb phrase. In the sentence analyzed below, the infinitive phrase is playing the role of subject:

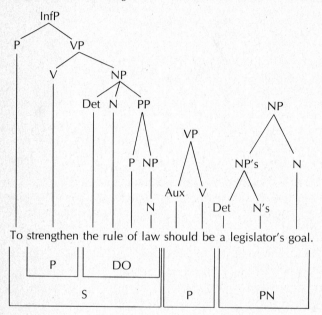

There is another variety of infinitive phrase that resembles a noun clause even more closely than the one illustrated in the sentence above. Compare the first sentence below, which illustrates this other type of infinitive phrase, with the second sentence, where the same idea is expressed as a noun clause:

> *For the ambassador to miss that appointment* was inexcusable.
> *That the ambassador missed that appointment* was inexcusable.

In the infinitive phrase in the first sentence above, the preposition *for* and a noun phrase precede the preposition *to* which marks the structure as an infinitive phrase. Even though, structurally, the italicized sequence in the first sentence is an infinitive phrase and not a clause, the functions of the groups within it are the same as if it were a clause: *The ambassador* is subject; *miss* is predicate; and *that appointment* is direct object.

Exercises

a. Each numbered item in this exercise consists of two sentences. Combine the two into one sentence by turning the second sentence into a noun clause and inserting it into the first sentence in place of the italicized word or words. Be prepared to discuss the function of the noun clause in the sentence you create. Here is the answer to number (1):

That a person can succeed in life without working hard is a foolish idea.

(1) *Something* is a foolish idea.
   A person can succeed in life without working hard.
(2) I used to think *something*.
   The moon was made of green cheese.
(3) I do not know *something*.
   Can I remain active in athletics and still maintain a high scholastic average?
(4) The messenger informed the mayor about *something*.
   A snow plow had buried the mayor's car.
(5) The solution to the energy crisis depends on *something*.
   Are the American people ready for sacrifice?
(6) When I was sixteen, I wondered about *something*.
   Where was life going to lead me?

b. Each numbered item in this exercise also consists of two sentences. Combine the two into one sentence by turning the second sentence into a gerundive phrase and inserting it into the first sentence in place of the italicized word or words. Be prepared to discuss the function of the gerundive phrase in the sentence you create. Here is the answer to number (1):

Worrying about the future is an activity reserved for the human species.

(1) *Something* is an activity reserved for the human species.
   Members of the human species worry about the future.
(2) *Something* can help preserve our natural resources.
   We recycle our newspapers.
(3) I can't stand *something*.
   I have to wait two weeks to find out my grades.
(4) Scientists must avoid *something*.
   Scientists confuse just one experimental result with a new law of nature.
(5) A healthy person is especially capable of *something*.
   A healthy person works hard and thinks clearly.
(6) Harry was upset with *something*.
   Mary left early.
(7) Teachers usually dislike *something*.
   Students eat in class.

c. Each numbered item in this exercise also consists of two sentences. Combine the two into one sentence by turning the second sentence into an infinitive phrase and inserting it into the first sentence in place of the italicized word or words. Be prepared to discuss the function of the infinitive phrase in the sentence you create. Here is the answer to number (1):

The surgeon tried to remove the bandage very carefully.

(1) The surgeon tried *something*.
   The surgeon removed the bandage very carefully.

(2) *Something* should be every person's dream.
Every person makes a significant contribution to the good of humanity.
(3) The King and Queen of Spain told Columbus *something*.
Columbus should sail west and see what he could find.
(4) Parents often seem to expect *something*.
Their children act like angels.
(5) I would like *something*.
I have time to enjoy a challenging profession and also to enjoy art and music.
(6) The object of the game of chess is *something*.
Someone checkmates the opponent's king.

Sentences as adjectives

These sentences were given earlier as examples of complex sentences with relative clauses (clauses that, like adjectives, modify nouns):

I once climbed a tree *that was planted by my grandfather.*
Students *who plan a literary career* should read broadly.

These two sentences can be viewed as combinations of the following pairs. of sentences:

I once climbed a tree. The tree was planted by my grandfather.
Certain students should read broadly. Certain students plan a literary career.

The context will determine whether to express ideas like those above as two simple sentences in succession or whether to make one of the sentences into a relative clause modifying a noun in the other sentence. For two sentences to be combined into a complex sentence with a relative clause, each of them must contain some noun in common. Both sentences in the first pair above talked about the same tree; both sentences in the second pair mentioned the same group of students. In the sentence that becomes the relative clause, the noun held in common becomes the relative pronoun *who* (or *whom*) if it refers to a person, and it becomes *which* if it refers to a thing or idea. Alternatively, the relative pronoun *that,* which is slightly less formal than *who, whom,* or *which,* can be used instead of any of these three.* Here are a few more examples of pairs of sentences and complex sentences with relative clauses combin-

---

* In edited English, when a relative pronoun refers to a person, some writers prefer *who* and *whom* to *that.* However, when a relative pronoun refers to a thing or idea, they prefer *that* in restrictive relative clauses (*Universities that need money often hire fund raisers*) and *which* in nonrestrictive relative clauses (*Universities, which need money, deserve our support*). See p. 145 for a discussion of the distinction between restrictive and nonrestrictive relative clauses.

ing them. In each set, examples with *who, whom,* and *which* on the one hand and *that* on the other are given.

John bought the bench. Albert made the bench.
John bought the bench *which Albert made.*
John bought the bench *that Albert made.*

I paid the women. The women delivered the refrigerator.
I paid the women *who delivered the refrigerator.*
I paid the women *that delivered the refrigerator.*

We saw earlier (p. 156) that an infinitive phrase can function like a noun clause. Let us now take a look at some sentences where infinitive phrases function like relative clauses and thus modify nouns. In the sentence diagrammed below, *to build for her brother* acts like a relative clause because it gives information about *which* models were given to Kathy.

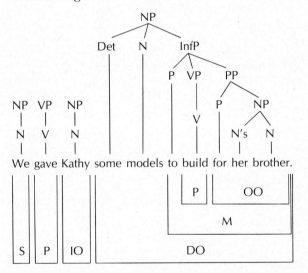

The above sentence can be viewed as a combination of the following two sentences:

We gave Kathy some models.
She would build the models for her brother.

Here are some other examples of infinitive phrases used as noun modifiers. First is given a pair of sentence; then a combined sentence where the second sentence of the original pair has been combined with the first by turning it into an infinitive phrase:

I need some money. I will invest the money in gold bullion.
I need some money *to invest in gold bullion.*

Married couples need more time. They spend the time in relaxing conversation.

Married couples need more time *to spend in relaxing conversation.*

You can make a sentence behave like an adjective in yet another way. In addition to creating relative clauses and infinitive phrases that act as noun modifiers, you can also turn a sentence into a *participial phrase.* Participial phrases are like gerundive and infinitive phrases in that they resemble clauses, but unlike gerundive and infinitive phrases, they can *only* function as noun modifiers. A *participle (Par)* may be defined as an inflected form of a verb occurring without an auxiliary. *Present participles* end in *-ing,* and *past participles* end in *-en* or *-ed.* The first sentence diagrammed on page 161 has a participial phrase with a present participle; the phrase modifies the noun *woman.* The second sentence has a participial phrase with a past participle; the phrase modifies the noun *car.* The first sentence can be viewed as a combination of the first pair of sentences printed below; the second sentence can be viewed as a combination of the second pair of sentences.

The car hit a woman. The woman was wearing dark glasses.
A car was found in Maryland. The car was stolen in Texas.

Exercises

a. Combine each of the following pairs of sentences into one complex sentence with a relative clause by inserting the second sentence into the appropriate place in the first sentence. Here is the answer to number (1) (the relative pronoun *that,* in place of *who,* would also be acceptable):

The country needs some leaders who have new ideas about inflation and energy.

(1) The country needs some leaders.
    The leaders have new ideas about inflation and energy.
(2) Hank Aaron's home-run record is an achievement.
    The achievement will endure for many decades.
(3) The candidate will have an uphill fight against the incumbent.
    The convention nominates the candidate.
(4) The pictures of the planet Jupiter were spectacular.
    Voyager II sent back the pictures of the planet Jupiter.
(5) My sister worked for ten months to earn the money.
    The money paid for our new stereo.

b. Turn the second sentence in each of the following pairs into an infinitive phrase and insert it into the appropriate place in the first sentence. Here is the answer to number (1):

All I need for a restful evening is a book to read in a quiet atmosphere.

(1) All I need for a restful evening is a book.
    I read the book in a quiet atmosphere.

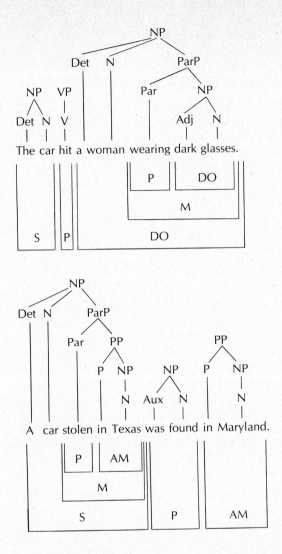

(2) Many young parents do not have enough experience.
Experience helps them cope with the problems of raising children in a period of uncertain values.

(3) The children of the rich often have too much money.
They spend the money on useless gadgets.

(4) Most underdeveloped countries ask only for adequate technological assistance.
Technological assistance helps them grow their own food and build their
own housing.

c. Each numbered item in this exercise also consists of two sentences. Combine
the two into one sentence by turning the second sentence into a participial phrase

(whether it has a present or past participle depends on the structure of the second sentence) and then inserting the participial phrase into the first sentence in place of the italicized word or words. Here is the answer to number (1):

The fittest person participating in the race won the Boston Marathon.

(1) The fittest person *who did something* won the Boston Marathon.
     The person participated in the race.
(2) A woman *who does something* should get rid of all her junk.
     The woman moves to another city.
(3) Serious health problems can afflict people *who do something*.
     People diet without a doctor's supervision.
(4) Students *of some kind* should read more.
     Students are confused by basic philosophical ideas.
(5) Thomas Jefferson was a man *of some kind*.
     Thomas Jefferson was respected and appreciated by his fellow citizens.
(6) During a play *of some kind* the audience may be attacked by the actors.
     The play was written by an avant-garde author.

Sentences as adverbs

Adverb clauses, like all adverbial modifiers, give information about how, where, when, why, or how often the action or state described in the predicate occurs. Here are some examples of sentences with different types of adverb clauses. Each one can be viewed as a combination of the pair of sentences printed just below it. In each case the italicized adverb clause replaces the italicized prepositional phrase in the first sentence of the pair.

Prices will come down *when we all start conserving fuel.*
Prices will come down *at some time.* We all start conserving fuel.

Long-distance swimmers can often endure *until they become too tired to stay awake.*
Long-distance swimmers can often endure *up to some limit.*
They become too tired to stay awake.

The third-world countries refused to take responsibility for the crisis *because they had nothing to do with its causes.*
The third-world countries refused to take responsibility for the crisis *for some reason.* They had nothing to do with its causes.

Notice that adverb clauses are introduced by words like *when, until,* and *because*. These are called *subordinating conjunctions* and they signal to a reader or listener the fact that a dependent adverb clause is part of a sentence. They also signal the nature of the relationship between the dependent clause and the main clause.

Sentences can also become adverbial modifiers in other sentences when you turn them into infinitive phrases. Here is a sentence in which the italicized infinitive phrase is an adverbial modifier telling *why* John studied intensely:

To pass the test, John studied intensely.

The above sentence combines these two ideas:

John studied intensely *for some reason.* John wanted to pass the test.

Here are a few other examples of infinitive phrases used as adverbial modifiers. Below each is a pair of sentences that the sentence seems to combine:

Lincoln accepted war *to preserve the Union.*
Lincoln accepted war *for some reason.* Lincoln preserved the Union.

You should be honest and hard working *to earn the right to use the fruits of others' work.*
You should be honest and hard working *for some reason.*
You earn the right to use the fruits of others' work.

Exercises

a. Use the subordinating conjunction given at the end of the pair of sentences to turn the second sentence into an adverb clause. Then put the adverb clause into the first sentence in place of the italicized phrase. Here is the answer to number (1):

Most of the children waited at the camp site while the adults searched for a way out of the storm-damaged canyon.

(1) Most of the children waited at the camp site *during some activity.*
    The adults searched for a way out of the storm-damaged canyon. (while)
(2) Motor cyclists should wear helmets *for some reason.*
    Many head injuries to cyclists result in epilepsy. (because)
(3) Some tyrants continue to waste the resources of their countries, *despite opposing views.*
    The majority of the people in their countries want to use them wisely. (although)
(4) Proponents of abortion focus on the feelings of the mother *despite opposing views.*
    Opponents of abortion focus on the basic right to life of all living human beings. (whereas)
(5) You should always study your facts very carefully *before something.*
    You decide to argue with a professional. (before)

b. Turn the second sentence in each of the following pairs into an infinitive phrase and insert it into the first sentence in place of the italicized words. Here is the answer to number (1):

> Most high school graduates go to college to learn skills they need to compete effectively in the job market.

(1) Most high school graduates go to college *for some reason.*
    They learn skills they need to compete effectively in the job market.
(2) *For some reason,* farmers use modern chemical fertilizers.
    Farmers make the earth produce more grain than ever before.
(3) *For some reason,* emergency workers are very careful about accident victims.
    They avoid worsening internal injuries.
(4) Control of English sentence structure is necessary *for some reason.*
    Writers shape sentences to fit appropriately into larger discourse contexts.

Seven | *Sentence Repair*

All English varieties—standard and vernacular, written and spoken, careful and casual—structure sentences according to the principles discussed in the past two chapters. But each variety has some special structural features of its own. Certain vernacular dialects use *right* as an intensifier of adjectives (*That's a right nice tie you're wearing*). Edited English limits it to use with adverbs (*The committee wishes to have the report right now*). Casual style readily allows the objective form of the pronoun to function as a predicate nominative (*The person who called yesterday was her*). Edited English requires that the subject form of pronouns function as predicate nominatives (*The person who called yesterday was she*). This chapter closely examines such special requirements of edited English in sentence structure. It focuses on issues that you probably will have most trouble with because, in these matters, edited English differs from most spoken styles and informal written styles. This chapter emphasizes matters that have a general application to sentence structure. Matters that depend on special needs of particular words (such as the difference between *lie* and *lay*) are treated in the usage glossary in the Appendix (pp. 329–340).

Fragments, Splices, Run-ons

The first problem in writing edited-English sentences is the problem of *recognition:* You have to know where one sentence ends and the next begins. You signal this to your reader with punctuation (which is treated in detail in Chapter Eleven). For now, the problem can be put this way: (1) Sometimes writers end a set of words with a period, but those words do not constitute a sentence, and (2) sometimes writers *fail* to end a set of words with a period, although that set *is* a sentence. These inexpert writers either use a comma instead of the required period, or they use no punctuation at all. If you use a period to set off words that are not a sentence you have written a *sentence fragment:*

> You should obey every law. *Even if you don't think it treats you fairly.*

The italicized words above are not a sentence but a dependent clause and should be set off by a comma (without capitalization of *even*). Here is another fragment:

> There is one thing that really bothers me about some salespeople. *Telling one customer one thing and another customer something else.*

Notice that the italicized words do not contain a subject. Only imperative sentences may appear without a subject. The word *telling* should be replaced by *They tell.*

The reverse problem occurs when two sentences are punctuated as one. The following sentences are examples of an error known as the *comma splice* (everything after the italicized words constitutes an entirely new sentence and should be separated by a period and capital letter, not by the comma):

> *Carbohydrate diets can be dangerous,* too many starches and fats can lead to heart disease.
> *My older sister loves rock music,* my younger sister can't stand it.

The third type of recognition error is very much like the second, but here the two sentences are not even separated by a comma. In the following sequence an entirely new sentence begins where the italics end, but there is no indication of this in the punctuation:

> *Don't fall for easy money schemes* the consequences could ruin you financially.

Sometimes *run-on sentences* like the above actually fuse two sentences together creating an impossible grammatical structure. Notice how the writer of the following sentence tries to use the words *our civic league* simultaneously as object of a preposition in one sentence and subject in another:

> The commissioner mailed a reply to the president of our civic league voted unanimously against the proposed project.

Here are some ways of solving the above problem:

The commissioner mailed a reply to the president of our civic league. *Our civic league* voted unanimously against the proposed project.

Instead of writing an entirely new sentence, the second idea could be expressed as a clause:

The commissioner mailed a reply to the president of our civic league, *which* voted unanimously against the proposed project.

For many writers, all of the above sentence faults are merely punctuation problems. If such is the case, then the treatment of punctuation in Chapter Eleven is the place to find help. If such problems indicate a real difficulty in recognizing exactly what a sentence is, then additional work with the matters treated in the past two chapters will be necessary.

Exercise

Read the following passage, and identify and label all the sentence faults as fragments, comma splices, or run-ons. Then rewrite the entire passage to correct the errors:

I got a new car last week I just walked into a used-car dealer and picked it out. One of those late-fifties models with big fins in the back and chrome all over. I knew I wanted it as soon as I saw it, the colors were red and black. The dealer was asking $200.00. A price that was $50.00 more than I could afford. So I offered $150.00, he took it. I was relieved when I drove the car out of that place was a real clip joint. I don't feel I was cheated. Because I know a lot about cars. I've worked on it every day, keeping it running won't be too hard.

Agreement Between Subject and Predicate

The subject and predicate in an English sentence must agree. This means that the choice of a certain noun or pronoun as head in the subject group determines the form of the first item in the predicate group. At the top of page 168 is a diagram that shows how this works.

Break and *have* are typical of all the rest of the verbs in English. Notice that an *s* is added when the subject is *he, she, it,* or a singular noun (and only in the present tense). The verb *to be* (both auxiliary and linking verb) is a special case. It has two columns in the chart. The first represents its present-tense forms; the second, its past-tense forms. Notice that it must change its spelling to agree with the subject, both with *he, she, it* and singular nouns, on the one hand, and with *I* on the other. And, unlike any other verb in English, it also agrees with the subject in the past tense, requiring the use of *was* with *I, he, she, it,* and singular nouns.

If the head word in the subject group is:	Then any of the following, if it is the first word in the predicate group, must be spelled:			
I ⟶ break	have	am	was	*(Italicized forms*
you ⟶ break	have	are	were	*are those that*
he, she, it or singular ⟶ *breaks* noun	has	is	was	*show agreement by changing from the typical*
we ⟶ break	have	are	were	*spelling.)*
they or plural ⟶ break noun	have	are	were	

The basic facts of subject–predicate agreement are easy enough to understand. Problems arise, however, in identifying what the subject is; if the writer is not sure of this, then there is no way the verb can be chosen to agree with it. Here are some typical problems and suggestions on how to deal with them:

(1) Treat subjects conjoined by *and* the same as the pronoun *they:*

The president and his cabinet *are* (not *is*) meeting.
Hard work and a little luck *make* (not *makes*) for success.

There is an exception: If the conjoined subject represents a single idea, treat it the same as *he, she,* or *it:*

Bacon and eggs *is* (not *are*) a good breakfast.
Bread and butter *goes* (not *go*) with meat and potatoes.

(2) Treat subjects conjoined by *or* the same as the pronoun that matches the one closest to the verb:

Ford or *Chrysler is* developing an electric car.
Peas or *carrots are* included with the entree.

Either the president or *the courts have* jurisdiction.
Either the courts or *the president has* jurisdiction.

(3) Expressions of amount, distance, weight, fraction, time, or money should ordinarily be treated the same as *he, she,* or *it:*

Two weeks *is* (not *are*) long enough for a vacation.
Five miles *is* (not *are*) not far to drive to work.
I think 75¢ *is* (not *are*) a lot for a candy bar.

Two and two *equals* (not *equal*) four.
Three fourths of eight *is* (not *are*) six.

(4) Treat *the number* the same as *he, she,* or *it:* treat *a number* the same as *they:*

The number of people in this auditorium *is* against fire regulations.
A number of people *are* trying to leave the room.

(5) Treat a word or series of words introduced by *every* or *many a* the same as *he, she,* or *it:*

Every student, professor, and administrator *is* asked to conserve electricity.
Many a young woman *joins* the armed forces nowadays.

(6) When initial adverbials cause the subject to follow the verb, be sure the subject and verb still agree:

Where *are* my *socks?*
There *is* one *sock.*
Here *is* the other *sock.*

(7) Do not lose track of the subject and mistakenly make the verb agree with the noun in a modifying prepositional phrase:

A *teacher* with several degrees *finds* (not find) it hard to get a job.
One of those custom-home builders *is* (not *are*) coming over tonight to give us an estimate.

Exercise

Choose the verb form that agrees with the subject:

(1) One of the scientists who developed the moon rocket (has, have) recently died.
(2) Either my next-door neighbors or the woman who lives across the street (is, are) considering moving.
(3) The shipment of packages (arrives, arrive) tomorrow.
(4) Here on my desk (is, are) a large dictionary and a smaller one.
(5) My two sisters and my brother (builds, build) houses for a living.
(6) A number of petitions (was, were) filed with the zoning board last month.
(7) There (is, are) a new job or two additional courses awaiting the results of my exams.
(8) Three months (is, are) a long time to spend away from people you love.
(9) A carton of eggs (is, are) in the refrigerator.
(10) Either the passangers or the driver (was, were) responsible for the accident.
(11) The reason for so many homework assignments (is, are) to give you all the practice you can get.

Agreement Between Pronoun and Antecedent

Pronouns usually refer back to a noun or nouns already mentioned in a discourse:

John lost *his* money.
Mary and I decided that *we* should exercise.
The children want their parents to allow *them* to stay up late.

The noun that a pronoun refers back to is called its *antecedent*. The pronoun must agree in number with its antecedent: In the first sentence above, *John* and *his* are both singular; in the third sentence *children, their* and *them* are all plural. A pronoun must also agree in person with its antecedent: In the first sentence above, *John* and *his* are both third person; in the second sentence both the phrase *Mary and I* and the pronoun *we* are first person. A pronoun must also agree in gender with its antecedent: In the first sentence above, *John* and *his* are both masculine.

Writers do not usually find it hard to make pronouns agree in person and gender with their antecedents, but number agreement can cause difficulty. Here are some typical problems and suggestions on how to deal with them:

(1) Use singular pronouns to refer to singular antecedents and plural pronouns to refer to plural antecedents.

A *person* must do *his or her* (not *their*) best to conserve energy.
The *members* of the team showed their (not *his or her*) appreciation to the coach.

If the antecedent is a compound noun joined by *and,* use a plural pronoun:

My mother and my aunt allowed me to lend *their* skis to my friends.

If the antecedent is a compound noun joined by *or* or *nor,* use a pronoun that agrees with the nearest antecedent:

Neither my cousins nor *my brother* would allow me to lend *his* skis to my friends.

Sometimes compound antecedents with *or* or *nor* can create awkward situations, and complete rewording is called for. The first of the following two sentences should probably be revised to read like the second.

Either John or *Sally* asked me to help *her;* I can't remember who.
Either *John* asked me to help *him* or *Sally* asked me to help *her;* I can't remember who.

(2) Use singular pronouns to refer to antecedents such as: *anybody, anyone, one, everybody, everyone, each, either, neither, somebody,* and *someone.*

Each of the candidates has to disclose *his or her* (not *their*) finances. *Anyone* who uses the facilities must agree that *he or she* (not *they*) will help to keep them clean.

Usage is rapidly changing on this matter, and increasing numbers of writers are using plural pronouns to refer to antecedents such as those listed above. Most careful writers, however, still use singular pronouns. If you find phrases like *he or she* and *his or her* awkward, then you may want to revise your sentences to avoid this agreement problem altogether. For help in doing this, reread the section on generic pronoun reference in Chapter Four (pp. 108–110), where issues closely related to this were discussed in the framework of paragraph consistency.

(3) Choose either singular or plural pronouns to refer back to collective nouns according to whether the collective noun is used in a singular or plural sense:

The *committee* should consider *its* annual budget.
The *committee* should not argue among *themselves.*

(4) Use pronouns only when their antecedents are clear to the reader. The reference of *she* is not clear in the following sentence, because there are two possible antecedents, *Mary* and *Helen.*

Mary told Helen that *she* was eating too much.

Depending on what the sentence is intended to mean, it could be rewritten in one of the following ways.

Mary said to Helen, "I'm eating too much."
Mary told Helen that Helen was eating too much.

The reference of the italicized *it* in the following set of sentences is not clear because it is too far from its antecedent, *car.*

That *car* was a beauty. I bought it just after I had gotten out of college and started my first job. *It* wasn't very expensive.

Either the italicized *it* should be replaced by *the car,* or the last sentence should be moved next to the first sentence.

Exercise

Correct any problems of agreement between pronouns and antecedents in the following sentences.

(1) The jury could not agree whether it should adjourn or continue deliberating through the night.

(2) A student who holds a job and goes to school at the same time must make certain that they have enough time to study.

(3) I studied the records of both candidates and found that neither had kept the promises that they had made in earlier campaigns.

(4) The Board of Supervisors spent several hours considering their agenda.

(5) When Mary introduced John and Bob, I could tell that he didn't recognize him.

(6) Someone obviously stole the bicycle while we were out of town, but no clues were left to help us identify them.

(7) The senator and the representative generally support programs that benefit people who have supported him.

(8) The school play was the product of many months of hard work by many people. Production money was very hard to find. It was very enjoyable.

(9) Even though the ordinary citizen is willing to sacrifice for the good of the country, they resent it when some people are exempted from sharing the hardship.

Placement of Modifiers

The freedom you have to move around both groups and clauses in sentences can sometimes get you into trouble. A noun or verb modifier sometimes expresses the central idea of a sentence and thus sounds best toward the end of the sentence. Or the modified word itself may express the new idea and appear at the end, but its modifier may make a nice transitional expression at the beginning. Such needs of coherence are important, but do not let them confuse the basic message of the sentence. Always make sure that the modified word is in fact expressed in the sentence and placed as close as possible to its modifiers. The italicized gerundive, participial, and infinitive phrases in the following sentences are called *dangling modifiers* because the word each modifies is not even expressed in the sentence:

Standing in line, the rain was drenching.
Exhausted from the climb, the mountain was conquered.
To get into college, a high school diploma is necessary.

How would you rephrase these sentences to express the word modified by the introductory phrases? Think about it before you read the following suggested revisions:

Standing in line, *we* were drenched by the rain.
Exhausted from the climb, *I* had conquered the mountain.
To get into college, *an applicant* needs a high school diploma.

The italicized words in the following sentences are called *misplaced modifiers* because they are not close enough to the word they modify to make their role clear:

The Nigerian ambassador *only* speaks English at press conferences.
Give me all applications from foreign firms *that were filed on time.*

If read literally, the first sentence above states that the Nigerian ambassador spends all day every day speaking English at press conferences. The writer of the sentence probably did not mean to assert that. Rather, one of the following two meanings was probably intended. *Only* should be placed to show which of these two was meant:

The Nigerian ambassador speaks *only* English at press conferences.
The Nigerian ambassador speaks English *only* at press conferences.

Try rephrasing the other sentence to make the reference of the italicized modifier clear. Think about it before you read the following suggested revisions:

Give me all applications *that were filed on time* from foreign firms.

Notice that *applications* is modified by a clause (italicized) and a phrase (*from foreign firms*). Moving the clause before the phrase does not completely solve the problem, because the reader might now think that *from foreign firms* modifies *time*. Here is a more drastic revision that seems to work better:

Give me all *foreign* applications *that were filed on time.*

The italicized word in the following sentence is called a *squinting modifier* because it is next to two words either of which it might relate to logically:

Swimming *often* helps your heart.

Do not read the following revisions until you have thought of two rewordings of the sentence, each of which makes one of the possible functions of *often* clear. The problem is not so easy to solve as it may seem. The one meaning expresses the idea that a lot of swimming helps your heart. The other expresses the idea that (any amount of) swimming can often help your heart. Moving *often* either to the very beginning or to the very end emphasises the *second* meaning:

Often, swimming helps your heart.
Swimming helps your heart often.

To relate the idea of *often* only to *swimming*, a comma can help:

Swimming often, helps your heart.

Or a complete rewording may be needed:

A lot of swimming can help your heart.

The placement of modifiers is a complex and subtle problem in edited English. Many of the problems just illustrated do not occur in spoken English because pauses and loudness often clarify relationships not expressed in the word order. You must become sensitive to this problem and work out any deficiencies in clarity, especially when you are revising a paper.

Exercise

Identify the problem with placement of modifiers in the following sentences (dangling, misplaced, or squinting), and then rewrite the sentences to resolve the problem:

(1) The former president has not even granted one interview to the press.
(2) John said today to buy a new dish.
(3) To write an effective paragraph, it should be unified and coherent.
(4) Delighted by the victory, the trophy was proudly accepted.
(5) While drinking a glass of wine, a cat sat on the guest's lap.
(6) Rewriting the paper, it received an A.
(7) The pilot of the plane radioed the tower having engine trouble.

Case in Pronouns

The case of a noun or pronoun is its function in the sentence. In many languages the actual spelling of a noun will change according to whether it is subject, direct object, indirect object, etc. In English, only the pronouns make significant changes in their spellings according to the grammatical role they play.

Pronouns that play the role of *subject* and *predicate nominative* must be spelled as follows:

I, you, he, she, it, we, they, who, whoever

Pronouns that play the role of *direct object, indirect object,* and *object of a preposition* must be spelled as follows:

me, you, him, her, it, us, them, whom, whomever

Pronouns that play the role of *noun modifier* (i.e., that fill the same position as a noun with apostrophe and *s*) must be spelled as follows:

my, your, his, her, its, our, their, whose

The choices seem simple, but for a variety of reasons there are a number of problems in choosing the correct pronoun case in edited English. Here is a list of things you need to watch out for to choose the correct case for pronouns in edited English:

(1) Do not be confused by compound subjects; choose from the list of subjective pronouns:

You and *they* (not *them*) are going to be blamed for the accident.

(2) Choose from the list of subjective pronouns to fill the role of predicate nominative:

Though Harold and Mary discussed the amendment, the one who actually wrote it was *she* (not *her*).

(3) Remember that pronouns in many comparative sentences are implied subjects; choose from the list of subjective pronouns:

Chris and Tommy both play tennis, but she is better than *he* (not *him*).

(4) Do not be confused by compound objects; choose from the list of objective pronouns:

The attorney general appointed John and *them* (not *they*) to investigate the scandal. (Direct object)
The mayor sent that police officer and *me* (not *I*) a letter of commendation. (Indirect object)
The winnings of this hand will be divided between you and *me* (not *I*). (Object of a preposition)

(5) In edited English use *whom* and *whomever* (instead of *who* and *whoever*) to fill the roles of direct object, indirect oject, and object of a preposition:

Whom did NASA pick to pilot the first space shuttle?
The government will pay *whomever* the judges choose.
Elizabeth I was a monarch *whom* the people admired.

In the second sentence above, *whomever* is the direct object of *choose* in the dependent noun clause. Here is a sentence where *whoever* is the appropriate choice because it is the subject of *designs* in the dependent clause (the choice of *whoever* or *whomever* in dependent noun clauses depends on the function of the pronoun in the noun clause):

The government will pay *whoever* designs the best electric car.

(6) Choose from the list of noun-modifier pronouns before a gerund (i.e., a verb that is functioning as a noun and that ends in *-ing*):

I can't stand *your* (not *you*) complaining about everything I ask you to do.

The Air Force approved *his* (not *him*) borrowing the plane for a mercy mission.

Exercise

Choose the correct form of the pronoun in each of the following sentences and state why it is correct.

(1) You should try your best to marry someone (who, whom) you love.

(2) The mayor who did most for this city was (she, her).

(3) Some local politicians are upset about (me, my) asking them to reveal their financial sources.

(4) (Who, Whom) would be a better choice for entertainer of the century than Elvis?

(5) For you and (they, them) the decision about solar heat is an important one.

(6) My parents and (I, me) have dinner together every Friday night.

(7) (Whoever, Whomever) the team selects, I will support.

(8) I don't know to (who, whom) that letter was addressed.

(9) Our neighbors are much more athletically inclined than (we, us).

(10) The IRS has already mailed Joe and (I, me) our refunds.

(11) Be sure to admit (whoever, whomever) arrives on time.

(12) The State Department appointed eight citizen-ambassadors but sent only Mary and (he, him).

Overuse of Passives

In the previous chapter (pp. 150–151) I suggested that passive sentences help serve the needs of creating coherent discourses in English. When a writer wishes to present the agent of some action as new information at the end of a sentence, a passive sentence like the following is appropriate:

Such problems must be faced head-on by an effective chief executive.

Or if the action of the verb itself is the key new information and the agent is either unknown or irrelevant an agentless passive sentence like the following is appropriate:

Such problems must be solved.

But too many passive sentences in a discourse tend to make it dull and uninteresting. At best the reader feels that actions and states are occurring on their own with little human involvement or control. Sometimes writers write such discourses to avoid responsibility—they know who the agent is but do not want to admit it:

The assignment sheet was misplaced, and as a result the paper was not written on time.

What the writer meant was this:

I lost my assignment sheet, so I did not write my paper on time.

Scientists and technical writers sometimes prefer passives to give their writing the air of objectivity; they want the writer to feel that their doings have an inevitable character, that it is not people who are responsible but immutable laws of nature:

The nuclei of the atoms were bombarded for many hours by subatomic particles. After several series of trials, three new types of particles were discovered.

The above passage might also have been written like this, but with less of a scientific air:

We bombarded the atoms for several hours with subatomic particles. After several series of trials, we discovered three new types of particles.

Be aware of passive sentences when you write. Do not use them unless you intend to use them and unless they clearly strengthen your writing's coherence.

Exercise

Here is a paragraph whose effectiveness and vividness are significantly weakened by overuse of passives. Rewrite it and name names: Who wasted the water? Who is prohibiting additional waste? Who will pay the consequences of further waste?

Reference is made to the problem created during the recent dry spell. Water was wasted because lawns were watered too much and cars were washed needlessly. Your neighborhood has been designated as a special problem area. Water pressure will be reduced during daylight hours and lawn watering and car washing will be prohibited. The prohibition will be enforced rigorously. Violators will be issued a summons and if improvement is not made, they will be fined. Through these means, the problem should be solved.

Faulty Parallelism

When I treated the paragraph in Chapter Four, I recommended the use of parallel grammatical structure as a means of strengthening the coherence of the paragraph: Sentences expressing similar or logically related ideas should follow the same grammatical patterns. But parallelism is also at work within the sentence. And here it is not just recommended; it is required. What this means is that items joined by conjunctions should represent the same grammatical class. Not only simple conjunctions such as *and, but, or,* and *nor,* but also correlative conjunctions such as *both . . . and, either . . . or, neither . . . nor,* and *not only . . . but also* have this requirement. It means that sentences like the following are not permitted in edited English:

> John is a *worker* and *productive.* (*And* joins a noun and an adjective.)
> My daughter likes *swimming, boating,* and *to water ski.* (*And* joins two gerunds and an infinitive phrase.)
> I like to work in my yard not only *in the morning* but also *when it's cloudy.* (*Not only . . . but also* joins a prepositional phrase and a dependent clause.)

Instead of the above, sentences like the following are preferred:

> John is a *worker* and an *achiever.* (Two nouns are conjoined.)
> John is *diligent* and *productive.* (Two adjectives are conjoined.)
> My daughter likes *swimming, boating,* and *water skiing.* (Three gerunds are conjoined.)
> I like to work in my yard not only *in the morning* but also *on cloudy days.* (Two prepositional phrases are conjoined.)

Faulty parallelism can also result from misplacing the conjunction:

> The IRS will *not only* be happy to advise you about your taxes *but also* to help you fill out your returns.

The items intended for conjoining are *to advise* and *to help,* thus *not only* should immediately precede *to advise,* not *be happy:*

> The IRS will be happy *not only* to advise you about your taxes *but also* to help you fill our your returns.

You must take great care in edited English to conjoin only elements of similar grammatical structure and to place your conjunctions carefully.

Exercise

Correct the faulty parallelism in each of the following sentences. Sometimes you need only move a conjunction to another position in the sentence. Usually you need to reword the sentence so that conjoined items represent the same grammatical class.

(1) The president should try not only to govern efficiently but also he should set ideals for the country.

(2) Not only is she fair with her employees but also with her colleagues.

(3) All college students should have a course in composition and how to speak in public.

(4) To apply was easy, to get the reply letter was scary, but reading the acceptance letter was a relief.

(5) The forestry department wants you to buy trees, to plant them, and fertilizing should be accomplished.

(6) Political dictators are interested neither in consulting the people, nor do they want to please the people.

(7) Their criticisms of the seniority system arose from its inefficiency, its unfairness, and failing to allow for flexibility.

(8) I attend college not only to learn but also because I hope to get a better job.

(9) The alumni awarded trophies both to coaches and players.

(10) She is not only proficient in swimming but also in diving.

Eight | *Words*

As a speaker of English, you already know thousands of words—their pronunciations, spellings, and meanings. However, one thing a writer learns early is that using words effectively presents a never-ending challenge. To help you face that challenge, this chapter takes a close look at English vocabulary: where words come from, how they communicate meaning, and how they affect people. And the next chapter looks at dictionaries, focusing on how to use them efficiently to learn more about words. You will read much about individual words in this chapter and the next, but your real aim should be to understand the general concepts so that you can apply them to the task of building a larger and more effective vocabulary. You especially want to learn to use words accurately and effectively in edited English, choosing the word that best suits your purpose and influences your reader just the way you want. The study of vocabulary with this kind of effective rhetorical use in mind is called *diction*.

Sources of Words

Words are at the center of the symbolic function of language. When children begin to speak, they name things; only months later do they begin to combine words into sentences. Most language scholars believe that language originated in the human species in much the same way: that generations of early humans had names for things in their environment long before any of them learned to combine words into sentences.

180

But the dawn of language is so many centuries back, we can never fully know the origin of words. However, we do know a lot about the history of English vocabulary during the past 1500 years or so.

A history of English vocabulary

The English language came to England beginning in the fifth century. It was the tongue of several Germanic tribes who began raiding the coasts of what was then an island peopled by Celtic tribes who had been ruled for 200 years by the Romans. The Germanic invaders eventually gained control over most of what is now England. Many of the Celts were pushed westward to Wales and Cornwall; others, northward to Scotland. Many remained and intermarried with the Germanic conquerors. The language spoken by the conquering tribes and their descendents from the fifth to the middle of the eleventh centuries is called *Old English.* Its vocabulary originated in the tribal homelands in northern Europe before the dawn of history. But from the time these earliest speakers of English settled in England, they borrowed words eagerly from the languages of peoples around them. Many Latin words in use in Celtic Britain found their way into Old English. Later waves of invasions by Danish tribes beginning late in the seventh century added Danish vocabulary to Old English. Here are some examples of modern vocabulary that come from these three sources during the Old English period:

(1) Native Germanic words:

wife, food, stone, winter, good, corn, blood, hand, land, heart, father, head, love, sleep, sit, knave, loaf, brother, ground

(2) Latin words from the time of the Roman occupation of Britain:

camp, toll, pound, chalk, copper, wine, pea, pepper, plant, belt, cup, dish, pan, kitchen, pin, line, wall, fever

(3) Danish words from the late Old-English period:

band, dirt, egg, fellow, freckle, leg, sister, skin, sky, steak, window, gap, guess, trust, scare, ill, meek, sly, they, their, both, same, though, till

In 1066 William the Conqueror, Duke of Normandy (a province in France), conquered England. His language and that of his court was Medieval French. For the next 200 years England was ruled by French-speaking nobles and clergy. The English of this period, called *Middle English,* borrowed many thousands of French words. Here are some of them:

(4) Middle-English French borrowings:

> justice, prince, image, reason, saint, religion, fruit, crown, council, discipline, city, dangerous, silence, joy, story, chair, peace, uncle, aunt, change, poor, rich, arrive

French is itself a descendent of Latin; so all words borrowed into English from French come ultimately from Latin. But many words were borrowed directly from Latin during the Middle-English period. Here are some of them:

(5) Middle-English borrowings directly from Latin:

> conspiracy, custody, distract, history, include, incredible, individual, private, quiet

The English of the period from about the middle of the fifteenth to the end of the seventeenth centuries is referred to as *Early Modern English*. From then to the present the language is called *Modern English*. These periods of Early Modern English and Modern English encompass the Renaissance, the Industrial Revolution, and the whole array of advances spanning the birth of modern science to the present age of technology. During these centuries England and later America were deeply involved in trade and sometimes conflict with many cultures. Here is a sampling of some modern English vocabulary borrowed from other languages during these periods (the lists of words and even of languages are far from complete):

(6) Arabic:

> algebra, arsenal, monsoon, assassin, jar, apricot, giraffe, hashish, alcove, sofa, harem, candy, safari, zero

(7) German:

> plunder, sauerkraut, hamster, cobalt, quartz, nickel, iceberg, poodle, vermouth, protein, semester, seminar, noodle, hex, frankfurter, hamburger, poker, bun, loafer, nix, liverwurst

(8) Hebrew (often through Latin, Greek, or French):

> amen, manna, rabbi, sapphire, babel, jubilee, hallelujah, kosher

(9) Italian:

> umbrella, bandit, motto, balcony, concert, opera, soprano, finale

(10) Japanese:

> sake, hara-kiri, tycoon, geisha, zen, kamikaze, karate

(11) North American Indian languages:

raccoon, moccasin, moose, muskrat, hickory, succotash, chipmunk, squash, powwow

(12) Slavic languages (e.g., Russian and Polish):

Czar, vodka, polka, intelligentsia, robot, sputnik

(13) Spanish:

anchovy, comrade, tornado, canyon, alligator, mosquito, banana, guitar, cafeteria, vanilla, plaza, marijuana, cigar, rodeo, stampede, bonanza

(14) Turkish:

horde, tulip, vampire, turban, fez

The vast majority of the words we use every day are either native Germanic words or Middle-English French borrowings, but English surpasses all the world's languages in the variety of sources from which it has taken its vocabulary. Hardly a day goes by that each one of us does not use some words borrowed from a half dozen languages.

Exercises

a. Below are four versions of one verse from the Parable of the Prodigal Son (Lk. 15:13). As you read the four versions, pay special attention to the italicized words. Notice how the various forces just described not only added words to the list of English vocabulary, but caused some to disappear. Look up the italicized words in a dictionary and find out how they got into the English language. (If you do not know how to find this information in a dictionary, consult pp. 212–217 in the next chapter.)

(1) Modern English (twentieth century):

A few days later, the younger son got together everything he had and left for a *distant country* where he *squandered* his *money* on a life of *debauchery*. (From *The Jerusalem Bible*)

(2) Early Modern English (sixteenth century):

And not many days after the younger son gathered all together, and took his *journey* into a *far country*, and there *wasted* his *substance* with *riotous* living. (From *The King James Bible*)

(3) Middle English (fourteenth century):

And not after many *daies*, whanne alle *thingis* weren gederid togider, the gonger sone wente forth in *pilgrymage* in to a *fer cuntre*; and there he *wastide* hise *goodis* in lyuynge *lecherously*.

(4) Old English (tenth century):*

> þā æfter fēawum dagum eall his þing gegaderode sē gingra sunu, and fērde wræclīçe on feorlen rīçe, and forspilde þǣr his ǣhte, libbende on his gǣlsan.
>
> (Then after few days all his things gathered the younger son and journeyed (fared) wandered-like (wretch-like) in far land, and wasted (for-spilled) there his wealth, living in his wantonness.)

b. Below are reprinted the words given earlier as representative of the native Germanic vocabulary that survives in modern English. Virtually all of the words have changed their spellings and pronunciations since the Old-English period and some have changed their meanings. Consult a dictionary and find out both the Old-English spelling and meaning of each word and also the Middle-English spelling and meaning. (If you do not know how to find this information in a dictionary, consult pp. 212–217 in the next chapter.)

> wife, food, stone, winter, good, corn, blood, hand, land, heart, father, head, love, sleep, sit, knave, loaf, brother, ground

c. Consult a dictionary to determine the language from which English borrowed each of the following words. (If you do not know how to find this information in a dictionary, consult pp. 212–217 in the next chapter.)

> alcohol, avocado, candle, cheese, cockroach, coffee, concert, cousin, frustrate, ghetto, give, journey, judo, kindergarten, mile, obedience, piano, podunk, popular, pretzel, satan, sherry, skirt, skunk, submit, them, tundra, zinc

Word formation

Many modern English words are neither native, in the sense that they have been in the language for thousands of years, nor borrowed, with little or no change, from another language. Some English words have simply been invented out of thin air. Many have been formed out of other words by a variety of processes. Let us look at some of them.

Invention. Only very few words have been invented out of thin air. Two frequently mentioned examples are *Kodak* and *Nylon*. The following common nouns derive from proper names, and in a sense appeared from nowhere at a given period in history with the meanings they now have: *lynch, boycott, sandwich, ohm.* Each of these words has a fascinating story associated with it. Did you know for instance that no one was ever said to "boycott" anything until it happened to Charles C. Boycott in the middle of the nineteenth century? He was the land agent for an Irish

---

* Pronounce þ the same as the *th* in *think;* pronounce ç the same as the *ch* in *chin;* pronounce g̣ the same as the *y* in year.

earl and lost his job when the earl's tenants got together and refused to pay their rents.

Prefixes and suffixes. New words may be formed by adding prefixes to old words:

*bi*focal, *post*war, *pre*school, *inter*marry, *sub*conscious, *hyper*active, *ultra*-modern, *un*zip, *dis*infect, *non*conformist

Or new words may be formed by adding suffixes to old words:

sister*hood*, lecture*ship*, mob*ster*, imperial*ism*, rapid*ity*, clever*ness*, approv*al*, employ*er*, puzzle*ment*, deaf*en*, null*ify*, modern*ize*, cheer*ful*, self-*ish*, commend*able*, odd*ly*, alarm*ist*

Compounds. New words may be formed by combining two old words:

doghouse, facecloth, daybreak, headache

English has hundreds of such compound words in common use. Some words may be formed by a combination of processes. Here are two words formed by both compounding and adding suffixes:

beekeeper, songwriter

Blends. Some English words have been formed by fusing only parts of two old words:

smog (from *smoke* and *fog*), *brunch* (from *breakfast* and *lunch*), *motel* (from *motor* and *hotel*), *moped* (from *motor* and *pedal*).

Clipped words. Some new words have been formed by clipping off parts of old words:

fan (from *fanatic*), *van* (from *caravan*), *auto* (from *automobile*), *photo* (from *photograph*), *exam* (from *examination*), *intro* (from *introduction*)

Acronyms. These are really extreme cases of clippings. Some acronyms consist simply of the first letters of what was a phrase; the letters retain their alphabetical names and might be called *initialisms*:

YMCA, FBI, UN

Most acronyms are pronounced as though they were words, not sequences of letters of the alphabet; they derive nonetheless from the first letter or first few letters of several words in sequence: NATO (from *N*orth *A*tlantic *T*reaty *O*rganization), UNESCO (the *U*nited *N*ations *E*ducational, *S*cientific, and *C*ultural *O*rganization), WASP (*W*hite *A*nglo-*S*axon *P*rotestant); *Nabisco* (from *Na*tional *Bi*scuit *Co*mpany).

Folk etymologies. The spellings or pronunciations of both native and borrowed words are sometimes changed because speakers of English think they are hearing something they are not. The word *female* was originally spelled *femelle* because it was borrowed from French, where *fêmme* means "woman," and the suffix *-elle* means "little"; the English word *male* actually has nothing to do with the origin of this word. Similarly, the word *shamefaced* was spelled *shamefast* during the Middle-English period; *fast* is the same word part as occurs in *fasten* or the phrase *hold fast;* the English word *face* really has nothing to do with the origin of this word.

Back formation. A few English words have been formed by removing suffixes from words that were borrowed into English with them already attached. That is, the word with the suffix existed in English before the word without it did. (This can be considered a special type of clipping.) Here are some examples:

> *preempt* (from *preemption*), *electrocute* (from *electrocution*), *televise* (from *television*), *peddle* (from *peddler*), *swindle* (from *swindler*), *edit* (from *editor*)

Exercise

Each of the following words was formed by one (or a combination) of the eight processes just discussed. Consult a dictionary and find out which one it was. (If you do not know how to find this information in a dictionary, consult pp. 212–217 in the next chapter.)

> poisonous, snafu, paratroops, tricycle, pompadour, Dacron, fruity, flu, stockholder, burgle, memo, transplant, newscast, wooden, amoral, flowerbed, radar, cutlet, gym, crayfish, GI, semifinal, rainfall, SUNOCO, cockroach

The Meanings of Words

Every writer should be familiar with the rich history of English vocabulary and with the many word-formation processes even now at work in the language. But even more important is knowledge of what meaning is and how words convey it. These are complex issues. Let us approach them indirectly (inductively) by starting with some specific observations and working up to generalizations and definitions.

Read the following sentence, trying to notice what is happening in your mind as you do:

A crystal football hovers above the Astrodome.

What did happen? A scene was created inside you. A small world came into being in your mind. You pictured a "thing" shaped like a football, but transparent like glass. It hovered magically in space above an athletic arena in Houston, Texas, called the Astrodome. The definition of the word *meaning* depends crucially on this ability you have as a human being to create this kind of special world inside you. Its dimensions are limited only by the content of your experience and the creative powers of your imagination. You can close your eyes and seem to *be* somewhere else: by the sea or in the mountains. You seem to smell the air or even feel the sand or pine needles under foot. Often enough, this inner world takes its stimulus from direct experience: you look at a snow-capped mountain, turn away, but still "see" it in your mind. Later, a snapshot of the mountain may set you to thinking about it again. Or the word *mountain* could bring the reality back into consciousness. Notice that, unlike the photograph, there is nothing about the word *mountain* (its shape, its letters, its sounds) that in any way resembles a real mountain. But somehow those letters have the power to recreate the mountain inside you. Meaning is nothing more or less than that inner world. And the "meaning" of a word like *mountain* is just that portion of the inner world that recreates your experience of the mountain.

Human beings are especially fortunate in that the inner world of meaning is in no way limited by the outer world of reality. There does not have to be a real crystal football for you to be able to think of one. And if you invented a word, say *puntoid,* for such an object, it would have no less meaning than a word like *Astrodome.* Nor does real-world gravity keep it from floating in air above the Astrodome in your mind.

Anything that you see, hear, touch, smell, or taste, and that registers in your mind, has meaning. In this sense, the sight of a mountain has meaning if you pay enough attention to it to remember it. So does the smell of a flower or the taste of a pizza. But a shape or a sound or a smell can also have the power to mean something other than itself. If it does, it is called a *symbol.* If the feel of another's hand in yours makes you think of friendship, it is a symbol. If the sound of a siren makes you think of stopping your car, it, too, is a symbol. And if the eight letters that constitute the word *mountain* make you think of a mountain, then this word, too, is a symbol. *Words are sequences of letters or sequences of sounds that are symbols and that thus have the power to create an inner world of meaning in the human mind.* Let us now take a closer look at some of the ways they do this.

Concrete and abstract meanings

Words with concrete meanings, such as the ones on the left below, make you see, hear, touch, smell, and even taste things in your mind.

Abstract words, such as the ones on the right, do not. Some words, such as those in the middle, may or may not, for there can be degrees of concreteness.

Concrete		**Abstract**
blade	pain	suffering
scratch	wound	
cut		
blood		
numb		
clench		
scream		
wind	the elements	nature
snow		
ice		
frost		
slime	slum	poverty
rats		
rags		
dirt		
cockroach		
rose	flower	beauty
violet		
daisy		
tulip		
claws	attack	danger
teeth		
growl		
hiss		
rattle		
fang		
apple	fruit	sustenance
pear	juicy	succulent
plum		
orange		

When you write, you must take careful note of each word's ability to create a concrete image in your reader's mind. Your purpose will usually determine whether you should favor concrete or abstract meanings. A military officer informing parents that their son was killed in action would favor abstract vocabulary to describe his wounds and the circumstances of his death but concrete vocabulary to describe his bravery and his qualities as a friend so that they could have once more in words the experience of being with their son. For most purposes, concrete vocabulary is better than abstract vocabulary because it will force your readers to relate your message to their own life experiences.

Exercises

a. Below is a selection of abstract words. Write each one to the right on a sheet of paper and then make a list on the left of concrete words that have related meanings. If there are words that seem more concrete than the words on the right but less concrete than the words on the left, write them in the middle. When you finish, you should have several displays like those presented on page 188. Here are the words:

(1) authority
(2) confusion
(3) fear
(4) tenderness

b. Here are some sentences containing abstract words (in italics). Rewrite the sentences using concrete vocabulary. Choose words that will breath life into the message: that will make your reader see, hear, and feel what the sentence is about. Here is a sample problem sentence:

When I saw the *danger,* I called for help.

Here is a possible answer for the above sentence:

When I saw the claws and teeth and heard the growls, I called for help.

(1) Bruce Jenner won the decathlon at the 1976 Olympics because he had developed his skills in *sports.*
(2) When the firefighters arrived at the scene they *showed tenderness to* the fear-stricken children.
(3) During a course in composition, you are expected to *show progress.*
(4) Inside Fort Knox, Kentucky, there is room after room filled with *wealth.*
(5) The amateur set out cautiously to walk the high wire, but half way across she stopped and *showed fear.*
(6) Many corporations and individuals would like to get their hands on Howard Hughes's *assets.*
(7) The prices of packaged foods at supermarkets are skyrocketing because farmers are spending more to *produce commodities.*
(8) Elvis Presley was an entertainment sensation because he *had talent.*
(9) People flock to ski resorts on winter weekends because of *the enjoyment.*
(10) I live in Manhattan because I have a profound interest in *the arts.*

Literal and figurative meanings

The literal meaning of a word is its ordinary meaning, the one everybody uses, often unthinkingly. A figurative meaning is out of the ordinary; like a figure or drawing, it attracts a reader's attention and thus tends to be more forceful and dramatic. Below is a list, with examples, of some "figures of speech." It begins with the most dramatic of the figures, metaphor, and ends with allusion, a type of meaning that many do not consider dramatic enough even to qualify as figurative (I include it anyway).

Metaphor. The figurative force or drama is created by transferring a word from what it ordinarily designates to something entirely new, thus creating an implied comparison or analogy. The transfer may be quite explicit, as in the sentence *Politicians are worms,* where the word *worms* does not designate a small boneless, limbless, creeping creature at all but a certain group of humans (albeit ones with certain worm-like qualities). The transfer may also be implicit, as in the sentence *His life flickered precariously, but his spirit still blazed brightly,* where *flicker* and *blaze*—verbs usually describing fire—are transferred to a person, thus forcefully dramatizing the person's fight with death by creating an implied comparison of the idea of life with the idea of fire.

Simile. The force and drama of a simile are similar to metaphor; the only difference is that the comparison is expressed explicitly by the words *like* or *as*:

> Politicians are like worms.
> His life flickered as does a flame, but his spirit blazed as brightly as a fire.

Oxymoron. Here, the dramatic effect results from joining two contradictory terms (and thereby forcing the reader to look for new depths of meaning in each term). The phrase *cruel kindness* in the following sentence is an example:

> The professor's cruel kindness in giving me an F taught me that I needed to study.

Here are some other examples: *brilliant stupidity, roaring silence, impoverished wealth, make haste slowly, be conspicuous by your absence.*

Hyperbole. Here, the dramatic effect results from exaggerated overstatement, as in *I could eat a horse,* or *This typewriter weighs a ton.* The ordinary meanings of *horse* and *ton* are not literally intended.

Metonymy. Here, the meaning of a word is dramatically extended to cover some closely related idea that it does not literally designate. In the sentence *He lost his job because he could not give up the bottle,* the word *bottle* does not literally designate a glass container, but figuratively designates the contents of that container (alcoholic beverage) and even the habit of drinking too much of it. In the sentence *Washington has raised taxes,* the word *Washington* does not literally designate the city, but rather designates figuratively the people in that city who make up the federal government.

Allusion. This may be considered figurative when a word, or phrase, or even a whole sentence, adds force or drama to a discourse by referring indirectly to something else beyond the literal. If a student writes in an appeal to the faculty, *We students must have life, liberty, and the pursuit of happiness,* the last seven words, in addition to their literal meanings, have a figurative force because they allude to the Declaration of Independence and all the principles of freedom treated in that document. If strikers demand of management their *daily bread,* then these words, in addition to their literal meanings (enough bread for each day), allude dramatically to ideas contained in the Lord's Prayer.

Guidelines for using figurative language.

Here are a few guidelines, with examples, that can help you to use figurative meanings effectively when you write.

1. *Be sure that you, and your intended ideas, are firmly in control of any figurative meanings your words express; do not let them control you.* This sounds easy, but it is not, for the English language has very many worn-out figures of speech (worn-out metaphors are even called *dead metaphors*). And these seem to have a tendency to appear on their own. Here for example are some sentences from an early draft of the first paragraph of this chapter. I have italicized the figurative language:

This chapter *looks* closer at English vocabulary: where words come from, how they communicate meaning, how they affect people, how they *work together* in sentences. And the next chapter *looks* at dictionaries, *focusing* on how to use them efficiently to learn more about words.

When I wrote that passage, I did notice that the word *looks* and *focusing* were used figuratively when transferred to the word *chapter.* That is, a chapter is simply a collection of words on a page; it does not literally have eyes to look with or lenses to focus. But the figure did dramatize and clarify what was going to happen in this chapter by having the reader think of the chapter as if it were a person with eyes. I must confess, however, that I used the figurative expression *work together* without realizing it. It is transferred to *words*; by saying that words work together, I had the reader think about words as things or people capable of working. I'm not sorry that I used that particular implied metaphor. But if I had paid more attention to what I was doing, I might have *used* the metaphor more effectively by building on it in the following way:

This chapter looks at why we *employ* certain words for certain purposes, how they *get the job done,* how they affect people, and how they *work together* in sentences.

The revised sentence uses the transfer more effectively, by forcefully impressing on the reader the idea that words are like workers: If we hire them, and give them the right working conditions, they will do more for us than we tell them to do. (In revising the sentence, I considered changing *affect people* to *sell our ideas to our audience,* but I decided that would be overdoing it.)

2. *Try to create new figurative meanings whenever they strengthen your purpose and plan, and always prefer fresh figures to ready-made ones.* Read your drafts at least once to scrutinize your figurative language. Then make changes such as the one I illustrated above. If you discover that an unintended figure of speech does not contribute to your purpose, remove it. But think about it. Even very worn-out figures can be given new life if you lend them the help of your imagination. Here are some examples of some really worn-out expressions (in italics) that were given such help by very imaginative writers:

Baldwin occasionally *stumbles over the truth,* but he always hastily picks himself up and hurries on as if nothing had happened.

—WINSTON CHURCHILL

You don't tell a man he's in the *twilight of his life* when he thinks it's mid afternoon.

—Line from a television situation comedy

Kennedy won *by an eyelash* and some thought it was a false eyelash.

—HOWARD K. SMITH

.I don't want to be *thrown off the track* by every nutshell and mosquito's wing that falls on the rails.

—HENRY DAVID THOREAU

3. *Do not overuse figurative language, and, even more important, do not mix several figures when writing about one topic.* Here is a passage that (comically) illustrates this problem:

We've got talent here, but we obviously need some *shoring up* in several positions *depth-wise.* This year we have to do a lot of *weeding out* and see what *cream comes to the top.*

—Quoted in the Spokane *Spokesman-Review*

All the italicized words transfer meanings to a business or organization. But how can it be a building that needs shoring up, and at the same time be something with depth, and a garden or yard needing weeding, and also cow's milk waiting to settle! The figurative language does not add force or drama; it adds only confusion.

Exercises

a. Identify all of the figurative expressions you can in each of the following passages. Label them, using the six figures of speech discussed above. Evaluate the effectiveness of the figurative language in each passage.

In Pirandello's plays, the bait of appearance masks the hook of reality, but the mysterious fish of life is never caught.

—T. E. KALEM in *Time,* November 14, 1977

Their great love, in which she lived completely immersed, seemed to be ebbing away, like the water of a river that was sinking into its own bed; and she saw the mud at the bottom.

—GUSTAVE FLAUBERT, *Madame Bovary*

Arcadio had seen her many times working in her parent's small food store but he had never taken a good look at her because she had that rare virtue of never existing except at the opportune moment. But from that day on he huddled like a cat in the warmth of her armpit.

—GABRIEL GARCÍA MÁRQUEZ, *One Hundred Years of Solitude*

The author's polished images evoke whole landscapes and interiors. But on occasion they leave his characters as rigid as snapshots. Like the subjects of most candid portraits, the characters sometimes appear as unfocused, refugees wrenched by the camera from the context of their lives. The stop-and-start chapters abort their growth and development; some are simply dropped or disappear inexplicably for hundreds of pages.

—Adapted from a review by Paul Gray in *Time,* September 29, 1975

b. For each of the figures of speech listed below, find or invent two sentences containing a word or expression that illustrates the figure. Identify the word or expression and justify your claim about the figure of speech it represents.

(1) Metaphor
(2) Simile
(3) Oxymoron
(4) Hyperbole
(5) Metonymy
(6) Allusion

Denotative and connotative meanings

At the beginning of this section, I stated that words have the power to create an inner world of meaning in the human mind, and that the contribution of each word to that inner world is its meaning. But this inner world of meaning, like the outer world it mirrors, is a complex one. It is a world of facts and objective realities on the one hand, but it is also a world of feelings and subjective values on the other. When the biological life of a human being ends, we might say that the person "died" or that the person "passed away." As far as the objective facts are concerned, both words mean the same thing. But the subjective feelings evoked by each in that inner world of meaning are different. If the deceased is a loved one, it somehow does not hurt as much to say "passed away." This expression has less of the fear and pain of death associated with it than the word "died" has. The bare, unadorned, factual meaning of a word is called its *denotation*. The feelings, moods, or associations suggested by a word constitute its *connotations*. If we take the whole meaning of a word to be the sum of its denotations and connotations, then "died" and "passed away" do not in fact mean the same thing. They have the same denotation (termination of biological life) but vastly differing connotations.

The connotations of a word may be as varied as is the range of human feelings and emotions. Nonetheless, it is possible and useful to treat connotations as though they fell neatly into just three general categories: positive, neutral, and negative. Consider the following three words: *economical, inexpensive,* and *cheap.* All three have the power to denote the amount of money spent on a vacation:

> The Browns had an economical vacation.
> The Browns had an inexpensive vacation.
> The Browns had a cheap vacation.

The first sentence in no way implies that the Browns did not enjoy themselves, even though they limited their spending—that may even have added some to the adventure. The last sentence clearly implies that their "cheap" vacation was not much fun at all. The middle sentence is neutral: It is up to the reader to decide how much the Browns enjoyed themselves. Here is a table listing the above examples and a few others on a scale from positive through neutral to negative connotations. Notice as you examine it that the emotions that form the basis of the connotations vary and that there are degrees of positive and negative connotations:

Positive		Neutral		Negative
economical		inexpensive		cheap
hefty	stout	corpulent	overweight	fat
enterprise	project	job	chore	scheme
creative	probing	curious inquisitive	prying	nosey

The negative connotation of a word like *fat* derives from the feeling of embarrassment and self-consciousness people experience or see others experience when (especially as children) others make fun of them. But the negative connotation of the word *scheme* derives less from an intense personal feeling than from a judgment of illicitness or illegality.

It is extremely important for the writer of edited English to be sensitive to connotations. You can thoroughly undermine your purpose and confuse your reader if, in an expository essay, you use too many words with strong connotations (positive or negative). On the other hand, in an argumentative essay that aims to evaluate or exhort, appropriately chosen connotations can reinforce your purpose and sharpen your influence on your reader.

Exercises

a. Arrange each of the following columns of words on a scale from positive through neutral to negative connotations. Be prepared to discuss the reasons for your ranking.

(1) cop	(2) brave	(3) female	(4) casual	(5) fresh
smokey	audacious	chick	disordered	naive
pig	daring	woman	sloppy	untried
officer	cocky	libber	unkempt	green
fuzz	bold	lady	messy	new
police	foolhardy	fox	untidy	inexperienced

b. Examine the following three passages. For the most part, the denotations and the grammatical structure in each have been held constant. It is mainly the connotations of the differing vocabulary choices that distinguish the passages. Evaluate the effects of word connotations in each passage. What are the connotations of the individual words? What is the overall effect of each passage on the audience?

At the climax of 1977, President Sadat offered peace initiatives to Israel. Prime Minister Begin endorsed the initiatives and invited Sadat to visit Israel to initiate the reconciliation process.

At the end of 1977, Mr. Sadat proposed truce talks to Israel. Mr. Begin agreed with the idea and asked Sadat to come to Israel to begin the negotiation process.

At the close of 1977, the President of Egypt put the challenge of face-to-face negotiations to Israel. The Israeli Prime Minister accepted the challenge and called on his counterpart to journey to Israel to begin the bargaining process.

c. Here are some sentences in which a word is out of place because something about its connotation does not match the message, implied audience, or implied purpose of the rest of the sentence. Determine what the word is, prepare yourself to discuss the reason why it is inappropriate, and be ready to suggest and to justify an alternate word:

(1) The school psychologist advised the parents to seek help for their daughter because she was crazy.

(2) The princess, who was wearing a corsage, delighted the diplomatic corps; not only did she look beautiful, she also reeked of orchids.

(3) In the wake of Watergate, Americans determined never again to be victimized by naughty politicians.

(4) Federal law requires that girls with graduate degrees be given equal pay for equal work.

(5) Thomas Edison was such a famous inventor because he had a fidgety mind.

The Social Impact of Words

Recall that language was compared to clothing in the section on language variation in Chapter One. Clothes have a function, to cover the body, but they are also cultural symbols. A derby and a cowboy hat both protect the head from cold or sun, but the former generally labels one as British, the latter as American. Similarly, *lorry* and *truck* both denote the same thing, but the former labels the speaker as British and the latter as American. A pin-striped suit and coveralls both serve equally well the function of clothing the body, but the former labels one as upper class or a white-collar worker and the latter as working class or a blue-collar worker. Similarly, the words *philistine* and *jerk* may both denote a person whose actions indicate ignorance and lack of taste, but *philistine* tends to label its user as white-collar and *jerk* tends to label its user as blue-collar. The social aura accompanying a word, of course, contributes to its connotations. So in a real sense this section constitutes a closer look at certain types of word connotations and how to use them effectively.

Regionalisms, colloquialisms, and slang

All three types of phenomena to be treated in this section relate to words or expressions that are inappropriate in edited English because they are too strongly associated with another dialect or style of English.

Regionalisms. Regionalisms are words or expressions that are generally used and fully understood only in a certain part of the United States. They should be avoided in edited English not only because readers in your audience from other parts of the country may not understand them, but also because they tend to connote that the writer has a limited or provincial perspective (i.e., they can undermine your credibility with your audience). Actually, regionalisms will probably not cause you serious problems. Most of them refer to homey, everyday things you will not often find a need to discuss in edited English. But be sensitive to them nonetheless. Here are some examples:

carry (This means "take or drive a person" in parts of the South: *I carried my grandmother to the grocery store yesterday.*)
hoagie (This means "submarine sandwich" in parts of the middle Atlantic region.)
light bread (This means "white bread' in parts of the South.)
poke (This means "paper bag" in parts of the East.)
pulley bone (This means "wish bone" in parts of the South.)
snap bean (This means "green bean" in parts of the South.)

Colloquialisms. Colloquialisms present a different kind of problem for the writer. These are words or expressions (often originating in a regional vernacular dialect) that tend to be reserved for use only in spoken English. As a result, you should avoid them when you write, because they connote that the user is uneducated, or worse, that the writer intends subtly to insult the reader by being too casual and familiar. Using colloquialisms in edited English would be comparable to wearing tennis shoes along with the expected suit and tie to a formal occasion such as a wedding. Colloquialisms can have as many shades of connotations as there are social relationships in our culture. Here are some colloquialisms that tend to turn up in carelessly edited student papers. Watch out for them, and avoid them:

ain't
anyways
anywheres
being as
being that
broke (Do not use it as an adjective: *My car is broke.*)
can't hardly
could of
don't (Do not use this contraction with third-person singular pronouns: *She don't like school.*)
figure (Do not use this to mean "think": *I figure she'll be here later.*)
folks
gonna
gotta
had ought to
hadn't ought to
kind of (Do not use this as an intensifier: *I'm kind of sad.*)
learn (Do not use this to mean "teach": *She'll learn him chemistry real well.*)

might could
mighty (Do not use this as an intensifier: *We're mighty glad.*)
nowhere near
outside of (Do not use this phrase to mean "except": *Everyone outside of John got there on time.*)
plenty (Do not use this word as an intensifier: *They were plenty mad.*)
reckon
right (Do not use this word as an intensifier: *I'm right glad to see you.*)
scairt
should of
somewheres
sort of (Do not use this as an intensifier: *I'm sort of sad.*)
sure (Do not use this to mean "certainly": *I sure like ice cream.*)
theirselves
up and (Do not use this to mean "all of a sudden": *She up and died.*)
upside (Do not use this to mean "on": *He got hit upside the head.*)
ways (Do not use this to mean "distance": *We have a ways to go.*)
would of
you all, y'all
youse
y'uns

Slang. Slang is often confused with colloquialism. Indeed, the two types of vocabulary share certain characteristics. Slang words, like colloquialisms, tend to be used only in speech—but this is not their defining feature. Slang words, like colloquialisms, have a connotation of informality —but this is not their defining feature either. Slang consists of words characterizing casual style that have originated in a given cultural group or subgroup, are often short-lived, and carry a strong connotation of group membership.

The slang of college students may serve as an example. When students speaking among themselves use words like *prof, econ, cram, poly sci, all-nighter,* and *the pits,* they are not only denoting certain things; they are identifying themselves and their listeners as members of a group who share a certain comradeship as students.

The special slang in use among East-Coast naval personnel may serve as another example. When sailors speak of going to *the Med* (a sea tour in the Mediterranean Sea), when they refer to *the brass* (higher officers) or *airedales* (naval fliers) or *Brits* (British sailors), or when they ask about the latest *scuttlebutt* (gossip), they are not only conveying denotations, they are also connoting a sense of shared membership—even of shared values.

Whenever we use slang we connote that we are relaxed in the presence of our listeners and that they should be relaxed in our presence. Often, slang words and expressions that have originated in a certain group achieve a broader use (*scuttlebutt* is an example). But as long as such words retain the connotation of shared group membership they may still be considered slang.

When you write edited English, you are not necessarily required to avoid slang altogether. But you should certainly be fully aware when you use it, and you should make very sure that any slang expressions support your purpose and help your reader understand your message. You use such expressions inappropriately whenever they stand out too obviously and draw attention away from your message.

Exercises

a. The following sentences would probably be inappropriate in an essay in edited English because they contain regionalisms, colloquialisms, or slang. Identify and label any instance of these three phenomena. If you find slang, label the group from which it probably originated. Be prepared to justify your decisions. You may find reasons to apply more than one of the three labels to certain expressions.

(1) The Senate is trying to pull something over on the President.
(2) The pot pushers on the streets are ripping us off.
(3) The students were studying plant life in an arroyo near the university.
(4) I don't dig that cat's tempo but he's sure hip with a horn.
(5) The dean recommended to the medical students that they hit the books.
(6) We can snatch fifty grand and beat the rap if the fuzz don't snag us.
(7) A considerable amount of paper could be conserved if shoppers brought their own totes to the supermarket.

b. The examples of colloquialisms given in the discussion above tended to be drawn from vernacular dialects. But some colloquialisms do not have so strong a nonstandard connotation. Even so, they still seem inappropriate for use in writing (unless the writer is purposely seeking a conversational tone). The expressions, *pull something over on* and *hit the books,* which were given in numbers (1) and (5) in the previous exercise, are examples of this latter type of colloquialism (as well as being idioms and clichés). Listen to a casual conversation among friends (or tape record one if you can do so inconspicuously) and then identify in it any words or expressions that would not be appropriate for use in formal written English (edited English).

c. Compile lists of slang words and expressions characteristic of members of the following groups (or any other such groups of your own choosing):

(1) baseball players and fans
(2) show business people
(3) CB radio users
(4) professional wrestlers

Taboo words and euphemisms

Sometimes the emotional connotations of a word or expression are so strong that the word is avoided altogether not only in edited English but in all but the most intimate styles of spoken English as well. Offensive words with this type of strong social prohibition are called *taboo words.* (The word *taboo* came into English from the Tongan language of the South Pacific, where *ta* meant "mark" and *bu* meant "exceedingly." Thus, a *tabu* was something set apart, usually in fact something sacred and therefore a source of awe and even fear.) Often, taboo words refer to bodily functions or to sexual organs or activities. But words that vividly connote the reality of death and illness are also treated as taboo. Consider the words *die, death,* and *dead.* Two women faced with the need to discuss how one will go on after the other's dying husband is gone would carefully avoid saying things such as, "When John is *dead,* the children may have to get jobs." If such a reality has to be discussed, then expressions like *passed away, no longer with us,* or *deceased* would be used. These have the same denotation as *died* but somehow do not evoke the same painful feelings. Any word or expression expressly *used to substitute for* an offensive taboo word (i.e., one with strong emotional connotations) is called a *euphemism.*

In addition to euphemisms for death, English has many euphemisms for illness. One rarely uses words like *cancer* or *tumor* when speaking to sick people or their families; rather, euphemisms like *growth* or *tissue mass* are substituted. Among the many euphemisms that denote bodily functions but avoid the strong negative connotations that their taboo-word counterparts convey are *perspire, go to the bathroom, number two,* and a variety of others, such as *tinkle,* that are used especially with young children. Among the many euphemisms that denote the sexual organs or sexual activities but avoid the strong negative connotations of their taboo-word counterparts are *bottom, privates, make love,* and *have intercourse.*

The majority of euphemisms treat the three themes mentioned in the previous paragraph (death and illness, bodily functions, sexual organs and activities), but any offensive connotation can give rise to a euphemism. When one uses *refreshments* in place of *whisky* because some people in one's audience do not approve of drinking, one is speaking euphemistically. When, during the Vietnam War, military press officers used the phrase *protective reaction strike* in place of the more offensive *bombing raid,* that too was euphemistic. So, too, the phrase *borrow some ideas* is a student's euphemism for *cheat.*

Some contemporary language scholars urge writers to use taboo words and expressions instead of euphemisms and thus somehow reduce the shock power that taboo words have in our society. My advice to you (as usual) is to be extremely sensitive to your audience. On some occasions, the use of taboo words can give an essay force and vividness, whereas euphemisms may make it seem vague and insincere. On other occasions the use of a taboo word may so shock your readers as to distract them entirely from the point you are trying to make.

Exercises

a. Look up the following euphemisms in *The American Heritage Dictionary of the English Language*. Find out what the taboo counterpart of each is. Then look up the taboo expression in the same dictionary and find out what the dictionary says about the social restrictions on its use. *The American Heritage Dictionary* will probably also have entries for other taboo expressions known to you, whose entries you may also wish to consult. Here are the four euphemisms to look up:

(1) heck
(2) darn
(3) shoot² (second entry for *shoot* in the *AHD*)
(4) gosh

b. The following passages contain inappropriately used taboo expressions *or* euphemisms. Identify the relevant expression; label it as taboo or euphemism; and then state why, if it is a taboo expression, a euphemism would be more appropriate, or, if it is a euphemism, why a less euphemistic expression would be appropriate.

(1) During the lecture by the eminent urologist, the assembled doctors were again reminded that older men tend to have persistent difficulties making water.
(2) The account executive told his client that he preferred to golf in the evening because, in the afternoon sun, he had a tendency to sweat.
(3) As the enemy attack intensified, the patrol leader turned to his men and said, "Goshdarnit, men, we have to fight together or we'll all be killed!"
(4) The surgeon explained to the patient that during the operation the medical team would have to saw off a leg.
(5) A few years ago the Supreme Court made it legal to kill fetuses up to the third month.
(6) Auschwitz was the resettlement camp where the Nazis carried out the final solution to the Jewish problem.

Gobbledygook and wordiness

This section treats a loose assortment of phenomena you should certainly be able to recognize and for the most part avoid when you write edited English. Most of us fall victim to the weaknesses in word use discussed here without realizing it or intending it. However, some writers cultivate the misuse of words, for, as we shall see, several of the word uses treated here have the effect of giving the impression of communication when in fact they cloud meaning and mislead the reader. After devoting some paragraphs to three specific types of gobbledygook (idioms, clichés, and jargon), I will then go on briefly to discuss and exemplify wordiness.

Idioms. The word *idiom* has many technical and many popular meanings. Sometimes it even refers to an entire language or dialect (e.g., *He handles the American idiom very well*). Here I use the term to refer specifically to expressions like the following, where the meaning of the entire expression is something other than the sum of the meanings of the words that compose it:

bury the hatchet (reach an accommodation)
kick the bucket (die)
take off one's hat to (salute, praise)
fight *tooth and nail* (ferociously)
on pins and needles (nervous)
shoot the breeze (chat)

Note that in each expression above there are words (*hatchet, bucket, hat, tooth, breeze*) that neither the speaker not the hearer literally thinks of when the idiom is used. There are two things a writer should know about idioms:

(1) Most of them tend to be colloquial—reserved for use in speech.
(2) They tend to cloud rather than clarify the message—this may be because many of them derive from dead metaphors (once vivid figures of speech that have lost their concreteness).

Both the writer and the reader have heard these exressions so many times that they may be written and read without even stimulating the meaning centers in the brain. The label "idiomatic" is often applied to any group of words that have a tendency to stick together—even if each retains its meaning. Here are some two-word verbs in English that strongly resemble the idiomatic expressions given above (the two together mean something different from the two separately):

cough up (give)
water down (dilute)
set off (explode)
pipe down (lower voice)
throw up (vomit)

But here are some two-word verbs in which, though the two words tend to form a pair, the meaning of the whole is indeed the sum of the parts:

hand over
write down
throw in
send off

There are hundreds of verbs like the above in English; most tend to be colloquial. They vary in the degree to which they tend to cloud rather than clarify meaning (some are still quite concrete). It is your choice as a writer whether to use or not to use an idiom. You will not for the most part have any choice about changing the idiom (if you try to change *shoot the breeze* to *blast the breeze,* your reader will probably read it literally and not figuratively).

Clichés. Clichés are similar to idioms in that they are groups of words that have a strong tendency to remain together. But the words in them, for the most part retain their own identities. Here are some examples:

as fit as a fiddle
as light as a feather
as thin as a rail
as sharp as a tack
fought like a tiger
slept like a log
ate like a pig

Notice that whereas many idioms originated as metaphors, the above clichés were all once lively and original similes. But through overuse they have lost their power. They are not the products of the writer's own original thought, and, because they have been heard so many times, they will make little impression on the reader's mind. Any expression, worn out through overuse may be considered a cliché; it does not have to be a simile:

neat and tidy
in the not too distant future
at that point in time

Clichés tend to be more of a problem for writers than idioms. We often intuitively avoid idioms when we write because we sense that they are colloquial. Unfortunately, written English has as many clichés as spoken English, so you need to be on your guard against them. You will not be able to avoid all use of prefabricated expressions (notice that *on your guard* in my last sentence might be considered a cliché), but you should be in control. Work as hard as you can to assure that the words you use are products of and vehicles for your own ideas. Do not let the words slip onto the paper before you are finished formulating your thoughts.

Jargon. Jargon is the misuse of the technical vocabulary of some special field, as when a professional educator addressing a PTA meeting might tell the assembled parents that "preadolescents intermittently generate ego-oriented projection fantasies during shared-activation modules" when the message is no more than this: "Your children tend to day-dream about the future when we leave them alone in discussion groups." There is nothing wrong with technical vocabulary if it is carefully de-fined and if it labels some reality for which the language does not already have a word. But if it is a useless substitute for a familiar word already in existence, has no precise definition, or, worse, is used with the wrong au-dience, then it is jargon.

Doublespeak. Doublespeak is a relatively new label for what has often been called pompous or inflated diction. It may also be viewed as a type of jargon. It is characterized by the unnecessary use of long and unfamil-iar words, whether drawn from any particular field or not, when more familiar (and usually more concrete) words would serve just as well or better. This problem often arises when writers who are not comfortable writing edited English, but who know that it is more formal than casual English, overdo their attempts to avoid colloquial vocabulary. The itali-cized words in the following passage from a student paper on baseball techniques represent this tendency:

> *Affix* the eyes on the *projectile* and *rotate* the bat smoothly in order to *en-counter* the *projectile* at a point *perpendicular* to the *pectoral* plane.

Here is what the writer should have written:

> Keep the eyes on the ball and swing the bat smoothly so as to hit the ball directly in front of the chest.

Pompous diction becomes doublespeak in the strict sense when it is used purposely as a kind of extended euphemism to hide the true mean-ing of a passage. Military press officers would be most unlikely to report their unit's activities as follows:

> We killed all the people in the village so that the enemy could not recruit them.

They would be more likely to put it something like this:

> Pacification of the village's personnel through nullification guaranteed termination of their availability to recruitment by the enemy.

The term *doublespeak* has also been extended to apply to any type of gob-bledygook used purposely to misinform or mislead one's audience. (The intentional overuse of passives—see pp. 176–177 in Chapter Seven—is also a favorite doublespeak tactic.) Needless to say, honesty should be one of the writer's prime guides. But you should also be on the alert to avoid even unintentional impulses to use idioms, clichés, jargon, or pompous vocabulary that cloud rather than clarify your message and thereby subvert your purpose.

Wordiness. Wordiness may sometimes occur intentionally as a reinforcement of doublespeak. More often, it occurs unintentionally. It usually happens when the writer is still thinking about what to say, but lets the pen or typewriter run on at the same time. Here is an example of a wordy passage:

> In the event that a majority of the representatives of the student body should happen to decide that it might possibly be of the utmost necessity to bring it to the attention of the appropriate representatives of the faculty that their practices of grading are more or less fair, then they should consider bringing problems of this type to the attention of those people who are involved.

Notice that the passage, like most wordy passages, is characterized by excessive use of the words *of*, *to*, and *it*; by more than its share of qualifying expressions (*should happen to, might possibly, more or less*); and by long noun phrases (*a majority of the representatives of the student body, the appropriate representatives of the faculty, those people who are involved*). The passage really says no more than this:

> If most students think that faculty should examine unfair grading practices, then the faculty should be asked to do so.

There are three ways to avoid wordiness (and you usually need to use all three of them): (1) Think and plan carefully before you write; (2) attend carefully to paragraph structure, sentence structure, and word choice as you write; (3) carefully revise what you have written after you write, taking out any needless words.

Exercise

Each of the following passages represents at least one of the following problems with diction: (1) inappropriate use of idioms, (2) clichés, (3) jargon, (4) doublespeak, (5) wordiness. It is possible that more than one of these problems characterizes the passage. Identify the problem or problems. Be prepared to justify your analysis. Revise the passage to eliminate the problem.

(1) Henry Kissinger was as sly as a fox in generating suspicion between the Russians and the Chinese.

(2) The notice from the zoning board read: "Due to the municipality's right of eminent domain, your proprietorship over your residency must be abrogated within a period not to exceed thirty days."

(3) The problem of deciding on a career or occupation makes it necessary for students to consider taking courses in a variety of subject matters during the first few years of their college education.

(4) Earl Harold of England swore an oath to Duke William of Normandy that he would not oppose William's claim to the English throne when King Edward died, but in 1066 he asserted that he was only pulling William's leg when he did so.

(5) If there has been a tendency in past years for there to be the possibility of damage being caused to the skin by remaining in the sun for an excessively long period of time, then steps should most probably be taken to place a covering on the body when it becomes necessary to so expose oneself.

(6) When Pope John XXIII called for an Ecumenical Council in 1963, the responses of the bishops of the world was that it was no sooner said than done.

(7) Statistical evidence corroborates the assertion that samples of the population in lower socioeconomic strata are granted diminished remuneration for their productive activities.

(8) The overwhelming conclusion forced upon any reader of Richard Nixon's memoirs is that the bigger they are the harder they fall.

(9) The atmosphere in Washington during the Kennedy and Johnson administrations was like night and day.

(10) The foreign minister of the People's Republic of China proposed to the United Nations Disarmament Conference that peace could come to the world only when the United States and the Soviet Union buried the hatchet.

(11) The ecological impact of the refinery will consist primarily of the termination of biological organisms in the adjacent watershed.

(12) People who hold positions of authority in governmental or industrial places of business should probably make it their responsibility to be considerate of the feelings of the people who come to them with various types of inquiries.

(13) The child's ability to generate phonological sequences and to interpret lexicological units may be somewhat impaired by the neurological surgery.

(14) All personnel shall assure that their performance with respect to their fellow operatives is in accord with their expectations concerning the reciprocal performance of the aforementioned.

(15) The practice of repeating the skills required for any activity almost always makes it certain that the person involved acquires the skill to an almost perfect degree.

(16) In order to win seven gold medals at the Olympics, Mark Spitz certainly had to learn to swim like a fish.

(17) Copernicus hit the nail on the head when he asserted that the earth revolved around the sun.

(18) Our travel agency assures you that your hotel accommodations will be spic and span and that food served in the main dining room will be piping hot.

(19) The greatest and most prominent musicians in our time and in earlier times made it a point to concentrate on giving attention to playing their instruments on a daily basis from the time they were at an early age.

(20) John Dean was the first member of the Nixon administration to spill the beans about the Watergate burglary in testimony before a committee of the Senate.

Nine | *Dictionaries*

Words in edited English have a life of their own. As a writer, you must become aware that other writers have used every word you use, and by each use they have contributed something to the meaning of each word. You must also become aware that your reader will have read at least some of those writers, and having read them, will interpret what you write in part according to what *they* meant. But how can you have access to the meanings and uses of words by so many other human beings? You can do so by reading broadly and deeply. But even a lifetime is too short to read all the books that all your readers may have read. So how *can* you find out as much as possible about the contributions others have made to the meanings of words? The answer is, of course, by consulting dictionaries. I will discuss dictionaries in this chapter, not as ends in themselves, but as tools of the writer, focusing on uses you can and should make of them in order to make you a better writer of edited English.

Dictionaries come in two sizes: larger ones typically called unabridged dictionaries, and smaller ones typically called desk dictionaries. But even within the two general types, there is wide variation in size. There are perhaps a half-dozen dictionaries of English that claim to be unabridged. The most famous is *Webster's Third New International Dictionary* which was published in 1961 by the G. & C. Merriam Company. The largest and most authoritative is the *Oxford English Dictionary* (The *OED*) published between 1888 and 1928, with a supplement in 1933 and a new four-volume supplement now in process (A–G was published in 1972, and H–N in 1976). *Webster's Third* (as I will refer to it) is one very large volume containing more than a half-million entries. The *OED* (1933 reissue with supplement and two recent supplements) fills fifteen large volumes. Both of these dictionaries aim to present as complete as possible a list of all the words in edited English, including the vocabulary of special fields. The *OED* is so much larger because it aims to list all words and meanings from about the year 1200 to the present and to illustrate every definition of each word with a quotation from a printed source.

There are perhaps a dozen desk dictionaries available. These aim to provide information about the words most writers commonly use, and to do so in a book that is reasonably easy to handle. I will refer in this chapter to one such dictionary: *The American Heritage Dictionary of the English Language*. The *American Heritage* contains about 150,000 entries. In the subsections that follow on the various uses of dictionaries, I will typically illustrate with annotated entries first from one of the unabridged dictionaries and then from the *American Heritage*.

Spelling, Pronunciation, and Grammar

The spelling of a word comes first in a dictionary entry: Syllable division is indicated by dots; capitalization and hyphenation are also given. (As I wrote the first paragraph of this chapter, I wondered whether *lifetime* might be hyphenated and needed to consult my desk dictionary to find that it is not.) Immediately following the spelling, is a phonetic transcription of the word's pronunciation marked to indicate relative loudness of the word's syllables. Next comes the word's part-of-speech label (or primary label, if it functions as more than one part of speech) and an indication of how to spell the inflected variants of the word. If the word can be more than one part of speech, the other label and inflected variants in that part of speech follow the definitions in the primary part of speech. The first label is usually the first to appear in the history of English: *doubt* and *bottle* both can function as either a noun or a verb, but *doubt* is labeled first as a verb and then a noun because it was an English verb before it was a noun; *bottle* is labeled first as a noun and then as a verb because it was an English noun before it was a verb. Study the following entries for the word *comprise* and note how each presents the above types of information:

WEBSTER'S THIRD

○ Preferred spelling with syllable division indicated; this word is not capitalized; there are no hyphens in the spelling; it has no foreign language label and is therefore not italicized.

○ An alternative acceptable spelling. It is not equally acceptable; if it were, *or*, not *also* would precede it.

○ The pronunciation (in slanted lines). Consult the front of the dictionary for the values of the phonetic symbols—every dictionary has its own system. The raised line in front of the second syllable indicates that it is the loudest in the word. In three- and four-syllable words a second loudest syllable is indicated by a lowered straight line before it: See *Webster's Third* entry for *appreciate* on p. 221.

○ The part-of-speech label (*vb* = "verb") and the inflectional suffixes that may attach to the word (-ED/-ING/-S).

○ This word may be used as a transitive verb.

○ This word is also used as an intransitive verb. (No other parts of speech but verb are listed for this word.)

com·prise *also* **com·prize** \kəm'prīz\ *vb* -ED/-ING/-S [ME *comprisen*, fr. MF *compris* (past part. of *comprendre* to comprehend), fr. L *comprehensus*, past part. of *comprehendere* — more at COMPREHEND] *(vt)* **1 :** to include esp. within a particular scope **:** sum up **:** COVER, CONTAIN ⟨a whole religion *comprised* within one book⟩ ⟨his program was *comprised* in the party slogan⟩ **2** *obs* **:** UNDERSTAND **3** *obs* **:** to lay hold of **:** SEIZE **4** *obs* **:** ENCLOSE, HOLD **5 a :** to consist of **:** be made up of ⟨the fortress ∼s many miles of entrenchment and well-hidden artillery positions⟩ ⟨the thirty-five essays it ∼s . . . are mostly reprinted from previous collections —Harry Levin⟩ **b :** to make up **:** CONSTITUTE ⟨the chapters that ∼ the first part of the novel⟩ ⟨the estate ∼s some 500 acres⟩ ∼ *(vi)* **:** to be made up **:** CONSIST — used with *of* ⟨the funds of the association shall ∼ of members' subscriptions —*Education*⟩

AMERICAN HERITAGE

Preferred spelling with syllable division indicated by

a dot (as in *Webster's Third*); this word is not capitalized.

Note that this desk dictionary does not give the alternate

spelling.

The pronunciation is given in parentheses (not slanted

lines). Consult the front of the dictionary for the values

of the phonetic symbols. Notice that the loudest syllable

is here indicated by a bold-face accent mark *after* it. In

words of three or more syllables, a second-loudest sylla-

ble would be followed by an accent mark not in bold-

face type: See the *American Heritage* entry for appreciate

on p. 219.

The part-of-speech label

includes the designation

"transitive" (*tr. v.* =

"transitive verb"). Note

com·prise (kəm-priz′) *tr.v.* **-prised, -prising, -prises. 1.** To consist of; be composed of. **2.** To include; contain. —See Synonyms at **include.** [Middle English *comprisen,* from Old
French *comprendre* (past participle *compris*), to comprehend,
include, from Latin *comprehendere,* to grasp mentally : *com-,*
together in mind, mentally + *prehendere,* to seize (see **ghend-** in
Appendix*).] —**com·pris′a·ble** *adj.*
    Usage: By definition, the whole comprises the parts; the parts
do not comprise the whole, nor is the whole comprised of its
parts. In strict usage: *The Union comprises 50 states. Fifty states
compose* (or *constitute, make up*) *the Union. The Union is
composed of 50 states.* This rule restricting *comprise* and *compose* to separate senses is supported by a majority of the Usage
Panel, but returns indicate that *comprise* is increasingly used in
both senses: *Fifty states comprise the Union* (unacceptable to 61
per cent of the Panel); *the Union is comprised of 50 states* (unacceptable to 53 per cent).

that this desk dictionary

does not list the intransi-

tive use of this word. Note

also that the inflected

forms are spelled out (this

shows more clearly than

Webster's Third that the *e* is dropped when the *-ing* is added).

Exercises

a. Are the following spellings the only correct ones for these words? If alternates are given in your dictionary, are they equally acceptable or is one preferable?

ameba, catalog, catsup, enclose, judgment, hiccough, plough

b. Look up the pronunciations of the following words in your dictionary. If alternates are given, is one preferable? How do the pronunciations indicated in the dictionary compare with your pronunciation? (You will have to study the front matter of the dictionary—where the values of the phonetic symbols are discussed—in order to do this exercise.)

adult, alias, despicable, greasy, harass, mischievous, project, record, research, route

c. How many different parts of speech can each of the following words function as in English? What is its primary part of speech?

search, cash, attempt, mask, calm, skin, turn, answer, finger, yellow, brick

d. How do you spell the inflected forms of the following words? (If alternate spellings are given in your dictionary, is one preferable?)

lovely, equip, model, theater, picnic, occur, shy, bias

Etymology

The etymology of a word is its history. In it the dictionary states the source of a word and the development of its form (spelling and pronunciation) and to some extent its meaning. The etymology of a word is usually given in square brackets immediately following information about spelling, pronunciation, and grammar (some recent dictionaries, however, including the *American Heritage*, put the etymology near the end of the entry after the definitions). Although etymologies probably provide the least practical information for writers, they can be helpful nonetheless. The information in them is often hard to decode because many of the words are abbreviated and the emphasis is on the history of the form of the word rather than on the history of the meaning. Below are two entries for the word *fragile*. The etymology in the first (from the *OED*) is typical of most dictionaries. The etymology that follows it (from the *American Heritage*) represents a major departure from traditional practice: (1) No abbreviations are used, which makes the entry much easier to read, and (2) the reader is referred to an appendix where more detailed and practically useful information about the word and related words can be found. You should note, however, that even though the bracketed etymology in the *OED* is difficult to use, no dictionary matches the information given in the body of the entry about the historical development of the word's meaning. Study the following entries and comments very carefully.

OXFORD ENGLISH DICTIONARY

Etymology of the word given in square brackets. This is sometimes called the "form history," because it focuses on the history of the spelling, pronunciation, and grammatical status of the word with only incidental treatment of the history of the meaning.

Note that in the *OED* as in most dictionaries, the etymology immediately follows information on spelling, pronunciation, and grammar.

Note also how many abbreviations are used (a. = "adopted from," F. = "French, " c. = "century," ad. = "adaptation of, " L. = "Latin, f. = "from"). You must study the front matter of your dictionary to learn what such abbreviations mean.

Note that the *OED* (in the body of the entry) treats the history of a word's meaning implicitly by listing the meanings in historical order, and by providing many quotations to illustrate each of the developing meanings.

(This is a relatively short entry for the *OED*.)

The dagger indicates that this meaning is obsolete (notice that the last quotation is dated 1548).

Fragile (fræˑdʒil⟩, *a.* Also 6 **fragyll**, 8 **fragil.** [a. F. *fragile* (14th c.), ad. L. *fragil-is*, f. *frag-* root of *frangĕre* to break. See FRAIL *a.*]
1. Liable to break or be broken ; easily snapped or shattered ; in looser sense, weak, perishable, easily destroyed. Also *fig.*
1607 SHAKS. *Timon* v. i. 204 Throwes That Natures fragile Vessell doth sustaine In lifes vncertaine voyage. **1626** BACON *Sylva* § 841 Of Bodies, some are Fragile ; and some are Tough, and not Fragile. *a* **1668** DENHAM *Progr. Learn.* 188 When subtile Wits have spun their thred too fine, 'Tis weak and fragile, like Arachne's line. **1671** MILTON *P. R.* III. 388 Much ostentation vain of fleshly arm And fragile arms. **1756** BLACKLOCK *Soliloquy* 281 Secure, thy steps the fragile board could press. **1832** G. R. PORTER *Porcelain & Gl.* 248 Threads .. render the material [glass] extremely fragile. **1856** KANE *Arct. Expl.* I. xxvii. 356 We found the spot..hemmed in by loose and fragile ice.
b. Of persons, etc. : Of weak or tender frame or constitution, delicate (= FRAIL, but used with an allusion to the primary sense).
1858 FROUDE *Hist. Eng.* III. xvii. 435 The..people saw as yet but a single fragile life between the country and a disputed succession. **1883** OUIDA *Wanda* I. 43 An old lady, so delicate..so pretty and so fragile.
† **2.** Liable to err or fall into sin ; frail. *Obs.*
1513 BRADSHAW *St. Werburge* I. 1875 More lyke an angell ..Than a fragyll mayde of sensuall appetyte. *Ibid.* I. 2776 A wanton prynce folowynge sensualyte And his fragyll appetyte. **1548** HALL *Chron., Edw. IV* (an. 23) 248 b, Suche is the blyndnes of our fraile and fragile nature, euer giuen to carnal concupiscence.
3. quasi-*sb.* in *pl.* = fragile articles or goods.
1882 *Pall Mall G.* 19 June 10/1 Cases..marked..'Fragiles'.
Hence **Fraˑgilely** *adv.*, **Fraˑgileness.**
1727 BAILEY II, *Fragileness.* **1864** WEBSTER, *Fragilely.*

AMERICAN HERITAGE

Etymology of the word given in square brackets (as in the *OED*.)

Unlike the *OED* and most dictionaries, the etymology is here

placed toward the end of the main entry and not immediately

after the information on spelling, pronunciation, and grammar.

Note that no abbreviations are used in the etymology.

frag·ile (frăj′əl, -ĭl′) *adj.* **1.** Easily broken or damaged; brittle. **2.** Physically weak; frail. **3.** Suggesting fragility; light: *"she put her hand on my arm, a fragile touch careful not to waken"* (Truman Capote). **4.** Tenuous; flimsy: *a fragile claim to fame.* [Old French, from Latin *fragilis,* from *frangere,* to break. See **bhreg-** in Appendix.*] —**frag′ile·ly** *adv.* —**fra·gil′i·ty** (frə-jĭl′ə-tē), **frag′ile·ness** *n.*
  Synonyms: *fragile, breakable, frail, delicate, brittle.* These adjectives mean susceptible to being broken or injured. *Fragile* most often describes objects whose lightness or delicacy of material requires that they be handled with great care. *Breakable* refers to what can be broken, but makes a less strong implication of inherent weakness. *Frail,* applicable to persons and things, implies slightness of constitution, build, or structure and consequent lack of durability. *Delicate,* in this comparison, also suggests lack of durability or susceptibility to injury. *Brittle* refers to the hardness and inelasticity of some material that makes it especially subject to fracture or snapping when subjected to pressure.

Note this reference to *bhreg-* in the Appendix. The Appendix is a diction-

ary of root words in a hypothetical language called Proto–Indo–European,

which scholars have reconstructed by comparing the forms and the mean-

ings of words in languages of Europe and the Near East. It is presumed to

have been spoken in Central Europe around 4,000 B.C. Most of the lan-

guages of Europe and the Near East are claimed to have descended from it

through different changes in sound and meaning over the centuries. (See

the entry for *bhreg-* on page 215).

AMERICAN HERITAGE (Appendix entry for *bhreg-*)

First, the presumed meaning of the Proto-Indo-European root is given.

Next, the development of the root in the various branches of the Indo-European family tree is traced. (Note that the initial *bh* in *bhreg-* changed to a *b* in the Germanic languages but to an *f* in Latin. Thus, English has words descended from this root that begin with *b*, in its native Germanic vocabulary, and others that begin with *f*, in vocabulary borrowed directly or indirectly from Latin. *Fragile* is thus a distant cousin of *break*; it is no accident that *fragile* and *breakable* are synonyms.)

bhreg-. To break. **1.** Germanic **brekan* in: **a.** Old English *brecan*, to break: BREAK; **b.** (Old English *brecan* and) Old High German *brehhan*, to break: BREACH, BRECCIA, BRASH²; **c.** Old French *breier*, to break: BRAY²; **d.** Old French *brier* (dialectal) and *broyer*, to knead: BRIOCHE. **2.** Germanic **brak-*, bushes (< "that which impedes motion"), in: **a.** Old English *bracu*, thicket: BRAKE³; **b.** Old Norse **brakni*, undergrowth, bracken: BRACKEN. **3.** Germanic **brāk-* in Middle Dutch *braeke*, crushing instrument, stopping gear: BRAKE¹. **4.** Nasalized zero-grade form **bhr-n-g-* in Latin *frangere*, to break: FRACAS, (FRACTED), FRACTION, FRACTIOUS, FRACTURE, FRAGILE, FRAGMENT, FRANGIBLE, FRAIL¹; ANFRACTUOUS, CHAMFER, DIFFRACTION, INFRACT, INFRANGIBLE, INFRINGE, IRREFRAGIBLE, OSSIFRAGE, REFRACT, (REFRAIN²), (REFRINGENT), SAXIFRAGE, SEPTIFRAGAL. **5.** Latin *suffrāgāri*, to vote for (? < "to use a broken piece of tile as a ballot"), hence *suffrāgium*, the right to vote: SUFFRAGE, (SUFFRAGAN). [Pok. 1. *bhreg-* 165.]

All words printed in small capitals in the Appendix entry are modern English words that derive from *bhreg-*. Thus they all are related somehow in form and meaning. If you take the time to read and study such entries, you can learn to recognize such relationships and in the process enlarge your vocabulary.

The *American Heritage* is the only dictionary with an Appendix of this type.

Exercises

a. Here again are the native Germanic words listed in exercise *b* on p. 184. Consult their etymologies in a dictionary and list their Old-English spellings and meanings and their Middle-English spellings and meanings:

wife, food, stone, winter, good, corn, blood, hand, land, heart, father, head, love, sleep, sit, knave, loaf, brother, ground

b. Here are the borrowed words listed in exercise *c* on p. 184. Consult their etymologies in a dictionary and find out the language from which English borrowed each one:

alcohol, avocado, candle, cheese, cockroach, coffee, concert, cousin, frustrate, ghetto, give, journey, judo, kindergarten, mile, obedience, piano, podunk, popular, pretzel, satan, sherry, skirt, skunk, submit, them, tundra, zinc

c. Here are the words listed in the word-formation exercise on p. 186. Consult their etymologies in a dictionary and find out which process of word formation produced each one:

poisonous, snafu, paratroops, tricycle, pompadour, Dacron, fruity, flu, stockholder, burgle, memo, transplant, newscast, wooden, amoral, flowerbed, radar, cutlet, gym, crayfish, GI, semifinal, rainfall, SUNOCO, cockroach

d. Here is the entry from the appendix to the *American Heritage Dictionary* for the Proto-Indo-European root, *pel-*[6]. Read it carefully. Then list all the modern English words printed in it in small capitals. Next, underline the letters of each word that seem to descend from the *pel* of the ancestor word (e.g., *fil*ter, pro*pel*, ap*peal*). Finally, try to state the meaning of each of the modern words by a statement that contains the definition of the ancestor word (e.g., *propel* = "to thrust or drive forward"; *appeal* = "to drive—an argument—toward"). This last task may not be possible in every case since the meaning may have changed drastically in some words, but you may be surprised to discover how many words retain the meaning of the ancestor word and are thus still related not only in form but in meaning.

pel-[6]. To thrust, strike, drive. **1.** Extended form **peld-* in: **a.** Germanic **falt-*, to beat, in Old English *-fealt*, beaten: ANVIL; **b.** Germanic **feltaz*, **filtiz*, compressed wool, in (*i*) Old English *felt*, felt: FELT[1] (*ii*) Frankish **filtir*, piece of felt: FILTER; **c.** Latin *pellere* (past participle *pulsus*), to push, drive, strike: POUSETTE, PULSATE, PULSE[1], PUSH; COMPEL, DISPEL, EXPEL, IMPEL, PROPEL, REPEL; **d.** suffixed zero-grade form **pḷd-to-* in Latin *pultāre*, to knock, beat: PELT[2]. **2.** Extended form **pelə-* (present stem **pelnā-*) in: **a.** Latin *appellāre*, "to drive to," address, entreat, appeal, call (*ad-*, to, AD-): APPEAL; **b.** Latin *compellāre*, to accost, address (*com-*, intensive prefix, COM-): COMPELLATION; **c.** Latin *interpellāre*, "to thrust between," interrupt (*inter-*, between, INTER-): INTERPELLATE. **3.** Suffixed o-grade form **pol-o-*, fuller of cloth, in Latin *polire*, to make smooth, polish (< "to full cloth"): POLISH. **4.** Suffixed extended zero-grade form **plə-tio-* in Greek *plēsios*, near (< "pushed toward"): PLESIOSAURUS. [Pok. 2 a. *pel-* 801.]

e. Look up the following Proto-Indo-European roots in the appendix of the *American Heritage Dictionary* and do with each one what you did with *pel-*[6] in exercise *d* above:

bher-[1], *dwō, ghel-*[2], *ghend-, gnō-, ped-*[1], *spen-, wer-*[3]

Definition

The definition of a word is that part of the dictionary entry that lists the sense or senses of the word and often includes illustrative quotations. If a word can function as more than one part of speech, all the senses of its most common use as a part of speech are treated first, then those for other parts of speech. If a word may function as both a *transitive* verb (taking a direct object, as in *I appreciate the gift*) and an *intransitive* verb (lacking a direct object, as in *The value of the land appreciated*), then the senses for transitive are treated separately from those for intransitive. The *OED* and *Webster's Third* list the senses in historical order. The *American Heritage* gives what the editors consider the central and most current meaning first, and then lists other senses in the order in which they relate to the central sense, thus providing in effect a semantic analysis of the word and attempting to show the unity of its meanings. The unabridged dictionaries tend also to exemplify the senses with illustrative quotations; desk dictionaries contain a few quotations. In desk dictionaries many undefined words are listed at the very end of entries. These *run-on words* are usually close relatives of the defined word that have been formed by adding prefixes or suffixes; thus, you can assume that their meanings are the sum of the senses in the entry to which they are attached and the meanings of the prefixes or suffixes. Study the two illustrative entries and their accompanying explanatory notes in the following two pages.

OXFORD ENGLISH DICTIONARY

The main senses of the word are numbered in the *OED*, and sub-senses are lettered. The senses are listed in the historical order in which they developed. Often, the lower numbered senses will be obsolete and marked with a dagger (see the *OED* entry for *fragile* on p. 213). None of the senses of *appreciate* was obsolete in the 1880s when the *A* volume of the *OED* was published. The most special feature of the *OED* is that each sense and subsense is illustrated by at least one quotation for each century that the word was in use with a given sense. The first quotation is claimed to be the first appearance of the word in print with the given sense, and the last quotation is claimed to be its last appearance. Note that *appreciate* first appeared in print in English in 1769. One would have to consult the 1933 supplement or the supplement now being published to make certain that none of the listed senses

has become obsolete since this entry was published in the original dictionary.

Appreciate (ăprī·ʃi‚eⁱt), *v.*; also 8–9 **appretiate.** [f. L. *appretiāt-* ppl. stem of *appretiā-re* to set a price to, appraise, f. *ap-, ad-,* to + *preti-um* price. Cf. Fr. *apprécier* (15th c. in Godef.). The literal sense of the Fr. is supplied by APPRAISE, APPRIZE. In Eng., as in Fr., the med.L. spelling *appreciāre* has been followed. Neither this verb nor any derivative is in Johnson; but see sense 3.]

1. *trans.* To make or form an estimate of worth, quality, or amount.

1769 BURKE *Pres. St. Nat.* Wks. II. 59 Let us calmly .. appreciate those dreadful and deformed gorgons and hydras. **1817** W. TAYLOR in *Month. Rev.* LXXXIII. 458 The extreme want of candour..with which Priestley appretiated Hume. **1818** ACCUM *Chem. Tests* 496 The weight of the gold is to be appreciated. **1837** SIR W. HAMILTON *Metaph.* ii. (1877) I. 22 It was the bias of antiquity..to appreciate all knowledge principally by the higher standard.

2. To estimate aright, to perceive the full force of.

1798 FERRIAR *Illustr. Sterne* iv. 124 The physiological reader only can appreciate the profound sagacity of this conclusion. **1842** ALISON *Hist. Eur.* lvii. § 43 IX. 41 Napoleon..instantly appreciating the magnitude of the danger. **1875** GRINDON *Life* xiii. 167 Until the truth of any thing.. be appreciated, its error, if any, cannot be detected.

b. *esp.* To be sensitive to, or sensible of, any delicate impression or distinction.

1833 BREWSTER *Nat. Magic* ii. 32 The retina has not appreciated the influence of the simple red rays. **1862** F. HALL *Hindu Philos. Syst.* 236 In like manner, a blind man is able to appreciate sound, touch, etc., but not colours. **1879** PRESCOTT *Sp. Telephone* 7 If the number of vibrations exceeds forty thousand per second, the ear becomes incapable of appreciating the sound.

3. To esteem adequately or highly; to recognize as valuable or excellent; to find worth or excellence in.

1655 [See APPRECIATING.] **1742** BAILEY, *Appretiate,* to set an high Price, Value, or Esteem upon any thing. **1795** *Fragm. Pol. & Hist.* I. 230 Your labours will not be fully known and appreciated till the succeeding generation. **1858** GLADSTONE *Homer* I. 25 The mental culture necessary in order to appreciate Homer. **1858** HAWTHORNE *Fr. & It. Jrnls.* I. 171 It requires a finer taste than mine to appreciate him.

4. To raise in value; opposed to *depreciate.* (This and the following sense have been long in use in U. S.)

1779 P. WEBSTER *Pol. Ess.* (1791) 33 Any probable attempt to raise or appreciate the value of the money. **1880** R. MACKENZIE in *19th Cent.* 207 Rents have been unduly appreciated. **1881** H. H. GIBBS *Double Standard* Pref. 9 The resumption of specie payments in Gold, thus appreciating that metal.

5. *intr.* To rise in value.

1789–96 MORSE *Amer. Geog.* I. 323 A great demand for specie and bills, which occasioned the latter..to appreciate. **1882** P. TIDMAN *Gold & Silv. Money* 85 Gold has been steadily appreciating in value.

AMERICAN HERITAGE

The editors of the *American Heritage* list the meanings in a priority order
(rather than by historical order or simple statistical frequency). Thus, the
first is what they consider to be the central and most current meaning.
Other meanings are listed in an order of relationship to the central meaning. Notice that, because of this, the first meaning in the *American Heritage* entry corresponds to the third meaning in the *OED* entry.

Definitions for the transitive function of this verb
are given first.

ap·pre·ci·ate (ə-prē′shē-āt′) *v.* -ated, -ating, -ates. —*(tr)* **1.** To
estimate the quality, value, significance, or magnitude of. **2.** To
be fully aware of or sensitive to; realize. See Usage note below.
3. To be thankful or show gratitude for. **4.** To admire greatly;
enjoy. **5.** To raise in value or price. —*(intr)* To go up in value
or price. [Late Latin *appretiāre,* to set a value on : *ad-,* to +
pretiāre, to value, from *pretium,* price (see **per¹** in Appendix*).]
—**ap·pre′ci·a′tor** (-ā′tər) *n.*

Definitions for the in-
transitive function are
given next. (If *appreciate*
could function as another
part of speech, definitions
for that part of speech
would follow.)

Synonyms: *appreciate, value, prize, esteem, treasure, cherish.*
These verbs express having a favorable opinion of someone or
something. *Appreciate* applies especially to favor based on
judgment and assessment. *Value* implies high regard for the im-
·portance of the object, while *prize* emphasizes its specialness.
Esteem suggests respect of a formal sort; *treasure* and *cherish*
suggest affectionate regard mixed with pride of possession.
Usage: *Appreciate,* as a synonym for *be fully aware of* or
realize, is especially appropriate to situations calling for sensi-
tivity and understanding: *I appreciate your problems.* In lesser
contexts, *appreciate* is often regarded as an example of gen-
teelism: *I appreciate the lateness of the hour.* Only 47 per cent of
the Usage Panel approve the second example, although it is
defensible by the definition of *appreciate.*

The meanings of this run-on word can be taken as the sum of the meanings
of *appreciate* and the derivational suffix *–or.*

Exercises

a. Study the following two dictionary entries, focusing on the definition portions. Notice the use of illustrative quotations in the *Webster's Third* entry. Match the senses given in the one entry as best you can with those given in the other. Can you detect a difference in the order in which the senses are given? How can you explain this difference? Why do you think the *Webster's Third* entry does not contain run-on words?

WEBSTER'S THIRD

¹**apt** \'apt\ *adj, usu* -ER,'-EST [ME, fr. L *aptus* fastened, attached, suitable, fr. past part. of *apere* to fasten; akin to L *apisci* to reach, attain, *apud* near, Skt *āpta* fit, *āpnoti* he reaches] **1 :** having the necessary qualifications **:** unusually fitted or qualified **:** READY, PREPARED ⟨tall was he, slim, made ∼ for feats of war --William Morris⟩ **2 a :** having an habitual tendency or inclination **:** LIKELY ⟨the fish is ∼ to be lighter in shallower water --Francesca R. La Monte⟩ **b :** ordinarily disposed **:** GIVEN, INCLINED, PRONE ⟨are ∼ to believe what we like to believe --John Mason Brown⟩ **3 :** suited to its purpose **:** FITTING, SUITABLE ⟨picking out every term or figure ∼ for literary use --C.E.Montague⟩; *specif* **:** to the point **:** APPOSITE, APPROPRIATE, PAT ⟨words were ∼ and well chosen --Osbert Sitwell⟩ ⟨∼ quotations from classical Arabic travelers --W.L.Wright⟩ **4 :** keenly intelligent **:** mentally alert **:** QUICK-WITTED, QUICK ⟨an ∼ student⟩ ⟨an ∼ wit --Samuel Johnson⟩ ⟨the boy was observant and ∼ to learn --J.G. Cozzens⟩ **syn** see FIT, QUICK

AMERICAN HERITAGE

apt (ăpt) *adj.* **1.** Exactly suitable; appropriate. **2.** Likely. See Usage note below. **3.** Inclined; given. See Usage note below. **4.** Quick to learn or understand. —See Synonyms at **fit, relevant.** [Middle English, from Latin *aptus*, fit, suited, from the past participle of *apere*, to fasten. See **ap-¹** in Appendix.*] —**apt′ly** *adv.* —**apt′ness** *n.*

Usage: *Apt* and *likely*, when followed by an infinitive, are often interchangeable. *Likely* is always appropriate when mere probability is involved: *It is likely to snow. He is likely to leave soon.* When probability based on a natural or known tendency is implied, *apt* is the choice: *He is apt to stammer when he is excited.* In similar constructions, in careful usage, *liable* implies the possibility or probability of risk or disadvantage to the subject: *An angry man is liable to say more than he means.* Employment of *liable* in expressing only probability is loose usage: *We are liable* (preferably *likely*) *to go tomorrow.*

b. Look up the following words in these three dictionaries: *The OED, Webster's Third,* and the *American Heritage* (or any desk dictionary). Then do the following things:

(1) Compare the length of the entries especially noting how many illustrative quotations each dictionary uses.
(2) Note how many senses and subsenses each dictionary gives for each word.
(3) Check to see whether the two unabridged dictionaries have separate entries for run-on words listed in the desk dictionary entries.

dead, effect, exercise, general, help, load, pick

Synonyms

Toward the end of the entries for many words, are passages labeled *Syn* or *Synonyms*. These discuss and compare the senses and uses of words whose meanings are similar to the word defined in the entry. Typically, such passages are printed only with one of the synonyms and cross-referenced at the entries for all the other words in the synonym set. These passages make every dictionary a thesaurus. They can be extremely helpful to you as vocabulary builders. Whenever you are looking for information of any kind about a word and find a synonym passage, be sure to read it. These can be especially helpful if you are not sure about the connotations of a word, for the differences between sets of synonyms are usually differences in connotation. Here is an entry from

Webster's Third with a long synonym passage. Study it and compare it with the synonym passage given with the *American Heritage* entry for *appreciate* on p. 219. Note that the passage in the *American Heritage* is briefer and does not contain illustrative quotations. Note also that the *Webster's Third* entry discusses connotations explicitly.

WEBSTER'S THIRD

ap·pre·ci·ate \ə'prēshē͟,āt *sometimes* -rishē- *rarely* -rēsē-, *usu* -ād·+V\ *vb* -ED/-ING/-S [ML & LL; ML *appretiatus* (past part. of *appretiare* to value, esteem), fr. LL, past part. of *appretiare* to appraise, put a price on, fr. L *ad-* + *pretium* price, value — more at PRICE] *vt* **1 a** (1) **:** to evaluate highly or approve warmly often with expressions or tokens of liking ⟨to be loved, to be *appreciated*, to be admired and highly valued —Theodor Reik⟩ (2) **:** to judge or evaluate the worth, merit, quality, or significance of **:** comprehend with knowledge, judgment, and discrimination ⟨incapable of *appreciating* the difference between right and wrong —B.N.Cardozo⟩ ⟨*appreciated* that a new era was beginning —David Fairchild⟩ ⟨my power of *appreciating* your many charms and my desire that you should become my wife —Samuel Butler †1902⟩ **b :** to judge with heightened perception or understanding: (1) **:** to be critically and emotionally aware of delicate subtle aesthetic or artistic values ⟨he could not ∼ artistic quality⟩ (2) **:** to be fully sensible of often through or as if through personal experience ⟨must be experienced to be *appreciated* —Rudyard Kipling⟩ **c :** to esteem highly and express thanks or gratitude for ⟨I ∼ your kindness but I should be much happier alone —Louis Bromfield⟩ **2 :** to raise the value of **:** increase the market price of ⟨from 1820 onwards gold was mainly *appreciated* —J.A.Todd⟩ — opposed to *depreciate* ∼ *vi* **:** to rise in value or quantity ⟨apples *appreciated* 2 to 5 cents per box —*Wall Street Jour.*⟩ ⟨the calving and lambing season is good and numbers greatly ∼ —James Stevenson-Hamilton⟩
syn VALUE, PRIZE, TREASURE, CHERISH: APPRECIATE connotes recognition of worth or merit through wise judgment, analytical perception, and keen insight ⟨the author *appreciates* the historical development of the Roman law and the character of its various sources —H.O.Taylor⟩ ⟨he liked to be near people and have his talent as a whittler *appreciated* —Sherwood Anderson⟩ It is rarely used without these notions, although in less precise use it may carry added notions of warm hearty approval or full or delicate enjoyment ⟨attach herself to someone who knew how to *appreciate* the fullness of her ardor —Morley Callaghan⟩ ⟨youth *appreciates* that sort of recognition which is the subtlest form of flattery age can offer —Joseph Conrad⟩ In this series VALUE is less rich in suggestion than the others. It may suggest judgment blending the analytic and the subjective ⟨she only *valued* rest to herself when it came in the midst of other people's labor —Thomas Hardy⟩ ⟨suddenly Gard was smitten by the tragedy of plain women; to be *valued*, but not loved —Mary Austin⟩ PRIZE stresses high evaluation, often subjective; it may suggest a sense of pride in acquisition or possession and reluctance to lose or be deprived of the thing in question ⟨his grandfather's two *prized* standing cups —T.B.Costain⟩ ⟨we had *prized* our solitude when we had to fight for it —Virginia D. Dawson & Betty D. Wilson⟩ ⟨what is freedom and why is it *prized*? —John Dewey⟩ TREASURE, used with things considered or felt to be of extreme value, stresses notions of storing or of jealous guarding against loss or theft, notions of cleaving to and preserving ⟨that the volumes I write will be *treasured* up with the utmost care for ages —William Cowper⟩ ⟨ecstatic moments for him, to be *treasured* and conned over —T.B.Costain⟩ ⟨if . . . I have your friendship, I shall *treasure* it —Edna S. V. Millay⟩ CHERISH, rich in affective suggestion, adds the idea of deep-seated, perhaps tacit affection or intimate fond reflection on ⟨he *cherished* a painfully nostalgic memory of his childhood sweetheart —Saxe Commins⟩ ⟨troubled by the conflict of many ideas in his fruitful mind, and ardently *cherishing* those he thought true and good —Carl Van Doren⟩ ⟨*cherish* their allegiance to Christ in solitude and silence —Katharine F. Gerould⟩ **syn** see in addition UNDERSTAND

Following the entry for many words, a list of its synonyms is given and discussed. (These are words with similar meanings—often the same denotation but differing connotations.) This entry from *Webster's Third* not only discusses the different connotations of the synonyms, it also generously illustrates them with quotations. (The *OED* does not contain such synonym passages).

Note the reference to another discussion of synonyms of *appreciate* at the entry for *understand*. You will be referred to this passage at the entries for *value, prize,* etc.

Exercise

Consult both *Webster's Third* and a desk dictionary to see what they have to say about the following sets of synonyms (all of which were presented earlier, in the section on denotation and connotation). You may find that one or other of the dictionaries may not treat these sets at all or that the sets in the dictionaries contain fewer or more words than are listed here. In general, do the dictionary synonym passages treat the connotations adequately to help you make judgments about audience and purpose when you write?

(1) economical, inexpensive, cheap
(2) hefty, stout, corpulent, overweight, fat
(3) enterprise, project, job, chore, scheme
(4) creative, probing, curious, inquisitive, prying, nosey
(5) smokey, cop, pig, officer, fuzz, police
(6) audacious, brave, daring, cocky, bold, foolhardy
(7) female, chick, woman, libber, lady, fox
(8) fresh, naive, untried, green, new, inexperienced
(9) disordered, casual, sloppy, unkempt, messy, untidy

Usage

Dictionaries have traditionally provided information about the social impact of words by placing labels such as the following immediately after the spelling, pronunciation, and grammatical label: (1) regional labels, such as *British, Southern, Scottish,* and (2) social status labels, such as *nonstandard, colloquial, informal, slang, vulgar, obscene.* Such labels aim to help the user of a dictionary know what limits there are, if any, on the stylistic contexts in which words are used. *Webster's Third* greatly reduced the use of social status labels, and furthermore included for the first time entries for vernacular forms such as *ain't.* For the many members of our culture who looked to this unabridged dictionary more as an authority on how words should be used than as a description of how they are in fact used, this change in policy amounted to linguistic treason. The scholarly uproar that followed the publication of *Webster's Third* ultimately gave rise to the publication of the *American Heritage Dictionary,* and will surely result in a change in policy whenever a new edition of *Webster's Third* is published. (The desk dictionary based on it, *Webster's New Collegiate Dictionary,* has already reinstated extensive use of social status labels.)

The *American Heritage Dictionary* represents a radical innovation in dictionary treatments of usage. It not only uses the traditional social status labels; it also includes more than 800 *usage notes.* A usage panel of more than 100 members was consulted on a variety of questions of appropriateness. The panel consisted of members of American Society who were leaders in professions where the use of language and especially mastery of edited English are central to success. Many were writers, critics, or language scholars, but there were also anthropologists, legislators, and social activists. The usage notes report the opinions of the usage panel, giving percentages where opinions varied.

Examine the following three entries for the word *enthuse*. Notice the three distinct approaches to the social impact of words as you study both the entries and the annotations:

OXFORD ENGLISH DICTIONARY

The *OED* and most other dictionaries apply labels such as these (colloquial, humorous, vulgar, slang) to advise the dictionary user on the social impact of a word.

Enthuse (enþiū·z), *v. U.S. (colloq.* or *humorous.*) [An ignorant back-formation from ENTHUSIASM.] **a.** *trans.* To kindle with enthusiasm. **b.** *intr.* To grow enthusiastic ; to go into ecstasies.
1869 *Ohio newspaper* in *N. & Q.* Ser. IV. IV. 512 The only democrat whose nomination could enthuse the democracy of Ohio. **1872** LYTTON *Parisians* II. viii, The American.. whispered ..' I am not without a kinkle that you will be enthused '. **1880** GRANT *Confess. Frivolous Girl* iv. 180, I admit he began to enthuse a little. **1887** H. P. KIMBALL in *Pall Mall G.* 22 June 5/1, I don't get enthused at all, sir, over all this Greek business.

The *OED* even goes on to pass a social judgment on the etymology: It is not only a back-formation; it is an "ignorant" back-formation!

WEBSTER'S THIRD

The editors of *Webster's Third* discontinued the use of usage labels. There is no hint in this entry that writers of edited English should avoid this word.

en·thuse \ən'th(y)üz, en-\ *vb* -ED/-ING/-S [back-formation fr. *enthusiasm, enthusiast, enthusiastic*] *vt* **1 :** to make enthusiastic ⟨~ her with the potential pleasing power of the merchandise at her disposal *—Fashion Accessories*⟩ **2 :** to express (as an opinion) with enthusiasm ⟨''a sweet little town'', he *enthused* —Lawrence Constable⟩ ~ *vi* **:** to grow enthusiastic **:** express enthusiastic sentiments ⟨they are always ready to ~ over arms, the romance of heraldry and the family —L.G.Pine⟩

AMERICAN HERITAGE

The *American Heritage*

en·thuse (ĕn-thōōz′, ĭn-) *v.* -thused, -thusing, -thuses. *Informal.*
—*tr.* To stimulate enthusiasm in. —*intr.* To show enthusiasm.
—See Usage note. [Back-formation from ENTHUSIASM.]
    Usage: *Enthuse* is not well established in writing on a serious level. The following typical examples are termed unacceptable by substantial majorities of the Usage Panel. *The majority leader enthused over his party's gains* is disapproved by 76 per cent. *He was considerably less enthused by signs of factionalism* is disapproved by 72 per cent. Alternative phrasing might be *became* (or *waxed*) *enthusiastic* or *was less enthusiastic over.*

not only uses usage

labels, it also has added

the innovation of the

usage note.

Usage notes such as this report the findings of surveys sent to more than

100 people, who, though not necessarily language scholars, have achieved

recognition in our society for mastery of edited English. Typically, the

judgment of the usage panel is reported in percentages (as in this note).

This gives the user of this dictionary an opportunity to stand with the

minority if one is inclined toward an informal tone when writing a given

essay in edited English. Notes such as the one above make it quite clear

that there is no absolute consensus about the usage requirements of edited

English. You must let your audience and purpose be your primary guide.

(The *American Heritage Dictionary* is the only one with notes of this type).

Exercises

a. Consult the *OED*, *Webster's Third*, and a desk dictionary, and list any regional labels or social status labels included in the entries for the following words. (Be prepared to discuss general differences in the use of such labels among the three dictionaries.)

arroyo, bairn, begora, cram, embarcadero, irregardless, lorry, poke, tempo

b. Consult the appropriate usage note in the *American Heritage Dictionary* to discover the judgment of the usage panel concerning the italicized expression in each of the following sentences.

(1) The senator has *proven* his claim.
(2) Your new car is *different than* mine.
(3) The job was done by the man *who* Mary hired.
(4) I want to buy a car *whose* tires will last.
(5) She is the *eldest* of my two daughters.
(6) This report *infers* that you are to blame.
(7) This sentence *finalizes* this chapter.

Ten | *Spelling*

In the strict sense, spelling is the art of representing words in print with a sequence of letters that follows established custom. This aspect of language study is more technically referred to as *orthography* and is often distinguished from *orthoepy,* the study of the customary pronunciations of words. In this chapter I extend the meaning of the term *spelling* in a number of ways. I use it to include all aspects of the visual appearance of the letters in a word: (1) what letters compose a word and in what order, (2) whether any (or even all) are capitalized, (3) whether the letters are to be represented in standard (roman) type or in italic type, (4) whether numbers are to be spelled out in letters (and how) or represented by numerals, and (5) whether the representation of a word is to be abbreviated, and if so how.

Your primary resource for all of the above is your dictionary. And the basic principle of good spelling is this: *Unless you are absolutely sure about the spelling of any word, check in your dictionary.* Thus, my controlling purpose in this chapter is to provide you with general information about spelling that will, if you learn it, greatly reduce your need to consult a dictionary about questions of spelling. If you study this chapter carefully you can cut the time you will need to spend checking spellings in a dictionary to a fraction of what it might otherwise be. Remember, however, that only very few people become such proficient spellers that they never need to consult a dictionary at all.

The first three sections of this chapter deal with spelling in the strict sense: how to represent words in print with a sequence of letters that follows established custom. The three sections, taken as a whole, present a list of words that are hard to spell. You should compile a list of every word given as an example and every word given in an exercise and practice with that list. The lists given in the third section present only words that did not fit easily into one of the patterns discussed in the first two sections.

Spelling and Pronunciation

The fact that you know how to pronounce most of the words you will need to spell can be both a help and a hindrance to correct spelling. In this section I hope to point out ways in which pronunciations can help you spell and to warn you about situations where pronunciations might cause you to make mistakes in spelling.

I before e except after c

As I learned this well-known spelling rule, it went like this:

I before e except after *c,*
or when sounded like a as in *neighbor* and *weigh.*

English has dozens of words where a single vowel sound is spelled with the sequence of letters *ie* and dozens of others where a single vowel sound is spelled *ei,* but there is no obvious relationship between pronunciation and the two spelling alternates. This is the problem the above maxim attempts to address. It tries to show that there is *some* patterning in the relationship between the pronunciation and spelling of such words. Before I give examples, I wish to propose a slight revision in the rule:

I before e except after *c,*
or when sounded other than ee.

Here is the first fact: (1) in most words that cause trouble the vowel in doubt is pronounced like *ee* in *feet.* It is to these words that the first line in the rule applies:

(*I* before e . . .		except after c, . . .)
achieve	hygiene	ceiling
believe	piece	conceit
chief	shriek	deceit
grievous	thief	receive
handkerchief	wield	
hurriedly	yield	

Memorize these exceptions to this part of the rule (i.e., six words with the *ee* sound but the *ei* spelling *not* after *c* and one with *ie* after c):

either   seize   species
leisure   sheik
protein   weird

Here is the second fact: (2) In most words with this problem, where the vowel is pronounced other than *ee*, the vowel in question is spelled *ei*. It is to these words that the second line in the rule applies:

(. . . *or when sounded other than ee.*)

words with the *a* sound of *bate*
    vein
    freight
    eight
    weight
    neighbor

words with the short *i* sound of *bit*
    foreign
    forfeit

words with the long *i* sound of *bite*
    height
    sleight
    seismograph

Memorize this one exception (i.e., a word where the vowel is pronounced other than *ee* but where *i* is nonetheless before *e*):

fiery

Exercise

Fill in either *ie* or *ei* in the space in each of the following words:

(1) d__gn   (5) gr__f   (9) s__ge
(2) counterf__t   (6) kal__doscope   (10) sl__gh
(3) f__ld   (7) n__ce   (11) spec__s
(4) f__ry   (8) pr__st   (12) w__rd

Soft and hard c and g

It is useful to remember that English tends to pronounce the letters *c* and *g* "soft" in front of *i* and *e* and "hard" in front of other sounds. "Soft" *c* sounds like *s*, and "hard" *c* sounds like *k*. "Soft" *g* sounds like the *j* of *jet;* "hard" *g*, like the *g* of *get*. (And notice that *get* proves that this is only a tendency: It has a "hard" *g* sound in front of the vowel *e*, not the "soft" one that would be expected.) Here are some words that illustrate this tendency:

Soft *c* in front of *e* and *i*	Hard *c* elsewhere
cede	career
decide	careful
innocent	decade
license	decorate
parcel	particle
participate	significant

Soft *g* in front of *e* and *i*	Hard *g* elsewhere
angel	angle
changeable	argument
exaggerate	bargain
margin	elegant
merger	guarantee
sergeant	navigable

Awareness of this tendency can help you remember the spellings of words like the above. It also explains some otherwise puzzling and problematic spellings:

picnic*k*ing (the *k* keeps the "hard" final *c* of *picnic* from becoming "soft" in front of the *i* of *-ing*)

mimic*k*ing (the *k* keeps the "hard" final *c* of *mimic* from becoming "soft" in front of the *i* of *-ing*)

peac*e*able (the *e* remains to keep the "soft" *c* of *peace* from becoming "hard" in front of the *a* of *-able*)

Notic*e*able (the *e* remains to keep the "soft" *c* of *notice* from becoming "hard" in front of the *a* of *-able*)

chang*e*able (the *e* remains to keep the "soft" *g* of *change* from becoming "hard" in front of the *a* of *-able*)

serg*e*ant (the *e* serves the function of signaling that the *g* is "soft")

Exercise

How many words can you think of to add to the four lists of words given above that follow the pattern of hard and soft *c* and *g*? And can you think of other words, like *picnicking, changeable,* etc., that present spelling problems because of soft and hard *c* and *g*?

Reduced vowels

There is a strong tendency in English for vowels in unstressed syllables to be pronounced alike. They tend to sound like the "uh" sound that appears in the second syllable of the word *sofa*. The problem is that this sound may require a variety of letters to spell it, and thus the pronunciation seems to be of little help to you in deciding just what the spelling is. The unstressed "uh" is called a reduced vowel because the word or word part containing it may appear in other words with a distinct (i.e., unreduced) pronunciation. Here are two lists of words that cause spelling problems because they have reduced vowels. Each word in the first list is accompanied by a related word where the vowel is not reduced, and where the pronunciation clearly indicates the appropriate spelling. If you study these related words, you will find it easier to remember the letter that represents the reduced vowel in the problem word. In the second list you simply have to memorize the letter that represents the reduced vowel:

Problem words with related words
compar*a*ble (Comp*A*re)
expl*a*nation (expl*A*in)
gramm*a*r (gramm*A*tical)
imagin*a*tive (imagin*A*tion)

comp*e*tition (comp*E*te)
pr*e*sent (pr*E*sentation)
rep*e*tition (rep*E*at)

def*i*nition (def*I*ne)
hypocr*i*cy (hypocr*I*tical)
d*i*vide (d*I*vidend)
sim*i*lar (verisim*I*litude)

apol*o*gy (apol*O*gia)

Without related words

cat*e*gory	maint*e*nance
chall*e*nge	obst*a*cle
desp*e*rate	secr*e*tary
detr*i*mental	sep*a*rate

Sometimes knowledge of a word's etymology can help you remember the correct spelling of words like those in the second list above (e.g., that *separate* means to divide into *pArts*). But your surest solution is rote memory.

Exercises

a. Make a list of the words in the above text of my comments on reduced vowels that themselves contain reduced vowels. (I count more than a dozen of them.) For each word, try to find a related word—where the reduced vowel is distinctly pronounced—that gives you a clear indication in its pronunciation of the correct spelling of the reduced vowel.

b. Here is a paragraph with several misspellings attributable to reduced vowels. Identify the misspellings, first by looking for related words where reduced vowels are pronounced distinctly, and then by consulting a dictionary.

> The congrigation of the First Community Church was dissatesfied with its preacher because he was too speculitive in his sermons and tended to exaggarate financial problems. They elected a representitive to discuss the problem with him, and they hoped that there could be a resalution of the diffeculties without causing complecations.

Unpronounced letters and unspelled sounds

For most of the words listed in this section, pronunciation is a hindrance to correct spelling, because the typical pronunciation either leaves out a vowel or a consonant that must be spelled or puts in sounds or sound sequences that are not spelled. Some of the problem words have related words that do not cause spelling problems (these are given in parentheses) and that therefore provide helpful clues to the correct spelling of the problem words. Some spelling experts recommend that you change your pronunciations to match the spellings. If this seems to work for you, try it. It is probably just as easy in the long run simply to memorize the correct spellings.

Here, first of all, are some problem words where a typical conversational pronunciation gives no hint of a certain vowel that needs to be spelled:

accident*a*lly (accidental)	bound*a*ry
bus*i*ness (busy)	choc*o*late
comp*a*rable (compare)	desp*e*rate
fav*o*rite (favor)	extr*a*ordinary
light*e*ning (enlighten)	gen*e*rally
marr*i*age (marry)	math*e*matics
mem*o*ry (memorial)	mis*e*ry
nin*e*ty (nine)	priv*i*lege
	temper*a*ment
	vet*e*ran

Here are some problem words where a typical conversational pronunciation gives no hint of a consonant (or even a vowel and a consonant) that must be spelled:

condem*n*ed (condemnation)	pum*p*kin
environ*n*ment (environs)	su*b*tle

gover*n*ment (govern)
solem*n* (solemnity)

iden*t*ity
mor*t*gage

mali*g*n (malignant)
paradi*g*m (para*d*igmatic)
phle*g*m (phlegmatic)
reco*g*nize (cognizant)

can*d*idate
We*d*nesday

Feb*r*uary
lib*r*ary
su*r*prise

apos*t*le (apostolic)

ar*c*tic

lit*e*rature (sometimes pronounced "lit'rature," sometimes "lit'ature")
natu*ra*lly (sometimes pronounced "nat'rally," sometimes "natur'ly)
prob*a*bly (sometimes pronounced "proba'ly," sometimes "prob'ly")
temper*a*ment (sometimes pronounced "temp'rament," sometimes "temper'ment")
temper*a*ture (sometimes pronounced "temp'rature," sometimes "temper'ture," sometimes even "temp'ature")

Finally, here are some words where a typical conversational pronunciation (and in the case of the last two, the only pronunciation) either reverses the order of spelled letters or includes sounds that are not spelled at all:

child*re*n (sometimes pronounced "childern")
comfo*r*table (sometimes pronounced "comfterble")
envi*ro*nment (sometimes pronounced "envior'ment")
nuc*le*ar (sometimes pronounced "nucylear")
rel*ev*ant (sometimes pronounced "revelant")
ath*l*ete (sometimes pronounced "athelete")
mischievous (sometimes pronounced "mischiev*i*ous")
colonel (always pronounced "kernel")
Worcestershire (always pronounced "woostersheer")

Exercise

Here are some words spelled incorrectly according to the way they are sometimes pronounced in conversation. Correct the spellings. If you are not absolutely certain about the answer, consult a dictionary. (The asterisk in front of each word is simply a reminder that it is misspelled.)

(1) *benine	(5) *grievious	(9) *quanity
(2) *colum	(6) *incidently	(10) *sophmore
(3) *evrything	(7) *libral	(11) *suprise
(4) *genrally	(8) *perscribe	

Some Spelling Guides

This section provides some guides to correct spelling that are not based on the interaction of spelling and pronunciation, but on patterns in the letters themselves or on the interaction of spelling and word formation (i.e., the addition of prefixes and suffixes of various types).

Changing *y* to *i*

Many English words that end in *y* change the *y* to *i* when a suffix is added—except when the suffix is *-ing*. Here are some examples:

Base Word	Spelling with Suffix	Spelling with *-ing*
bushy	bushier	
crazy	crazier	
funny	funnier	
lazy	lazier	
fishy	fishiness	
lonely	loneliness	
carry	carries	carrying
hurry	hurried	hurrying
study	studies	studying
lay	laid (*but:* lays)	laying
pay	paid (*but:* pays)	paying
say	said (*but:* says)	saying

The last three examples listed above partially illustrate an exception to the change-*y*-to-*i* principle. The exception is this: When a vowel precedes the *y*, do not change it to *i*. Here are some examples where the exception always holds:

Base Word	Spelling with Suffix	Spelling with *-ing*
array	arrays	arraying
	arrayed	
play	plays	playing
	played	
buy	buys	buying

Exercise

See how many other example words you can find that follow the rule like those in the first list of examples. Then see how many exceptions you can find like those in the second list.

Problems with prefixes

Prefixes cause real spelling problems. Some of these problems can be diminished if you learn to recognize prefixes when they occur and if you remember that English tends to give prefixes their full allotment of letters, while the word they attached to also retains its full allotment of letters:

mis- + spell = misspell (with two *s*'s)
mis- + apply = misapply (with only one *s*)
dis- + satisfied = dissatisfied (with two *s*'s)
dis- + appoint = disappoint (with only one *s*)
in- + mature = immature (with two *m*'s—note that the *n* of *in-* changed to *m*)
in- + oculate = inoculate (with only one *n*)

This problem is further complicated because there are many words in English like *immature,* where a prefix is given its full allotment of letters, but the last letter in the prefix is *changed* to match the first letter of the word it attaches to. (As I wrote the first few sentences of this subsection, I had to look up the spelling of *allotment:* Did it have two *l*'s or one? I did not recognize that it is a combination of *ad-* and *lotment*—the *d* of *ad-* changed to *l*.) Here is a list of words that tend to be misspelled because writers fail to recognize a prefix (and which prefix) at the beginning of them:

abbreviate	dissolve	occupy
accept	extraordinary	occur
accommodate	forehead	offer
address	illegal	oppose
collapse	illuminate	suffix
commit	illusion	suppose
committee	immunity	suppressed
disappear	interrupt	syllogism
dissect	interrogate	unnoticed

Exercise

There is no easy way to learn to spell problem words like those listed above (and the list just given is far from a complete one). The most effective solution is simply to memorize the correct spelling of any such word that gives you trouble. Another, and possibly more interesting, approach is to become more familiar with etymologies. The more you learn about Latin and Greek prefixes and their meanings, the less trouble you will have. As a start, pick about ten words from the above list (words that have given you trouble in the past) and study their etymologies in a dictionary. Note the meanings of the prefixes attached to them, and especially note that even though the spelling of a prefix may change, it receives its full allotment of letters.

Problems with derivational suffixes

There are two kinds of problems caused by words that end in derivational suffixes. The first is the need to determine whether to include an *e* that occurs in related words without the suffix; the second is the need to choose between two spelled versions of the same suffix. Here is the general tendency (with exceptions) that governs the first problem:

(1) Leave out the *e* if the suffix begins with a vowel:
     blame + -ing = blaming
     come + -ing = coming
     fame + -ous = famous
     value + -able = valuable
   Exceptions:
     change + -able = changeable (The soft-*g* rule explains this.)
     courage + -ous = courageous (The soft-*g* rule explains this.)
     notice + -able = noticeable   (The soft-*c* rule explains this.)
(2) Do not leave out the *e* if the suffix begins with a consonant:
     care + -ful = careful
     entire + -ly = entirely
     fine + -ly = finely
     safe + -ly = safely
   Exceptions:
     argue + -ment = argument
     awe + -ful = awful
     due + -ly = duly
     true + -ly = truly

Here are lists (correctly spelled) of words that typically illustrate the second problem with derivational suffixes, i.e., the need to choose between two spelled versions of the same suffix:

-able	versus	*-ible*	
changeable		accessible	indivisible
conceivable		audible	infallible
indispensable		compatible	intelligible
irritable		contemptible	invisible
likable		convertible	irresistible
noticeable		deductible	permissible
[and most		edible	plausible
other words you		eligible	possible
commonly use]		feasible	reversible

	incomprehensible	sensible
	incredible	susceptible
	indigestible	

-ance	versus	*-ence*	
appearance		audience	
attendance		conscience	
balance		existence	
guidance		experience	
hindrance		innocence	
instance		intelligence	
maintenance		occurrence	
nuisance		precedence	
performance		residence	
perseverance			
resistance			

-ant	versus	*-ent*	
defendant		apparent	independent
dormant		competent	intelligent
hydrant		confident	permanent
important		descent	persistent
merchant		eminent	prevalent
persuant		equivalent	referent
pleasant			

-er	versus	*-or*
accounter		accelerator
arrester		author
bargainer		conveyor
computer		counselor
examiner		detractor
interviewer		director
partner		sponsor
		surveyor

Exercises

a. See how many words you can find that follow the tendency governing the dropping of *e* before suffixes that begin with a vowel and how many that retain the *e* before suffixes beginning with a consonant. Can you think of other exceptions to either tendency besides the ones listed?

b. Sometimes the dictionary lists either *-er* or *-or* as equally acceptable (e.g., *adviser* and *advisor*). Think of ten words other than those listed above that end in either -*er* or -*or*. Look them up in a dictionary to find out whether only one spelling is correct or whether both are acceptable. If both are acceptable, is one preferred?

c. Can you add words to the lists for -*able* versus -*ible*, -*ance* versus -*ence*, and -*ant* versus -*ent*?

Problems with verb and adjective endings

You need to know when to double consonants before -*ing*, -*ed*, -*er*, and -*est*.

Double a consonant in front of any of the above four suffixes when a vowel immediately preceding that consonant is stressed (i.e., pronounced louder than vowels in surrounding syllables) and spelled with only one letter:

bar + -ing = barring	plan + -ing = planning
+ -ed = barred	+ -ed = planned
bat + -ing = batting	big + -er = bigger
+ -ed = batted	+ -est = biggest
beg + -ing = begging	glad + -er = gladder
+ -ed = begged	+ -est = gladdest
drop + -ing = dropping	red + -er = redder
+ -ed = dropped	+ -est = reddest
occur + -ing = occurring	prefer + -ing = preferring
+ -ed = occurred	+ -ed = preferred
permit + -ing = permitting	
+ -ed = permitted	

Otherwise, do not double such consonants:

enter + -ing = entering
+ -ed = entered } The *e* before *r* is not stressed.

dread + -ing = dreading } The vowel before *d* is not spelled
+ -ed = dreaded } with a single letter.

exert + -ing = exerting
+ -ed = exerted } No vowel *immediately* preceding *t*

timid + -er = timider
+ -est = timidest } The *i* before *d* is not stressed.

brief + -er = briefer } The vowel before *f* is not spelled
+ -est = briefest } with a single letter.

rich + -er = richer
+ -est = richest } No vowel *immediately* preceding *h*

Words ending in *w* are exceptions to the above rules: The letter *w* is not doubled even if it is preceded by a stressed vowel spelled with a single letter:

plow + -ing = plowing
    + -ed = plowed
snow + -ing = snowing
    + -ed = snowed
 new + -er = newer
    -est = newest
slow + -er = slower
    -est = slowest

Exercise

Spell the *-ing* form and the *-ed* form of each of the following verbs:

(1) infer   (3) visit   (5) knead
(2) exit   (4) stab

Spell the *-er* form and the *-est* form of each of the following adjectives:

(6) sad   (8) great
(7) thick   (9) hot

Problems with noun plurals

The plurals of most English nouns are spelled simply by adding the letter *s* to their singular forms. There are, however, a large number of different types of exceptions to this general tendency.

The plurals of some nouns are formed by adding, not just *s*, but *es*:

(1) To nouns that end in *s, sh, ch,* and *x*:

buses	bushes	batches	boxes
fusses	flashes	matches	foxes
masses		watches	

(2) Many, but not all, nouns that end in an *o* that is immediately preceded by a consonant:

echoes	(but not these):		
heroes	avocados	gringos	provisos
innuendoes	banjos	halos	quartos
potatoes	dynamos	lassos	salvos
tomatoes	Eskimos	mementos	solos
vetoes	gauchos	pianos	twos
(and many other such nouns)	ghettos	piccolos	zeros

(nor these, where a vowel precedes the *o*):

cameos

rodeos

tatoos

zoos

(3) Some nouns that change *y* to *i* and add *es* – when the *y* is preceded by a consonant:

Singular	Plural
army	armies
body	bodies
city	cities
copy	copies
comedy	comedies
mercy	mercies
reply	replies
sky	skies

(but not if a vowel precedes the final *y*):

boys

days

guys

keys

The plurals of some nouns are spelled unpredictably because English retains the spellings of the foreign languages from which the words have been borrowed:

Singular	Plural	Singular	Plural
alumnus	alumni	codex	codices
locus	loci	analysis	analyses
stimulus	stimuli	axis	axes
genus	genera	basis	bases
		crisis	crises
alga	algae	diagnosis	diagnoses
alumna	alumnae	ellipsis	ellipses
larva	larvae	hypothesis	hypotheses
		oasis	oases
addendum	addenda	parenthesis	parentheses
bacterium	bacteria	synopsis	synopses
corrigendum	corrigenda	thesis	theses
desideratum	desiderata		
erratum	errata	criterion	criteria
ovum	ova	phenomenon	phenomena
stratum	strata		

There are words related to those on the above list that now have both regularly spelled plurals and foreign plurals in use. (Often you will need to consult a dictionary to see whether either one is preferable.) Here they are, with subtypes listed in the same order as on the previous list:

Singular	Regular Plural	Foreign Plural
cactus	cactuses	cacti
crocus	crocuses	croci
focus	focuses	foci
nucleus	nucleuses	nuclei
stylus	styluses	styli
syllabus	syllabuses	syllabi
terminus	terminuses	termini
corpus	corpuses	corpora
antenna	antennas	antennae
formula	formulas	formulae
vertebra	vertebras	vertebrae
aquarium	aquariums	aquaria
curriculum	curriculums	curricula
medium	mediums	media
memorandum	memorandums	memoranda
moratorium	moratoriums	moratoria
symposium	symposiums	symposia
apex	apexes	apices
index	indexes	indices
vortex	vortexes	vortices
appendix	appendixes (organs)	appendices (of books)
matrix	matrixes	matrices
automaton	automatons	automata
plateau	plateaus	plateaux
bureau	bureaus	bureaux
tableau	tableaus	tableaux

The word *data* presents a special problem. Historically, it is related to the words in the first list above that are grouped with *addendum/addenda* and to those in the second list grouped with *aquarium/aquariums/aquaria*. It came into English from Latin as a singular noun, *datum*, whose plural was *data*. It has not developed a native plural (**datums*) like the words on the second list. Instead, the Latin plural, *data*, has tended to be used in the singular as well as in the plural: *Only one data supports that claim; all of those data support that claim.* Thus, you have the following options in spelling the singular and plural of this word:

Foreign Singular	Native Singular	Foreign Plural
datum	data	data

In very formal writing, you should prefer *datum* as the singular; for most audiences, even in edited English, *data* is also an appropriate spelling of the singular.

Exercises

a. Spell the plurals of the following nouns. Apply the rules discussed above and consult the lists of exceptions. If you are uncertain, consult a dictionary:

(1) ax   (5) hello   (9) mercy
(2) bench   (6) industry   (10) mosquito
(3) dish   (7) kudo   (11) toss
(4) domino   (8) lady   (12) trench

b. Look up each of the following words, taken from the above lists of words with foreign plurals, and find out what foreign language it was borrowed from:

(1) appendix   (4) corpus   (7) index
(2) automaton   (5) focus   (8) medium
(3) bureau   (6) formula

Alternate spellings

Many words have more than one correct spelling. Some of the alternates are typically British and should be avoided so as to conform to standard American practice, but others are not. Here are some examples of British versus American spellings:

American	British	American	British
center	centre	connection	connexion
theater	theatre	inflection	inflexion
clamor	clamour	dreamed	dreamt
favor	favour	inquiry	enquiry
glamor	glamour	check	cheque
apologize	apologise	defense	defence
criticize	criticise	jewelry	jewellry

Here are some other alternate spellings where both are acceptable in American usage. It is generally advisable to use the first spelling listed in your dictionary; however, if you are more comfortable with the second, you are free to use it. In sets like those ending in *-og* or *-wards,* it is important to be consistent. I have listed the spelling that I prefer on the left. When a spelling rule applies (such as the one that calls for dropping the *e* before a derivational suffix beginning with a vowel, as in *likable*) I prefer the spelling that follows the rule:

analog	analogue
catalog	catalogue
dialog	dialogue
epilog	epilogue
monolog	monologue
prolog	prologue
travelog	travelogue
backward	backwards
downward	downwards
eastward	eastwards
forward	forwards
homeward	homewards
inward	inwards
northward	northwards
outward	outwards
southward	southwards
toward	towards
upward	upwards
percent	per cent
cannot	can not
racket	racquet
acknowledgment	acknowledgement
judgment	judgement
cigarette	cigaret
likable	likeable
fulfill	fulfil
develop	develope
goodbye	goodby
traveling	travelling

Exercise

Look up at least ten different kinds of words from the list of alternate spellings immediately above, and find out whether your dictionary prefers one of the spellings, and if so, which one. Then, look again at the list of British alternate spellings; can you think of any other British spellings besides those listed?

Frequently Misspelled Words

All the words discussed so far in this chapter are candidates for membership on a list of frequently misspelled words. So such a list has been begun already. Two extensions of that list are presented in this section.

First, I present a list of pairs and triplets that cause problems not because they are inherently difficult to spell, but because they are easily confused. Then, I present a list of words that did not fit easily into one of the earlier sections, either because the problem is not part of a general pattern or because the word presents more than one spelling problem. Words of the latter type may have appeared earlier but are repeated here simply because they are doubly troublesome.

Problematic pairs and triplets

Be sure to distinguish the following pairs and triplets. Often you need only remember which of the words you are writing. In some cases you may need to study the difference between the words. Your dictionary will be your best guide. Some of these pairs and triplets are discussed in the usage glossary in the Appendix:

accede, exceed
accent, ascent, assent
accept, except
aid, aide
advice, advise
affect, effect
all ready, already
all together, altogether
allusive, elusive, illusive
aural, oral
ascent, assent
allusion, illusion
baloney, bologna
break, brake
bare, bear
born, borne
breach, breech
bouillon, bullion
bloc, block
bough, bow
breath, breathe
cede, seed
cloths, clothes
callus, callous
canvas, canvass
capital, Capitol

carat, caret
caster, castor
ceiling, sealing
cereal, serial
chic, Sheik
choose, chose
climactic, climatic
complement, compliment
coarse, course
conscience, conscious
consul, council, counsel
chord, cord
cent, scent, sent
decent, descent
desert, dessert
device, devise
discreet, discrete
dyeing, dying
earn, urn
elicit, illicit
emigrant, immigrant
envelop, envelope
eminent, imminent, immanent
fain, feign
faint, feint

formally, formerly
founder, flounder
forth, fourth
farther, further
forbear, forebear
forward, foreword
gorilla, guerrilla
hear, here
holey, holy, wholly
idle, idol, idyll
instance, instants
its, it's
ingenious, ingenuous
install, instill
interment, internment
know, no
knead, need
later, latter
lead, led
loose, lose
manner, manor
marshal, martial
maybe, may be
moral, morale
morn, mourn
of, off
ordinance, ordnance

passed, past

peace, piece

personal, personnel

peak, peek, pique

peremptory, pre-
emptory

plain, plane

pore, poor, pour

precede, proceed

presence, presents

profit, prophet

pedal, peddle

principal, principle

quiet, quit, quite

right, rite, write

rye, wry

sense, since

shone, shown

stationary, stationery

straight, strait

stake, steak

suite, sweet

than, then

their, there, they're

toe, tow

thrash, thresh

timber, timbre

to, too, two

vain, vane, vein

weak, week

weather, whether

were, where

your, you're

Exercises

a. Study the pairs and triplets in the list just given. If you are not absolutely certain of the distinction in meaning and use between members of a pair or among members of a triplet, check the usage glossary in the Appendix (pp. 329–340) to find out the difference. If the items are not listed there, look up their meanings in your dictionary.

b. Here is an informal paragraph containing several words given on the list of pairs and triplets. Identify any misspelled words and replace them with the correct word. Be prepared to explain why each correction was necessary.

I would like to go back to college and finish my degree. I can take only a few coarses a semester, so I want to find professors who do not hand students a lot of bologna. I also cannot stand teachers who think they are sheik. In fact, I prefer teachers with a rye sense of humor. I do not morn the years I spent in low-paying jobs, because I earned a descent living, but I do hope to move to a higher plane. One advantage I will have is that I can peddle my bike to classes if climactic conditions permit.

Assorted problem words

Many of the words listed here do not fit into one of the problem patterns treated earlier. Many others do, and were already listed. Some fit into more than one problem pattern. Those that are listed here, in addition to many that do not fit into any pattern, are repeated because they tend to be misspelled especially often.

Ask a friend to read this list to you, and try to spell each word as you hear it. You will discover that you already know how to spell many of these words, but you will identify those that you do not in fact know how to spell.

accept	always	annual	beginning
accommodate	amateur	anonymous	calendar
across	analysis	awkward	career
address	analyzing	balloon	careful

Caribbean	fascinate	misspell	proceed
cannot	favorite	mileage	pronunciation
category	February	mustache	pursue
chauvinism	fluorescent	obstacle	questionnaire
commit	forehead	occur	racket
committee	fulfill	occurred	recommend
competition	government	occurrence	repetition
condemned	grammar	offense	roommate
conscious	guarantee	omit	sacrilegious
conscientious	guttural	omitted	secretary
controlled	harassment	operate	separate
curriculum	height	pamphlet	souvenir
dealt	hypocrisy	parallel	succeed
definitely	imitation	paralleled	successful
desperate	judgment	paroled	supersede
detrimental	knowledge	pastime	suppressed
develop	library	percent	temperament
disappear	license	phony	technique
disappoint	likable	picnic	therefore
disastrous	literature	picnicking	tomorrow
discipline	loneliness	possession	truly
embarrassment	magic	precede	twelfth
encyclopedia	maintenance	precedence	until
equipment	maneuver	preceding	unnoticed
exaggerate	marriage	privilege	vacuum
explanation	mischievous	procedure	Wednesday
			wholly

Exercise

After you have discovered which words on the above list, and any other words treated earlier, cause you spelling problems, study each word on your list and identify the letter or letters that seem to be the source of the difficulty. After you study each word, copy it several times. Begin a list of your special spelling gremlins. (The best place to keep this list is on the inside cover of your desk dictionary.)

Capitalization

The rules of capitalization apply not only to edited English but to more casual written styles as well. These rules typically require that the first letter of certain words be from the set of upper-case letters. The rules are complex and sometimes unpredictable. Therefore, as with spelling per se, your dictionary must be your constant guide. If you learn the contents of this section, you will need to consult your dictionary less. The section begins with capitalization requirements that operate on the level of the sentence and then moves down the scale of language structure to requirements operating on the level of the word.

Initial words

Capitalize the first word in a sentence, in an exclamation, or in a purposely used sentence fragment:

> The bigger they are, the harder they fall.
> Hurrah!
> There is one sure route to success. Telling the truth.

Capitalize the first word in a direct quotation, whether or not it is in quotation marks:

> The panelist said, "This problem deserves serious attention."
> His question was: Why are the American people so blind to the energy crisis?

The first word of a quoted fragment is not capitalized:

> She referred "to the problem, not to its causes."

Capitalize the first word in every line of a traditional poem:

> *Let me not to the marriage of true minds*
> *Admit impediments: love is not love*
> *Which alters when it alteration finds*
> *Or bends with the remover to remove*
>
> —WILLIAM SHAKESPEARE

Capitalize the first word in a complete sentence or in a formally introduced series of clauses after a colon if these are punctuated as sentences:

> Here is the problem: No one will take responsibility for the decision.
> Three principles must guide the writer: Think before you write. Organize as you write. Revise after you write.
> We must find answers to these questions: Where will we find more electric power? How shall we distribute it fairly?

Capitalize the first word in the salutation and in the complimentary close of a letter:

> Dear Ms. McCoy,
> My dear Mr. Rollo,
> Very truly yours,
> Sincerely yours,

Exercise

The following sentences contain mistakes in capitalization. Find them; correct them; and be prepared to state why they are mistakes.

(1) Nature, like liberty, is but restrained
   by the same laws which first herself ordained.
      [Two lines from a poem by Alexander Pope]
(2) And God said, let there be light. [—Gen 1:3]
(3) my Dear friend Harry,
      [Salutation from a letter]
(4) Emerson once wrote that the reward of a job well-done "Is to have done it."
(5) Justice is rooted in reason. mercy is rooted in feeling.

Words in titles

There are special rules for capitalizing in titles: Capitalize all words in titles except articles (*a, an, the*), short conjunctions (e.g., *and, but*), and short prepositions (e.g., *in, of, at*); capitalize *these also* if they are the first or last word in the title or if they appear after a colon. The rules apply to titles of books, magazines, articles, pamphlets, poems, etc.:

For Whom the Bell Tolls
   (A novel by Ernest Hemingway)
Canadian Journal of Linguistics
   (A scholarly periodical)
Field and Stream
   (A popular magazine)
"Japanese Beetles: A Treatment Farmers Need to Be Aware Of"
   (Title of an article in a magazine—with final *of* capitalized and *a* capitalized after a colon)
"Anecdote of the Jar"
   (Title of a short poem by Wallace Stevens)

Exercise

Think of at least two examples like each one on the list of examples just given and decide which words in them must be capitalized. They may be real titles, or they may be imaginary ones.

Proper nouns and proper adjectives

A proper noun designates a unique person, place, or thing (*Tom Jones, Africa,* the *Titanic*) and thus does not occur with certain modifiers (**the Tom Jones, *an Africa, *every Titanic*). A proper adjective (*African*) is an adjective that is derived from a proper noun and retains the noun's unique reference. Proper nouns and proper adjectives are capitalized. (But take care not to capitalize such words if they are used in contexts where they do not have the unique reference that characterizes a proper noun.)

Names of persons, including pets
Charles C. Boycott, Mohammed (Mohammedan), Ronald Mcdonald, Fido, Old Hickory

But: We have been boycotting lettuce.

Names of God, including pronouns
God, the Deity, Allah, the Supreme Being

But: I hate this god-awful weather.

Names of peoples and languages
Europeans, Blacks, Turks, Turkish, French, Swahili

But: french fries, turkish bath

Names of religions and their members
Protestantism, Protestants, Buddhism, Buddhist, Catholicism, Catholic

But: He has catholic (i.e., universal), interests.

Names of organized bodies
the Congress of the United States, the United States Senate, the Virginia General Assembly, the World Court, the Textron Corporation

But: He's attending a congress of legislators. They're forming a corporation.

Names of aircraft, spacecraft, and ships
the *Spirit of St. Louis,* the *S. S. United States, Apollo 11*

Trademarks
Coke, Kleenex, Xerox

Historical periods and events
the Renaissance, the Middle Ages, World War I, the Battle of Hastings, the Treaty of Versailles

But: another world war, a battle at Hastings, a treaty at Versailles

Days, months, holidays, and holy days
Monday, Tuesday, January, February, Passover, Easter, Thanksgiving

But not the seasons: winter, spring, summer, fall

The stars and the planets
>the Little Dipper, Mars, Venus

But: the earth, moon, sun—unless listed with others

Parts or chapters of specific books
>Part III, Chapter 9

But: The book has three parts. There is a chapter on food.

Remember that proper adjectives based on all proper nouns in the above listing are also capitalized. In addition to *Mohammedan,* which was listed, some others are *European, Protestant,* and *Martian.*

Exercise

Capitals are needed in certain of the following words and expressions but not in others. Place them where appropriate:

(1) a congressional proclamation
(2) the ohio legislature
(3) spokane
(4) italian
(5) fourth of july
(6) saturday
(7) september
(8) state of the union message
(9) swiss cheese

Titles and modifying words in proper names

Titles and terms of family relationship that precede a proper name are also capitalized; titles that follow are not [an exception is *the President* (of the United States), which may be capitalized].

President Carter
Ronald Reagan, the President
Senator McGovern
Uncle Joe
Professor Stein

But: George McGovern, the former senator;
Joe, my uncle;
Albert Stein, my English professor

Modifying words in proper names are capitalized:

Woodland Avenue
Union Station
Tampa General Hospital

But: a wide avenue,
the railroad station,
a general hospital

The definite article is capitalized only in very few proper names:

The Hague   *But:* the Middle East, the Congress, the Governor, the *Times,* the National Biscuit Company

Exercise

Add capitals where called for:

(1) the cape of good hope
(2) Churchill, a british prime minister
(3) the north pole
(4) eastern standard time
(5) John Danforth, the doctor who operated on me
(6) the new york city ballet

Words and expressions entirely in upper case

The title that you actually type on a term paper, the words designating the major divisions in a term paper, and the word *table* in the label of a table in a term paper are entirely in capitals:

THE ORIGIN OF LANGUAGE
(Title of a term paper as it appears on the cover)
CONTENTS, ENDNOTES, BIBLIOGRAPHY
(Headings of major sections of a term paper as they are typed at the tops of their respective pages)
TABLE 2:   Correlations of Average Weekly Incomes with Social Class
(A title under a table in a term paper)

Loudness can be indicated in transcriptions of dialog by writing certain words in all capital letters:

Joe said, "I didn't MEAN to lie; I just couldn't HELP it!"

Abbreviations are in all capitals if the words they abbreviate begin in capitals:

UCLA (University of California at Los Angeles)
NATO (North Atlantic Treaty Organization)
HUD (Department of Housing and Urban Development)

But: i.e. (Latin for "that is")

The words *I* and *O* (but not *oh*) are always capitalized:

Joe wondered if I could help him.
I prayed, O Lord, help us!

Exercise

Examine the specimen term paper printed in Chapter Twelve and notice instances of words typed in all capitals. What kinds of writing contexts might justify the use of all capitals to show emphasis in dialog? Should this be a frequent practice in edited English? List five abbreviations that appear in all capitals and also the proper name which each abbreviates.

Italics

When you write or type a paper, you indicate italics by underlining the words to be italicized. Italicize titles of books, periodicals, pamphlets, plays, long poems, works of art and music, and also the names of newspapers:

Roots (Title of a book by Alex Haley)
Ladies Home Journal (Title of a periodical)
A Streetcar Named Desire (A play by Tennessee Williams)
Paradise Lost (A long poem by John Milton)
The Last Supper (A painting by Leonardo Da Vinci)
The New York Times (A newspaper)

The following are not italicized, but are enclosed in sets of double quotation marks: titles of chapters or parts of books, titles of articles or essays in periodicals, titles of short stories and short poems, titles of songs, and names of TV and radio programs.

Italicize names of aircraft, spacecraft, and ships:

the *Spirit of St. Louis* (An aircraft)
Apollo 11 (A spacecraft)
the *Queen Mary* (A ship)

Italicize words, letters, and numerals when cited and discussed as such:

The word *capital* comes from a Latin word meaning "head."
The letter *e* is dropped before certain suffixes.
The first *3* on this sheet is smudged.

Italicize foreign words and phrases that have not yet been absorbed into the native vocabulary of English. (Usually such expressions either will not appear in your dictionary or will appear with a foreign language label.)

If the weather does not improve, I will have to say *adiós* to the Northeast.
Illiteracy is the *raison d'être* of college handbooks.
When I sneezed, Herman said, *"Gesundheit!"*

Italicize to show emphasis, but do so sparingly in edited English:

The test tubes must be shaken *very carefully* to avoid the possibility of an explosion.

Exercise

Add italics where they are called for in the following passage:

I plan to write a book about the TV show, "Star Trek." I think I will call it Our Future in Space. If it is well-written, it will be de rigueur in literary circles. I hope to show that Captain Kirk and his ship, the Enterprise, were not traveling in a fantasy world, but in the real world of the future. The word bestseller will have a new meaning when my book is published.

Numbers

There are several customs governing the use of numbers in edited English. These may be grouped under two headings: (1) You need to know when it is appropriate to spell out a number and when it is appropriate to represent it with numerals, and (2) you need to know about several special usage rules governing the use of numerals when they are appropriate.

Spelling out numbers versus using numerals

Ordinarily, you should spell out a number in edited English if you can do so in one or two words. This applies to cardinal numbers (*one, two, three*), ordinal numbers (*first, second, third*), and also fractions:

for four months	*But:*	for 255 years
forty-five minutes		122 minutes
the twenty-eighth President		the 108th prime minister
three thousand dollars		$3,550.00
one fourth of the class		$24\frac{1}{2}$

Spell out numbers (even if more than two words are needed) at the beginning of a sentence, or reword the sentence so that the number does not appear first:

Two hundred and fifty-five years is a long life for a tree.
A tree has a long life if it lasts 255 years.
Twenty-four and a half bushels of potatoes will last a month.
We will have a month's supply with $24\frac{1}{2}$ bushels of potatoes.

Round off and spell out very large numbers unless the context requires absolute accuracy or you wish to use the numerals to add emphasis:

The governor proposed a two and a half billion dollar budget.
Not: The governor proposed a $2,500,000,000.00 budget.
Also acceptable: The governor proposed a $2.5 billion budget.

If two or more numbers occur in parallel structure and one of them is written as a numeral, then all should be written as numerals—even those short enough to spell out:

The bill was defeated by a vote of 422 to 12.
I bought 3 apples, 28 bottles of juice, and 145 napkins.

Only in legal and commercial documents are numbers both spelled out and written as numerals:

The executor of this trust fund will receive not more than one hundred
   (100) dollars for each day administering the fund.
Also acceptable: . . . one hundred dollars($100) . . .

Exercise

Decide whether each number in the following sentences is correctly spelled out or represented by numerals. If it is correct, leave it alone; if it is incorrect, make the appropriate change and be prepared to state why you made the change:

(1) I got a hundred (100) on my math test.
(2) My son dated a woman who is 133rd in line for the throne of Belgium.
(3) A neighbor of mine told me about a woman in Asia who was one hundred and twenty-nine years old.
(4) California used to have a $5.5 billion surplus before the tax revolt.
(5) All we need is four volunteers, three sheets of plywood, and 250 nails, and we can do the job.

Special uses of numerals

Some of the following special uses constitute exceptions to the principle that numbers are spelled out if they take only one or two words. So study them carefully.

Notice how decimals and percentages are ordinarily represented:

(1) We had 3.2 inches of rain.
   (Use numerals even with decimals that could be spelled out in a few words.)
(2) We had a 20 percent (or 20%) return on our investment.
   (Use numerals to express percentages; either the word *percent* or the symbol % may be used with percentages of more than one numeral.)
(3) We had a $5\frac{1}{2}$ percent return on our investment.
   (Only the word *percent* may be used with percentages of one numeral.)

Do not spell out numbers in any of the following, even if only one or two words will do it; instead, use numerals as indicated here:

(1) **Dates**
   August 14, 1970   *But not:*   August 14th, 1970
   from 1978 to 1981   from 1978–1981
   1978–1981 (*or:* 1978–81)   from 1978–81

(2) **Time of day**
   4 A.M., or 4 o'clock in the morning   *But not:*   5:30 o'clock
   5:30 P.M., or half-past 5 in the af-
   ternoon

(3) **Addresses**
   P.O. Box 20
   614 South 70th Street
   Apartment 12

(4) **Ages**
   8 years old
   2 years 3 months and 17 days
   a 3-year-old girl

(5) **Book divisions**
   Part 3
   Chapter 5
   page 20

(6) **Numbers in proper names**
   George III (Roman numerals are usually used in names of people.)
   Soyuz 3 (A spacecraft)
   U.S. Highway 66
   Channel 15

Exercise

   Correct any errors in the representation of numbers in the following sentences. Be prepared to explain why you left a given number as is or made a given
change.

   (1) Only 3% of those surveyed agreed with the new policy.
   (2) I have so far read only Chapter 4.
   (3) They live in apartment three hundred.
   (4) Pope Paul VI headed the Roman Catholic Church during a period of
       change.
   (5) On my next birthday, I will be thirty-nine.
   (6) The mail arrives each day at 10:30 o'clock.
   (7) I was born on January first 1941.

Abbreviations

This section lists certain common abbreviations and some problems writers have in using them. It also lists several types of words that should not be abbreviated in edited English. But only very few of the many hundred abbreviations in English are treated here. As in all matters treated in this chapter, the dictionary will be your ultimate guide.

When to abbreviate

Abbreviate titles before proper names, and titles and degrees after proper names:

Mr. Edward Elsworth
John F. Kennedy, Jr. (note the comma before *Jr.*)
Ms. Helen Murray (note that *Ms.* may be pronounced *miz* or *em-es*)
Dr. Carlos Garcia, Ph.D.
Julie R. Cahill, M.D.
St. Thomas Aquinas

Abbreviate words and symbols used with numerals (but do not abbreviate them when the words are spelled out):

10 A.M. or 10 AM (No comma precedes
   the abbreviation. Notice that this abbreviation is set in small capitals.
   When you type or write a paper,
   you may use lower case letters.)
no. 12 or No. 12   *But not:*   no. twelve
$8.00
44 B.C. or 44 BC (These, too, are small
   capitals. When you write or type a
   paper; use upper case letters.)
35 mph, 40 rpm, 1000 kwh   *But not:*   thirty-five mph

Learn the abbreviations for familiar organizations, institutions, and individuals. Remember that *United States* is abbreviated only when used adjectivally, and *District of Columbia* is abbreviated only following *Washington:*

. . . a representative of the U.S. Government . . .
Washington, D.C.
UN, IRS, FBI, GOP, FDR, JFK, LBJ, TV

OK and *O.K.* are both okay, but not in very formal writing. (Notice that many common abbreviations are used without periods; consult your dictionary when in doubt about this.)

Learn how to write and say common Latin abbreviations such as the following. They are followed by a comma or colon in a text and are not italicized:

The Abbreviation	The Latin Expression It Abbreviates	Meaning—and English Reading
(1) etc.	*et cetera*	"and so forth," or "et cetera"
(2) i.e.	*id est*	"that is"
(3) e.g.	*exempli gratia*	"for example"

Do not confuse *i.e.* and *e.g.*; *i.e.* restates a point and *e.g.* presents an example of it. *He likes his leisure; i.e., he's lazy. You must eat more proteins, e.g., eggs.* The two abbreviations are not interchangeable in the example sentences.

(4) viz.	*videlicet*	"namely"
(5) vs. or v.	*versus*	"versus"

In edited English it is customary to avoid either abbreviation and simply use the full English word *versus*, which has been borrowed from Latin.

(6) et al.	*et alii*	"and others"

Notice that *et* is a complete Latin word and is therefore not followed by a period in the abbreviation, *et al.*

(7) cf.	*confer*	"see," or "compare"

When not to abbreviate

Do not abbreviate names of courses of study:

Sociology, Psychology, Political Science, Physical Education	*Not:* Soc., Psych., Poly. Sci., P. E.

Do not abbreviate words that refer to books and book parts (except in certain specified contexts, such as footnotes):

volume, part, chapter	*Not:* vol., pt., ch.

Do not abbreviate names of countries (except the USSR), states, months, days of the week, measurement words:

Canada, England, Libya	*Not:*	Can., Engl., Lib.
Kansas, Alaska, Delaware		Kan., Al., Del.
April, August, November		Apr., Aug., Nov.
Wednesday, Sunday		Wed., Sun.
pounds, feet, yards		lbs., ft., yds.

Do not abbreviate words like *street, avenue, boulevard, park, mount, company:*

		Not:	
The pavement needs repair on Spring-dale Court.			Springdale Ct.
He is going to work for Acme Wrench Company.			Acme Wrench Co.

Do not use the ampersand in the name of a company unless it appears in official publications of the company: *John Wiley and Sons, Publishers,* not *John Wiley & Sons;* however, *Harper & Row, Publishers* is correct.

Exercise

Correct any mistakes in the use of abbreviations in the following sentences:

(1) My boss claimed he caught a fish that weighed 45 pounds.
(2) Many more foreign tourists are traveling to the U.S.
(3) We all have to work very hard to win this race, e.g., do our best.
(4) This summer, our club plans to climb Mt. McKinley.
(5) The moral dilemma that often tests politicians is truth versus expediency.
(6) Our company considers the terms of the sale to be OK.
(7) It is possible that John F. Kennedy Junior may one day be a successful politician.
(8) One may drive 25 mph in a school zone in Virginia.
(9) During the month of Mar. I.R.S. offices are open after 5 P.M.
(10) Taxes are due on Apr. 15th.

Eleven | *Punctuation*

At the outset of Chapter Four, I noted that the focus from that point on in the book would be on the revision process, because conscious application of the principles of paragraph structure, sentence structure, diction, and spelling most commonly takes place as you revise your earlier drafts. Chapters Four through Ten treated principles that should guide your revisions of paragraphs, sentences, words, and spelling. But punctuation is not a level of language structure in the same sense. Its principles apply at all levels. Often, a given mark of punctuation can play a meaningful role on more than one level. The semicolon, for instance, can operate in paragraph structure; it does so when it closely connects two independent clauses (as it just did in this sentence). The semicolon can also do the job of a comma in sentence structure: joining a series of clauses, independent or dependent; joining a series of phrases, of any type; or joining a series of words when one or more of the items in any such series requires internal commas (as in this sentence).

I would like to be able to organize this chapter to treat paragraph-level punctuation, then sentence-level, and finally word-level punctuation. You would gain greater insight into the overall patterns of English punctuation if I did. But such an approach would require the uses of the semicolon to be treated in two separate places in the chapter, and uses of the period to be treated in three separate places. This would make this book very difficult to use as a reference. My compromise is to treat all uses of a given mark of punctuation together, but to arrange the uses according to the hierarchy of language structure: marks of punctuation whose uses are primarily on the paragraph and sentence levels are treated before those whose uses are primarily on the word level. And the several uses of each mark are ordered from higher to lower levels of language structure.

Periods /.

Use a period after a complete sentence that makes a statement or gives a command.

The sun is the center of the solar system.
The more he exercises, the weaker he seems to get.
Do your assignments on time.
Please help us control pollution.

Use a period after carefully chosen sentence fragments that play an important role in an essay.

Are today's youth as dedicated to the survival of democracy as their forebears? Up to a point.

Be very cautious about putting periods after fragments. And begin to do so only when you have gained a thorough feel for sentence structure and have no problems of sentence recognition such as those treated in Chapter Seven on pp. 165–167.

Use a period after an indirect question or after a question that is intended as a suggestion and does not therefore require an answer.

Harold wondered why William's fleet had not sailed.
The people want to know whether taxes will come down.
May we ask that you arrive on time.

Use three periods (ellipsis dots) to show that one or more words have been omitted in quoted material. (If the omission follows a complete sentence, a period should precede the three ellipsis dots.)

Fourscore and seven years ago our fathers brought forth on this continent a new nation . . . dedicated to the proposition that all men are created equal.

—ABRAHAM LINCOLN

I am thankful that the good God created us all ignorant. . . .

—MARK TWAIN

Use an entire line of periods (ellipsis dots) to show the omission of one or more lines when quoting the text of a poem:

> *The innocent brightness of a new-born Day*
> > *Is lovely yet;*
>
> . . . .
> *To me the meanest flower that blows can give*
> *Thoughts that do often lie too deep for tears.*

— WILLIAM WORDSWORTH

Use a period after numbers and letters in outlines, but not those enclosed in parentheses.

I. Problems caused by machinery
  A. Affecting the owner
    1. Maintenance
      a. Scheduled
      b. Unscheduled
    2. Breakdown
  B. Affecting society as a whole: pollution
II. Problems caused by people

The above sample is a part of the outline developed at the end of Chapter Three. If the paper had been longer, and further divisions were needed under I.A.1.a., they would appear in parentheses without periods: (1), (2), etc. And divisions under those would be small letters in parentheses without periods: (a), (b), etc.

Use periods in abbreviations, but remember that many common abbreviations appear without periods. Let your dictionary guide you.

Ph.D.
Mr., Mrs., Ms.
etc., i.e., e.g.

Refer to the section on abbreviation in the previous chapter (pp. 254–256) for additional information on when to abbreviate and when not to abbreviate words and expressions.

Use a period to separate integers from decimals:

$4.29
8.75 percent
12.5 meters

There is an exercise on p. 261 treating the uses of periods, question marks, and exclamation points.

Question Marks /?

Use a question mark with direct questions that seek an answer.

Can the federal government cope with the problems of the cities?
Does rock music damage the ear?
What will historians say about the 1970s?
Why has Western civilization lost its committment to absolute values?

Use a question mark even with statements when they are to be read as questions.

The defense budget has actually decreased in terms of the gross national product?
We are supposed to be there at six?

Use a question mark with each of a series of questions conjoined into one clause.

Was a new house bought by the Smiths? and the Joneses? and the Allens?

One question mark at the end would mean that the three families are joint owners of one house.

Use a question mark enclosed in parentheses to show doubt or skepticism about matter in the text.

The witness saw the suspect eat ten(?) pizzas before robbing the cashier.

The writer of the sentence is not sure whether the witness said "ten" or "two"; the writer is simply skeptical about the credibility of a witness who would make such a claim.

The newspaper reported that a pet(?) thundered over the beach.

The writer wishes to report accurately what the newspaper wrote but wishes also to express doubt about it. Perhaps it was a jet, not a pet. There is an exercise on p. 261 treating the uses of periods, question marks, and exclamation points.

Exclamation Points /!

Use the exclamation point to indicate extreme surprise, disbelief, approval, or other strong emotion expressed in a complete sentence. However, do so only very rarely in edited English, when it is especially appropriate to audience and purpose.

President Nixon resigned on August 9, 1974. The American constitutional system was vindicated!
How long will we continue destroying the natural environment!

Use the exclamation point with a phrase or a word that expresses strong emotion. When you do so, the phrase or word is capitalized as if it were a sentence. (This use of the exclamation point should be even less frequent in edited English than the first use.)

The outcome of the vote was not certain until the last delegate was heard from. Victory! The convention erupted in pandemonium.
Only six months after taking up distance running, Helen broke the state marathon record. On to the Olympics!

Use an exclamation point enclosed in parentheses to express surprise about matter in the text.

Amy Schuller, an eight-year-old(!), won the state spelling bee.
President Ford exercised the veto nearly 60 times(!) during his presidency.

This use of the exclamation point, like the other two uses, should be infrequent in edited English, and carefully attuned to requirements of audience and purpose.

Exercise

At several places in the following passage, parentheses indicate that a period, a question mark, or an exclamation point might be appropriate. Decide first whether *no punctuation* is needed (and be prepared to argue why). If you decide that punctuation *is* needed, pick which of the three is most appropriate (and be prepared to argue why). If more than one of the three marks of punctuation could fit the position, say so (and be prepared to discuss the different affect each mark would have on meaning, audience, and purpose).

When I was young, I wondered why I could not have everything I
wanted( ) I saw others indulging themselves( ) Pleasure, pleasure, and more
pleasure( ) That was their creed( ) Why couldn't I live like them( ) I
wanted fun, but I also needed knowledge( ) Fun took time and energy;
learning took more time and energy( ) More than I had available( ) Maybe
there wasn't time in life for a full dose of both( ) I had to choose( ) So will
you( ) May I suggest that you make your choice before it's too late( )

Single Commas /,

Use a comma between two independent clauses joined by a coordinating conjunction (in the absence of a conjunction, a period or semicolon must be used).

> Foreign auto makers have greatly improved the safety of their cars, and American manufacturers are taking notice.

Before I could even be sure that it was a mountain lion, it charged against the trap, but before it reached it something hit it and made it recoil.

—CARLOS CASTANEDA

If *but* were removed, either a semicolon or a period and a capital *b* on *Before* would have to replace the comma after *trap*.

Use commas between three or more clauses in a series. This includes placing a comma before the conjunction that must precede the last clause in the series.

> College students spend their time absorbing ideas from professors and books, college professors spend their time teaching and researching, and college administrators spend their time.
> When children develop a sense of security, when adolescents develop a sense of responsibility, and when adults develop a feeling of tolerance, then many of society's problems may begin to resolve themselves.

Use commas between three or more phrases or words in a series. This includes placing a comma before the conjunction that must precede the last phrase or word in the series.

These textbooks expound the body of accepted theory, illustrate many or all of its successful applications, and compare these applications with exemplary observations and experiments.

—THOMAS KUHN

> The elderly must be treated with dignity, with respect, and with compassion
> Prudence, justice, temperance, and fortitude—these are old virtues, but they are by no means out of date.

Use a comma to set off quoted materials from the text quoting it.

> "On with the show," he said. (Comma after quoted matter)
> He said, "On with the show." (Comma before quoted matter)
> Saying, "On with the show," he took his seat. (Commas before and after quoted matter)

Use a comma to set off adverbial clauses or phrases that introduce a sentence.

> Because I need to develop discipline, I have taken up distance running.
> When Harold heard that William had landed, he marched his army southward.

For love of country, many men and women have postponed careers and endured hardship.

A phrase of only two or three words in length need not be set off by a comma.

In the morning the sails of the enemy ships could be seen on the horizon.

Use a comma to set off other words or phrases that have been displaced from their typical positions and moved to the front of the sentence.

Books, I cannot get enough of.
Glorious urban renewal plans, we have; money to finance them, we do not have.

Use a comma to set off an introductory transitional expression that is not a functional part of the syntax of a clause.

Nevertheless, government must provide what services it can with the funds it has.
On the other hand, the business community has a role to play in urban renewal too.

Use a comma to separate a tag question from the sentence it accompanies.

Abraham Lincoln was the sixteenth president, wasn't he?
The Spanish settled in Florida long before the English, didn't they?
We are required to file a notarized report on automobile accidents, are we not?

Use a comma to indicate gaps the reader can fill by reference to an immediately preceding parallel clause or phrase.

The adolescent is sure of everything; the senior citizen, of nothing.
Theodore Roosevelt signed the first Panama Canal Treaty, and Jimmy Carter, the second.

Use a comma to avoid ambiguity or add emphasis, but try to avoid all unnecessary uses of commas in edited English.

For John, Smith was a saviour.
Workers who like to help their families, eat healthy lunches.

Use a comma for all of the following conventional purposes.

(1) Dates
October 19, 1942
Early on the morning of October 19, 1942, Carol was born.

(2) Addresses
Who lives at 1600 Pennsylvania Avenue, Washington, D.C.?
Virginia Beach, Virginia, is the largest resort city in the world.

(3) Salutations in informal correspondence
Dear Bill,
Dear Dad,

(4) Complimentary closes in formal and informal correspondence
Cordially,
Sincerely,
Yours sincerely,
Very truly yours,

(5) Before abbreviated titles following proper names
Henry Kissinger, Ph.D.
Jonas Salk, M.D.

(6) In large numbers
1,234,579
4,678

An exercise on the use of commas appears after the section on pairs of commas (see p. 265).

Pairs of Commas /, . . . ,

Use a pair of commas to set off a clause, phrase, or word that interrupts the grammatical flow of a sentence but does not radically interrupt the flow of ideas (if it radically interrupted the flow of ideas, parentheses or pairs of dashes would more appropriately set it off).

I thought, when I was young, that I would have resolved at least a few basic questions by the time I reached forty.
Work persistently, he thought, toward one key goal at a time.
The committee agreed, however, that many more hearings needed to be held before a bill could be drafted
I must, therefore, advise you to seek the advice of a lawyer.

Use a pair of commas to set off a nonrestrictive relative clause or nonrestrictive phrase modifying a noun.

Women, who are equal to men in intelligence, must be given equal educational opportunity.

Without the commas the clause would restrict the class of women who are equal to men, stating that only some are. With the commas, the clause is really a variant of the type of parenthetical additions to a sentenced listed in the use immediately above. See Chapter Five, pp. 145–146 for a discussion of the distinction between restrictive and nonrestrictive relative clauses.

> Women, representing more than half of the people on earth, should have equal rights.

The modifying phrase set off by commas is nonrestrictive; it applies to all women. Thus, the writer of the sentence asserts that all women should have equal rights.

Use a pair of commas to set off words or phrases in apposition (i.e., words or phrases that simply rename or reidentify someone or something in a sentence).

> Dorothy Alphonso, a candidate for city council, will address the Chamber of Commerce on Tuesday.
> Harold Jones, a doctor, administered first aid.
> After a committee searched for months to find the best administrator to do the job, the governor appointed Harold Farley, his uncle.

Exercise

Insert commas where needed in the following sentences. If no comma is needed in a given sentence, write *No* beside it. Be prepared to discuss the reasons for your decision in each case.

(1) Early in the spring fifteen citizens were appointed to the task force.
(2) Was it Churchill who said "If a man is not liberal in his youth he has no heart; if a man is not conservative in his old age he has no mind"?
(3) Next month we will meet on the company picnic grounds.
(4) Your adviser will meet with you next Thursday but she will not sign your card until Friday.
(5) Susan Schrantz who was formerly president of the company refused to agree to the merger.
(6) The teacher who graded this paper was unfair.
(7) Jerry Brown the governor vowed to implement the tax cut.
(8) Your claim that she was enrolled at Harvard from September 10 1963 to June 8 1967 has not been substantiated.
(9) The accused was seen in the company of the victim was she not?
(10) Red white and blue are the colors of the Cuban flag.
(11) It is true nonetheless that overuse of any substance can be dangerous to health.
(12) After I learned of the beauty of the Andes I was eager to visit them.
(13) Next type up the payroll lists because checks are due on Friday.
(14) Linda designed the house and Beth built it.

(15) The movie "Star Wars" had been running for over a year.
(16) Visiting our vacation resort does not obligate you to buy any property.
(17) The President's original energy program before Congress for over a year represented only the first steps toward solving the problem.
(18) You may write a paper on a sociological problem you may read three books by a noted sociologist or you may do a field study in which you gather sociological data.
(19) The winner reaps glory; the loser bitterness.
(20) I lived in Tampa Florida for two years.

Semicolons /;

You may use a semicolon to join two independent clauses (which could otherwise be separated by a period or joined by a comma and coordinating conjunction) when you wish the reader to note a close connection in their meanings. Often, but not always, the two clauses express sharply contrasting ideas.

Hard work built this country; laziness may destroy it.
The law applies to the poor; it must apply equally to the rich.
Weed the young plants carefully; water them frequently.
Literacy breeds knowledge; illiteracy, ignorance.

Use a semicolon, rather than a comma, to join a clause with a following clause that is introduced by a transitional expression or abbreviation (a period will often serve this purpose as well).

You arrived late; consequently, you will be paid less.
Wordsworth is the most lyrical of the early Romanticists; furthermore, I enjoy him more than any of the others.
Physics is one of the more abstract natural sciences; i.e., it requires a greater knowledge of mathematics.

Use a semicolon to take the place of a comma to join three or more clauses or phrases in series, where one or more of the items in series require internal use of commas.

The members of the committee are Jennifer B. Anderson, a noted jurist; John Garcia, president of the State Bar Association; and Warren Jones, warden of the state penitentiary.

(Notice that the semicolon and the coordinating conjunction, which are usually mutually exclusive, occur together in this instance.)

The bargainers agreed that goods, services, and money should be shared equally; future negotiations should commence earlier in the year; and all parties should consult their constituents, if time permits, as early as possible.

Exercise

Insert semicolons and commas where appropriate in the following sentences. In each place where you can correctly use a semicolon, a period (with appropriate capitalization following it) or a comma might also fit correctly. In such cases, be prepared to state why you think the semicolon is the more appropriate mark of punctuation.

(1) Fear brings out the worst in us determination the best.
(2) Exercise is often blamed for heart attacks on the contrary it can prevent heart attacks if it causes mild symptoms that lead one to seek medical help.
(3) Conquerors do not always win because of superior numbers e.g. Cortez was greatly outnumbered by the Aztecs but he eventually won anyway.
(4) When I think of the starvation, sickness, and death in the world when I see how little is being done about it and when I realize that I have talents that could help solve some of the problems I give serious thought to a career of service.
(5) Franklin Roosevelt was a great president he had the courage to act.
(6) There are students living in my college dorm who come from Lincoln Nebraska Dallas Texas and Knoxville Tennessee.

Colons I:

Use a colon to introduce a clause, phrase, or word that illustrates, explains, or gives an example of something just mentioned in the sentence.

The esthetic standards of the general public in American are mediocre at best: One need only sample the fare that television offers on any night of the week.

There is one motive that stands out above all the rest in matters of energy conservation: the good of our children and grandchildren.

One concern guided the justices of the Supreme Court in considering that case: justice.

Use a colon to introduce a series of clauses, phrases, or words that extend or amplify something just mentioned.

These things are certain: that America does not have enough oil; that it is importing too much oil; that its national security is threatened.

She wore jeans and a neat shirt, briskly American: bright, clean, competent. . . .

—A. ALVAREZ

Use a colon when quoted material is formally and explicitly introduced as quoted material.

I quote from the transcript of the trial: "Mrs. Elsberg told me that she had heard strange noises in the next apartment."
Here is the general's statement: "Nuts to you!"

Use a colon to introduce the body of a formal letter following the salutation.

Dear Professor Stanforth:
Dear Sir or Madam:
To Whom It May Concern:

Use a colon for all the following conventional purposes.

(1) In bibliography entries, between place of publication and name of publisher
New York: Harper & Row, Publishers, Inc.
(See pp. 310–311 for more details.)

(2) In Biblical references
Luke 4:3
I Corinthians 13:4

(3) In subtitles of books and articles
The Able Writer: A Rhetoric and Handbook
"Causes of the Cuban Revolution: A Journalist's Notebook"

(4) In stating the time of day
10:15 A.M.
12:30 P.M.

There is an exercise on p. 271 treating the uses of colons and other marks of punctuation.

Dashes / —

Use a dash (typed with double hyphens and no space on either side) to indicate an abrupt break in the continuity of ideas in a sentence. The break is usually accompanied by an abrupt break in the syntactic coherence of the sentence as well.

Hitler's racist policies were evil because—the evil is self-evident.
The American constitution guarantees certain freedoms, but it also assumes certain responsibilities—that goes without saying.

When writing dialog, use a dash to indicate that a speaker did not finish a sentence (for whatever reason):

> The driver yelled, "We're going to—" The car exploded in flames.
> The defense counsel argued, "In view of the new evidence, I ask the court to grant a—" "I object," interrupted the prosecutor.

Use a dash to introduce a summary statement following a series of clauses, phrases, or words:

> He came, he saw, and he conquered—that summarizes Julius Caesar's exploits in Gaul.
> Food, shelter, and clothing—these are our needs.

Use a dash preceding the attribution of a direct quotation.

We have nothing to fear but fear itself.

—FRANKLIN D. ROOSEVELT

Love is always patient and kind; it is never jealous; love is never boastful or conceited; it is never rude or selfish; it does not take offense, and is not resentful.

—I Corinthians 13:4–5

An exercise treating the uses of dashes and other marks of punctuation is on p. 271.

Pairs of Dashes /—. . .—

Use pairs of dashes to set off a word or group of words that very abruptly interrupts the flow of ideas in a sentence in addition to interrupting the syntactic coherence. Pairs of dashes are similar to pairs of commas in this use, because pairs of commas also set off expressions that interrupt the grammatical coherence; however, matter set off with commas usually does not interrupt the flow of ideas so abruptly as matter set off with pairs of dashes.

The line between man and beast—between the highest ape and the lowest savage—is the language line.

—SUZANNE K. LANGER

Having a light—a candle flame is ideal—behind or below the neck of the bottle makes it easier to see when the dregs start to move. . . .

—HUGH JOHNSON

An exercise treating the uses of pairs of dashes and other marks of punctuation is on p. 271.

Parentheses /(. . .)

Use parentheses to set off a word or group of words that interrupts not only the grammatical coherence but also the flow of ideas in a sentence. (Rhetorically, parentheses stand between pairs of commas, which set off mild interruptions, and pairs of dashes, which set off abrupt interruptions; the punctuation you choose often depends on your judgment about how you want your audience to view the interruption.) As the parentheses around the previous sentence indicate, they may also be used (but pairs of commas or dashes cannot) to indicate that a given sentence may interrupt the coherent flow of a paragraph.

Punctuation rules are not contained in desk dictionaries (at least not in *The American Heritage*) but they should be.
In June of 1978 the Supreme Court ruled (but by the slimmest of margins) in favor of Alan Bakke.

Use parentheses to enclose numbers or letters accompanying items in series (note that periods do not accompany the numbers or letters).

In case of emergency, the order of boarding will be (1) children, (2) women, (3) men.
Empirical scientific method entails (a) making observations about discrete phenomena, (b) noting patterns within these observations, (c) discovering laws that govern the patterns, and (d) formulating theories to explain the laws.

Use parentheses to enclose numerals that restate numbers already written out in commerical and legal correspondence:

The terms of this contract shall become applicable one hundred (100) days following the date on which it is signed and notarized.

An exercise treating the use of parentheses and other marks of punctuation is on p. 271.

Brackets /[. . .]

Use brackets to enclose either summarizations or editorial comments within quoted material.

"The federal government cannot ignore [the problems of the cities] any longer."

(The speaker had actually said "them," having mentioned the problems of the cities in an earlier sentence. But the writer wanted to quote only this sentence, and thus needed to insert an explanation to make it clear what the quoted speaker actually meant.)

The candidate made the following statement: "I will cut taxes in half [City Council does not have the power to do this] within a month of my election."

(The statement, *City Council does not have the power to do this,* is not part of the quotation; it is an interpolation by the writer who is citing the statement by the candidate.)

Use brackets to enclose the abbreviation, *sic,* which is inserted into a direct quotation to indicate that a mistake in spelling, grammar, or fact is indeed part of the quoted material and not a misprint or a misquotation:

The governor then said, "I ain't [sic] going to put up with any more waste of funds."
The text of the document reads as follows:
"All parties to the contract shall provide their own transportion [sic]."

Exercise

In the following sentences, internal punctuation is missing. Please insert colons, dashes, pairs of dashes, parentheses, and brackets where appropriate. You may also need to insert commas, pairs of commas, or semicolons. Be prepared to justify your choice of any mark of punctuation. If alternative choices were available, be prepared to discuss the different effects these would have had on the rhetoric of the sentence.

(1) My boss recently wrote from Europe, "They simply do not know how to broil a medium-rare stake sic on this continent."
(2) The voters must admit if they consider the inflation rate in some Latin American countries that a 10 percent rate is at least bearable.
(3) Anna Lyons Mary Louise Lyons Mary von Phul Emilie von Phul Eugenia McLellan Marjorie McPhail Marie-Louise L'Abbe Mary Danz Julia Dodge Mary Fordyce Blake Janet Preston these were the names I can still tell them over like a rosary of some of the older girls in the convent the Virtues and the Graces.

—MARY MCCARTHY

(4) Three factors are causing subtle changes in weather patterns a developments on the surface of the sun b chemical changes in the atmosphere and c shifts in the ocean currents.

(5) At his press conference last week the President promised again how often have we heard presidents do so that he would reduce government spending next year.

(6) The Declaration of Independence holds out the promise of "life, liberty and the pursuit but not the guarantee of happiness."

(7) We must assure we must at least try to assure equal treatment for everyone.

(8) Aristotle's *Physica* Ptolemy's *Almagest* Newton's *Principia* and *Opticks* Franklin's *Electricity* Lavoisier's *Chemistry* and Lyell's *Geology* these and many other works served for a time implicitly to define the legitimate problems and methods of a research field for succeeding generations of practitioners.

—THOMAS KUHN

(9) "If only I" she cried softly as I closed the door behind me.

Quotation Marks /". . ." /'. . .'

Place all commas and periods occurring at the end of quoted matter inside the quotation marks; other punctuation is placed inside only if a part of the quoted matter.

Use sets of double quotation marks to enclose a direct quotation.

My answer is, "Yes."
"I will help you," Harold said, "only if you agree to my terms."

Notice that each part of an interrupted direct quotation begins and ends with quotation marks.

Marie asked, "Why can't they eat cake?"
Who said, "If elected I shall refuse to serve"?

Use sets of single quotation marks to indicate a quote within a quote.

The witness repeated her testimony: "Every time I asked my neighbor if she was afraid of something, she said, 'No.'"

In Great Britain, sets of single quotation marks are used commonly, and sets of double quotation marks are used only to indicate a quotation within a quotation.

Use a set of double quotation marks at the beginning of each stanza of a quoted poem or at the beginning of each paragraph of a long quoted text of prose. However, use a set of closing quotation marks only at the end of the last stanza of the poem or the last paragraph of the prose text. If an extended citation of either poetry or prose is indented or blocked off (e.g., by single spacing in a double-spaced paper) then no quotation marks are used at all.

Use sets of double quotation marks to enclose titles of chapters or parts of books, articles or essays in periodicals, lectures, short stories, short poems, songs, and names of TV and radio programs.

> "The Creative Mind," a lecture by Jacob Bronowski given at MIT in 1953 and later published as the first chapter of his book, *Science and Human Values,* demonstrates that a great scientist must have many of the same qualities as a great poet.
>
> Anyone who would understand the task of the writer should read "Anecdote of the Jar," a poem by Wallace Stevens.
>
> "All in the Family" was the first of a series of television shows that eventually changed the direction of the medium as a whole.

Use quotation marks to enclose slang words or expressions or other words used in a special way. The purpose is to call the reader's attention to the fact that the word is not to be read in its typical sense or that the author wishes not to be held accountable for certain aspects of the word's meaning or social impact.

The electric fan is designed not to make too much noise; you use the blast of air and you don't use the "kick-back."

> —WOLFGANG LANGEWIESCHE

Too often we are concerned only with the tactics of "correct" grammar, too seldom for the strategy of good design in writing.

> —GORDON ROHMAN AND ALBERT WLECKE

Exercise

Insert sets of quotation marks (double or single, as appropriate) wherever they are needed in the following sentences. Be especially careful to position the closing quotation marks correctly with respect to other punctuation: All commas and periods go inside quotation marks; other punctuation is placed outside, unless it is part of the quoted matter.

(1) Julie yelled, Cut down the noise; I can't concentrate.

(2) Some of his students consider professor Tenslow to be a jive professor.

(3) The ambassador from Costa Rica will address the graduates on The Changing Role of Agriculture in Central America.

(4) My grandmother used to tell us, Remember the saying, A penny saved is a penny earned, and you will never be poor.

(5) Did the letter actually say, All students late for class will be suspended?

(6) I agree with the thrust of the resolution, the senator said, but I would hope the assembly will accept a minor amendment.

(7) Have you ever heard Hopkins' poem, The Windhover, read aloud?

(8) The professor asked, Who can relate Descartes' statement, I think; therefore, I am, to some of the philosophical issues we have been discussing in class?

(9) The psychotherapist testified to the grand jury that the accused was indeed a junkie.

Hyphens /-

Use a hyphen between words that together form a long modifying phrase *preceding* a noun. (Such phrases are often used for humorous effect, and are uncommon in edited English.)

The judge recommended to the feuding neighbors that they should all develop a live-and-let-live attitude.

The threat of federal regulation is encouraging land developers to take a grab-all-you-can approach to community development.

Use a hyphen between compound adjectives modifying a noun. This is actually a specification of the same principle described immediately above, but it applies much more frequently in edited English.

The water-soaked picnic basket was retrieved from the bay.

The sale-priced items were of inferior quality.

Scores of government employes perform the time-consuming task of editing the *Congressional Record*.

A two-thirds vote is required to close off debate in the United States Senate.

Note that fractions used as adjectives are hyphenated; used as nouns they are not: *Two thirds will suffice.*

Either two- or three-inch banners are permissible in the parade.

Notice that the hyphen is written after the first element of a compound modifier, two-, even when, through conjoining, the second element is deleted.

Use hyphens with many compound nouns and other fixed compounds in English. In the vast majority of cases, you will need to consult a dictionary to be sure whether to use hyphens or not. There are, however, some general patterns:

(1) Compounds with prepositions and pronouns are usually hyphenated.

good-for-nothing
forget-me-not
brother-in-law
know-it-all

(2) Written out numbers from 21 to 99 are hyphenated.

thirty-three, fifty-five, sixty-one, ninety-nine

In most other cases the dictionary must guide you in deciding whether compounds are to be written solid, hyphenated, or written as two words. The following examples illustrate the general lack of pattern in such matters.

Written Solid	Hyphenated	Written as Two Words
housekeeping	air-conditioning	
dressmaking	book-keeping	
matchmaker	gate-crasher	cigar smoker
songwriter	radio-operator	crime reporter
haircut	birth-control	book review

Use a hyphen between a prefix and a proper noun or adjective, use a hyphen with the prefix *ex-* meaning "former," and use one whenever an odd combination of sounds or letters would otherwise occur.

Pre-Colombian art
Proto-Germanic
ex-husband
re-creation (meaning "act of creating again," not "act of enjoying one's self")
ill-lighted
pro-opera

Use the hyphen to indicate spans of years or hours, or spans of pages.

1978–1980, or 1978–80
8–11 P.M.
pp. 257–289, or pp. 257–89

Use a hyphen to indicate that a word is not complete at the end of a printed, typed, or written line and that the rest of the word is on the next line. Words may be divided thus only between syllables. When in doubt about syllable divisions, consult a dictionary, where syllable divisions are indicated in the main entry by dots between letters. (Avoid hyphenating a word when this would leave only one letter on a line.)

Use hyphens between letters of a word to indicate that it is to be read as a spelling of a word.

The English adjective which means "prudent" is spelled d-i-s-c-r-e-e-t; the adjective which means "distinct" is spelled d-i-s-c-r-e-t-e.

Exercise

Insert hyphens where appropriate in the following sentences. Be prepared to state why the hyphen is needed, whenever you insert one.

(1) The back to the basics movement may cause a disproportionate emphasis on mechanics and weaken the treatment of rhetoric in composition classes.

(2) Neither pro nor antiChinese mercenaries are currently active in central Africa.

(3) As they stood dazzled by the beauty of the Grand Canyon, they glared at each other with I thought *you* were going to bring the camera expressions on their faces.

(4) Both paragraph and sentence level coherence depend on correct use of punctuation.

(5) The Common Market countries are suspicious of nonEuropean currencies.

(6) Increasingly, in the years ahead, urban communities will have problems finding clean drinking water.

(7) During the period 1952 1960, there was domestic calm in the United States.

(8) Nancy won the spelling bee when she said, "Dilettante is spelled d i l e t t a n t e."

Apostrophes /'

Use the apostrophe in contractions to signal that certain letters (or even words) have been deleted.

o'clock (of the clock)
wouldn't (would not)
they're (they are)
it's ("it is", do not confuse this with the pronoun *its;* see below.)
spirit of '76 (spirit of 1776)
ne'er (never)
I've (I have)

Use the apostrophe (followed by *s*) to indicate the possessive case of most singular nouns and indefinite pronouns, but not personal pronouns.

Harold's opinion	*But:*	hers, his, its, ours,
a dollar's worth		yours, theirs (and also
someone's suggestion		whose)

The apostrophe and *s* tend to appear at the end of the noun phrase next to the item possessed (rather than on the head noun of the phrase):

The Governor of Alabama's decision
My brother-in-law's debts
everyone else's money

In compound phrases showing joint possession, the apostrophe and *s* appear only on the second noun:

Harry and Mary's house (i.e., they are joint owners)

In conjoined or disjoined phrases showing separate possession, the apostrophe and *s* appear on both nouns:

Harry's and Mary's houses (i.e., they own separate houses)
Either the husband's or the wife's testimony is false.

The use of the apostrophe and *s* to show possession actually grew out of the use of the apostrophe to signal a contraction. During the Middle English period the possessive case was spelled *es* (Chaucer, for example, uses the phrase *Goddes love* where we would write *God's love*). The apostrophe thus signaled the deletion of the letter *e*. Unfortunately, contemporary usage of the apostrophe with possessives has strayed far from this original function (as the next three uses will illustrate). Study the conventions carefully, for they are among the most forceful and socially significant defining features of edited English.

Use the apostrophe (followed by *s*) to indicate the possessive case of a few plural nouns that end in letters other than *s*.

Those women's views are as diverse as those of any group of men.
Children's toys are less dangerous than they used to be.

Use the apostrophe (not followed by *s*) to indicate the possessive case of plural nouns that end in *s*.

The workers' paychecks will be distributed at 4:00 P.M.
All my friends' spouses attended the reception.

Use the apostrophe (not followed by *s*) to indicate the possessive case of a few singular nouns which end in *s* or *ce*.

I need Mr. Jones' assistance.
For conscience' sake, help us right this wrong!
Not even a soothsayer could predict Prince Charles' future.

(Some writers treat words like this the same as the majority of singular nouns, writing *Jones's, conscience's,* and *Charles's;* if you pronounce the extra *s*, you may opt for the apostrophe and *s* rather than the apostrophe alone.)

Use the apostrophe (followed by *s*) to indicate the plurals of letters, numerals, and words referred to as words.

Because Johnny doesn't dot his *i's*, they look the same as his *e's*.
Professor Albertini was dismissed because, on a scale of five, her students circled too many *3's* on evaluation forms.
There are just too many *of's* and *to's* in government memoranda.

Exercise

Place apostrophes where they belong in the following sentences. Be prepared to discuss the reasons why you have done so.

(1) Her friends and neighbors card cheered her up in the hospital.
(2) Last winters snows surpassed even those of the notorious winter of 92.
(3) Its very difficult to teach a dog not to chase its tail.
(4) "When twas time to go to war, my generation went," Grandpa said.
(5) Wallace Stevens poetry challenges the imagination.
(6) My neighbors yards are all fenced in.
(7) Many college students remain hopelessly confused about their *whos* and their *whoms*.
(8) Those congressmens expense accounts all show numerous irregularities.
(9) Marys arriving late to the wedding bothered the groom.
(10) We ll either give the award to their entry or to the Smiths.

Twelve | *Research*

A research paper is a unified and coherent essay in edited-English style that presents an original perspective on a carefully chosen topic and supports its claims with formally documented references to the writings of others. This chapter will focus on how to give the research paper an original perspective, how formally to document references to the writings of others, and, most important, how to reconcile these two seemingly contradictory elements in the above definition: maintaining originality while referring to the work of others. There will be little in this chapter about the unity or coherence of the research paper or about its conformity to the stylistic norms of edited English; earlier chapters have already addressed these qualities (of course, they apply fully when you write a research paper).

The chapter is divided into eight sections, each treating a distinct phase in the highly structured research process. I wrote it for you to use as a guide while you are actually writing a paper. There are some exercises you can do even if you are not in fact writing a paper as you read the chapter, but most of the exercises call on you to move one step closer to a completed paper of your own.

Before we turn to the first phase of the research process, let us look at the phrase, "formally documented," from the above definition of the research paper. The word *documented* means that you must list all books and articles you have read in preparing the paper and credit their authors with all words and ideas you took from them. You do so in numbered notes that appear either at the end of the paper (endnotes) or at the foot of the page on which an author's words or ideas occur (footnotes). But the complete phrase, *"formally* documented," means more. It means that you must list the books and articles, position the notes, and type both the list and the notes in a particular *format:* You cannot write a research paper unless you have at hand a particular research manual (or handbook) to guide you. You must refer to it constantly and follow its every directive, from those concerning the sizes of margins to those concerning the placement of punctuation marks in your notes. If you are learning the research process in an elementary college course, this chapter may serve as such a manual. But it is probably not comprehensive enough to serve all your needs in upper-division courses in particular fields.

The research format presented in the body of this chapter is based on the standard research handbook used in the fields of language and literature:

> The Modern Language Association of America. *MLA Handbook for Writers of Research Papers, Theses, and Dissertations.* New York: Modern Language Association, 1977.

Alternate acceptable formats are fully described in the following research manual (probably the most widely used manual in various fields in the United States):

> Turabian, Kate L. *A Manual for Writers of Term Papers, Theses, and Dissertations.* 4th ed. Chicago: The University of Chicago Press, 1973.

Each academic discipline usually has a standard research manual of its own. Professors in advanced courses may require you to purchase and use one. Here are a few:

Biology:

> Council of Biology Editors, Committee on Form and Style. *CBE Style Manual.* 3rd ed. Washington, D.C.: American Institute of Biological Sciences, 1972.

Chemistry:

> American Chemical Society. *Handbook for Authors of Papers in the Journals of the American Chemical Society.* Washington, D.C.: American Chemical Society, 1967.

Engineering:

> Engineers Joint Council, Committee of Engineering Society Editors. *Recommended Practice for Style of References in Engineering Publications.* New York: Engineers Joint Council, 1966.

Linguistics:

Linguistic Society of America. *LSA Bulletin,* No. 88 (Dec. 1980).

Mathematics:

American Mathematical Society. *Manual for Authors of Mathematical Papers.* 4th ed. Providence, R.I.: American Mathematical Society, 1971.

Physics:

American Institute of Physics, Publications Board. *Style Manual.* Rev. ed. New York: American Institute of Physics, 1973.

Psychology:

American Psychological Association. *Publication Manual of the American Psychological Association.* 2nd. ed. Washington, D.C.: American Psychological Association, 1974.

My purpose throughout this chapter is to emphasize the process of writing a research paper and to give enough information on the details of documentation to serve the needs of most users of this book. But you may, nonetheless, find it necessary to consult the *MLA Handbook* on some matter of detail. Before you begin to work on your paper, become aware of where you can find an *MLA Handbook* just in case you need to refer to it.

Phase One: Audience and Purpose

Write for yourself (to learn)

For you, the research paper is a very special learning experience. Knowledge you gain from it is deeper and more durable than the knowledge that comes from listening to a lecture or reading a book or even studying for a test. This knowledge lasts longer because it is personal and because acquiring it requires discipline:

(1) You must actively seek the truth, often working for several long days in the library finding sources and taking notes. You do not just passively hear or read.

(2) You must use your own initiative, carefully specifying your topic, formulating your own questions about it, and then seeking answers to your own questions.

(3) Even though you use many ideas from other writers, you must create your own perspective. It is impossible to do this unless you truly understand these ideas.

One of the distinguishing characteristics of the human species is that the knowledge of each generation is preserved and passed on intact to the next, which can thus take up the learning process where others left off and progress to greater achievements. The research paper is a key tool that makes this cumulative growth in knowledge possible. In mastering its techniques, you are learning to participate more fully in this amazing process of human intellectual growth because you learn how to find out what the status of human knowledge is on matters that interest you and where the openings are for your creative contribution.

Write for your teacher (to prove yourself)

Research papers are typically written as requirements in college courses. In an elementary composition course, you may write a research paper to learn *how* to write one. In all courses, you write research papers to learn more about the course matter. This is not surprising, since, as I have pointed out, the research paper is such an excellent learning tool. In both situations, you should remain fully aware that your teacher is your primary audience. In the composition course, your best way to prove that you have indeed mastered the research process is to focus on the same objectives that will guide you in later courses. Thus, in both instances, you should keep these points firmly in mind:

(1) The paper has been assigned to help you learn something on your own. Understand what that something is, and make certain that you demonstrate clearly that you have learned it.
(2) The paper has been assigned so that your teacher can evaluate (a) your specific skills in seeking out facts, interrelating them, and presenting them in an organized way and in a specified research format and (b) your overall intellectual creativity as shown by the originality of the perspective that governs the organization of your paper.

Write for a wider audience (because your ideas matter)

Even though your primary purpose in writing any research paper should be your own intellectual growth, and your secondary purpose should be the demonstration of that growth to your teacher, you will not in fact write your best paper unless you believe that it will interest a wider audience. If your perspective is truly original, then the world should know about it. If you do not believe this, you will just not give the paper your best.

Your wider audience may be none other than your closest friend. Or it may be other students in the course for which you are writing the paper, or fellow members of a campus organization who share your interest in the paper's topic. It may be your mother or father, a brother or sister. If you are ambitious, your intended wider audience may be the readership of a certain publication or even the public at large. Try not to let attention to a wider audience overpower attention to your primary audience, yourself and your teacher, but do think about it and let it motivate you.

A few of you will go on to careers in scholarship; others, to careers in government, business, and industry, where you will use the research process in your work. But most of you probably will do neither. This makes it all the more important to get the most out of research papers you write in college. If you do, you will carry even specific insights from these papers with you through the years. But most important, you will have learned something about the research process: When you have questions that need answers, you will know where and how to find those answers.

Exercise

Read the research paper printed toward the end of this chapter and then answer these questions about it:

(1) How does it fulfill the primary purpose of a research paper; i.e., what do you think the author learned by writing it?

(2) How does it fulfill the secondary purpose; i.e., what aspects of it show mastery of the research process, and what aspects show originality of perspective and organization?

(3) How does it fulfill the tertiary purpose of a research paper; i.e., how does it appeal to a wider audience? You can answer this third question by simply asking whether it appealed to you. Was it interesting and informative? If so, why? If not, why not?

Phase Two: Choice of Topic

Beginning in this section, I will exemplify the phases by actually working through the process that produced the sample paper presented with commentary toward the end of the chapter.

Choose an interesting topic

Even in a beginning composition course it is rare that a specific topic will be assigned. Sometimes the choice is yours within certain limits, but often it is completely open. If it is, you have a rare opportunity to learn more about a topic very dear to you. Your choice of a topic on such a paper could ultimately determine what your college major will be; it could even help you choose a career. Whether the topic is open or in some way limited, choose a topic that interests you: an interesting comment of one of your professors, an idea from a textbook or a campus lecture, an issue currently stimulating student interest on campus. Even the frustrations of college—bad teaching, red tape, inferior food, prejudice, loneliness—should motivate you to learn. You will never again have so much time available for serious study of issues that affect you and people around you, for asking serious questions and having time and resources to find answers. If you have kept a writer's notebook throughout the course, as suggested in Chapter Two, it should be bulging with topics for term papers, and your problem will be to select the one from among the many that is the most important and the most promising.

Margaret Poole, the writer of the sample paper printed toward the end of this chapter, had a free choice of topic. Her professor had suggested that she look for an idea or theme that had come up in more than one of her classes. (This would indicate that the issues were important and therefore showed promise of being interesting.) In an introductory speech course, she had been surprised to hear for the first time that language capacity in humans tended to be localized in one side of the brain. In an introductory psychology course, her professor had mentioned a controversial Princeton psychologist named Julian Jaynes who has suggested that there may be some connection between the tendency for the two sides of the human brain to specialize and the origin of language. Her interest was given a third stimulus when a fellow student mentioned reading in a textbook for yet another course that most of what has been written about the origin of language amounted to little more than groundless speculation. She wished she knew more about the brain and language, and she wondered why Jaynes was considered controversial; was it because he too specialized in "groundless speculation"? The topic certainly interested her, and because it had come up in two of her courses and one of a friend's, she had reason to believe that it would interest a wider audience.

In estimating how interesting *your* topic is, be sure to keep your teacher and some type of broader audience in mind. At the very least, read your teacher's directions carefully; if you have any doubts, ask your teacher's opinion about the topic you have in mind. Then ask yourself whether there is at least one other person who would be interested in the paper you plan to write. If you can think of no one, you should probably search for another topic.

Choose a specific topic

If you think carefully about your purpose and also resolve that the paper must be filled with concrete images, you should have little trouble making your topic specific. Recall that the basic question of purpose is whether you wish to inform or persuade; the next is whether you are informing about a person, place, thing, or event or persuading to agree, to evaluate, or to act. If you cannot fulfill your purpose by evoking images of concrete things, then the paper is probably too abstract.

If you are interested in tennis, do not plan a paper on how to play tennis; rather, write on the back hand. Do not even plan a paper on Billie Jean King; rather, write one about her special style of play, or about her income, or about her greatest achievement. If you are interested in the Civil War, research the role of a particular general in a particular battle, or write about the effects of the burning of Atlanta on the city's economy. If you are interested in marketing, do not write about inflation's effect on retail sales; rather, study the effect of higher meat prices in a particular year on the sale of hamburgers by a particular fast-food chain.

It is difficult to decide beforehand just how broad your topic is and how to narrow it; you need to begin the research process and discover just how much or how little information is available to you before you can be sure. But do be aware, as you read, take notes, and organize, that you should aim to write a paper that treats specific people and things and that favors concrete vocabulary.

At this stage in the planning of her paper, Margaret Poole wondered whether further reading would lead her to narrow her topic to the origin of language in some specific place in the world, or to one particular scholar's views on the origin of language, or to the role of the brain in the origin of language. But the topic was so new to her that she could only wonder until she read more.

Choose a workable topic

Strange as it may seem, there is a danger of picking a topic that is too specific—not too specific in the sense that such a topic would not be interesting, but too specific in the sense that there is not enough information available to find enough sources. Professors in introductory courses delight in telling students about the latest developments in their fields. A psychology professor might mention that chimpanzees have been taught to use human sign language and that researchers are now waiting to see whether they pass it on to their offspring. The idea is so exciting that a student might decide to write a paper comparing how humans and chimps teach grammar to their offspring. The student will go to the library only to find that there is virtually no information available on the topic. Someone wishing to write on dolphin poetry, or on the meanings of specific Mayan hieroglyphic transcriptions would be similarly frustrated.

How then can you assure that your topic is workable? You could of course ask your professor, but usually one of the purposes of a research assignment is to give you experience in using tools of research that will tell you just how workable the topic is. The primary tools for this phase of the research process are reference works: dictionaries, almanacs, and encyclopedias. You should have a dictionary, and perhaps an almanac, as part of your personal library. If a topic for a paper occurs to you, look it up in the dictionary to see how it is defined; then look up words in its definition. If your topic is factually oriented, the almanac should give you an indication of how generally interesting it is. If you find much useful information in these reference works, that is a good sign. If you find little or nothing, that is a bad sign, but do not give up. Go to the library and consult a general encyclopedia. Here are the names of some:

Chambers Encyclopedia	*Encyclopedia International*
Collier's Encyclopedia	*New Columbia Encyclopedia*
Encyclopedia Americana	*The Random House Encyclopedia*
Encyclopaedia Britannica	*World Book Encyclopedia*

Most of these are multivolume sets, but the *Columbia Encyclopedia* and *The Random House Encyclopedia* are single volumes. Remember that you are consulting them to discover whether your topic is workable—you have not yet begun your research, and ordinarily you should not refer to an encyclopedia article, or to a dictionary or almanac entry, in a research paper. Use the encyclopedia to focus your topic and to discover something about how it fits into the overall structure of human knowledge.

Margaret Poole looked at *The Random House Encyclopedia* to check on the workability of her topic. She found its main article on language to be four pages long. Since approximately one-sixth of the text in that article was devoted to the origins of speech, she assumed rightly that there would be enough material available to her in writing the paper. In fact, she wondered whether the topic might not be too broad and she resolved to look for ways to make it more specific if necessary.

Exercises

a. List at least five possible topics for research papers. Try to base them on issues that interest you, such as hobbies, or on matter in one or more of your courses that attracted your attention when it was covered. Then check each topic in at least two encyclopedias to see how workable it is. If you are totally at a loss to think of some topics, here are some general suggestions:

(1) A historical issue: the role of a specific person in a specific historical event
(2) A social issue: specific people or events that have affected issues like human rights, family life, human starvation, medical care, adequate energy supplies
(3) A technological issue: the role of specific people or products in the development of and marketing of products such as solar electric cells or electric cars
(4) A cultural issue: the role of particular persons or works in particular movements of art, architecture, and literature
(5) A life-sciences issue: the role of a particular animal or plant in its local ecological system or in broader systems; the causes and cures of certain diseases

b. If you are writing a paper as you read this chapter, test the interest, specificity, and workability of the topic you have chosen.

Phase Three: Finding Books

Books form the superstructure of the great storehouse of accumulated human knowledge. Ideas do not ordinarily find their way into a book until they have been tested and carefully related to other ideas. For this reason, books will ordinarily provide the strong foundation of any papers you write. It is important to find just those books that relate most closely to the topic you have chosen. The following subsections tell you what you need to know and do to find them.

Learn how books are shelved in the library

By the phase *the library* in this section, I ordinarily mean the library at your college. If, however, you are attending a community college or a branch campus of a larger institution, you may need to use several libraries. Do not assume that all are the same; you must learn the system and get to know the people at each library you use.

Books are shelved systematically, acording to subject matter. They are given *call numbers* that indicate something about their content and also tell the librarians where to put them and you where to find them. Smaller libraries tend to use the Dewey Decimal System. Here are its ten major divisions:

000–900 General works
100–199 Philosophy
200–299 Religion
300–399 Social Sciences
400–499 Philology

500–599 Pure Science
600–699 Useful Arts
700–799 Fine Arts
800–899 Literature
900–999 History

Each of the ten major divisions has ten subdivisions. Here, for instance, are the subdivisions under Philology:

400 Language
410 Linguistics
420 English and Anglo-Saxon languages
430 Germanic (Teutonic) languages
440 Romance languages, French
450 Italian, Romanian, Rhaeto-Romance
460 Spanish and Portuguese languages
470 Italic languages, Latin
480 Hellenic languages, Classical Greek
490 Other languages

And each of the subdivisions has ten additional subdivisions. Here are the ten subdivisions under Language:

401 Philosophy and theory
402 Miscellany
403 Dictionaries, encyclopedias, concordances
404 (Unassigned)
405 Serial Publications
406 Organizations
407 Study and teaching
408 Collections
409 Historical and geographical treatment

Additional subdivisions are indicated by decimals. *On the Origins of Language: An Introduction to the Evolution of Human Speech,* a book cited in the sample paper later in this chapter, has the following complete call number in the Dewey Decimal System: *401.9.* The numbers before the decimal label it as a work on the philosophy and theory of language; the number after the decimal indicates its place within the whole array of books on this topic.

Larger libraries use the Library of Congress classification system in assigning call numbers. Here are its major divisions:

A   General Works
B   Philosophy-Religion

C	History-Auxiliary sciences
D	Foreign history and topography
E–F	American history
G	Geography-Anthropology
H	Social sciences
J	Political science
K	Law
L	Education
M	Music
N	Fine Arts
P	Language and Literature
Q	Science
R	Medicine
S	Agriculture
T	Technology
U	Military Science
V	Naval Science
Z	Bibliography-Library science

Under these major divisions, the first set of subdivisions is also indicated by letters, thus allowing many more books to be distinctly numbered without making the call numbers excessively long. Subdivisions below the first two sets are indicated by numbers as in the Dewey system. Here is the Library of Congress call number for *On the Origins of Language: An Introduction to the Evolution of Human Speech:* P 116.L5.

Your library probably provides a booklet or a handout that maps the building and indicates where books in each classification are stored. Obtain a copy of it, and walk through the library carrying the map. Find all of the books under each division of the classification system used in the library. Stop occasionally and look at a book, noting how the call number does indeed indicate its topic.

Search the card catalogs in the library

The card catalogs do for the entire library what an index does for a book. There is at least one card in the catalogs for every book in the library, and there are usually three or more. Each book has a card filed alphabetically by the author's last name, another card filed alphabetically by its title, and one or more cards filed alphabetically by the subject or subjects treated in the book. The format and content of these cards are represented below. Notice that the title card and the subject card are reproductions of the author card but with the title or the subject typed at the top.

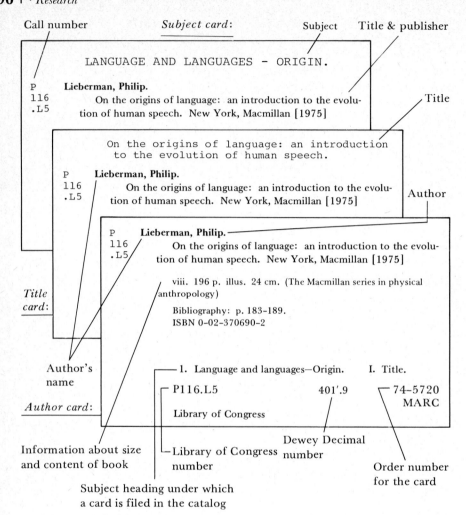

Call number   *Subject card:*   Subject   Title & publisher

LANGUAGE AND LANGUAGES - ORIGIN.

P
116
.L5

Lieberman, Philip.
On the origins of language: an introduction to the evolution of human speech. New York, Macmillan [1975]

Title

On the origins of language: an introduction
to the evolution of human speech.

P
116
.L5

Lieberman, Philip.
On the origins of language: an introduction to the evolution of human speech. New York, Macmillan [1975]

Author

P
116
.L5

Lieberman, Philip.
On the origins of language: an introduction to the evolution of human speech. New York, Macmillan [1975]

viii. 196 p. illus. 24 cm. (The Macmillan series in physical
anthropology)

*Title
card:*

Bibliography: p. 183-189.
ISBN 0-02-370690-2

Author's
name

Author card:

1. Language and languages—Origin.   I. Title.

P116.L5   401'.9   74-5720

MARC

Library of Congress

Information about size
and content of book

Library of Congress
number

Dewey Decimal
number

Order number
for the card

Subject heading under which
a card is filed in the catalog

In some libraries, all three types of cards are filed together alphabetically. In others, all three types are in separate alphabetical catalogs. In still
others, author and title cards are in one catalog, and subject cards are in
another. No matter how they are filed, the subject cards will be of most
help to you at this stage in your research project. You know the subject
you want to write about, so you know where to look in the subject catalog; it will tell you about authors or titles that treat your subject.

Margaret Poole found the book listed on the cards above by looking in the subject catalog under the heading *Language and Languages—
Origin.* As the research process develops, you will come across titles of

books and names of authors in other books, and to locate these sources in the library you will of course use the author cards and the title cards.

Some libraries are replacing card catalogs with computer catalogs (which they call COMCAT), in which separate entries by author, title, and subject are entered on small microfiche films (which look and feel much like four-inch by six-inch black-and-white photograph negatives). You insert these into a viewing machine and read their contents on a screen. The advantage of the system is that hundreds of books may be entered on one card and as many as two dozen entries can appear on the screen at one time. It is like viewing many cards from a card catalog at one time and it is easier to take notes from the screen than from a card catalog because you do not need to use one hand to hold a card in place as you write with the other. The format of an entry in a COMCAT is very similar to that in a card catalog. The major difference is that the call number is printed at the bottom of the entry and not off to the side. Compare the following COMCAT author entry with the author card portrayed earlier for *On the Origins of Language: An Introduction to the Evolution of Human Speech.*

```
Lieberman, Philip.
   On the origins of language; an
introduction to the evolution of human
speech. -- New York, Macmillan [1975].
viii, 196 p. illus. 24 cm. -- (The
Macmillan series in physical
anthropology)
   Bibliography: p. 183-189.
   I. Language and languages--Origin.
P116 .L5
```

Browse in the stacks and the reference room

The library is usually the quietest place on campus and often one of the more comfortable places. Try to make it a habit to visit and spend time there even when you do not have a specific reason for going. Before you settle down to read or study, or when you have finished doing so, spend some time simply walking along the stacks of books, stopping to examine titles that catch your eye, and noting the call number of any book you handle. When you decide on a major field in college, you should concentrate your attention on books in your field. Notice how they are arranged; discover areas where the library's holdings are plentiful and other areas where they are sparse. For each new course you take, discover where the books are that treat the special emphasis of the course. When you read a chapter in a course text, check to find out how many complete books are in the library on the chapter's theme. I have found this kind of habitual browsing to be much more interesting than the cold and monotonous activity of searching the card catalogs. Knowledge I had thus gained about my library's collection often played an important role even in the early decisions about audience, purpose, topic, and plan for assigned research papers when I was a college student.

The reference room deserves special attention. There is no reason why you cannot become thoroughly familiar with virtually all of the reference works in your major area, and still have time to develop a good feeling for the available references in all the fields you will study in college. In the reference room, shelved according to the classification system in use in the library, you will find general indexes, encyclopedias, dictionaries, catalogs, yearbooks, atlases, who's-who anthologies, and bibliographies.

Make a bibliography card for each book you find

You may learn of a book by finding its card in a card catalog (or COM-CAT), by picking it off the shelves as you browse, or by seeing it listed in the bibliography of a reference book. But you have not officially "found" it until you make a bibliography card for it. Since most of the books you find will ultimately be listed in the bibliography of your paper, and since the research format demands that they be listed in a very specific format, it is most important for you to learn that format now and to use it from the very outset. That is, *write down the information about each book you find in the exact format you will need to use when you type your bibliography.** At the top of page 293 you will find the bibliography card Margaret Poole made for the book by Lieberman as soon as she located it in the library. And here is the bibliography entry ultimately typed from it in her final paper (see also p. 336).

```
Lieberman, Philip. On the Origin of Language: An Introduction to
    the Evolution of Human Speech. New York: Macmillan, 1975.
```

Study pp. 310–311, where the format for the bibliography entries for all types of books and articles is discussed and exemplified in detail. Learn to follow it as you make your cards and before you have begun to take notes from the books and articles you have found.

---

* The bibliography is usually typed last—when you are exhausted from the task of writing the paper. You will appreciate the saving in time and effort if you need only copy information from your cards exactly as it appears on them.

```
Lieberman, Philip.  On the
   Origins of Language: An Intro-
   duction to the Evolution of
   Human Speech. New York:
   Macmillan, 1975.
```

Exercises

a. Take a tour of the library at your college or university. While there, do the following:

(1) Find out if it uses card catalogs, a COMCAT, or both.

(2) If it has a card catalog, find out whether author, title, and subject cards are mixed or whether they are in separate sets of drawers.

(3) Find out which system of classification is in use: the Dewey Decimal System or the Library of Congress System.

(4) If the Dewey system is in use, locate each of the ten major classes of books it lists; if the Library of Congress system is in use, locate each of its twenty major classes of books.

(5) Locate the reference room and while you are there, find out how many of the encyclopedias listed above on p. 286 are there. Take them off the shelves and look at them. While in the reference room, locate copies of the *Oxford English Dictionary, Webster's Third New International Dictionary,* and *The American Heritage Dictionary.*

(6) Do some browsing in the stacks and in the reference room. While you are at it, find the shelves in both places for books like this one on English composition.

(7) Find at least two books in the library on each of the following topics; referring to pp. 310–311, make a bibliography card for each one as you find it:
   (a) Karl Maria von Clausewitz
   (b) The Social Status of the Native Indian Populations in the Highlands of Peru
   (c) Mary Wollstonecraft
   (d) Breeder Reactors: Dangers and Benefits
   (e) The Significance of Monticello in the Development of Architecture in America
   (f) Hypoglycemia: Its Causes and Cures

b. If you are working on a paper as you read this chapter, find the books you need: Search the catalogs, the shelves, and the bibliographies of books you have already found. As soon as you decide a book may be useful, make a card for it, carefully following the format described on pp. 310–311.

Phase Four: Finding Articles

Articles, contained in periodical publications of all kinds, provide the most recent developments in a field or the most current views on a variety of issues. You will find it necessary to use older articles when their insights were indeed lasting but too specific to require book-length treatment. The task of finding exactly those articles most suited to your topic is in some ways more challenging than finding the books you need. This is a problem not only because there are many more articles published each year than there are books, but especially because each library does not contain a catalog of only those articles it holds. You need to look in general indexes of article titles and then go to find out whether the titles you have listed are indeed in the library. Here are some suggestions that should make the search reasonably efficient.

Learn how periodicals are stored in the library

Articles appear in journals, magazines, and newspapers. These are all referred to as periodicals and are kept in a special room in the library: the periodicals room. It often fills an entire floor of the library. Most libraries display current (unbound) periodicals separately from back issues (which are bound). Some libraries shelve them together. Smaller libraries shelve periodicals alphabetically by title; larger ones shelve them according to their call numbers, thus putting all periodicals in one field together. Learn the custom in use in your school's library.

Search the periodical indexes and volumes of abstracts in the reference room

Several sets of publications in the reference room (not the periodicals room itself) attempt to list and index by subject and author most of the articles published in a given year. These are called periodical indexes. Several other sets of publications (each usually focusing on a given field) contain short summaries of important articles in that field. The summaries are called abstracts, and they are indexed by subject and author in the volume in which they appear. Here are the names of some of the more important periodical indexes:

Reader's Guide to Periodical Literature
Humanities Index
Social Sciences Index
New York Times Index
Poole's Index

One of these indexes is no longer in print (*Poole's Index*), and others are successors to indexes with different names (*Humanities Index* and *Social Sciences Index*). When you locate them in the reference room, it will be obvious from the shelving arrangements which indexes with other titles precede a given index and which years each index spans. In addition to the general periodical indexes listed above, there are numerous others specializing in particular fields. The reference librarian will tell you whether the library contains one in the subject you are researching and will also help you locate it.

Let us look more closely at the most frequently used of the indexes, *The Reader's Guide*. It is published in sections throughout the year and again as one volume at the end of the year. Here is a portion of a page in the volume spanning March 1975 to February 1976.

612   READERS' GUIDE TO PERIODICAL LITERATURE March 1975–February 1976

LANGSETH, Marcus G. See Keihm, S. J. jt
    auth
LANGUAGE, Obscene. See Words, Obscene
LANGUAGE, Psychology of. See Language and
    languages—Psychology
LANGUAGE, Universal
    English—best hope for a world language. G.
    C. McGhee; discussion. Sat R 2:7-8 F 22 '75
LANGUAGE and languages
— From language to linguistics and beyond.
    R. J. Trotter. Sci N 108:332-4 N 22 '75
        See also
    Africa—Languages
    Canada—Languages
    Children—Language
    Conversation
    Grammar, Comparative and general
    Languages, Modern
    Linguistics
    Metaphor
    Rhetoric
    Sign language
    Speech
    Translations and translating
    Women—Language
        also names of languages. e.g. English
        language. French language

        Philosophy
    Black, white, language, and decalang. J. A.
        Rogers. bibl f Engl J 64:30-4 Ap '75
    Living principle. by F. R. Leavis. Review
        Nat R 27:1487-8 D 19 '75 H. Kenner
    Message in the bottle. by W. Percy. Review
        New Repub 173:28-9 Jl 19 '75. J. Boat-
        wright

LANKER, Brian
    Brian Lanker. R. Burns. il Pop Phot 76:76-
        85+ Ap '75 •
    Shows we've seen. D. Turner. Pop Phot 77:
        127+ O '75 •
LANSFORD, Henry
    Climate outlook: variable and possibly
        cooler. il Smithsonian 6:140-2+ N '75
LANSING, Kenneth
    Leadership in education; address, February
        28, 1975. Vital Speeches 41:506-9 Je 1 '75
LANTERNS, Blacklight. See Ultraviolet rays
        —Lamps
LANZEROTTI, Louis J. See Akasofu, S.-I. jt
    auth
LAOS
    Accord with history. K. Willenson and oth-
        ers. il Newsweek 85:40+ My 26 '75
    Cambodia's cry for help. N. Cousins. Sat R
        2:4-5 Ap 19 '75
    From feudalism to communism in Laos. R.
        Butwell. bibl f Cur Hist 69:223-6+ D '75
    Laos: after 30 years, peace has come. il
        Newsweek 85:30 Je 2 '75
    Laos as Hanoi's province. D. Kirk. Sat R
        2:23 Ag 23 '75
    Laos: the last domino in Indo-China falls.
        W. S. Merick. il U.S. News 78:23 My 26
        '75
    Notes and comment. New Yorker 51:25 S 8
        '75
    Polite revolution. il Time 106:38 D 15 '75
    Preserving a thin façade. il Time 105:26-7
        My 26 '75
    Removing the last obstacle. il Time 105:24-5
        Je 2 '75
    Ripe for the Communists. il Time 105:28 My
        19 '75

— An article used by the writer
    of the student paper printed
    toward the end of this chapter

— A subject entry

— An author entry

— Articles listed alphabetically
    under a subject entry

Compare the information given in *The Reader's Guide* above with the content and format of the bibliography entry for the article by R. J. Trotter in Margaret Poole's term paper on p. 326 at the end of this chapter. Notice that *The Reader's Guide* uses more abbreviations than does the bibliography entry. To use *The Reader's Guide* (and other such indexes) you need to familiarize yourself with the system of abbreviations used, especially for the titles of periodicals.

Search the bibliographies of books and articles you have already found

Most books and articles contain a list of references of their own. Thus, the process of finding sources for your own paper can become simpler as it progresses: Each source you find will lead you to other sources. You should especially follow up on the references contained in books or articles you find interesting or especially relevant to your topic.

Several of the works listed by Margaret Poole in her bibliography (see p. 325) were found by following up references in other works she had found. She discovered, for instance, that the article listed above in *The Reader's Guide* was the first of a two-part article summarizing the proceedings of a major conference on the origin of language sponsored by the New York Academy of Sciences. This led her not only to look up the second part but to look for the complete published proceedings of the conference. That book, when she found it, provided more material for her paper than any one other source.

Make a bibliography card for each article you find

Just as with books, you have not officially "found" an article until you have made a bibliography card for it. Study the format carefully for how to enter articles in the bibliography of the final typed paper (see pp. 310–311) and then enter the information on the preliminary bibliography card in that exact format. On page 297 is the card Margaret Poole made for the Trotter article listed in *The Reader's Guide*. She made it as soon as she found that it was indeed available to her in her school's library.

Exercises

a. Continue your tour of your college or university library.

(1) Go to the periodicals room and find out (a) whether current and bound periodicals are displayed together or separately and (b) whether they are shelved alphabetically by title or by call number.

(2) Go to the reference room and locate the periodical indexes listed in this book on p. 295.

(3) Find at least two articles of each of the following types and, referring to pp. 310–311, make a bibliography card for each one:

Trotter, Robert J. "From Language
to Linguistics and Beyond."
Science News, 108 (1975),
289 - 311.

(a) The City of St. Augustine, Florida, Under Spanish Rule
(b) Educational Programs for Gifted and Talented Children
(c) The Spread of "Killer Bees" Throughout South and Central America
(d) The Language of Gypsies
(e) The Relationship Between Alcoholism and Cancer of the Liver
(f) (Any two articles by Gary Wills)

b. If you are working on a paper as you read this chapter, find the articles you need. Search the periodical indexes in the reference room; browse among the bound and unbound periodicals in the periodicals room; study the bibliographies of books and articles you have already found. As soon as you decide an article may be useful, make a bibliography card for it, carefully following the format described on pp. 310–311.

Phase Five: Reading and Note Taking

This is the phase in the research process where the most learning takes place. Here is where you read and study your sources, and make the notes from which you will eventually write the paper. Here is where you should begin to take care to guard against plagiarism. Plagiarism is the presentation of the ideas or words of another as if they were your own. It is a serious violation of ethical standards, and in most colleges and universities it can lead to serious consequences such as suspension or even expulsion from school. You are expected to know what it is and how to avoid it. Unless you take notes with great care, you may unwittingly use the words of others in your paper without giving them proper credit.

Let your topic guide your reading

You will not ordinarily have time to read in their entirety the books and articles you have found. Nor do you have to. Begin by scanning the chapters or sections to discover the parts that most directly relate to your topic. (Occasionally, the entire work will be relevant and you will have to read all of it.) Read the relevant sections carefully. Passages that seem to treat very explicitly the ideas you have in mind should be copied out exactly onto 3 × 5″ index cards, noting the source and the page number. If the main ideas of a chapter or in several paragraphs seem relevant, you may summarize them in your own words, but still note the source and the page number on the note card.

When the writer of the sample paper consulted *People of the Lake: Mankind and Its Beginnings,* a book by Richard Leakey and Roger Lewin, she scanned the table of contents and decided not even to consult the chapters on subjects such as "The Human Family Unearthed," "An Ancient Way of Life," or "The First Affluent Society." She read only the chapter entitled "The Origin of Language."

Make note cards from your sources

The notes you take on 3 × 5″ index cards are of two types: paraphrases and direct quotes. Here are some paragraphs Margaret Poole read in Peter Farb's book, *Word Play,* and on page 300 is a copy of the note card on which she summarized their contents. Read the paragraphs from Farb carefully and then compare their wording with that on the note card:

Since sentences do not leave anything equivalent to the fossils and pottery shards that allow anthropologists to trace the prehistory of human beings, linguists can only speculate about the origins of language. Theories have been advanced, have won adherents for a while, then later were shown to be fanciful—and given derisive baby-talk names. Because some of these theories occasionally reappear today in new guises, let me mention several of them as a guide to the wary.

The Bow-Wow Theory states that language arose when humans imitated the sounds of nature by the use of onomatopoeic words like *cock-a-doodle-doo, cuckoo, sneeze, splash,* and *mumble.* This theory has been thoroughly discredited. It is now known that many onomatopoeic words are of recent, not ancient, origin and that some of them were not derived from natural sounds at all. But the most telling argument against the Bow-Wow Theory is that onomatopoeic words vary from language to language. If the human species had truly based its words on the sounds of nature, these words should be the same in all languages because of the obvious fact that a dog's bark is the same throughout the world. Yet the *bow-wow* heard by speakers of English sounds like *gua-gua* to Spaniards, *af-af* to Russians, and *wan-wan* to Japanese.

The Ding-Dong Theory dates back to Pythagoras and Plato and was long honored, but nowadays it has no support whatsoever. This theory claims a relationship between a word and its sense because everything in nature is supposed to give off a harmonic "ring," which humans supposedly detected when they named objects. But the Ding-Dong Theory cannot explain what resonance a small four-footed animal gave off to make Englishmen call it a *dog* rather than any other arbitrary collection of vowels and consonants—and what different resonance it communicated to Frenchmen to make them call it a *chien* or to Japanese to make them call it an *inu*.

Still other explanations for the origin of language are the Pooh-Pooh Theory, which holds that speech originated with spontaneous ejaculations of derision, fear, and other emotions; the Yo-Heave-Ho Theory, which claims that language evolved from the grunts and groans evoked by heavy physical labor; the Sing-Song Theory, which placed the origin of speech in the love songs and the rhythmic chants of early humans; and the Ha-Ha Theory, which states that languages evolved out of laughter. All these speculations have serious flaws, and none can withstand the close scrutiny of present knowledge about the structure of language and about the evolution of our species.

—PETER FARB, *Word Play*

On the card on page 300 only the author's name and page numbers are used to identify the source. This saving of space and effort is possible because complete information on the source has been entered on the bibliography card, which is easily accessible when the time comes to type the complete note. Notice especially that when Ms. Poole wrote even a few words on the card exactly as Farb did (such as "shown to be fanciful" in the second line of the front of the note card), she put them in quotation marks. Had she failed to do so, and then later used this exact phrase in her own paper without quotation marks, she would have been guilty of plagiarism.

Take a look now at the second paragraph on the first page of text in the finished sample paper (p. 315 below) where Ms. Poole uses the information on the note card. In studying her paragraph notice that (1) she did not feel the need to name all the fanciful theories of language origin that Farb names in order to make *her* point; (2) she rephrased the ideas entirely in her own words; (3) she thus did not need to put any words in quotation marks; but (4) she still needed to credit Farb with the *ideas* contained in her paragraph—as she did, with the note at the end of the paragraph. Had she not credited the ideas to her source, even though they were presented entirely in her own words, this too would have constituted plagiarism.

On page 301 is an example of a note card containing a direct quotation. Compare its contents with the citation from it on the second and third pages of the sample research paper (pp. 316–317), where ellipsis

(a) Front of note card:

> Most theories of language origin
> have been "shown to be fanciful."
> - Bow - Wow: "Humans imitated
>   sounds in nature ..."
> - Ding - Dong: Everything in
>   nature sends out a harmonic
>   ring, which early humans
>   detected in order to name things.
> - Pooh - Pooh: "Speech originated with
>   spontaneous ejaculations of derision."
>
> (over)

(b) Back of note card:

> Yo-Heave-Ho: Grunts and groans
> of physical labor gave rise to
> language.
> Sing - Song: Love songs and
> rythmic chants gave rise to
> language.
> Ha - Ha: "Language evolved
> out of laughter."
>
> Farb
> pp. 266 - 267

dots indicate that certain material from the source (and the note card) was left out when the source material was adapted for use in the paper.

It is extremely important to copy notes onto cards with special care —especially for punctuation in direct quotes. Your cards will ordinarily be your only sources when you type your paper, and any inaccura-

(a) Front of note card:

"*By a million years ago, some stone tool makers were producing objects that impress us as much more refined. They involve more definite design and control. Balanced, symmetrical objects such as a handaxe are much harder to manufacture; they require a stronger sense of purpose, more example and instruction, and more practice. By 100,000 years ago, some stone tool assemblages really*

(over)

(b) Back of note card:

begin to look elaborate, even to our technologically conscious eyes, and to learn how to make them properly, takes years of practice.
By 30,000 or 40,000 years ago, a kaleidoscopic diversity of forms and techniques were being utilized, and changes begin to be breathtakingly rapid by the standards of the early periods."

Isaac
p. 276

cies on them will also appear in the finished paper. Some researchers avoid this problem by photocopying key passages from their sources. This practice is not prohibited, but I strongly recommend against it when writing short papers and especially when writing papers in freshman composition classes. First, photocopied notes are not so easy to organize and reorganize as index cards, and, second, photocopying deprives you of the meditative understanding that comes from the admittedly time-consuming task of taking notes in longhand.

Exercises

a. Pick a topic of special interest to you, or pick one of the topics listed in exercises at the end of the previous two sections of this chapter, and then find two books and two articles on the topic. In each source try to find a key passage and make a direct-quotation note card of that passage. Elsewhere in each of the four sources, find several interesting paragraphs and make a note card in your own words, summarizing the ideas contained in those paragraphs.

b. If you are writing a paper as you read this chapter, read your sources carefully and take as many direct-quotation notes and as many paraphrase notes as you think necessary.

Phase Six: Preparing to Write

In many respects, the research process is a cycle, rather than simply a linear set of phases as I am presenting it. This means that even as you are reading your sources and taking notes, you may be discovering new sources and adding bibliography cards to your inventory. You may even find it necessary to refine your topic and, in light of the refinement, remove some cards from your list of sources. This cycle is especially apparent in the relationship between the reading/note-taking phase and the preparing-to-write phase.

Prepare an outline

You may have a very general outline in mind even before you begin to read your sources. But this is unusual. Ordinarily, you should have done some reading and note taking before you draft a preliminary outline. When you sit down to do it, your notecards will be spread about a desk top in very much the random manner that words were spread about a sheet of paper during the brainstorming phase of making an outline (see the display on p. 75 at the end of Chapter Three). Read and reread the cards; let them suggest a grouping to you. When you do, proceed with the process of making an outline exactly as that process was explained at the end of Chapter Three. Work on the outline. Do your best to refine it, for it will guide your reading and organize your note cards throughout the remainder of this phase.

Here is the outline that Margaret Poole developed during this phase of work on the sample paper:

I. The questions
  A. When did language originate?
  B. Why did language originate?
II. The evidence
  A. Cultural
  B. Physiological
III. The conclusions
  A. As to when
  B. As to why

As she continued her reading she discovered a number of things. First, she found out that although much had been written about the origin of language, very little of it was scientifically based. This meant that even though in one sense her topic, the origin of language, seemed too broad, in another sense it was not. It was not too broad when one considered the limited scientific evidence on the subject. She reconsidered retitling her paper, "Recent Scientific Evidence on the Origin of Language," but then decided to keep the more general title because the evidence did indeed address the general issues and did so effectively. As she read more, she also expanded the outline. You may want to compare the above preliminary outline with the final one she included in the paper (see p. 314 below).

Code your note cards according to the outline

As soon as you have prepared your outline, take each of your note cards and indicate in the upper right hand corner which section of the outline the note card relates to. Then arrange the cards in the order of the outline. At the top of page 304 is a representation of how the two note cards depicted earlier were thus coded.

The card coded as *I.B.* is the one taken from Farb, where he discusses fanciful theories about the origin of language. The card coded *II.A* is the one from Isaac, where he discusses developments in tool-making technology. Each author used the material on the card for a purpose different from Ms. Poole's, and the matter was placed in their works according to a different organizational plan. She took their ideas and arranged them to suit *her* purpose and *her* plan. It is at this point in the research process, more than any other, that she exercised originality as a writer. And it is at this point that you should take the greatest care. The ideas from your sources take on new relationships in the mechanical act of coding and arranging your note cards.

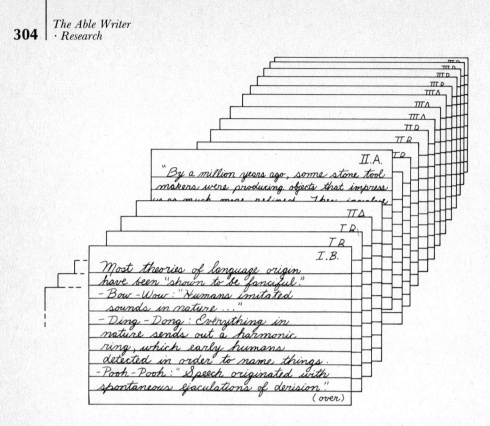

II.A.

" *By a million years ago, some stone tool makers were producing objects that impress*

II.A.

I.B.

I.B.

I.B.

Most theories of language origin have been "shown to be fanciful."
– Bow-Wow: "Humans imitated sounds in nature ... "
– Ding-Dong: Everything in nature sends out a harmonic ring, which early humans detected in order to name things.
– Pooh-Pooh: "Speech originated with spontaneous ejaculations of derision."

(over)

Study the cards as ordered by the outline

You are not yet ready to write. You need to test your perspective and your plan. To do so, set your outline before you, and while constantly referring to it, read all your note cards through several times. Do they make sense in the order you have given them? Are some of them unnecessary (i.e., unrelated to the outline section in which you have placed them)? Do some notes belong elsewhere in the stack? Is there insufficient information (not enough notes) for some sections of your outline? If the answer is yes to the last question, then you should consider either revising your outline or doing more reading and note taking in order to fill in the gaps. When you feel that you have fully absorbed the content of the note cards into *your* plan as expressed in *your* outline, then you are ready to begin drafting your paper.

Exercises

a. If you are not writing a paper as you read this chapter, but wish nonetheless to gain some experience in writing an outline from note cards and then evaluating it by rereading the cards, then you can take the eight notes you made for exercise *a* at the end of the last section (p. 302) and work with them. You will not of course be able to develop a very complex outline from only eight notes, but you should be able to find some basis for a plan in them. At the very least, once you draft an outline, you will be able to see where you would need to do more reading and note taking if indeed you intended to develop materials for a complete research paper.

b. If you are writing a paper as you read this chapter, then spread out your notes on a table and begin the process of developing an outline. When you have it drafted, code and arrange your cards according to it. Then read them through several times, evaluating your plan and looking for ways to improve it, either by more reading or by rearranging.

Phase Seven: Drafting the Paper

As you write, your stack of note cards should be at one hand and your outline at the other. This insures that you follow your plan and at the same time remain fully aware when ideas derive from your sources, and especially when you are using the exact words from a given source. You must write in your own words, giving your paragraphs their own coherence, and not rely on the organizational structures that the authors of your sources used in their works. When you quote a particular sentence from a source, be sure to make it fit coherently into the paragraph structure you have decided on.

Occasionally, several consecutive sentences from one of your sources will state a given idea better than you could and in a manner that fits perfectly into your plan. In such instances you may quote the entire passage exactly.

Margaret Poole used two such extended quotations in the sample paper (see pp. 316 and 318). The first such passage, on her second and third pages, is so clear and direct a description of the significant advances in toolmaking she wishes to discuss that she felt she could neither have summarized it nor restated it better than the source she quotes. And notice how the passage on her fourth page blends smoothly into her own paragraph.

Draft your notes as you write

An important preliminary point to remember is this: If you have done enough reading and taken enough notes, you should have many more note cards than you will actually use as you draft the paper. Much of the information will have been absorbed into your mind and will show up in the paper so indirectly that you will not be able to trace it to one source. Do not feel that you have wasted effort if you do not refer to every card. This is in the very nature of the research process.

The exact format to use in writing notes is presented in the discussion of Phase Eight below (pp. 308–310). You will need to study it, and to refer to it, in order to follow the suggestions I make in this section. When it comes time to type the paper, you will save yourself much extra effort, if you have taken the trouble to draft your notes in the proper format even in the rough draft of your paper. But, on the other hand, it is unnecessary to give them numbers in your draft (for you may decide to delete some in revision), and it is certainly unnecessary to worry about where they will eventually be in the text. Therefore, I recommend that you simply draw a line across the page of your draft at the point where a note's number will appear; then draft the note, draw another line, and continue with the text. On page 307 is a representation of the draft of a portion of the sample paper (it starts with the second full paragraph on the paper's second page of text; see p. 316 below). The first two notes in the handwritten draft on page 307 follow the format for a first-reference note; the third note follows the format for a subsequent-reference note. This distinction is illustrated fully in the discussion of Phase Eight (pp. 310–311).

Use edited-English style

It goes without saying that all the conventions of paragraph structure (Chapter Four), sentence structure (Chapters Five to Seven), word choice (Chapters Eight and Nine), spelling (Chapter Ten), and punctuation (Chapter Eleven) should guide you as you draft and revise and carefully edit the revised draft of your paper. At the very least you should plan to mark up your first written draft, tightening up sentence structure and working on word choice. Then you should make a rough *typed draft* from your revised written draft. It will be easier to work with. Make additional changes in sentence structure and word choice, but concentrate on the format of your notes and on details of punctuation and spelling. Only after two *or more* such preliminary drafts will you be ready to type the final version.

Exercises

a. If you are not writing a paper as you read this chapter, you should continue the small research project you began in exercise *a* after Phase Five and continued in exercise *a* after Phase Six. You took notes from four sources on a topic of your choice and then sorted the note cards and made an outline. Now try to draft a short paper from the outline. Insert at least four notes in it sim-

Ancestors of the human species first began to make crude stone tools approximately two and a half million years ago.

Glynn L. Isaac, "Stages of Cultural Elaboration in the Pleistocene: Possible Archaeological Indicators of the Development of Language Capabilities," in Harnad et al., pp. 275-288.

The methods used then and for at least the next million and a half years were very simple, much like the process of whittling a point on a piece of wood (though stones were used to "whittle" sharp edges on other stones). Contemporary professors of archaeology have taught their students this technique in a few hours.

Philip Lieberman, *On the Origins of Language: An Introduction to the Evolution of Human Speech*, (New York: Macmillan 1975), pp. 167-168.

By a million years ago, some stone tool makers were producing objects that impress us as much more refined... By 100,000 years ago, some stone tool assemblages really begin to look elaborate, even to our technologically conscious eyes, and to learn to make them properly takes years of practice. By 30,000 or 40,000 years ago, a kaleidoscopic diversity of forms and techniques were being utilized, and changes began to be breathtakingly rapid by the standards of early periods.

Isaac, p. 276

This technological explosion which...

ply so that you get some practice in drafting them. Do your best to make the draft coherent and well written.

b. If you are writing a paper as you read this chapter, then draft it. Pay careful attention to your cards and your outline as you write. Remember that you do not need to use every card in the paper. Follow all the principles of good writing you have learned throughout this book. Revise and rewrite as many times as needed to make the last preliminary draft as good as it can be.

This will allow you to concentrate on the research format as you type the final version.

Phase Eight: Typing and Editing

Ordinarily, you should type your paper yourself. If you do not know how to type, you should make every effort to learn, even if this means learning which fingers go with which keys and pecking your way through the paper; you will be surprised how soon you begin to peck faster. In an emergency, someone else may type a paper for you, but you may not rely on that person to correct grammar or punctuation or spelling, or to arrange your notes and bibliography for you. To do so would constitute another form of plagiarism besides the forms already discussed. Make sure that your typewriter has a ribbon that leaves dark letters, and, if necessary, clean the keys with an old toothbrush to avoid dark centers in open letters such as *o* and *e*.

Know the correct format for notes

Ordinarily, it is equally acceptable either to place notes at the bottom of the page of text to which they refer or to group them all together at the end of the paper. Your professor may have a preference, however. Below is a list of sample notes. Notice that the first citation gives complete information, but subsequent citations may be briefer. A much more complete list of sample notes is available in the *MLA Handbook*.

(1) A book with a single author

First note: ¹Philip Lieberman, On the Origins of Language: An Introduction to the Evolution of Human Speech, (New York: Macmillan, 1975), pp. 167–168.

Subsequent note: ²Lieberman, 152–153.

(2) A book with two authors

First note: ³Patrick J. Aspell and George F. McLean, Ancient Western Philosophy: The Hellenic Emergence (New York: Appleton–Century–Crofts, 1971), pp. 135–137.

Subsequent note: ⁴Aspell and McLean, p. 140.

(3) A book with three or more authors

First note: ⁵Randolph Quirk et al., A Grammar of Contemporary English (New York: Seminar Press, 1972), p. 1077.

Subsequent note: ⁶Quirk et al., 1080.

(4) A book with a corporate author

First note: [7]The Modern Language Association of America, <u>MLA Handbook for Writers of Research Papers, Theses, and Dissertations</u> (New York: Modern Language Association, 1977), p. 32.

Subsequent note: [8]<u>MLA Handbook</u>, pp. 36–38.

(5) A work in a collection of pieces by different authors

First note: [9]Mary R. Haas, "Interlingual Word Taboo," in <u>Language in Culture and Society</u>, ed. Dell Hymes (New York: Harper & Row, 1964), p. 489.

Subsequent note: [10]Haas, p. 491.

(6) An edition

First note: [11]Sir Thomas More, <u>Utopia</u>, ed. Robert M. Adams (New York: Norton, 1975), pp. 65–67.

Subsequent note: [12]More, p. 85.

If the editor's commentary is being cited, the editor's name should come first.

(7) A translation

First note: [13]Leo Tolstoy, <u>Anna Karenina</u>, trans. Constance Garnett (Indianapolis: Bobbs–Merrill, 1978), p. 205.

Subsequent note: [14]Tolstoy, p. 551.

(8) An article in a journal where pages are numbered by volume

First note: [15]Adrienne Lehrer, "Talking About Wine," <u>Language</u>, 51 (1975), p. 909.

Subsequent note: [16]Lehrer, p. 912.

(9) An article in a journal where pages are numbered by issue

First note: [17]Philip H. Rhein, "Two Fantastic Visions: Franz Kafka and Alfred Kubin," <u>South Atlantic Bulletin</u>, XLII, No. 2 (1977), p. 63.

Subsequent note: [18]Rhein, p. 66.

(10) An article in a monthly magazine

First note: [19]James Crockett, "Help for Your Houseplants," <u>Family Circle</u>, Oct. 1978, p. 58.

Subsequent note: [20]Crockett, p. 67.

(11) An article in a weekly magazine or newspaper

First note: [21]Merrill Sheils, "Why Johnny Can't Write," <u>Newsweek</u>, 8 Dec. 1975, p. 58.

Subsequent note: [22]Sheils, p. 60.

(12) An article in a daily newspaper

First note: [23]Tim Morton, "Copland: His Talents Run to
                     Extremes," The Virginian-Pilot and the Ledger-Star,
                     10 Sept. 1978, Sec. F. p. 4 col. 3.

Subsequent note: [24]Morton, p. 4 col. 6.

(13) An unsigned article

First note:)   [25]"The Year That the Building Stopped," Time,
                     28 Oct. 1974, p. 88.

Subsequent note: [26]"Building Stopped," p. 89.

(14) A review

First note: [27]Margaret M. Bryant, "Nevada Names," rev. of
                     Nevada Place Names: A Geographical Dictionary, by
                     Helen S. Carlson, American Speech, 49 (1974), p.
                     287.

Subsequent note: [28]Bryant, p. 288.

Know the correct format for bibliography entries

Below are sample bibliography entries for each of the types of sources illustrated in the section above on notes. All sources you consult in preparing your paper (even if you do not refer to them in a note) should be listed on a separate sheet alphabetized by the author's last name. If you list two works by the same author, do not retype the author's name in the second (or subsequent) entry; rather, type ten spaced hyphens (as in the sample paper on page 326 below) or type an underscore the length of the author's name in the previous entry. A longer list of example bibliography entries is given in the *MLA Handbook*.

(1) A book with a single author

Lieberman, Philip. On the Origins of Language: An Introduction
      to the Evolution of Human Speech. New York:
      Macmillan, 1975.

(2) A book with two authors

Aspell, Patrick J., and George F. McLean. Ancient Western
      Philosophy: the Hellenic Emergence. New York: Appleton-
      Century-Crofts, 1971.

(3) A book with three or more authors

Quirk, Randolph, et al. A Grammar of Contemporary English.
      New York: Seminar Press, 1972.

(4) A book with a corporate author

The Modern Language Association of America. MLA Handbook for
      Writers of Research Papers, Theses, and Dissertations.
      New York: Modern Language Association, 1977.

(5) A work in a collection of pieces by different authors
Hass, Mary R. "Interlingual Word Taboo." In <u>Language in Culture
and Society</u>. Ed. Dell Hymes. New York: Harper & Row, 1964.

(6) An edition
More, Sir Thomas. <u>Utopia</u>. Ed. Robert M. Adams. New York: Norton,
1975.

Alternatively, if the editor's commentary was your main source:

Adams, Robert M., ed. <u>Utopia</u>. By Sir Thomas More. New York: Norton, 1975.

(7) A translation
Tolstoy, Leo. <u>Anna Karenina</u>. Trans. Constance Garnett. Indianapolis: Bobbs-Merrill, 1978.

Alternatively:

Garnett, Constance, trans. <u>Anna Karenina</u>. By Leo Tolstoy. Indianapolis: Bobbs-Merrill, 1978.

(8) An article in a journal where pages are numbered by volume
Lehrer, Adrienne. "Talking About Wine." <u>Language</u>, 51 (1975), 901-
923.

(9) An article in a journal where the pages are numbered by issue
Rhein, Philip H. "Two Fantastic Visions: Franz Kafka and Alfred
Kubin." <u>South Atlantic Bulletin</u>. XLII, No. 2 (1977), 61-66.

(10) An article in a monthly magazine
Crockett, James. "Help for Your Houseplants." <u>Family Circle</u>. Oct.
1978, p. 58; pp. 67-68

(11) An article in a weekly magazine or newspaper
Sheils, Merrill. "Why Johnny Can't Write." <u>Newsweek</u>, 8 Dec. 1975,
pp. 58-65.

(12) An article in a daily newspaper
Morton, Tim. "Copland: His Talents Run to Extremes." <u>The
Virginian-Pilot and the Ledger-Star</u>, 10 Sept, 1978, Sec. F.
p. 4, cols. 3-6.

(13) An unsigned article
"The Year That the Building Stopped." <u>Time</u>, 28 Oct. 1974, pp.
88-92.

(14) A review
Bryant, Margaret M. "Nevada Names." Rev. of <u>Nevada Place Names</u>:
<u>A Geographical Dictionary</u>, by Helen A. Carlson. <u>American
Speech</u>, 49 (1974), pp. 287-289.

Follow the format of this sample paper

On the following pages, you will find a representation of the final typed version of the sample paper we have been discussing throughout this chapter. Study it carefully, noting especially the aspects of format pointed out in the marginal notes. Be sure to read and do the exercises that are printed after the sample paper on p. 327.

The paper must measure exactly
8½ × 11″.

Use plain white bond paper,
not onion skin paper.

8½ inches

11 inches

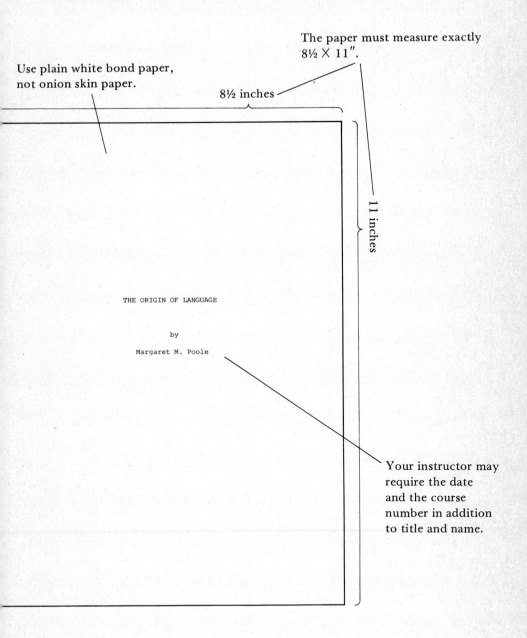

THE ORIGIN OF LANGUAGE

by

Margaret M. Poole

Your instructor may
require the date
and the course
number in addition
to title and name.

Your instructor may
require a statement of
the paper's main idea
in the outline.

Note the lack of
page number.

OUTLINE

Page

I. The questions — 1

    A. When did language originate? — 1

    B. Why did language originate? — 1

II. The evidence — 2

    A. Cultural — 2

        1. Toolmaking — 2

        2. Art — 3

    B. Physiological — 4

        1. Brain development — 4

        2. Vocal tract development — 6

III. The conclusions — 7

    A. When language originated: during the last
       ice age — 7

    B. Why language originated — 7

        1. Survival value — 7

        2. Physiological readiness — 7

This is a topic
outline; you or
your instructor
may prefer a
sentence outline.

Indent each paragraph five spaces.

Leave a 1½-inch margin at the top.

Center the title in all capitals.

Do not number the first page of text, but count it.

Quadruple space between title and text.

Double space between lines of text and between paragraphs.

Leave a one-inch margin on the left, right, and bottom.

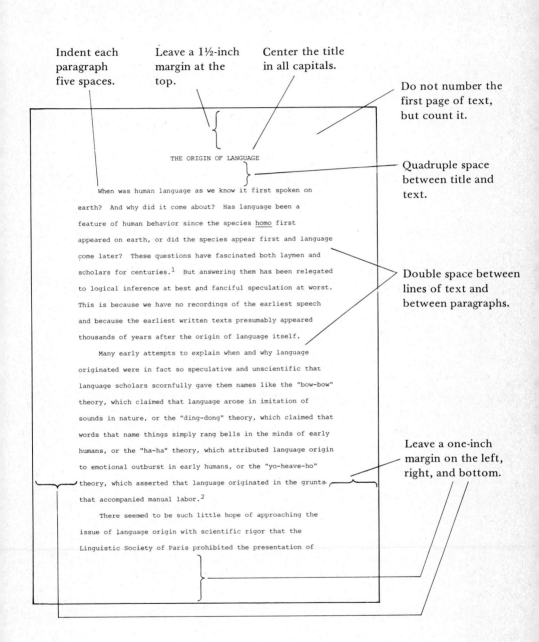

THE ORIGIN OF LANGUAGE

When was human language as we know it first spoken on earth? And why did it come about? Has language been a feature of human behavior since the species homo first appeared on earth, or did the species appear first and language come later? These questions have fascinated both laymen and scholars for centuries.[1] But answering them has been relegated to logical inference at best and fanciful speculation at worst. This is because we have no recordings of the earliest speech and because the earliest written texts presumably appeared thousands of years after the origin of language itself.

Many early attempts to explain when and why language originated were in fact so speculative and unscientific that language scholars scornfully gave them names like the "bow-bow" theory, which claimed that language arose in imitation of sounds in nature, or the "ding-dong" theory, which claimed that words that name things simply rang bells in the minds of early humans, or the "ha-ha" theory, which attributed language origin to emotional outburst in early humans, or the "yo-heave-ho" theory, which asserted that language originated in the grunts that accompanied manual labor.[2]

There seemed to be such little hope of approaching the issue of language origin with scientific rigor that the Linguistic Society of Paris prohibited the presentation of

It is a good idea to
type your name on each page.

Note that the number is 2,
even though no number appeared
on the previous page.

```
                                    Poole    2

papers on the subject in 1866 and renewed the prohibition in

1911.³  Skepticism about this subject among scientists per-

sisted throughout the first two-thirds of the present century,

but beginning about ten years ago, fragmentary scientific

data, drawn from fields of study unrelated to language itself,

began to make it possible to ask when and why language origi-

nated and to hope that finally some answers based on sound

scientific methodology might begin to emerge.  Much of the

evidence is circumstantial, but it is evidence nontheless.

     The first two types of evidence derive from archaeological

studies of early human cultures, especially from studies of the

types of tools made by early humans and from studies of when

representational art emerged.

     Ancestors of the human species first began to make crude

stone tools approximately two and a half million years ago.⁴

The methods used then and for at least the next million and a

half years were very simple, much like the process of whittling

a point on a piece of wood (though stones were used to "whittle"

sharp edges on other stones).  Contemporary professors of arch-

aeology have taught their students this technique in a few

hours.⁵

        By a million years ago, some stone tool makers were

     producing objects that impress us as much more refined

     . . . .  By 100,000 years ago, some stone tool assemblages
```

Note numbers
should be raised
one half space above
the line, outside any
punctuation but
immediately up
against it.

Leave a triple space
between your text
and blocked quo-
tations. (Some
instructors prefer
you to type block-
ed quotations single
spaced, in which
case you can leave
a double space
between the
blocked quote and
your text).

Read the final typed copy very carefully. Errors
may be corrected in pen. If you find more than
three small errors on one page, retype the page.

Poole   3

really begin to look elaborate, even to our technolo-

gically conscious eyes, and to learn to make them proper-

ly takes years of practice. By 30,000 or 40,000 years

ago, a kaleidoscopic diversity of forms and techniques

were being utilized, and changes began to be breathtak-

ingly rapid by the standards of early periods.[6]

This technological explosion that took place between 30,000

and 40,000 years ago surely signals a point of significant

advance in human cognitive ability. Such an inference is

reinforced by the second type of evidence from archaeology:

That is the fact that representational art did not exist

prior to 30,000 years ago and emerged in different forms, at

different places, and in a highly developed state at just about

the same time as the "kaleidoscopic" diversification of tool-

making techniques was taking place. A 2½-inch carved horse,

found in Germany in 1931, has been dated to 30,000 B.C. and

is thus the earliest representational art image known.[7] High-

ly sophisticated drawings of reindeer on cave walls in France

have similarly been dated to this same period.[8]

    What might have caused this burst in human cognitive pro-

gress and what, if anything, did it have to do with the origin

of language? Here we turn to paleontology and what it has

learned from studying the fossilized remains of early human

skulls. By making casts of the insides of fossil skulls and

Poole   4

measuring the casts in precise ways, certain inferences can be

made about the brains that once inhabited those skulls. The

study of such casts shows a steady increase in brain size

relative to body weight from three million years ago down to

the present.[9] More importantly, such studies suggest that:

> there may have been a genetic breakthrough in laterali-
> zation some 50,000 years ago, bringing about a sudden
> increase in effective cerebral storage capacity and
> obviating the need for any further expensive growth of
> the brain. The evidence, to be sure, is all indirect:
> the fossil record apparently shows no significant brain
> growth since the data given . . . and something has to
> account for the sudden sharp jump in technological com-
> lexity, diversity, and rate of change as of about 40,000
> years ago. On the expanded storage capacity, the notion
> is that in a symmetrical brain everything must be stored
> in parallel in the two hemispheres, whereas with our
> brand of lateralization one gets cross-connections so
> designed that, although a lot of information is laid down
> in only one hemisphere, it is nevertheless available for
> use on both sides of the body.[10]

Here we have an explanation for the quantum leap in tool-making

ability and for the sudden appearance of representational art:

the ability of the brain to store and process information had

increased dramatically because humans had developed lateralized
brains: brains where each side had its own functions, but
where each side nonetheless had contact with the other side.
This in effect doubled the capacity of the human brain without
doubling its size.

But it is still not completely clear what all of this
has to do with the origin of language. The line of reasoning
goes something like this: Only humans have lateralized brains;
only humans acquire language and pass it on to their offspring;
furthermore, language skills are localized in one side of the
brain; therefore, the advent of lateralization must have had
something to do with the origin of language. A related argument uses the evidence discussed earlier in a different way.
It goes like this: The processes involved in making the complex tools dating from 30,000 years ago and in learning the
skills required to produce representational art that dates
from the same period are so complex that merely watching someone else do it could not preserve them from generation to
generation; these skills had to be explained; therefore,
language must have been part of human behavioral equipment
from at least 30,000 years ago.[11]

The evidence is diverse, and the reasoning may seem a bit
forced, but it is hard scientific evidence nonetheless, and it
provides grounds for a reasonably specific answer to the
questions of when language arose (some time between 50,000 and

30,000 years ago), and for a partial answer to why it arose
(because genetic change in the structure of the brain--the
advent of lateralization--made it possible). But there is
another kind of evidence from the fossil record that both
supports the above answer to when language originated and adds
a different perspective to the question of why it originated.

Philip Lieberman and Edmund Crelin have recently developed a complex method of studying the speaking ability of
early humans by studying their fossilized skulls.[12] They
made casts of the mouth and throat (vocal tract) of several
fossilized skulls and compared them with casts made from skulls
of newborn and adult humans of the twentieth century. They
developed a computer program that was able to project the
types of vowels that a vocal tract shaped like a given cast
would be able to produce. They found that whereas the twentieth-
century adult human would (of course) be able to produce the
vowel sounds in the words eat, ooze, and ah (sounds that
occur in all known languages) both the twentieth-century
newborn infant and fossilized skulls dating from about
3,000,000 B.C. to about 75,000 B.C. would be incapable of producing the sounds, or in the case of fossilized skulls from
later in that period, would produce only very fuzzy versions
of the sounds. However, a skull dating from 40,000 B.C. was
entirely like the modern skull in possessing a vocal tract
capable of producing these vowels.

Poole   7

What is the meaning of the evidence described in the last paragraph? It means that sometime after 50,000 B.C. early humans not only developed brains capable of language as we know it, but they also seem to have developed the vocal abilities to enunciate language as we know it. This confirms the period of 50,000 to 30,000 B.C. as the age when language originated. It also indicates another reason why language originated: Humans had become physiologically capable of controlling the vocal productive mechanisms commonly used today by all speakers of all languages.

There is one question yet to be addressed: Why should evolutionary processes have produced two major genetic changes (a lateralized brain and a refined vocal tract) in so relatively short a period of time (50,000 to 30,000 B.C.)? Major evolutionary changes tend to occur during periods when a species is under great pressure in its fight to survive, and interestingly enough, the period in question was one of great strain on the human species: 35,000 B.C. marked the coldest point in the last great ice age. It was a time when ice covered much of the Northern Hemisphere and when humans needed all of the mental powers and communicative powers they could muster in order to survive. In many places, it seems, only those with developing lateralization and greater vocal control did indeed survive: The principle of natural selection was operating in high gear.[13]

And so, we have intriguing, if not decisive, answers to

the questions with which this paper opened. When did language
originate? Sometime during the last ice age, probably between
50,000 and 30,000 B.C. Why did language originate? Environ-
mental pressure on the human species during the ice age led
to brain lateralization and refined control of the organs of
speech, both of which seem essential for language as we know
it. As further evidence of the essential accuracy of both of
these answers we have the tremendous advances in tool making and
the sudden appearance of representational art about 30,000 B.C.
Both of these indicate that something most unusual had happened
to the species homo. That something was language.

This page may also be labeled
ENDNOTES; do not label it
FOOTNOTES, for the notes
are not at the foot of the
page.

Notice that notes can do more than
simply cite the sources of material;
this one does that, but it also
suggests how the reader can learn
more about an idea not treated in depth
in the paper.

Poole   9

Quadruple space.

NOTES

[1] For a review of some of the more serious attempts to address these questions, see Robert J. Trotter, "From Language to Linguistics and Beyond," Science News, 108 (1975), pp. 332-333; for a more thorough review, see Hans Aarsleff, "An Outline of Language-Origin Theory Since the Renaissance," in Origins and Evolution of Language and Speech, ed. Stevan R. Harnad et al., Annals of the New York Academy of Sciences, 280 (1976), pp. 4-13.

[2] Peter Farb, Word Play: What Happens When People Talk (New York: Bantam Books, 1975), pp. 266-267.

[3] Dwight Bolinger, Aspects of Language, 2nd ed. (New York: Harcourt Brace Jovanovich, 1975), p. 306.

[4] Glynn L. Isaac, "Stages of Cultural Elaboration in the Pleistocene: Possible Archaeological Indicators of the Development of Language Capabilities," in Harnard et al., pp. 275-288.

[5] Philip Lieberman, On the Origins of Language: An Introduction to the Evolution of Human Speech, (New York: Macmillan, 1975), pp. 167-168.

[6] Isaac, p. 276.

[7] Alexander Marshack, "Some Implications of the Paleolithic Symbolic Evidence for the Origin of Language," in Harnad et al., p. 289.

[8] Lieberman, p. 181.

Compare the format
of each of these notes
with the list of
sample notes on
pp. 308-310.

[9]Lieberman, 152-153.

[10]C. F. Hockett, "In Search of Jove's Brow," <u>American</u>
<u>Speech</u>, 53 (1978), p. 286.

[11]Both arguments are engagingly summarized and with good
additional discussion of some evidence already described here
in Richard E. Leakey and Roger Lewin, <u>People of the Lake:</u>
<u>Mankind and Its Beginnings</u>, (Garden City, N.Y.: Anchor Press/
Doubleday, 1978), pp. 208-216.

[12]The method was first described in Philip Lieberman and
Edmund S. Crelin, "On the Speech of Neanderthal Man," <u>Linguistic</u>
<u>Inquiry</u>, II (1971), 203-222; the summary in this paragraph is
based on Lieberman, pp. 121-148.

[13]For a detailed discussion of the effects of the ice
age on language origin see Julian Jaynes, "The Evolution of Language in the Late Pleistocene," in Harnad et al., 312-317;
Julian Jaynes, <u>The Origin of Consciousness in the Breakdown</u>
<u>of the Bicameral Mind</u>, (Boston: Houghton Mifflin, 1977), pp.
129-133; and, for a summary of Jayne's argument, Robert J.
Trotter, "Language Evolving: Part Two," <u>Science News</u>, 108 (1975),
pp. 378-378, 383.

Quadruple space.

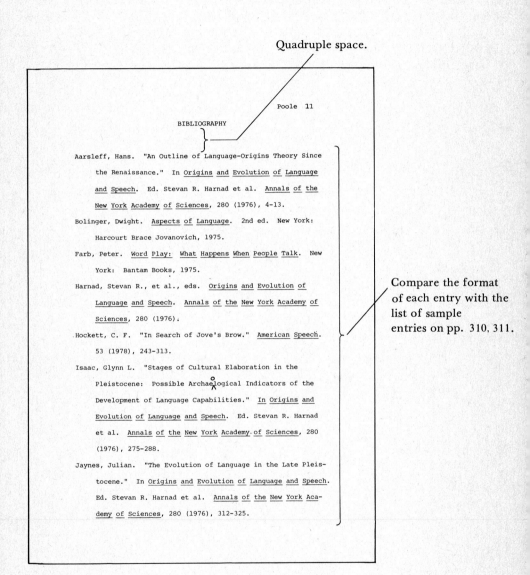

Poole 11

BIBLIOGRAPHY

Aarsleff, Hans. "An Outline of Language-Origins Theory Since

the Renaissance." In Origins and Evolution of Language

and Speech. Ed. Stevan R. Harnad et al. Annals of the

New York Academy of Sciences, 280 (1976), 4-13.

Bolinger, Dwight. Aspects of Language. 2nd ed. New York:

Harcourt Brace Jovanovich, 1975.

Farb, Peter. Word Play: What Happens When People Talk. New

York: Bantam Books, 1975.

Harnad, Stevan R., et al., eds. Origins and Evolution of

Language and Speech. Annals of the New York Academy of

Sciences, 280 (1976).

Hockett, C. F. "In Search of Jove's Brow." American Speech.

53 (1978), 243-313.

Isaac, Glynn L. "Stages of Cultural Elaboration in the

Pleistocene: Possible Archaeological Indicators of the

Development of Language Capabilities." In Origins and

Evolution of Language and Speech. Ed. Stevan R. Harnad

et al. Annals of the New York Academy of Sciences, 280

(1976), 275-288.

Jaynes, Julian. "The Evolution of Language in the Late Pleis-

tocene." In Origins and Evolution of Language and Speech.

Ed. Stevan R. Harnad et al. Annals of the New York Aca-

demy of Sciences, 280 (1976), 312-325.

Compare the format
of each entry with the
list of sample
entries on pp. 310, 311.

The second time a work by a given author is cited the name is represented by ten spaced hyphens.

Poole 12

- - - - - - - - - -. The Origin of Consciousness in the

    Breakdown of the Bicameral Mind. Boston: Houghton

Mifflin, 1977.

Leakey, Richard E. and Roger Lewin. People of the Lake:

    Mankind and Its Beginnings. Garden City, N.Y.: Anchor

    Press/ Doubleday, 1978.

Lieberman, Philip. On the Origins of Language: An Introduction

to the Evolution of Human Speech. New York: Macmillan,

    1975.

- - - - - - - - - - and Edmund S. Crelin. "On the Speech of

    Neanderthal Man." Linguistic Inquiry, II (1971), 203-222.

Marshack, Alexander. "Some Implications of the Paleolithic

    Symbolic Evidence for the Origin of Language." In

    Origins and Evolution of Language and Speech. Ed.

    Stevan R. Harnad et al. Annals of the New York Academy

    of Sciences, 280 (1976), 289-311.

Trotter, Robert J. "From Language to Linguistics and Beyond."

    Science News, 108 (1975), 332-334.

- - - - - - - - - -. "Language Evolving: Part Two." Science

News, 108 (1975) 378-379, 383.

Exercises

a. Look again at the notes and bibliography entries in the sample paper you have just read. Carefully check each note against the list of sample notes on pp. 308–310. Identify by number just which sample note corresponds to each note in the sample paper. Do the same for the bibliography entries. Which numbered sample entry on pp. 310–311 corresponds to each entry in the bibliography of the sample paper?

b. If you are writing your own paper as you read this chapter, carefully type and edit the final version. Attend to all matters of detail: the title page, the format of the outline, the numbering of the pages, the positioning of the note numbers in the text, the proper spacing between headings and text, and especially the exactly correct format of the notes and the bibliography.

c. Think about this book. I hope that you have read most or all of it by this time. Plan an essay about this book. It may be expository or argumentative; i.e., you may wish to discuss how the book was used in your course, or you may wish to evaluate it. I hope you will be able to think of strengths as well as weaknesses. I am the audience for your essay. Try to show what you have learned about writing in the way you write the essay. When you finish it mail it to: John P. Broderick, c/o College Division, Harper & Row, Publishers, Inc., 10 East 53d Street, New York, NY 10022. Your essay *will* influence the structure and the content of the next edition. Thank you.

Appendix | *A Glossary of Edited-English Usage*

In this Appendix, you will find a list of language features, most having to do with word choice, that often cause problems for writers. This is because edited English requires particular choices, but informal written English and conversational English may not. Many of the "do nots" in the following glossary may seem strange to you, for they recommend against usages that are often familiar in conversation. Remember, this is a guide to edited English only; the recommendations here need not affect the way you speak English or write it informally.

I have tried to limit the glossary to high-frequency and troublesome items and to those that a clear majority of the *American Heritage Dictionary* usage panel agreed on. If you disagree with a directive given here, then consult the *American Heritage* usage note and find out how large a minority of panel members agreed with you. In the end, always let your audience and your purpose be your guide.

a, an: Use *a* before words beginning with a consonant *sound* (*a book, a house, a historical novel*). Use *an* before words beginning with a vowel *sound* (*an apple, an honest politician, an hour*).

accept, except: *Accept* means "to receive" (*She accepted a bribe*). *Except* has two meanings: As a verb it means "to leave out" (*Pregnant women will be excepted from the draft*); as a preposition it means "but" (*Everyone contributed except Richard*). Do not confuse these words or meanings.

advice, advise: *Advice* is a noun (*They gave me advice*). *Advise* is a verb (*They advised me*). Do not confuse these spellings.

affect, effect: As a verb, *affect* means "to act on" (*Pollution affects all of us*). *Effect* means "to create," or "to bring about" (*Political action will effect social change*). The noun *effect* names the result of *both* verbs (*The effect of pollution on all of us is* *serious; The effect of political action is social change*). The verb *affect* has another, less common meaning: "to pretend" (*She affected to be mad*). There is a noun, *affect,* which is used only as a technical term in psychology. Do not confuse these words or meanings.

all ready, already: *All ready* is a combination of a noun and an adjective, and thus means "all were ready" (*The students were all ready to board the bus*). *Already* is an adverb meaning "by a certain time" (*They have arrived already* or *They have already arrived*—note that *They have arrived all ready* would mean "They have arrived and they are all ready"). Do not confuse these words or meanings.

all right: Do not misspell this expression as *alright.*

all together, altogether: *All together* is a combination of a noun and an adjective, and thus means "all were together" (*My uncles were all together for the reunion*). *Altogether* is an adverb meaning "completely" (*It is altogether fitting and proper that we should do this*). Do not confuse these words or meanings.

allusion, illusion: *Allusion* means "a reference to" (*When the speaker asked for "our daily bread," she was making an allusion to the Lord's Prayer*). *Illusion* means "a mistaken hope or idea" (*It is an illusion to think that government can solve all problems*). Do not confuse these words or meanings.

a lot: Never write this as one word (*alot*).

also: Do not use this in place of *and: Americans are guaranteed life, liberty, and* (not *also*) *the pursuit of happiness; Jefferson designed Monticello, and* (not *also*) *he designed the Rotunda at the University of Virginia.*

among, between: Use *among* when three or more parties are involved (*The negotiations among the U.S., Great Britain, and the Soviet Union are moving slowly*).

amount of, number of: Use *amount of* with uncountable heaps (*An enormous amount of energy is needed to work twenty straight hours*). Use *number of* with countable sets (*A large number of push-ups can damage the heart of a middle-aged person*).

and etc.: Since *etc.* means "and so forth," it is a needless repetition to write "and etc."

and/or: Avoid this except in legal or business communication.

ante-, anti-: *Ante-* means "before" (*ante-World War II*). *Anti-* means "against" (*antiwar activists*). Do not confuse these prefixes.

any: When this is used as a pronoun, use either a singular or a plural verb according to the meaning (*Any of the students has a chance to win* [there will be one winner]; *Have any of the hors d'oeuvres been eaten?* [*any* means "some"]). Avoid overuse of *any* as an adjective; write *The most serious problem is pollution* instead of *The most serious of any problem is pollution.*

any more, anymore: *Any more* is an adjective and a noun (*Are there any more arriving today?*) or an adjective and an adjective (*Are there any more grapes arriving today?*) Do not write either of these as one word. *Anymore* is an adverb that appears only in negative sentences (*She does not study anymore*). Avoid using this adverb in affirmative sentences to mean "nowadays" (*Anymore, there seem to be fewer honest politicians*).

anybody: Do not write this indefinite pronoun as two words (*Does any body need help?*) The phrase *any body,* as in *Any body needs nourishment for its cells,* is of course two separate words.

anyone: Do not write this indefinite pronoun as two words.

anyplace, someplace: Do not substitute these for *anywhere* and *somewhere*. (The two-word phrases, *any place* and *some place* have meanings of their own.)

as: Do not use *as* to mean "because": *Because* (not *as*) *he arrived late, he missed his turn.* Do not use it to mean "since": *There is no mail today, since* (not *as*) *it is a holiday. As* may of course be used to mean "while": *Nero fiddled as Rome burned.*

as, like: *As* may function as a subordinating conjunction; *like* may not: *The President holds frequent news conferences, as* (not *like*) *he promised he would. As* may function as a preposition in prepositional phrases of manner (those that tell "how"): *She excels as a pilot.* However, avoid using *as* in place of the preposition *like: Many problems, like* (not *as*) *health, money, or love-life, can distract college students.* (The phrase *such as* may be used in place of the preposition *like* in this sentence.)

as . . . as, so . . . as: In affirmative sentences making comparisons, use *as . . . as* (*Mary runs as fast as Hal*); in negative sentences making comparisons, use *so . . . as* (*Hal does not run so fast as Mary*).

as if, as though: Prefer the subjunctive after these phrases: *He acted as if he were* (not *was*) *guilty; They ate as though it were* (not *was*) *their last meal.*

as to: Do not use this to mean "about": *The committee has not been informed about* (not *as to*) *the senator's stock holdings.* Before *whether,* leave it out altogether: *They are not sure whether* (not *as to whether*) *he will testify.*

at: Do not use *at* after where: *Where is it?* (not *Where is it at?*)

author: Do not use *author* as a verb: *D. H. Lawrence wrote* (not *authored*) *Lady Chatterly's Lover.*

awhile, a while: *Awhile* is an adverb telling "how long" (*They stayed awhile*). *A while* is a phrase consisting of a determiner and a noun (*They stayed for a while*). Do not confuse these two expressions.

bad, badly: Use the adjective *bad* after verbs of sense like *feel* and *look* (*They feel bad; They look bad*). Use the adverb *badly* after other verbs (*The car runs badly; He cooks badly*).

because, reason: Do not use both of these in introducing one clause; use the one or the other: *The reason is that they lied* or *Because they lied . . .* (not *The reason is because they lied*).

being as, being that: Do not use either of these in place of *since: Since* (not *being as*) *it is Friday, we can stay longer; Since* (not *being that*) *you forgot my birthday, I do not regret forgetting your anniversary.*

beside, besides: *Beside* is a preposition (*The garage is beside the house*). *Besides* is an adverb (*Besides arriving late to work, that clerk did not do his job*). Do not confuse them

better than, more than: Do not use *better than* in place of *more than: More than* (not *better than*) *300,000 people attended the rock concert.*

between, among: See *among, between.*

both: Do not use *both* in reference to more than two persons or things: *The faculty, the students, and the administration should make concessions* (not *Both the faculty, the students, and the administration . . .*).

burst, bursted: *Burst* is the present, past, and past participle of this verb: *They burst balloons every day: Yesterday, they burst a balloon; The balloons have burst.* Do not use *bursted* in place of any of these three.

but: *But* is ordinarily a conjunction, joining grammatically equal but logically opposite items (*They try hard, but they usually fail*). When *but* joins two nouns, the first is usually an indefinite pronoun, and *but* may be paraphrased as *except* (*The boss promoted everyone but them*). In such sentences, *but* is often considered a preposition. In conversational sentences like the following, *but* is clearly a preposition because the verb agrees with *everyone,* and *them* (even though it is in the subject noun phrase) represents the case form of the pronoun that must follow a preposition: *Everyone but them was promoted.* However, in edited English you should avoid this prepositional use of *but* and instead use *except: Everyone except them was promoted.*

But (meaning "only") may also be used as an adverb. In this sentence it modifies the adjective *one: I regret that I have but one life to give for my country.* It modifies the verb *opened* in this sentence: *She had but opened her eyes, when she heard the crash.* Because the adverb *but* has a negative meaning, avoid using it with other negatives: *I have* (not *haven't*) *but one life to give; she had* (not *had not*) *but opened her eyes.*

but that, but what: Avoid *but that* and *but what: I have no doubt that* (not *but that* or *but what*) *you are right.*

can, may: *Can* expresses power or ability (*The President can veto legislation passed by Congress*). *May* expresses possibility or permission (*Employees may report to work two hours later because of the weather*). Do not confuse them.

cannot, can not: Prefer *cannot* to *can not.*

compare to, compare with: *Compare to* emphasizes similarities: *Swimming compares favorably to running as a health aid. Compare with* emphasizes both similarities and differences: *The report compared inflation with unemployment and found both to be unacceptable.* Be sensitive to this distinction.

complement, compliment: A complement completes: *The wine complements the meal.* A compliment praises: *The queen complimented the pianist on her artistry.* Do not confuse these words or meanings.

consensus of opinion: Since *consensus* already means "a jointly held opinion," this phrase is needlessly repetitious. Prefer *consensus.*

continual, continuous: *Continual* means "repeated": *After continual meetings over a period of ten months, the House and the Senate reached agreement on energy legislation. Continuous* means "uninterrupted": *After thirty-six continuous hours of negotiation, the union and management reached an agreement.* Avoid confusing these words or meanings.

couple of: Do not omit the word *of.* Prefer *a couple of books* to *a couple books.*

critique: Do not use *critique* as a verb: *The sales staff evaluated* (not *critiqued*) *McNally's presentation.*

differ from, differ with: Two people or things that are not alike *differ from* each other. Two people who disagree *differ with* each other. Do not confuse the two expressions.

different from, different than, differently than: Use *different from* when contrasting two nouns: *Peaches are different from pears.* Use *different than* only with *more* when contrasting degrees of difference: *The taste of a peach is different from the taste of a pear. The taste of a banana is more different than that of a peach.* Use *dif-*

ferently than when contrasting two verbs: *Jenny writes differently than Hal.* Do not confuse these three expressions.

discrete, discreet: *Discrete* means "distinct or unrelated": *Inflation and unemployment are discrete problems. Discreet* means "prudent" or "careful": *The company president was discreet when he waited until after the board meeting to tell the vice-president he was fired.* Do not confuse them.

due to: Do not begin a sentence with *due to:* substitute *because of.*

due to the fact that: Avoid this expression; use *because* in its place.

each and every: Avoid this expression; prefer either *each* or *every.*

each other, one another: *Each other* refers to two persons: *The two of them argued with each other. One another* refers to three or more persons: *The four of them argued with one another.* Be sensitive to this distinction.

effect, affect: See *affect, effect.*

either, neither: Both of these words, when used as pronouns, require a singular verb: *Either is* (not *are*) *capable of doing the job. Neither was* (not *were*) *there on time.*

enthuse: Avoid this word either as a verb or as an adjective. Prefer *be enthusiastic about.*

equally as: Avoid this expression. Instead of writing *An abacus is equally as good as a calculator,* write either *An abacus is as good as a calculator* or *An abacus and a calculator are equally good.*

etc.: See *and etc.*

every day, everyday: *Every day* is a noun phrase that consists of an adjective and a noun, and it is often used as an adverbial modifier: *They read the newspaper every day: Everyday* is an adjective: *Danger is an everyday experience to police officers.* Do not confuse these two expressions.

everyone, everybody: These are singular pronouns. Thus, you should avoid using *their* to refer back to them: *Everyone lost his* (not *their*) *money.* If you wish to avoid the sexist connotation of generic *he,* which is grammatically correct, then find an alternate wording that avoids the issue. (See pp. 108–110 for a discussion of such alternates.)

everyplace: Do not use this as a substitute for the adverb *everywhere: Everywhere* (not *everyplace*) *they go, they find trouble.*

except, accept: See *accept, except.*

farther, further: *Farther* refers to literal distance: *Australia is farther from California than Hawaii is: Further* refers to figurative distance: *further from my mind; further in the future.* Do not confuse these words or meanings.

fewer, less; *Fewer* refers to a number and answers "How many?" (*There are fewer candidates this year than last*): *Less* refers to quantity and answers "How much?" (*There is less sand arriving by rail*). Do not confuse them.

finalize: Avoid this verb; prefer the phrase *make final.*

flaunt, flout: *Flaunt* means "to show off brazenly": *Even though he won it by cheating, he flaunted his trophy: Flout* means "to show contempt for someone or something": *They flouted the law when they sped through the traffic light as the police watched.* Both of these words share the connotation of brazenness, but their denotations differ markedly. Do not confuse them.

former, latter: *Former* refers back to the first of two antecedents; *latter* refers back to the second of two: *Ms. Altschul and Mr. Hargrave were appointed to positions in the administration; the former is now commissioner of revenue and the latter is vice-chancellor of taxation.* If more than two persons or things are involved, use *first, second, . . ., last.* Avoid using *former* and *latter* when more than two referents are involved. Clarity is often better served when you do not use *former* and *latter* at all, but simply rename the antecedents.

funny: *Funny* means "humorous"; do not use it to mean "odd" or "unusual": *Europeans write the number seven in an odd* (not *funny*) *way: They draw a line through the stem.*

further, farther: See *farther, further.*

gift: Do not use *gift* as a verb: *They gave him* (not *gifted him with*) *a new car.*

good, well: As evaluative terms, *good* is an adjective, and *well* is an adverb. Do not use *good* as an adverb: *The generator works well* (not *good*). Do not use *well* as an adjective after a verb of sense or cognition: *She felt so good* (not *well*) *that she thought she could break a world record.* There is also an adjective, *well,* which is not an evaluative term, but which means "not ill"; it may of course be used after a verb of sense or cognition: *Now that she is well, she hopes to return to work.*

a half a: Avoid this expression; instead use either of the following: *They delivered a half* (not *a half a*) *ton of gravel; They delivered half a* (not *a half a*) *ton of gravel.*

hanged, hung: *Hanged* is the past and past participle of the verb that means "execution by hanging": *They hanged the murderers at dawn; The murderers have been hanged. Hung* is the past and past participle of the verb *hang* in all other senses: *They hung up their coats; They should have hung their coats in the lobby.* Do not confuse them.

hardly, scarcely: These are negative adverbs. Thus, you must avoid using them with a negative predicate: *I can* (not *can't*) *hardly see it; They had* (not *hadn't*) *scarcely arrived, when they heard the bad news.*

illusion, allusion: See *allusion, illusion.*

imply, infer: *Imply* means "to suggest" or "to hint," and it is an activity usually attributed to a speaker or writer: *In his memoirs, the former President implied that the CIA plotted his downfall. Infer* means "to draw a conclusion from logical premises" (the rules of logical inference are implicitly alluded to); this is an activity usually attributed to a reader or listener, or to a person pictured as a thinker: *The jury knew the documents were missing; it also knew that only the defendant had access to the vault; it therefore inferred that the defendant was guilty.* Do not confuse them.

in, into: *In* indicates location: *She raced in a car. Into* indicates direction: *She raced into a car.* Do not use *in* to indicate direction: *The speaker walked into* (not *in*) *the auditorium through the rear door.*

infer, imply: See *imply, infer.*

inside of, outside of: Do not use *inside of* to mean "within a time period": *Within* (not *inside of*) *an hour, the results will be known.* Do not use *outside of* to mean "except": *All members agreed on the policy except* (not *outside of*) *us.*

in regards to: Avoid this. Instead use *in regard to* or *as regards.*

irregardless: This word is a double negative (both the prefix and the suffix have a negative meaning); avoid it. Instead, use *regardless: Regardless* (not *irregardless*) *of the effect on inflation, the Congress intends to pass the bill.*

is when, is where: Do not use these phrases in definitions: *Integrity is a virtue that leads one to do what is right even when no one is watching* (not *Integrity is when one does what is right* . . .).

its, it's: *Its* is a possessive pronoun: *The committee will stand by its decision. It's* is a contraction of *it is: It's important to make decisions quickly.* Do not confuse them.

ketchup, catsup: You may use either of these spellings.

kind, sort: These are both singular nouns: *this* (not *these*) *kind of person.* Both words may of course be used in the plural: *those kinds of problems; these sorts of things.*

kind of a, sort of a: Do not use the indefinite article in these expressions: *this kind of solution* (not *this kind of a solution*).

lady, woman: Except for the standard greeting, "Ladies and gentlemen," avoid the term *lady* when referring to a professional woman. Unless the person's sex is specifically relevant, prefer simply *doctor, lawyer,* or *police officer,* say, to *lady doctor, lady lawyer,* or *lady police officer;* if sex is relevant, then write *woman doctor, woman lawyer,* or *woman police officer.*

latter, former: See *former, latter.*

lay, lie: *Lay* is a transitive verb. Its direct object names the person or thing in a reclining position: *They lay their books on the table when they enter the room each night. Lie* is an intransitive verb. Its subject names the person or thing in a reclining position: *Their books lie on the table during the meeting each night.* The past tense and past participle of *lay* are both *laid: They laid their books on the table; they have laid their books on the table.* The past tense of *lie* is *lay: Last night, during the meeting, their books lay on the table.* The past participle of *lie* is *lain: During every meeting, their books have lain on the table.* Do not confuse any of the three principal parts of either verb with any of the three principal parts of the other.

leave, let: Do not use *leave* to mean "permit": *Let* (not *leave*) *him do it; Let* (not *leave*) *us go now.*

less, fewer: See *fewer, less.*

lie, lay: See *lay, lie.*

like, as: See *as, like.*

literally: Do not use *literally* as an intensifier, especially when an idiomatic meaning retains its nonliteral meaning: *The committee meeting exploded* (not *literally exploded*) *into a shouting match.*

loan: This word is a noun. do not use it as a verb: *Will you lend* (not *loan*) *me ten dollars?*

loose, lose, loosen: *Loose* is an adjective: *The problem was caused by a loose electrical connection. Lose* is a verb meaning "to possess no longer": *If you lose a credit card, you should notify the company immediately. Loosen* is also a verb, but it means "to free": *When they arrived on the scene, the medics loosened the victim's tie.* Do not confuse these words or meanings.

lots, lots of: Avoid these when you write. Prefer *This city has many problems* to *This city has lots of problems.*

may, can: See *can, may.*

may be, maybe: *May be* is a phrase consisting of an auxiliary and a verb: *They may be there when we arrive. Maybe* is an adverb meaning "perhaps": *Maybe the judge will reconsider her ruling.* Do not confuse them.

myself: This pronoun may be used as the direct object of a verb that has *I* as its subject (*I pushed myself too hard*) or as an appositive adding emphasis (*I myself hold the same opinion*). Do not use it in other grammatical contexts where *me* is called for: *The petition was handed to the mayor and me* (not *myself*).

Ms.: This form of address may be used with any woman regardless of her marital status. Do not limit its use either to divorced women or to single women.

nauseated, nauseous: *Nauseated* is an adjective that describes someone feeling queasy or disgusted; *The scene at the crash made even hardened news reporters feel nauseated. Nauseous* is an adjective that describes something *causing* the feeling of queasiness or disgust: *The stench of burning flesh at the crash sight was nauseous.* Do not confuse these two adjectives: *I feel nauseated* (not *nauseous*).

neither, either: See *either, neither.*

not . . . no: Do not use double negatives. Instead of *They did not provide no proof of their allegations,* write *They provided no proof* or *They did not provide any proof.*

nevertheless: Do not spell this word *never-the-less.*

none: You may use either a singular or a plural verb with this word: *There are twelve students and none is going to pass; there are twelve students and none are going to pass.*

noplace: Do not use this in place of *nowhere: They looked, but the children were nowhere in sight.*

number of, amount of: See *amount of, number of.*

a number, the number: The expression *a number* takes a plural verb: *A number of senators are under investigation.* The expression *the number* takes a singular verb: *The number of dishonest legislators is probably small.* Do not confuse these usages.

off of: Write simply *off: The criminal jumped off* (not *off of*) *a moving train.*

O.K., OK, okay: Do not use this word in any of its forms except in informal business communications.

one another, each other: See *each other, one another.*

outside of, inside of: See *inside of, outside of.*

per: Except in certain Latin expressions (*per diem, per capita*) avoid this word: prefer *She earns $800 a month* to *She earns $800 per month.*

percent, percentage: Use *percent* with numbers: *Ten percent of the population may have been exposed to the virus;* use *percentage* with less definite modifiers like *a, large, small,* or *certain: a percentage of the population; a small percentage of the population.*

plus: Do not use *plus* as a transitional expression in place of *also, in addition,* or *besides.* One of these should replace *plus* in the following sentence: *State legislators do not need a raise; they received one last year; plus, many of them have law practices on the side.*

practicable, practical: *Practicable* means "capable of being put into practice": *Building a tunnel under the English Channel is practicable. Practical* means "useful" and usually also "economical": *Building a tunnel under the English Channel is not practical.* Do not confuse them.

prepositional usage: Many verbs and even nouns and adjectives require a certain preposition to accompany them. There is relatively little system to explain the verb's preference in each case. And edited English usually requires that only the specified preposition be used. Only by careful attention to prepositional usage in your reading will you fully master this most open-ended of usage problems. Here, however, are many of the more common pairings for your attention and study:

accede *to*

accord *with*

according *to*

accused *by* (a person)

accused *of* (a deed)

acquiesce *in*

adapted *for* (a purpose)

adapted *to* (a situation)

adapted *from* (= changed from)

addicted *to*

adept *in*

adhere *to*

adverse *to*

affinity *with*

agree *about* (a subject)

agree *to* (a proposal)

agree *with* (a person)

angry *with* (a person)

angry *at* (a thing)

approve *of*

apply *for* (a position)

apply *to* (a person)

argue *against, for* (a policy)

argue *with* (a person)

arrive *in* (a city)

arrive *at* (a small place)

blame *for* (a deed)

blame *on* (a person)

comply *with*

concur *in* (an option)

concur *with* (a person)

conform *to*

conformity *with*

contend *against* (an obstacle)

contend *for* (a principle)

contend *with* (a person)

convenient *for* (a purpose)

convenient *to* (a place)

correspond *to, with* (a thing)

correspond *with* (a person)

dabble *in*

deal *with*

depend *on*

deprive *of*

desire *to*

desirous *of*

destructive *of*

devoid *of*

die *of*

differ *about, over* (an issue)

differ *from* (a thing)

differ *with* (a person)

differ *in* (opinions)

differ *on* (amounts)

different *from*

disagree *on* (a plan)

disagree *with* (a person)

disappointed *in*

disdain *for*

dissent *from*

enter *into* (agreements)

enter *upon* (duties)

envious *of*

expert *in*

identical *with*

impatient *for* (something)

impatient *with* (someone)

impose *on*

improvement *in* (something)

improvement *on* (a prior state)

independent *of*

infer *from*

inferior *to*

inseparable *from*

knack *of*

oblivious *of*

part *from* (a person)

part *with* (a thing)

proceed *with* (a project)

proceed *to* (a beginning)

proficient *in*

profit *by*

prohibit *from*

rely *on*

reward *for* (a deed)

reward *with* (a gift)

sensitive *to*

surrounded *by* (people)

surrounded *with* (things)

sympathy *for* (a person)

sympathy *with* (feelings)

talk *to* (a group)

talk *with* (a person)

treat *of* (a subject)

treat *with* (= negotiate)

vie *with*

wait *at* (a place)

wait *for* (a person)

wait *on* (a customer)

presently: Do not use *presently* to mean "now" or "soon": *Helen is now* (not *presently*) *studying medicine; Soon,* (not *presently*) *they will be here.*

principal, principle: *Principal* may be a noun or an adjective and means "first" or "most important": *Mrs. Brown is the principal of the school; Mrs. Brown was the principal force behind the new collective bargaining law; The principal aim of the strikers is more wages. Principle* is always a noun, never an adjective, and means "an idea," "a general truth," or "a standard of behavior": *The administration's position is based on the principle that people who do the same work should get the same pay.* Do not confuse these two words or their meanings.

precede, proceed: Precede means "to go before": *A buffet dinner will precede the concert.* Proceed means "to move ahead, figuratively, to something else": *After making the toast, the speaker proceeded to insult the host.* Do not confuse these words, and do not use *proceed* to refer to literal movement: *After dinner the guests went on* (not *proceeded*) *to the auditorium for the concert.*

profit, prophet: *Profit* refers to financial gain: *One usually makes a profit in selling a house.* A *prophet* is a person who foretells the future: *Prophets are rarely popular in their own time, because they usually predict catastrophes.* Do not confuse them.

proved, proven: Use either of these as past participle of the verb *prove: They have proved their theory; They have proven their theory.* However, prefer *proven* as a purely attributive adjective: *a proven* (not *proved*) *cure.*

provided, providing: Do not use either of these words to mean "if": *The House will agree to a compromise if* (not *provided* or *providing*) *the Senate agrees as well.*

put across, put down, put on: Avoid these expressions when you write. Find a more appropriate item of edited-English vocabulary: *She supported her plan* (not *put it across*); *They criticized her* (not *put her down*); *They teased him* (not *put him on*).

raise, rise: *Raise* is a transitive verb: *Automakers have raised the prices of new cars again. Rise* is an intransitive verb: *New car prices are always rising.* Do not confuse *raise* (or its past and past participle: *raised, raised*) with *rise* (or its past and past participle: *rose, risen*).

rarely ever: Do not use *rarely ever* when *rarely* alone will do: *The mayor rarely* (not *rarely ever*) *consults the City Council.*

reason . . . is because: Avoid this wordy and redundant expression. Instead of *The reason the administration is in trouble is because the President lacks political experience,* write *The administration is in trouble because the President lacks political experience* (leaving out *the reason . . . is*).

regards to, in: Instead of *In regards to your inquiry,* write *In regard to,* or *Regarding.*

respectfully, respectively: *Respectfully* means "in a respectful manner": *The employees presented their grievances to the owner respectfully. Respectively* means "in the same order that was previously given": *Helen and Mary married Jim and Ed, respectively.* Do not confuse them.

scarcely, hardly: See *hardly, scarcely.*

seldom ever: Instead of *They seldom ever agree,* write simply *They seldom agree.*

sensuous, sensual: Both of these words denote a stimulation of the senses, but their connotations differ markedly. *Sensuous* connotes pleasure of an artistic nature: *the sensuous delights of art, music, and dance. Sensual* connotes physical, often sexual, stimulation of the senses. Do not confuse these words or meanings.

set, sit: *Set* is a transitive verb. Its object names the person or thing located on a surface: *They set their books on the table when they enter the room each night.* The past tense and past participle of *set* are also *set: Last night, they set their books on the table; They have always set their books on the table.* *Sit* is an intransitive verb. Its subject names the person or thing located on a surface: *Their books sit on the table during the meeting each night.* The past tense and past participle of *sit* are both *sat: Last night, during the meeting, their books sat on the table; Their books have always sat on the table.* Do not confuse any of the principal parts of either of these verbs with those of the other.

so . . . that: Do not use *so* as an intensifier of an adjective unless a *that* clause follows the adjective: Instead of *They were so happy,* write *They were very happy* or add a *that* clause: *They were so happy that they shouted.*

so . . . as, as . . . as: See *as . . . as, so . . . as.*

someplace, anyplace: See *anyplace, someplace.*

sort, kind: See *kind, sort.*

stationary, stationery: *Stationary* means "not moving": *The potted plants are stationary.* *Stationery,* which names paper and other items related to writing, used to be sold by a person called a *stationer* (one who rented a station in the market place); thus the *-er* derivational suffix is part of the word *stationery.*

than, then: *Than* is a conjunction used in comparisons: *Basketball is more exciting than baseball.* *Then* is an adverb of time, telling "when": *Life was more exciting then.* Do not confuse them.

their, there, they're: *Their* is a possessive noun modifier: *That is their car.* *There* is an adverb telling "where": *I put the tools there.* *They're* is a contraction of *they are: They're coming to visit us.* Do not confuse them.

to, too, two: *To* is a preposition used in prepositional phrases or infinitives: *The courier delivered the papers to the embassy; I hope to travel.* *Too* is either an intensifier modifying adjectives and adverbs (*The tomatoes are too ripe; you drive too recklessly*) or it is a transitional expression meaning "also" (*The Europeans are suffering the effects of inflation too*). *Two* is a number: *Many American families have two cars.* Do not confuse them.

too: Do not use *too* (meaning "also") to introduce a clause: *The third applicant has the best academic record; besides,* (not *too*) *she has the best letters of recommendation.*

try and: Do not use this phrase to mean "try to": *You should try to* (not *try and*) *persuade the opposition to consider a compromise.*

type: Do not use *type* to mean "type of": *That type of* (not *type*) *compromise serves no useful purpose.*

uninterested, disinterested: See *disinterested, uninterested.*

unique: *Unique* means "one of a kind"; you should avoid modifying it with *more* and *most,* since it is hard to imagine degrees of being one of a kind. Instead of phrases like *the most unique diamond* or *the more unique of the two speakers* prefer *the most nearly unique diamond* and *the more unusual of the two speakers.*

up: Do not use *up* as a verb: *The Russians want to increase* (not *up*) *the stakes in the international arms race.*

use to: This is a common incorrect spelling of *used to.*

wait on: Do not use *wait on* to mean *wait for: They waited for* (not *on*) *her for twenty minutes, but when she did not arrive, they had to leave without her.* It is, of course, appropriate to use *wait on* to mean "serve": *Because the waiters were on strike, the management of the restaurant had to wait on the customers.*

well, good: See *good, well.*

whether, if: See *if, whether.*

who, whoever; whom, whomever: *Who* and *whoever* are used as subject: *We need judges who resist political pressure; we should elect whoever will put the common citizen first.* *Whom* and *whomever* are used as direct and indirect objects and in prepositional phrases: *She is the candidate whom the people elected; The President will appoint whomever the Congress approves of.* Do not confuse *who* or *whoever* with *whom* or *whomever.* (This issue is treated in more detail in Chapter Seven, pp. 174–176.)

who's, whose: *Who's* is a contraction of *who is: I know the woman who's about to be appointed Attorney General.* *Whose* is the possessive form of the interrogative and relative pronouns: *Whose book is this? I know a woman whose nomination is assured.*

-wise: Avoid coining new words with this suffix, words like *candidatewise, collegewise,* or *gradewise.* Well-established words with this suffix (e.g., *clockwise*) are appropriate.

woman, lady: See *lady, woman.*

Index

Neither, either, 333
Nevertheless, 336
New Columbia Encyclopedia, 286
Newspapers, 294
New York Times Index, 295
Nominalizers, 144
None, 336
Nonrestrictive relative clauses, 146, 264
Noplace, 336
North American Indian languages, 183
Not . . . no, 336
Note cards, 298–307
Notes, 279–280
  format for, 308–310, 323
  numbers for, 316
Note taking, 297–302
Noun clauses, 144–145
  questions as, 153
Noun phrases, 126–133
  conjoined, 139–140
  expanded, 148
Nouns, 4–5, 123
  collective, 171
  compound, 128, 185, 274–275
  dependent clauses modifying, 144
  plurals of, 237–240
  proper, 246–249, 253
  sentences as, 153–158
Nowhere near, 198
Number agreement, 170–171
Number of, amount of, 330
Numbers, 251–253, 264
  in outlines, 78–79, 259
Numerals, 251–253

Objective complement, 117–118
Object of a preposition, 129–130, 174–175
Oblique objects, 117, 119, 130
  ordering of, 149
Off, of, 336
O.K., OK, Okay, 336
Old English, 181
Organization
  for an audience, 45–49
  importance of, 44
  in paragraphs, 89–97. *See also* Paragraphs
  planning and, 56–73
  for a purpose, 49–55
Ortheopy, 225
Orthography, 225
Outlines, 73–74
  developmental phase of, 76–78
  preliminary phase of, 74–76
  punctuation in, 259
  for research papers, 302–303, 314
  revision phase of, 78–81
Outside of, inside of, 198, 334

Oxford English Dictionary (OED), 209, 212–213, 217–218, 223
Oxymoron, 190

Paragraphs
  coherence in, 97–113
  functions of, 82–84
  unity in, 83–97
Parallel grammatical structure
  in paragraphs, 105–108
  in sentences, 177–179
Parentheses, 264, 270
  numbers in, 261
Participial phrases, 160
Participles, 160
Parts of speech, 4–5
  adjectives, 131, 246–249. *See also* Adjectives
  adverbs, 123, 162–164
  conjunctions, 138, 141, 143, 146, 162
  dictionary information on, 209–212
  nouns, 4–5, 123, 144. *See also* Nouns
  prepositions, 4–5, 123, 129
  pronouns, 131, 170–172. *See also* Pronouns
  verbs, 110–113, 135, 236–237. *See also* Verbs
Passive sentences, 151
  overuse of, 176–177, 205
Passive voice, 111–112
Past participles, 160
Per, 336
Percent, percentage, 336
Periodical indexes, 294–295
Periodicals, 294–295
Periods, 258–259
Personal pronouns, 131
Phonology, 18
Phrases
  adjective, 133–135, 140
  adverb, 123, 135–138, 140–141
  conjoined, 126–133, 138–143, 148
  gerundive, 154–156
  infinitive, 154–156, 159–160, 163
  noun, 126–133, 139–140, 148
  participial, 160
  prepositional, 122, 129–132, 134, 137
  structural, 123
  verb, 123–125, 138–140
Plagiarism, 297, 299, 308
Planning, 56–73
Plenty, 198
Plural nouns, 237–240
Plus, 336
Poetry, 245, 272–273
Polish, 183
Poole's Index, 295
Possessive nouns, 128

CORRECTION CHART

Here is an alphabetically arranged list of typical corrections that teachers make on student papers. Your teacher may choose to use the suggested correction symbols or may ask you to cross some out and write in different ones. Space is provided for adding other corrections and symbols to the chart. Beside the items are page numbers where you will find information to help you make the needed corrections.

Correction	Symbol	See Pages
Abbreviation problem	ab	254–256
Adjectives and adverbs confused or misused	ad	133–138
Agreement problem: pronoun and antecedent	agr:pa	170–172
Agreement problem: subject and predicate	agr:sp	167–169
Apostrophe needed or misused	apos	276–278
Audience not clearly identified	aud	45–49
Brackets needed or misused	[ ] /	270–272
Capitalization problem	cap	244–249
Case problem	case	174–176
Coherence weak	coh	97–113
Colon needed or misused	: /	267–268
Comma or commas needed or misused	, /	261–266
Comma splice	cs	165–167
Consistency problem: mood	cons:md	110–111
Consistency problem: pronoun	cons:pro	108–110
Consistency problem: tense	cons:tns	110–111
Consistency problem: voice	cons:vc	111–113
Dash or dashes needed or misused	—/	268–270
Delete (omit)	_e_	
Dialect is a problem	dial	11–16, 196–199
Diction: problem with connotation	d:con	193–196
Diction: problem with figurative language	d:fig	189–193
Diction: problem with gobbledygook and wordiness	d:wdy	201–207
Diction: problem with taboo and euphemism	d:euph	200–201
Diction: regionalism, colloquialism, or slang	d:colloq	196–199
Diction: too abstract	d:ab	187–189
Documentation problem	doc	308–327
Exclamation point needed or misused	! /	260–261
Grammar problem	gr	114–147
Hyphen needed or misused	- /	274–276
Ideas too unoriginal	id	24–40
Italics problem	ital	250–251
Logic problem	log	71–73
Lower case should be used	lc	244–249

82 83 84 85 9 8 7 6 5 4 3 2 1